Wireless Web Development with PHP and WAP

RAY RISCHPATER

Wireless Web Development with PHP and WAP

Copyright ©2001 by Ray Rischpater

ISBN (pbk): 1-893115-93-3

Printed and bound in the United States of America 12345678910

Editorial Directors: Dan Appleman, Gary Cornell, Jason Gilmore, Karen Watterson

Technical Editor: Charles Stearns

Developmental Editor: Martin Minner

Copy Editor: Nancy Rapoport

Project Editor: Carol A. Burbo

Compositor: Susan Glinert

Cover and CD Label Designer: Karl Miyajima

Distributed to the book trade in the United States by Springer-Verlag New York, Inc., 175 Fifth Avenue, New York, NY, 10010

and outside the United States by Springer-Verlag GmbH & Co. KG, Tiergartenstr. 17, 69112 Heidelberg, Germany

In the United States, phone 1-800-SPRINGER; orders@springer-ny.com; http://www.springer-ny.com

Outside the United States, contact orders@springer.de; http://www.springer.de; fax +49 6221 345229

For information on translations, please contact Apress directly at 901 Grayson Street, Suite 204, Berkeley, CA, 94710

Phone: 510-549-5931; Fax: 510-549-5939; info@apress.com; http://www.apress.com

Contents

Acknowledgments

IT'S NOT UNTIL YOU WRITE A BOOK that you recognize how many other people contribute to the process. In fact, I have a hunch that the only reason the publisher lists the author's name on the book's spine is because there's not enough room to mention everyone else as well!

I must first thank all those who have contributed to the open-source software around which this book is built: The Apache Group, responsible for the Apache Web server, the developers of PHP, developers of MySQL, and the independent developers who have all contributed code, documentation, comments, and fixes receive my everlasting gratitude. This would be a very different book if not for their efforts.

My deepest thanks go to the fantastic staff at Apress, including Carol Burbo, Martin Minner, Nancy Rapoport, Susan Glinert, Grace Wong, and Gary Cornell, for their efforts and support throughout the creative process. Working with them is truly a pleasure, and together they make even the hardest parts of the creative process easier.

While on the subject of creation, I must also express my hearty appreciation to Frank and Francis Adamson for their warm hospitality, friendship, and musical Thursdays. Time with them was a welcome respite from the hours of coding and writing and offered me the opportunity to compost my thoughts for this project.

Thanks to the generosity of Yospace and Nokia, this book includes two separate development environments with which you can hit the ground developing your WAP content. I appreciate the efforts of David Springall at Yospace, and Matt Volpi and Paul Chapple at Nokia for working with me to arrange distribution rights.

Of course, I owe Charles Stearns a debt of gratitude for his work as the technical reviewer of this book. Apress's commitment to technical excellence puts large demands on technical reviewers; Charles rose to the task admirably. I owe him thanks for a number of other contributions, too, many of which are the intangibles that constitute a wonderful friendship and working relationship. As is only fair, I will remind you that despite Charles's diligence throughout I alone bear the responsibility and beg your indulgence for any errors you might find herein.

My deepest appreciation must be expressed for my family's support. Jarod supported this book through his endless smiles and playtime; without his naps, I would have never finished. And Rachel, my soulmate and partner in all endeavors, contributed immensely to this work with her support, tireless care for both Jarod and me, engaging conversation, and comments on the manuscript and diagrams.

Introduction

THE WEB IS ON THE CUSP of a startling change: within three years more devices than computers will access the Web. The majority of these devices will be non-computer wireless devices such as screen phones, two-way pagers, and handheld computers. Consequently, there will be an across-the-board revolution in content management. Today's heavyweight content technologies such as HTML, DHTML, JavaScript, and Java will be augmented with lightweight counterparts such as the Wireless Markup Language (WML) and WMLScript. Behind the scenes, an increasing number of content providers will turn to active servers using technologies like PHP: Hypertext Processor to serve increasingly diverse formats to different clients. Together, these active servers and lightweight clients will become a Web of their own; already many people refer to this network as the Wireless Web.

Producing content for the Wireless Web is, at the same time, similar to and vastly different than producing content for the Web. While many of the fundamental technical aspects are the same—networks, markup languages, and so on—many of the requirements are different. Given the vast differences between a handheld device and desktop computer, a wireless network and the Internet, and a user at her desk and the same user on the go, you must bring additional tools to bear when writing content for the Wireless Web.

This book is about two of those tools: the Wireless Markup Language and PHP: Hypertext Processor. The Wireless Markup Language (and its scripting companion, WMLScript, which this book also covers) is part of the Wireless Application Protocol, a set of protocols designed to meet the needs of mobile wireless devices. PHP is the premier open source language for building active server pages. Together, these tools help you create dynamic Wireless Web sites for your customers, colleagues, and friends.

Who Should Read This Book

I wrote this book for a number of people, quite likely including you. If you're interested in building a Wireless Web site, of course, you should read this book. In it, I show you how to use WML, WMLScript, and PHP to build a real wireless Web site. If you're considering using another active server technology, such as Microsoft Active Server Pages, that's okay, too: the concepts you learn about when learning PHP apply to any active scripting technology.

Even if you're only interested in learning PHP, this book is for you. Everything I tell you about PHP and WML content applies equally to PHP and HTML content. Not only that, but you will quickly find that knowing about the Wireless Web will open new doors to you.

I'm assuming you already work with Web content as a designer, illustrator, publisher, or programmer. I *don't*, however, assume you know how to program. In fact, if you're not a programmer, you're in luck: one of the goals of this book is to teach you how to program using PHP and WMLScript. Because these languages are easy to learn, and the concepts behind them a subset of what you have to learn if you want to program in Java, C++, or another language, PHP and WMLScript offer a great place to start. On the other hand, if you're a programmer, you can quickly skim the introductory material and then dive into the details.

While I focus on technical details primarily of interest to technical professionals and enthusiasts, others may find this book interesting as well. If you're responsible for Wireless Web application development, as a manager, system administrator, marketing or sales professional, you'll find that this book gives you a better perspective on how things work.

What You Will Find in This Book

Broadly, this book is organized into four parts. In the first, you get a thumbnail view of several basic concepts common to Web application development. In the second, you learn how to create Wireless Web content with WML. In the third, you learn how to program using PHP and WMLScript. Finally, you put all these things together and build a Wireless Web application with me.

In **Chapter 1**, I lay out the fundamentals you need to understand as you read this book. Regardless of your background, I encourage you to read this chapter, even if you've encountered the material before. Because I may define concepts differently, or present things in a different light, you're likely to gain new insights.

In **Chapter 2**, I introduce you to the Wireless Web. After showing you how the Wireless Web is different from the Web, I show you the Wireless Markup Language. Together, we use the Nokia SDK to create pages in WML, and learn how to mark up content for the Wireless Web. After you read Chapter 2, you will be able to create your own static Wireless Web pages.

In **Chapter 3**, I step back from content and look at programming with PHP: Hypertext Processor. I show you how to install, configure, and use PHP, and I show you how to create simple active Wireless Web pages using PHP. After reading Chapter 3, you will know how to make simple active pages that use your input and other factors to create their content.

In **Chapter 4**, I introduce WMLScript, the scripting language created for lightweight clients such as screen phones and palm top computers. WMLScript lets clients do simple tasks such as input validation, which eliminates many of the network transactions that clients typically perform. Using WMLScript in your applications adds a level of professional polish you can't find elsewhere, so you should definitely look into it.

In **Chapter 5**, I build on your experience from previous chapters and show you how to use databases and other features within PHP. PHP is known for providing a dizzying array of interfaces and tools to other system facilities. After reading Chapter 5, you'll have your feet planted firmly on the ground, and will be able to take advantage of the tools PHP affords you.

In **Chapter 6**, I continue exploring PHP's interfaces and show you how to build a Wireless Web application that supports electronic mail. Equally important, I show you an exciting feature of the Wireless Web: *server notifications* that push content to the wireless handset.

In **Chapter 7**, I review important tactics you can use when something goes wrong. Invariably, programming has its pitfalls, and it's up to you to find them, root them out, and make your application work correctly. After reading this chapter, you'll be appropriately armed and will be able to debug PHP and Wireless Web applications.

In **Chapter 8**, I take a break from programming and dive into something fun: graphics. I show you how you can add graphics to your Wireless applications. You'll learn when graphics are appropriate, why they aren't widely used in the Wireless Web, and what to do if you want to use them.

In **Chapter 9**, I show you how to create client-independent content suited for both the Web and the Wireless Web. This is a growing area, with rapid advancement being made by a host of technologies. I show you how you can use content written in the eXtensible Markup Language (XML) to provide content to both Wireless Web users seeking WML and traditional desktop users looking for HTML. After you finish this chapter, you'll be able to identify which solution is right for you, and will have the tools you need to build an environment that supports multiple client types using PHP.

Of course, no technical book is complete without a host of appendices. In **Appendix A**, I survey a number of online references you'll find helpful as you read this book. In **Appendix B**, you'll find a quick reference guide to WML. **Appendix C** contains a quick reference guide to WMLScript.

In the back of the book, you'll find a CD-ROM that contains a number of helpful goodies, including the contents of every code listing in this book. As you learn, you'll find that one of the most valuable things you can do is take a working example and tinker with it to make it do your bidding. Of course, nothing's more frustrating than setting out to do this and finding you have to debug your typing mistakes, so I've taken the liberty of doing the typing for you. Also on the CD-ROM is a fully functional Wireless Web application, MobileHelper, which I wrote to support many of the examples in this book. This application meets the needs of small volunteer organizations that need to track a roster of volunteers as they proceed to and from assigned stations at particular dates and times. The problems this application solves (including user profiles, scheduling, messaging, and administration) are common items many wireless applications must address and, by working through MobileHelper, you'll gain the ability to tackle these in your own projects.

How You Can Read This Book

Because each chapter builds on material from the previous chapter, I suggest you read the entire book sequentially, rather than skipping to different chapters as your whim takes you. Even if you're familiar with some of the concepts, you may be missing important background, either about the material or about something I've shown you through specific examples in a section you've skipped. Once you've read—or at least skimmed—the entire book once, you can return to the chapters and sections that interest you most for a second reading.

Foremost, I intend this book to be educational. As you read, I hope you'll not only learn the material, but get a flavor for the gestalt of wireless development. To help you do this, each chapter includes a section at the end titled "Food for Thought." These sections are a review of the chapter's contents, cast as questions, which I believe will help you extend your understanding of the material. If you're reading this book with colleagues also interested in creating Wireless Web sites, these are excellent places to start a discussion; if you're working alone, you can mull them over as you like in your free time. If you prefer a more structured approach, you can treat them as exercises you should do before starting the next chapter, but you don't have to. Unlike exercises in other books, you don't have to do them and I don't put answers in the back of the book. I just suggest you think about them, and see where that thinking takes you.

A Word Regarding Presentation

In this book, I use several styles to make my meaning clear. Most of this is so you can tell what people are supposed to read and what computers are supposed to read; other times, it's so you can distinguish between what you read and what you enter or see on a Wireless Web browser.

Any text that looks `like this` is in one of the languages—WML, WMLScript, or PHP—that I'm discussing. (Of course, you'll be able to tell which language by the context of the discussion.) Whole listings of code look like this:

```
01: <?xml version="1.0"?>
02: <!DOCTYPE wml PUBLIC "-//WAPFORUM//DTD WML 1.1//EN"
03:   "http://www.wapforum.org/DTD/wml_1.1.xml">
04: <wml>
05:   <card title="Hello">
06:     <p>
07:       Hello, intrepid reader!
08:     </p>
09:   </card>
10: </wml>
```

The leading numbers in a listing, like 06:, are not part of the code itself. If you look on the enclosed CD-ROM, you'll see that the listings don't have these numbers. If you decide to type a listing in, be sure you don't include the numbers. Neither PHP nor WMLScript requires line numbers, and you're likely to get a lot of confusing error messages if you leave them in! They're there to help you stay oriented within each listing as I describe how the listing works.

Text **like this**, on the other hand, is text either from a Wireless Web browser's display, or something you're supposed to type into a browser or other program. Because an important element of Web design is visual appearance, you'll find many illustrations throughout this book. Many of these illustrations are screen shots, showing you what one or another wireless browser actually displays when given a bit of code. Other illustrations are figures in the Unified Modeling Language (UML) showing you how something works. If you don't know UML, that's okay—you'll learn enough to follow along in Chapter 1.

Looking Ahead

The Wireless Web is an exciting place, full of challenges and opportunities. Enough of the formalities: grab this book, your screen phone, and let's create some Wireless Web content!

About the CD-ROM

THIS **CD-ROM** INCLUDES all of the numbered listings and examples from each chapter of the book.

Requirements

Each of the applications on the CD-ROM requires a specific platform on which to run. The server utilities—Apache and PHP—run on Microsoft Windows 98 or later, Linux, or UNIX. The CD-ROM includes precompiled binaries for Microsoft Windows, but you need to build these from the source code for Linux, UNIX, or Mac OS X. Alternately, you can visit the Web sites `http://www.apache.org` and `http://www.php.net` to download precompiled binaries for your system. These applications are open-source software; see the enclosed license agreement that comes with each application for details on your rights to reproduce these applications.

The WAP toolkits require a Java runtime as well. The Nokia WAP Toolkit, which only runs on Microsoft Windows, also requires the Java runtime from Sun Microsystems. The Yospace SPEDE, on the other hand, is 100 percent pure Java, and runs on any platform on which you have a Java runtime installed, including Microsoft Windows, Linux, or Mac OS. Unlike the Apache Web server and PHP scripting engine, these are *not* open-source applications. Please consult the license agreement that comes with each application for details on your rights to reproduce these applications.

Organization

Within each of the directories named ch0n, you will find the numbered listings and separate examples from the corresponding chapter of the book. (These listings are formatted as IBM-compatible text files with both carriage returns and line feeds.) Note, however, that if you want to experiment with the MobileHelper implementation that uses MySQL, shown in Chapter 5 and later chapters of the book, you will need to download MySQL from `http://www.mysql.com`.

This CD-ROM includes source and precompiled binaries for selected platforms of the popular Apache Web server and the PHP scripting engine within the platform directories (Mac OS, UNIX, Windows). Please see the appropriate directory for your platform for installation and software license information applicable to these products.

Similarly, the CD-ROM includes the Nokia WAP Toolkit, courtesy of Nokia, and an evaluation version of the Yospace Smart Phone Emulator Developer Edition, courtesy of Yospace. Please see the appropriate directory for your platform for installation and software license information.

On the Net

Most of the material on this CD-ROM continues to evolve. For the latest releases of the Apache Web server, PHP scripting engine, and WAP tools, be sure to consult the Web sites for these applications for updates, new features, and bug fixes. You can find a list of the relevant URLs in Appendix A.

CHAPTER 1
Fundamentals of Wireless Development

REGARDLESS OF THE SUBJECT, having a firm grasp of the fundamentals is crucial. Often, it's what distinguishes the professional from the amateur. Also, a deep understanding of the fundamentals may enable you to make an important contribution to the state of the art. More importantly, you're better prepared to fix something in your own work when it goes wrong.

This chapter reviews the fundamentals of Wireless Web development, beginning with the basics, including covering networks, client-server relationships, markup languages, and even a few words on how you go about writing software. You'll also be introduced to the wireless application that is built throughout this book.

I encourage you to read this chapter, even if you're familiar with some of the material because you may find that it helps you expand your understanding of the material, or that it presents things in a different light. If you find the material's already familiar to you, so much the better: you'll read it that much more quickly!

The Network

Although it's hard to believe, the notion of pervasive network computing is a relatively new concept. As recently as five years ago, most computers were on small, closed networks, or they didn't talk to each other at all.

As you develop Wireless Web applications, it's important to have at least a nodding acquaintance with how your creations flow across the network between service provider and user. Of course, you don't often have to worry about the individual bits and bytes as they fly through the air, but you'll want to have a basic understanding of how a network moves data from place to place.

Protocols

Today's computers are connected via *networks* that enable applications that run on different computers to pass data, including documents such as Web pages, movie clips, sounds, or application-dependent information such as database records, user authentication, or electronic mail.

Computers on a network (often simply called *hosts*) operate according to a well-defined specification called a *protocol*. Following a protocol ensures that different vendors' computers and applications can talk to each other, a crucial part of a network's success. Protocols describe the format of the individual messages, or *packets*, passed between applications. There's a dizzying array of network protocols. These include the ubiquitous *Transport Control Protocol / Internet Protocol* (TCP/IP), which is the backbone of the Internet, along with protocols such as Apple's AppleTalk, Microsoft Windows NetBIOS, and others. Fortunately, in most cases, you don't need to know the details behind the protocol you use, because the applications and operating system you use hide the protocol's implementation.

Most protocols are designed for use on a *packet-switched* network. In a packet-switched network, the individual messages between computers are broken up into small pieces called packets, and each packet is sent one at a time. In these networks, some of the protocols are actually responsible for describing how computers can split data into packets, how computers should put the packets back together, and what to do when a computer discovers that some of the pieces are missing. In contrast, a few networks are *circuit switched*. In a circuit-switched network, the two computers exchanging data have a dedicated connection for the lifetime of their conversation. The existing telephone network behaves as a circuit-switched network; you pick up the handset, make a phone call, and for the duration of your call, you're occupying a single circuit.

Protocols can be *layered*, so that one protocol uses the capabilities provided by another protocol. When system designers do this, it is said that the protocol that uses the other protocol's features is *above*, whereas the protocol providing the base capabilities is *below*. For example, the TCP/IP protocol can sit above the Ethernet protocol, which defines how computers can use electrical signals to transmit data across wires. When protocols are layered such as this, each protocol can build on the capabilities of the one below. Often, you'll see pictures such as that shown in Figure 1-1, which shows that the HyperText Transfer Protocol (HTTP) sits on top of the Transmission Control Protocol, which sits on top of Internet Protocol. (You'll hear more about HTTP in the section "The HyperText Transport Protocol.") When talking about a group of protocols layered like this, the group is often referred to as a *stack* because it visually resembles a stack of objects.

Layering protocols has several advantages. Chief among these is that when applied properly, a given protocol—say, TCP/IP—can be used on top of several

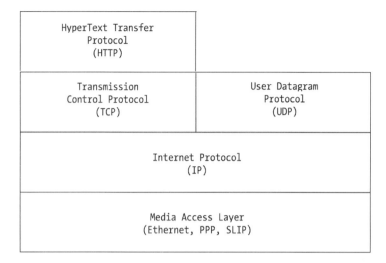

Figure 1-1. The HyperText Transfer Protocol

other protocols. For example, TCP/IP can run on top of both the Ethernet and Point-to-Point (PPP) protocols, enabling computers to use the same network protocols to talk over different physical networks such as Ethernet and phone lines. By doing this, each protocol can provide specific features, and the overall stack can offer a suite of features through the protocols it contains.

Fortunately, you don't often have to concern yourself with the details of a protocol, unless you'll be actually writing the software that implements the protocol. What you will want to understand, however, are the kinds of messages the protocol exchanges, and how these messages relate to what you need to do. For example, HTTP provides messages for receiving a document from a host, and sending a document to a host. You certainly don't want to use the former message to send data!

Many protocols distinguish between a computer that provides a datum, called a *server*, and a computer that consumes that datum, called a *client*. These protocols are called *client-server* protocols to reflect this. Client-server protocols are often used when the data being accessed is stored in a central repository, or when there's other obvious imbalances between one kind of host and another on the network. Figure 1-2 shows a typical client-server relationship, in which the client first asks the server for a document, and then the server returns the contents of the requested document.

In addition to clients and servers, a computer may play a third role in a protocol: that of a *gateway*. A gateway bridges a gap, such as between networks or different protocols, between the client computers and the server. Figure 1-3 shows a client-server relationship including a gateway.

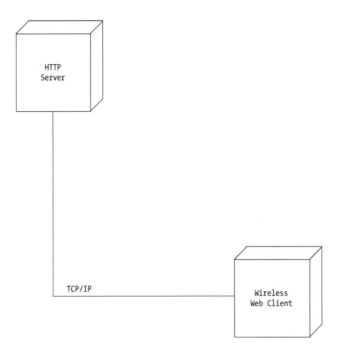

Figure 1-2. A client-server relationship

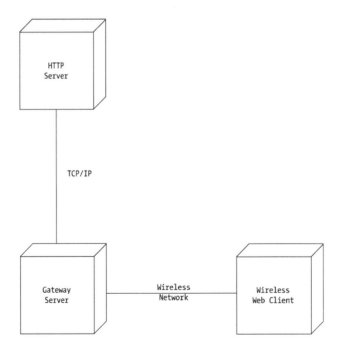

Figure 1-3. A client-server relationship via a gateway

A special kind of server called a *proxy* server is also a gateway that acts as a client when talking to the server, and as a server when talking to its clients. Clients seeking a datum make a request of the proxy, which in turn forwards the request to the server, called the *origin server*, and then returns the response. (The name *proxy* defines the proxy server's responsibility as a host acting on behalf of other hosts, the clients themselves.) Proxy servers are often used to provide additional processing of server responses for clients, or to lessen the number of client requests a server has to answer. Some gateways perform these functions as well as translating between one protocol and another, blurring the distinction between proxy servers and gateways. I'll use the terms interchangeably, choosing to call a server a *gateway* to emphasize it's protocol translation or network bridging features, and calling the server a *proxy* for you to think more about what it does on behalf of the server or client. Figure 1-4 shows a client-server relationship including a proxy server.

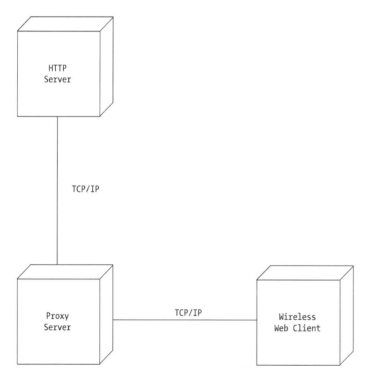

Figure 1-4. A client-server relationship via a proxy server

Anatomy of a Protocol

Let's turn our attention from generalities to a specific protocol: the HyperText Transfer Protocol (HTTP). As you'll soon see, HTTP plays an integral role within the Wireless Web.

Evolving from a research effort to speed the exchange of scientific documents, HTTP has become the workhorse of the World Wide Web. In practice, knowing how HTTP works enables you to understand how WAP handles sending information from the handset to the server, how phones cache pages for fast access, and other details.

With HTTP, clients send a message to make a request of a server. In turn, the server processes the request and responds with its own message. While HTTP is a general-purpose protocol, the lion's share of HTTP client requests are from clients seeking documents and the server's response message is the document sought by the client. Each message includes a unique identifier on the remote server called Universal Resource Identifier (URI) of the document the client is seeking.

The request message itself has several parts. The *request method* specifies what the client is asking the server to do, and includes both a URI and the version of HTTP supported by the client. Then comes a series of *request modifiers*, or *HTTP headers* (often simply just called *headers* when the meaning is clear), which provide information about the request, such as the kind of client making the request, in what formats the request should be returned, and other information. After these headers the client may send a document associated with the request if appropriate. In return, the client sends a message that begins with a status line, showing a numeric status code and a human-readable status message indicating the success or failure of the request. Immediately following this status line is a series of *response modifiers*, also often called HTTP headers, that includes information such as the server's identity, information about the entity of interest to the client, and so on. After these headers, the server can send a document if requested by the client.

HTTP headers are written as a single line consisting of a header description, followed by a colon, and the value of the header, such as this:

```
User-Agent: Nokia7110/1.0 (04.78)
```

(You'll see in a moment just what this header means.) This header is called the User-Agent because the header's description is the words User-Agent, and has a value of Nokia7110/1.0 (04.78). In general, clients and servers can specify their headers in any order.

Have you noticed that HTTP doesn't specify what the actual messages are about? That's because the protocol is general purpose; it doesn't care what kind of stuff the client and server talk about. In fact, HTTP can just as easily be used to exchange mail or news as Web pages. Moreover, in the process of supporting the

Web, HTTP already handles numerous file formats, including HTML, WML, WBMP, GIF, JPEG, PNG, WAV, and even QuickTime and MPEG movies. In fact, HTTP is a format-independent protocol.

Some HTTP servers don't even serve files per se. These servers are often referred to as *active* servers because they use scripts to generate content on the fly in response to HTTP messages. Scripts can be written in a programming language such as Java (using Java Servlets), or in a scripting language explicitly conceived for the Web such as Microsoft's Active Server Pages or PHP: Hypertext Processor. Chapter 3 discusses how you can build Wireless Web sites that perform compli-cated actions on behalf of the user using PHP, one of the most popular active server technologies.

Listing 1-1, together with Figure 1-5, shows an HTTP request and response from a screen phone and a Web server. Let's look at each line of the exchange to see what it says. (Figure 1-5 is a *sequence diagram* showing what happens between the client and server. Time progresses vertically from top to bottom along the diagram.) Figure 1-6 shows the screen phone display after downloading this doc-ument, which prompts you to enter a weather station's name.

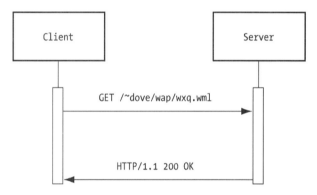

Figure 1-5. A client-server exchange with HTTP (Sequence Diagram)

```
01: GET /~dove/wap/wxq.wml HTTP/1.1
02: Host: kona.lothlorien.com
03: Accept: application/vnd.wap.wmlc, application/vnd.wap.wmlscriptc,
    image/vnd.wap.wbmp, application/vnd.wap.wtls-ca-certificate,
    text/plain,text/vnd.wap.wmlscript,text/html,text/vnd.wap.wml
04: Accept-Language: en
05: Accept-Charset: ISO-8859-1, UTF-8; Q=0.8, ISO-10646-UCS-2; Q=0.6
06: User-Agent: Nokia7110/1.0 (04.78)
07: Via: Nokia WAP Server 1.0.2
08: X-Network-Info: UDP,127.0.0.1,security=0
09: Accept-Encoding:
10: Connection: Close
```

```
11:
12: HTTP/1.1 200 OK
13: Date: Wed, 06 Sep 2000 03:18:25 GMT
14: Server: Apache/1.3.12 (Unix) PHP/4.0.1pl2
15: Last-Modified: Wed, 06 Sep 2000 03:15:22 GMT
16: ETag: "fb1c-1b0-39b5b6ca"
17: Accept-Ranges: bytes
18: Content-Length: 432
19: Connection: close
20: Content-Type: text/vnd.wap.wml
21: <?xml version="1.0"?>
22: <!DOCTYPE wml PUBLIC "-//WAPFORUM//DTD WML 1.1//EN"
       "http://www.wapforum.org/DTD/wml_1.1.xml">
23: <wml>
24:   <card id="entry" title="Weather">
25:   <p>Enter a station
26:     <input name="station" title="station"
       type="text" emptyok="false"/>
27:   </p>
28:   <do type="accept" label="Fetch">
29:     <go href="wx.php3" method="post">
30:       <postfield name="station" value="$station"/>
31:     </go>
32:   </do>
33:   </card>
34: </wml>
```

Listing 1-1. A client-server exchange with HTTP

Figure 1-6. Screen phone display

The message sent by the client—the screen phone's browser—is contained in the first 12 lines. The first line is the HTTP request method, telling the server that it should return the contents of the document named `/~dove/wap/wx.wml` using the HTTP `GET` method using version 1.1 of the HTTP protocol. This method simply instructs the server to fetch and return the requested document. The remaining lines are the client's HTTP headers.

The second line specifies the host that maintains the document requested using the `Host` header. Together, the `Host` header's contents and the URI form a network-wide unique identifier for the document called a *Universal Resource Locator*, or URL. In this example, the client is requesting the URL `http://kona.lothlorien.com/~dove/wap/wx.wml`.

Lines 3–6 inform the server what document types the client can understand. Line 3 uses the `Accept` header to specify which formats the client can display using Multipurpose Internet Mail Extension (MIME) types. MIME is a well-established standard used by the Web and electronic mail services to provide unique names for document formats, such as HTML, WML, Microsoft Word, and so on. Line 3 says that this client can display documents formatted in any of the following ways:

- A compiled Wireless Markup Language application (`application/vnd.wap.wmlc`)

- A compiled WMLScript application (`application/vnd.wap.wmlscriptc`)

- A Wireless Application Protocol Bitmap image (`image/vnd.wap.bmp`)

- A secure Wireless Application Protocol certificate (`application/vnd.wap.wtls-ca-certificate`)

- A plain text document (`text/plain`)

- A Wireless Markup Language document (`text/vnd.wap.wml`)

- A WMLScript application in text form (`text/vnd.wap.wmlscript`)

- An HTML document (`text/html`)

Line 4 uses the `Accept-Language` header to specify the human language the document should be in; in this case, the client desires documents in English. The International Standards Organization (ISO) has defined a multitude of (usually) two-letter codes that are used by various protocols to specify natural languages in the ISO-639 Standard. Table 1.1 shows some of the more commonly used codes and their meaning.

Table 1.1. Some ISO-639 Language Abbreviations

IDENTIFIER	LANGUAGE
ar	Arabic
bg	Bulgarian
bo	Tibetan
chi	Chinese
da	Danish
de	German
en	English
eo	Esperanto
fi	Finnish
fr	French
he	Hebrew
ia	Interlingua
it	Italian
ja	Japanese
nl	Dutch
ru	Russian
swe	Swedish
vi	Vietnamese
x-klingon	Klingon
zho	Chinese

Line 5 contains the `Accept-Charset` header to tell the server which character sets it can use to represent the characters in the document. A *character set* denotes the relationship between characters and numbers. A multitude of different character sets for different languages exist. Two of the most common are ISO-8859, which is a superset of the age-old ASCII character set, and Unicode, which supports a number of non-English characters including the Cyrillic alphabet and characters for Asian languages such as Japanese and Chinese. In this header, the client accompanies each character set it can support with a quality rating denoted by the Q, so the server knows that ISO-8859 is preferable to ISO-10646-UCS-2. (ISO-10646-UCS-2 is actually the ISO standard describing Unicode, although Unicode has additional features over ISO-10646-UCS-2.)

Line 6 specifies the type of encoding the server may return content using the Accept-Encoding header. This header is similar to the Accept header, except that while the Accept header specifies a document's format, the Accept-Encoding header specifies any compression or other encoding scheme allowed. This client has left this field blank, indicating that only the default coding for a specific type is acceptable.

The next two lines specify the type of client making the request. As discussed in Chapter 2, this header is one of the most important for a content developer. With this information, you can tailor your page's formatting for a specific device, such as taking advantage of a larger screen. Line 7 contains the User-Agent header, describing the kind of client making the request. In this case, the client is a Nokia 7110 screen phone. Line 8, the Via header, says that the client request is coming via a Nokia WAP gateway server. The term "user agent" that you often see in specifications and other documentation is actually a fancy way of saying client. It's derived from the notion that the client is an application agent operating on behalf of a user, such as a Web browser or other application. Unless it's important for you to recognize that the client isn't necessarily a browser, the simpler term *client* or *browser* is used throughout this chapter.

Line 9 is an example of an *extension* header, one not explicitly defined by the HTTP specification. All optional headers must begin with the letter X to indicate that they are extensions to the HTTP protocol. This header, the X-Network-Info header, specifies additional security information about the request. It specifies the originator of the request and the network protocol the client used to make the request. This request came from a client using the IP address 127.0.0.1 using the User Datagram Protocol.

The last header, the Connection header on line 10 tells the server to close the connection to the client after the request has been handled. Clients can use this header to instruct the server to leave the network connection open after completing the current request. Some clients do this and leave the connection open in anticipation of further requests because it's more efficient to do so.

The message returned by the server is in the remaining lines, starting with line 12. The first line of the response gives the version of HTTP supported by the server, in this case HTTP 1.1, along with the status for the request. The status code for this request is 200, indicating that the request completed successfully. The OK message associated with the status code is a human-readable version of the status code, which programmers can use when they're debugging problems by watching the protocol directly.

There are numerous status codes; you'll probably recognize several of them from using the Web. Each status code is a three-digit number followed by a human-readable phrase giving a reason for the status. The first digit of the status code represents the status type, and the remaining two digits represent a specific status within the type of status indicated by the first digit. HTTP defines five status types: "Informational," "Success," "Redirection," "Client Error," and "Server Error," corresponding to the type codes 1-5, respectively. For example, the status code 200 shown in Listing 1-1 indicates that the class of status is "Success," and the remaining two digits 00 indicate that the request was OK. Table 1.2 shows some of the more common status codes and their meanings.

Table 1.2. HTTP Status Codes and Their Meanings

CODE	MEANING
101	Switching Protocols
200	OK
201	Created
202	Accepted
203	Nonauthoritative Information
204	No Content
205	Reset Content
206	Partial Content
300	Multiple Choices
301	Moved Permanently
302	Found
304	Not Modified
305	Use Proxy
307	Temporary Redirect
400	Bad Request
401	Unauthorized
402	Payment Required
403	Forbidden
404	Not Found
405	Method Not Allowed
406	Not Acceptable
407	Proxy Authentication Required
408	Request Time-out
413	Request Entity Too Large
414	Request URI Too Large

Table 1.2. HTTP Status Codes and Their Meanings (Continued)

CODE	MEANING
415	Unsupported Media Type
416	Unable to Satisfy Requested Range
500	Internal Server Error
501	Not Implemented
502	Bad Gateway
503	Service Unavailable
504	Gateway Time-out
505	HTTP Version not supported

Line 13 uses the Date header to report the date and time at which the server handled the request. In HTTP, all dates and times are expressed using a twenty-four hour clock in Greenwich Mean Time (GMT).

Line 14 contains the Server header. This header tells the client the type of server handling the request. In Listing 1-1, it's a build of the popular Apache server running on a UNIX workstation with PHP enabled.

The Last-Modified header in line 15 shows the last time and date (again, always using GMT) that the document was modified. Together with the ETag header in line 16, the Last-Modified header enables a client to manage their *cache*, or local copy, of documents. Clients can keep cache of documents stored locally to avoid making lengthy network transactions to download identical copies of the same document. Understanding how to control what gets cached is an important part of Wireless Web development, which is addressed in greater detail in Chapters 2, 6, and 7. For now, you should know that when a client downloads a document, it usually stores the document, its URL, its last modified date, and its *entity tag*. The entity tag is constructed based on the document's contents and changes when the document changes. By including the last modified date and entity tag of a cached document in a request, a client can ask for a new document only if it's changed, avoiding the need to download the same document over and over again.

The Accept-Ranges and Content-Length headers, shown in lines 16 and 17, give hints as to the position and the number of the bytes in the response. Using the Accept-Ranges header, a client can request individual chunks of a document. Line 16 states that the entire document was returned in this case, and that the server providing the document can handle requests for parts of a document specified by a range of bytes. While not often used by clients, this enables clients with severe memory constraints to make requests such as "give me the first thirty-two bytes of this document," or "give me the contents of the document starting at byte 74 and ending at byte 102." The Content-Length header, on the other hand, tells the client exactly how many bytes are in the response document. Bear in mind that the Content-Length header refers to the length of the content, not the entire message.

The Connection header in line 18 informs the client that the server will close the connection after this response, acknowledging the request Connection header sent by the client.

The last header, the Content-Type header in line 19, tells the client about the format of the requested document. The value of this header is the MIME type of the content being returned. In this case, it states that the server is returning a text document containing Wireless Markup Language because a client can request a host of document types using the Accept header, and the content may not necessarily contain an identification of the format.

After the Content-Type header, starting on line 20, is the contents of the requested document. This is a simple WML document, which is examined in more detail in the following chapter. The request and response you've seen here is typical of the millions that occur over both the Wireless Web and the Web. In general, a user requests a document using a client application (the user agent, generally a Web browser of some kind) and a server returns the document's contents. But another kind of request can also occur and it's worth the time to take a quick look at it before moving on.

Some Web requests occur by submitting data to a remote server for processing, such as when you fill out a form using a Web browser and send the results to the server, or when you answer a questionnaire, or work with a Web application, or buy something (this book, perhaps). Servers can accept your information in one of the following two ways: as an extension to the document's URI with a GET method request, or as a document submitting using HTTP's POST request method.

The first way to send content to a server—extending the document's URI with a GET request method—is the simplest, and dates back to the earliest days of the World Wide Web. With this scheme, the client constructs a URI by appending the document's URI with a question mark and the content to be sent. While simple, this method has disadvantages: it creates unwieldy URLs, is awkward to use for long chunks of content, and challenges the built-in limits to the size of the URI that many servers can handle. For these reasons, submitting data with GET has been deprecated in HTTP, and isn't often used.

The second way—using the POST request method—is far simpler. With this scheme, the client sends a POST request, and includes the content as part of the request. Listing 1-2 shows the client-server exchange where the client does this. (Jumping ahead to our discussion of WML in following chapters, this exchange took place after entering **KF6GPE** on the screen phone and pressing Options, followed by pressing Fetch. Figure 1-7 shows the results.)

```
01: POST /~dove/wap/wx.php3 HTTP/1.1
02: Host: kona.lothlorien.com
03: Content-Type: application/x-www-form-urlencoded
04: Accept: application/vnd.wap.wmlc, application/vnd.wap.wmlscriptc,
    image/vnd.wap.wbmp, application/vnd.wap.wtls-ca-certificate,
    text/plain,text/vnd.wap.wmlscript,text/html,text/vnd.wap.wml
05: Accept-Language: en
06: Accept-Charset: ISO-8859-1, UTF-8; Q=0.8, ISO-10646-UCS-2; Q=0.6
07: User-Agent: Nokia7110/1.0 (04.78)
08: Via: Nokia WAP Server 1.0.2
09: X-Network-Info: UDP,127.0.0.1,security=0
10: Accept-Encoding:
11: Content-Length: 14
12: Date: Wed, 06 Sep 2000 03:15:28 GMT
13: Connection: Close
14:
15: station=kf6gpe9
16:
17: 18 HTTP/1.1 200 OK
18: Date: Wed, 06 Sep 2000 03:19:08 GMT
19: Server: Apache/1.3.12 (Unix) PHP/4.0.1pl2
20: X-Powered-By: PHP/4.0.1pl2
21: Connection: close
22: Transfer-Encoding: chunked
23: Content-Type: text/vnd.wap.wml
24: <wml>
25:   <card title="Weather">
26:     <p>Current readings at station kf6gpe<br/>
27:       Last reading at <b>09/01/2000 18:37</b><br/>
28:       Wind: <b>0 mph</b> from <b>202</b><br/>
29:       Temperature: <b>57 F</b><br/>
30:       Humidity: <b>63</b><br/>
31:      Barometer: <b>1015.9</b><br/>
32:       Rain: <b>0.01</b>/<b>0.25</b> hr/day
33:     </p>
34:   </card>
35: </wml>
```

Listing 1-2. A client-server exchange with HTTP using the POST request method

Figure 1-7. Screen phone display after form submission

On line 1, you see that the request is a POST request. Most of the headers are similar to those shown in the preceding example. The client's POST request includes a Content-Type header on line 3, indicating that the document being sent to the server is a WWW form whose contents have been encoded to preserve the structure of URL's. The POST request also includes a Content-Length header, indicating that the content enclosed in the client's message is fourteen bytes long. After all the headers, you can see the document being sent: the single line station=kf6gpe.

The server's response headers are similar, too. Note, however, that when handling this form, the server decided to include an HTTP extension to state that the server was handling the form submission using PHP with the X-Powered-By header.

While HTTP supports other methods and header types, the two are typical Wireless Web exchanges. In Chapter 3, you learn to write PHP scripts that serve Wireless Web content, and you'll learn how to set the server's response headers to control the remote client's behavior. You'll also learn how to see what headers the client sends you, so you can make determinations about what should be sent back.

Seeing HTTP in Action

One of the best ways to get a firm grasp of how the Wireless Web works is to watch the actual requests and responses, examining each header as you have in this section. While it's not easy to do with real-world servers and screen phones (and most users wouldn't want you eavesdropping as they use the Wireless Web anyway!), it's fairly easy to do in a controlled environment.

For example, to capture the traces you've read about in this section, two machines on their own networks were arranged in my office. One machine, called Client, ran the Nokia SDK (see the following chapter), simulating a screen phone. The other machine, called Kona, ran Linux, including the Apache Web server and PHP processor (discussed in Chapter 3). After writing and testing the documents that Client would download (wx.wml and wxq.php3), I used Linux's tcpdump utility to save the packets exchanged between Client and Kona on my network. The following was the actual command used:

```
tcpdump -i /dev/eth0 -w /tmp/result host kona
```

This command tells the tcpdump program to copy all packets to and from Kona on its Ethernet port to the file /tmp/result.

Then with Client, I downloaded a document using the Nokia SDK's screen phone emulator. When finished, I hit **control-c** on Kona to stop the tcpdump program. Then, I could peruse the file /tmp/result at my leisure, seeing not just HTTP messages, but the actual TCP/IP packets, too. (The TCP/IP packet contents often appear as garbage or control characters; to see what they mean, you can use tcpdump to parse the file you saved using the command `tcpdump -r file`.)

Because being able to see network traffic is an obvious security hole, you'll either need to have super-user access on your Linux machine or have the permission of your system administrator to use tcpdump. If you don't have access to a Linux server and you want to do this, you can use one of the many network-monitoring packages available for Microsoft Windows or Mac OS such as AG Group's EtherPeek. You get a better understanding of how HTTP handles client-server interaction, when you can both watch as you browse existing WAP sites with a simulator and create your own pages to see what happens.

Markup Languages

In computing, just as in life, sometimes the oldest concepts pervade the newest ideas. In printed publishing, authors have used *markup* in their documents, indicating to publishers how things should be typeset. This practice predates desktop publishing by years, perhaps even centuries. But as computers became more powerful, they were used to format and typeset documents, using *markup languages* derived from the ones publishers and typesetting machines accepted. Over the last twenty years, several markup languages have become popular in various parts of the computer and publishing industry, including TeX, nroff, LaTeX, Standard Generalized Markup Language (SGML), and HTML (HyperText Markup Language). More recently, the Wireless Markup Language (WML) has become the language used by most of today's Wireless Web clients.

History

By the mid-1960s, several groups were discussing a key aspect of document markup: the need to separate content and its structure. A document's content consists of the symbols it contains (words, punctuation, images, and so on), whereas its structure is how the document itself is organized. Separation of content and structure has many advantages, including freeing the author from worrying about both issues at the same time. Other advantages include the capability of having a single document's contents appear to be uniform when printed in different venues (say, a scientific paper in a journal and later in an anthology), and the capability to preserve a document's content over the lifetime of different markup languages.

As a result of numerous efforts SGML was created by designers who hoped it would provide a *lingua franca* for all markup languages. As with many attempts to unify a field, the results were broad, generally applicable, and, quite frankly, wholly unfathomable to many of the people SGML was supposed to help. SGML's wide applicability made it complex. While relatively few computer professionals have ever probed its depths, some have used SGML to create simpler markup languages, relying on SGML as a foundation to meet specific needs.

The most widely known example of this is HTML. Derived from SGML (some dialects of HTML are actually well formed markup languages that can be formally defined in SGML), HTML gave scientists, authors, programmers, and artists a simple markup language for creating richly formatted documents that could be linked to other documents. HTML's markup capabilities are vastly inferior to other existing markup languages for printed document preparation, and they are well suited to readers accessing documents over a network. With the advance of HTTP and HTML, the World Wide Web was born.

As HTML evolved, numerous efforts were made to bring HTML browsers to mobile and wireless devices. By 1995, a number of handheld computers used in academic and corporate research institutions could view HTML; the trend continues today with Web browsers available for handheld computers from Palm, Hewlett-Packard, Compaq, Psion, and many others.

At the same time, other developers were examining how the human-machine interface for handheld computers differed from that used by conventional computers, and the impact that these differences had on a document's content and structure. As you'll see in Chapter 2, many limitations exist such as small screens, limited bandwidth, and limited memory. Plus, a number of differences arise from the way users interact with wireless devices and their desktop kin. For many, these differences require a different approach. One company, Phone.com (previously Unwired Planet) developed a markup language to meet the needs of mobile devices.

Phone.com created the Handheld Device Markup Language (HDML), which is a markup language largely based on HTML that provides structure elements uniquely tailored to small-screen devices. Phone.com also aggressively marketed both their HDML specification and a browser implementation to a number of phone vendors. Over time, Phone.com and these vendors worked together, forming the Wireless Application Protocol Forum (WAP Forum), a forum of telecommunication companies working in concert to establish inter-operating standards for wireless data exchange.

Among the standards maintained by the WAP Forum is the Wireless Markup Language. WML's roots are in HDML, just as HDML's roots are in HTML. Readers familiar with any one of these markup languages—SGML, HTML, or HDML—will doubtless find much that they recognize in WML, although new elements exist as well. In addition, WML is a well-formed markup language when viewed from the perspective of XML, the eXtensible Markup Language. Many view XML as the successor to SGML, albeit with significantly less complexity and a corresponding improvement in public adoption.

Anatomy of a Markup Language

Markup languages such as HTML and WML share basic conceptual building blocks. These blocks include *tags*, *attributes*, *comments*, and *entities*.

A marked-up document contains text and *tags* dictating the document's structure. These tags are special groups of characters with well-understood meanings, such as "make the enclosed text a page title" or "make the following text stand out." In HTML, XML, and WML, greater-than and less-than symbols enclose tags, such as this <TAG>. Listing 1-3 shows an example of a marked-up document using WML.

```
01: <?xml version="1.0"?>
02: <!DOCTYPE wml PUBLIC "-//WAPFORUM//DTD WML 1.1//EN"
    "http://www.wapforum.org/DTD/wml_1.1.xml">
03: <wml>
04:   <card title="Weather">
05:     <p>Current readings at station kf6gpe<br/>
06:       Last reading at <b>09/01/2000 18:37</b><br/>
07:       Wind: <b>0 mph</b> from <b>202</b><br/>
08:       Temperature: <b>57 F</b><br/>
09:       Humidity: <b>63</b><br/>
10:       Barometer: <b>1015.9</b><br/>
11:       Rain: <b>0.01</b>/<b>0.25</b> hr/day
12:     </p>
13:   </card>
14: </wml>
```

Listing 1-3. A marked-up document in WML

For now, the tags themselves aren't important, but in reading Listing 1-3, you see three things:

- Many tags, such as the `<wml>` tag shown in line 3, contain content between the beginning tag and a corresponding *closing* tag, consisting of the same tag name with a preceding solidus (/) character. (For consistency, the pair of tags, opening and closing, are referred to as a single tag, even though there are really two components.)

- Other tags are *empty*, that is, they have no corresponding closing tag. The `<br/>` tag found in line 5 is an example of an empty tag.

- Some tags, such as the `<card>` tag in line 4, have *attributes* that modify the tag's behavior. The `title` attribute of the card tag supplies the card the browser presents with a title of Weather.

Although Listing 1-3 doesn't show it, a marked-up document can also contain *comments*. A comment is a markup element that's meant for human readers of the marked-up content, rather than either the software that's responsible for showing the markup or the end-user reading the markup. Comments usually refer to aspects of the markup, rather than the content of the document. See how to make comments in WML in Chapter 2.

Most markup languages also provide *entities*, atomic character units built from separate characters. An entity is a primitive element of the markup language that stands for something else. For example, because you have to use the greater-than and less-than symbols in WML to create a tag, WML provides the `&gt;` and `&lt;` entities to represent the < and > symbols in the final document.

Programs

Writing programs of any kind is part craft and part engineering. Even though a body of knowledge has been accumulated about how to make computers do things, writing a program still requires an ineffable skill that's only acquired with practice, effort, and experience. While distilling the essence behind the craft of software development exceeds the limits of this chapter, some of the important things you need to know to write a program are discussed. If after reading this section, you still feel you're out of your league, don't panic. After discovering how to write scripts in PHP and WMLScript, you'll have ample opportunity to hone your skills. Rome wasn't built in a day, and it generally takes more than a one-chapter lesson to learn how to write a program.

For more reading about the craft of software development, look at Dan Appleman's *How Computer Programming Works* or Kernigan & Pike's *The Practice of Programming*.

Anatomy of a Program

Software, or a computer program, is a collection of instructions that you write in a language the computer understands that tells the computer what to do. In the simplest sense, markup languages such as the ones discussed in the last section can be considered programs because they tell a computer how to present words and images to the user. In the case of a markup language, the program is the marked-up document, which is presented by another program such as a Web browser or document viewer. Other times, however, the program may be translated directly into a representation that the computer understands that controls the computer's hardware directly.

Both approaches have their advantages. *Interpreted languages*—those languages that are interpreted by a separate program when they are run—are often easy to learn quickly. As you learn an interpreted language, you can quickly make small changes to your program to see what happens. In addition, interpreted languages are easily ported from one computer to another. By comparison, *compiled languages*—those languages that require additional steps to translate the human-readable language to a compact machine-readable form—generally create programs that run faster and are more flexible. This book focuses on two interpreted languages (three, if you count WML as a programming language): WMLScript, the scripting language used by the Wireless Web, and PHP, a scripting language used to create active Web pages.

Interpreted and compiled languages share common elements such as *literals, statements, operations, variables, blocks, comments, flow control*, and *functions*. Programs are made up of these basic building blocks. At the heart of the differences between programming languages is how these building blocks are expressed. Listing 1-4 shows a simple program written in PHP. In Chapter 3, you learn what each line actually does; for now, let's just look at some of the elements in the program itself.

```
01: <?php
02:    /*
03:     * SaveAndShowHeaders
04:     * Iterates over the given array and prints each header to
05:     * the client and a log file.
06:     */
07:    function SaveAndShowHeaders( $header )
```

```
08:    {
09:      $f = fopen( "hdr", "a" );
10:      fputs( $f, date( "Y-M-d H:i\n" ) );
11:      for ( reset($header); $index=key($header);
12:        next($header) )
13:      {
14:        $value = $header[ $index ];
15:        print("$index: $value<br/>\n");
16:        fputs( $f, "$index: $value\n" );
17:      }
18:      fputs( $f, "\n" );
19:      fclose( $f );
20:    }
21:
22:    header("Content-type: text/vnd.wap.wml");
23:    echo( "<?xml version=\"1.0\"?>\n" );
24:    echo( "<!DOCTYPE wml PUBLIC " );
25:    echo( "\"-//WAPFORUM//DTD WML 1.1//EN\" " );
26:    echo( "\"http://www.wapforum.org/DTD/wml_1.1.xml\">\n" );
27:    echo( "<wml>\n" );
28:    echo( "<card title=\"Headers\">\n" );
29:    echo( "<p>" );
30:    $header=getallheaders();
31:    SaveAndShowHeaders( $header );
32:    echo( "</p></card></wml>\n" );
33: ?>
```

Listing 1-4. A simple PHP program

The program shown in Listing 1-4 defines a single function, SaveAndShowAllHeaders, and uses several PHP functions to obtain a client's HTTP headers and log them to a file on the server and show them on the client, as shown in Figure 1-8.

Figure 1-8. Listing 1-4 executed on a server when accessed by a screen phone

A *literal* is a token with an atomic meaning. In line 29, for example, you see the literal "`<p>`", which represents the characters `<`, `p`, and `>`. This is an example of a string literal, commonly called a string. Strings contain groups of characters between delimiters (in this case, quote marks) that can be searched, combined, separated, and displayed. Literals also represent numbers such as integers and floating-point numbers, although Listing 1-4 doesn't have any of these examples.

In conjunction with literals, *statements* tell the computer to do something, such as make a decision or exit the current program. Line 11 is an example of a *flow control* statement, the `for` statement. This statement directs the computer to perform an action a specific number of times, until a desired situation occurs. You separate each statement by a specific character. In the case of PHP, statements are separated by the semicolon `;`. For clarity, I usually put each statement on its own line, although there's no requirement to do this in most languages.

Programs are broken up into *blocks* of statements. In the case of PHP, blocks are enclosed by the curly braces `{` and `}`. Blocks are used to indicate the scope of another statement's behavior. For example after the `for` statement on line 11, you can see a group of statements in a block. When the computer executes the `for` statement, it repeats the block starting on line 13 and ending at line 17.

Some statements are actually *operations*, instructions to do something to something else. An operation usually represents a single step that the computer takes, such as an mathematical operation (addition, subtraction, multiplication, or division), or comparison, and so on. Operations are used sparsely in Listing 1-4, but you see one operation, the `=` or assignment operator, on line 11.

As it turns out, the assignment operator is closely related to the use of a *variable*. A variable is a named container that stores something. The notion of computer variable is similar to the notion of a variable in mathematics, but there are important differences. You can assign values, either literals or the contents of another variable, to a variable using the assignment operator. On line 30, you can see that something's being assigned to the variable `$header`. In the following line, the value of the variable `$header` is being used. Unlike mathematical variables, the value of a computer variable can change, and you can use one computer variable in different ways. You also can't solve for the values of computer variables.

Variables play an important role in *functions*. A function is a block of statements that you've given a unique name. Later, you can use this name to cause the statements to be executed. Lines 7 through 20 define a single function, `SaveAndShowAllHeaders`. This function has one input, the variable `$h`. When you use the function `SaveAndShowAllHeaders`, you must include a value for `$h`. In Line 29, I call the function, giving it the value of the `$header` variable, which is assigned to the variable `$h` for the duration of the function. It is said that `$h` has scope over the function `SaveAndShowAllHeaders`, meaning that `$h` only contains a valid value while the function is executing. Elsewhere, `$h` simply doesn't exist—if you try to access it, you get an error or a meaningless value.

When you write a program, most of what you write is intended for the computer. Sometimes, though, you want to make a note to yourself, explaining why you did what you did, or so you can understand what you're doing later. To do this, you can use a *comment*, which is a bit of text that the computer ignores that you can read. A comment is used in lines 2–6 to describe what the SaveAndShowAllHeaders function does in a human-readable way, so the next time this program is examined, it won't be necessary to stop and figure out what the code is doing. Comments are a very important and oft-overlooked part of programming. By liberally commenting your program (and keeping your comments up-to-date with what your program does) you won't spend your time trying to think as a computer to understand what you've already written.

A great deal of the work behind writing a program is simply deciding what steps the computer must take to accomplish your desired action. Making these decisions becomes an exercise in *decomposition*, that is, taking a big problem and breaking it into smaller problems. For example, Listing 1-4 started with a problem that could be phrased as the question "How do I see what headers my screen phone sends?" Then it was broken into several smaller questions, which were answered with specific pieces of the program as follows:

- "How do I show and save the headers?" This question was answered with the function SaveAndShowAllHeaders, used on line 31.

- "How do I tell the client what kind of document I'm displaying?" This was answered with the statement on line 22.

- "How do I start the document?" This was answered with the series of calls to PHP's echo function starting on line 23.

- "How do I end the result document?" This question was answered with the call to PHP's echo function on line 33.

Two popular approaches to decomposition are *functional* decomposition and *object* decomposition. In functional description, you break a problem down into smaller and smaller problems, each of which can be addressed by a specific function. In object decomposition, you break a problem down by looking at different objects in the problem, such as clients, records of data, and so on. Then you define parts of your program to model the behavior of each kind of object. Some languages, such as Smalltalk, C++, or Java, have special facilities to make object decomposition easier, although with discipline you can use the practice with any language. Much of what separates experienced programmers from novices is that as you gain experience, you learn how to decompose problems more efficiently.

The Program

Throughout the remainder of this book, most of the listings shown are from parts of a single program. While the users and constraints of this program are imaginary, the program itself is real; you'll find a copy of it on the CD-ROM that accompanies this book. Before jumping headlong into developing content for the Wireless Web, let's take a closer look at the application itself.

MobileHelper

This book's application addresses one of the most common mobile application targets: organizing the efforts of people serving the needs of other people. The MobileHelper application on the accompanying CD-ROM is designed to meet the needs of small volunteer organizations that track volunteers as they proceed to and from assigned stations at particular dates and times.

MobileHelper was written for an imaginary volunteer organization, the Mountain Neighbors Network (MNN), located in a quaint rural community. Members of the MNN check on each other and their neighbors after regional incidents such as earthquakes and floods. In the process, they often provide much-needed first-tier relief before larger organizations such as the county's emergency response services or the Red Cross can deploy their staff to provide services.[1]

Volunteers in the MNN perform two roles: emergency coordinator and relief volunteer. Members may fulfill either role, although additional training is necessary to fulfill the role of emergency coordinator. After an incident begins, the emergency coordinator is responsible for directing the tasks and responsibilities of each relief volunteer. Typically, relief volunteers check in with their neighbors, making sure that people are okay and determining what, if any help (such as medical attention, additional shelter, food, or water) may be required. Presently, MNN has one emergency coordinator, Sandy, and a handful of relief volunteers, including Chris and Pat.

Sandy uses MobileHelper to assign Chris and Pat specific tasks to perform such as checking with neighbors at a set time or visiting the local Red Cross shelter. Sandy can do this either at home using her PC or in the field from her screen phone. Similarly, Chris and Pat can check with MobileHelper to determine what they need to do or where they need to be at a particular time. Once they've completed a task, they check with MobileHelper to inform Sandy, rather than having to contact Sandy directly.

---

1. Imaginative readers are encouraged to believe that this neighborhood is quite like the one I live in, albeit with an improved and fault-tolerant wireless service supporting the application.

MobileHelper itself must meet the following needs:

- Store a list of tasks (dates, times, locations, and status) for volunteers.

- Provide access at two levels: an administrative access where a user can create new tasks, assign tasks to volunteers, obtain reports regarding the status of tasks, and so on.

- Be accessible to handheld phones and Web browsers running on a desktop computer.

- Send messages between volunteers.

These needs are similar to that for a number of wireless services, including field dispatch tools, wireless mail clients and personal information systems, sales force automation applications, and so on. However, by restricting MobileHelper's scope to that of a volunteer organization, it avoids many of the messy details involved in creating a larger system as you focus on learning how to write Wireless Web content.[2]

Software Notation

To help software developers visualize how a program operates, they use a variety of higher-level techniques. These techniques enable them to think in more abstract ways about how a program operates, rather than at the level of variables, statements, and operations.

The three techniques are to use cases, deployment diagrams, and sequence diagrams. Each technique provides a level of precision and brevity that's hard to achieve in a natural language such as English, and gives a level of abstraction you won't find in a programming language. And each is a valuable tool you may want to learn to use when describing how your own programs operate. These diagrams are all part of a formal notation called the Unified Modeling Language (UML), which aims to provide developers with a common language for representing system behaviors of all kinds.

---

2. I admit to an ulterior motive in selecting a scenario for volunteer applications as well: it may remind you that volunteering your time for public service, with whatever skills you have, can be deeply rewarding.

Use Cases

A *use case* is a pictorial diagram that shows the relationship between those that depend on part of an
application, the *actors*, and the tasks performed by
the application. An actor is anything outside the
application that interacts with the application in
some way. You can identify actors by making a list of
the kinds of things—people or other applications—
that will use your application. Divide them up into

Figure 1-9. An actor

similar groups, such as "system administrators," "end users," "power users,"
"managers," and so on. Each group represents a single actor. Figure 1-9 shows the
symbol used to represent an actor in a use case.

Let's look at an actual use case and see what the different symbols mean.
Figure 1-10 is a use case used by two actors: the Coordinator and the Volunteer.
The Coordinator actor represents MNN volunteers that are emergency coordinators,
whereas the Volunteer actor represents the relief volunteers. This use case
demonstrates how users prove their identity to MobileHelper. All users must
prove who they are; volunteers can simply use their mobile phone number (called
a Mobile Identification Number, or MIN), whereas a Coordinator must also enter
a private Personal Identification Number (PIN) before performing administrative
functions. In the figure, you see that the Volunteer actor uses the Auth use case.
This use case relies on two other use cases, the Check MIN use case and the Reject
User use, which the diagram shows with the dashed arrow and the <<include>>
label. In contrast, the Coordinator actor relies on the AuthAdmin use case to perform administration tasks (as well as the Auth use case to access MobileHelper
when the Coordinator is simply accessing the system as a volunteer does). The
AuthAdmin use case is an *extension* of the Auth use case; alternately, it can be said
that the Auth use case is a *generalization* of the Authenticate Coordinator use
case. Regardless, a solid line with a hollow error is used, pointing to the more general
of the two use cases. In the AuthAdmin use case, a simple description of the nature of
the extension is also included. Finally, the little sticky-note-like box in the bottom
left-hand corner is a comment; it holds a note for readers pointing out that the
Coordinator actor only uses the AuthAdmin use case when it needs to perform an
administrative function.

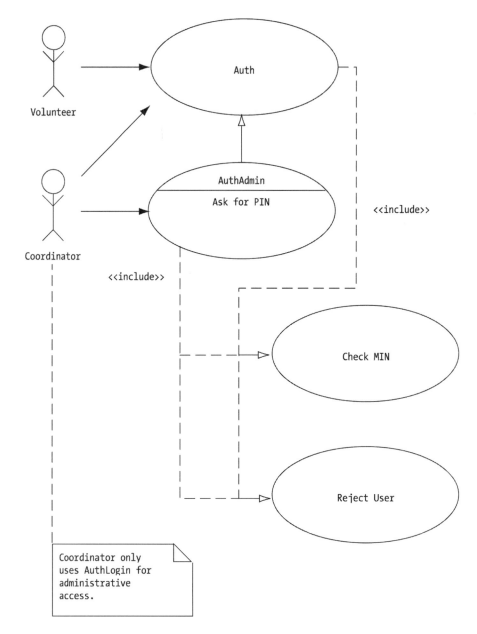

Figure 1-10. Login use case for MobileHelper

Use case diagrams are often accompanied by a textual description of the use case, including the name of the use case, what actors use the use case, and the steps the actor and system must perform in order to fulfill the use case. For example, the Auth use case is shown in Listing 1-5.

```
01: Use Case: Auth
02: Purpose: Used by actors to prove their identity to the
03:          system.
04: Includes: Check MIN, Reject User
05: Flow of Events:
06: 1. The user accesses the main page for MobileHelper.
07: 2. The MobileHelper application obtains the MIN from the
08:    client's HTTP headers.
09: 3. If no MIN is available, the MobileHelper application
10:    redirects the client to a page prompting the user for
11:    their MIN.
12: 4. Use the Check MIN use case to verify the identify of
13:    the user.
14: 5. If the identify of the user cannot be validated, use
15:    the Reject User use case and return to step 1.
16: Otherwise show the user the main page.
```

Listing 1-5. The Auth use case

The listing begins with the name of the use case and its description. Even though you can look at the diagram to see who uses the use case, it is displayed in the use case as well, so you don't have to flip back and forth. A list of the use cases that use this use case is also included.

After that, the use case lists the flow of events that make up the use case. These are a natural language description of what the user and application do to complete the use case. It's helpful if you number the steps because you can have steps pointing at each other, the way it's done in step 5. Listing 1-5 looks as if it's a program a little bit more than Figure 1-10 does. As you learn in following chapters, the text of a use case is often where you start converting a description of how the program should behave into the program itself.

Deployment Diagrams

While a use case shows how someone uses an application, a deployment diagram shows how you've organized the computers that run the application. You've seen three examples of deployment diagrams in Figures 1-2, 1-3, and 1-4. Figure 1-11 shows yet another deployment diagram, that of how a wireless network can be organized.

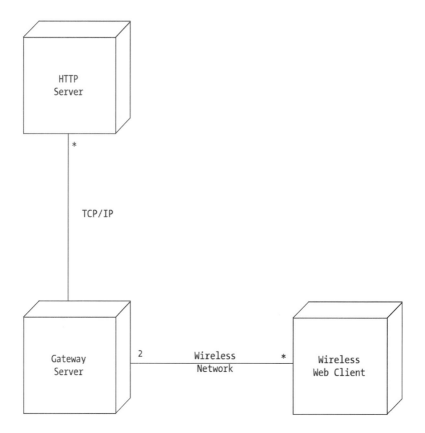

Figure 1-11. A wireless network

Deployment diagrams represent each computer as a three-dimensional box. The solid lines between each box show how the computers are connected. In Figure 1-11, you see that the HTTP Server computer is connected to the Gateway Server via TCP/IP, whereas individual wireless clients connect to the Gateway Server via the wireless network. The little symbols by the individual solid lines show how many individual machines are on a specific side of the connection. For example, the figure shows two Gateway Servers serving the clients. The * by the Wireless Web Clients and HTTP Server boxes indicates that there can be any number of these machines.

Sometimes you want to show in greater detail the individual components within a given computer and how they relate in the context of a deployment diagram. Figure 1-12 shows such a diagram, in which MobileHelper is actually a bunch of PHP scripts that the Apache Web server accesses. The smaller boxes contained in the HTTP server cube refer to specific system components: the Apache Web server and the PHP script interpreter.

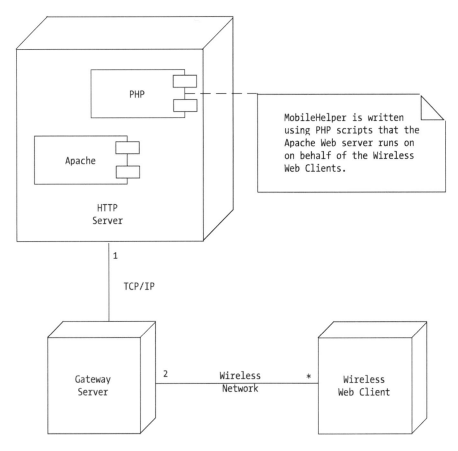

Figure 1-12. MobileHelper deployment diagram

Sequence Diagrams

You've seen an example of a sequence diagram, too, back in Figure 1-5. Sequence diagrams show the progression of a series of activities over time as objects take action. Within a sequence diagram, each object that participates in the activity is shown as a box along the top of the diagram, while time increases as you look from top to bottom. The vertical line below an object is called its *lifeline*, and shows how long the object exists. Objects send messages to each other. These messages are shown as solid arrows with labels describing the message. Figure 1-13 shows a sequence diagram for the two HTTP requests examined in Listings 1-1 and 1-2. Here, the Wireless Web Client is shown, as are the network connection (called a *socket)* that's used for each request, and the HTTP server.

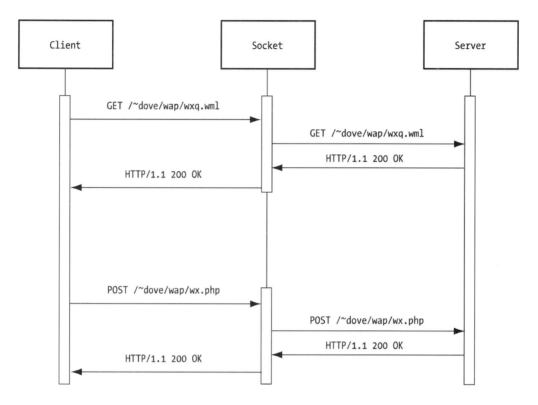

Figure 1-13. Sequence diagram of HTTP GET *followed by HTTP* POST

This diagram shows the Wireless Web Client first fetching the page using a GET request, and the server sending the response. A single network socket is used to carry this request and response; after the messages are passed, the server closes the socket, and the socket's lifeline ends. Later, when the Wireless Web Client wants to submit user input, it creates a new socket, and uses the new socket to send the second message (the POST message) to the server, which in turn processes the POST message and returns a response. You can see clearly from the diagram the impact of the HTTP Connection header: two different network sockets are used between client and server. After each message, the socket object disappears, shown by the end of its lifeline.

Software Development Process

While many people have the impression that programmers simply sit down at a keyboard and write programs, nothing could be further from the truth. In fact, programming is an orchestrated harmony of planning, investigation, experimentation, documentation, and construction. Ask most professional programmers what they do most in their jobs and they're apt to tell you that they spend most of their time either thinking or writing. Determining what a program should do, how it should look, and decomposing the problem are all steps you have to take before writing the program itself.

Understanding how to organize a software project—the collection of tasks that constitutes writing a program—enables you to write better programs. This understanding gives you a framework for organizing your thoughts. By viewing the writing of a simple program as a software project instead of simply a handful of lines of code you'll write, you gain the ability to organize your thoughts and create a better program. Later, as you gain experience with this method, you'll have greater confidence and the skills you need to attack the problems that arise when you create a larger program.

To reflect this aspect of programming, people refer to the software development life cycle. There are a number of life cycle models; each emphasizing particular kinds of activities that you undertake as you create a software product. One especially successful life cycle is the *iterative life cycle*, also known as the *Rational Model*.

In the iterative life cycle, creating a program is broken into four phases: *inception*, *elaboration*, *construction*, and *transition*. In each step, you focus on only some of the tasks you need to accomplish to create an application. In one sense, the software life cycle is simply another example of decomposition: it's an exercise in decomposing how people write programs.

A key aspect of the iterative life cycle is that you don't stop after one pass through each phase. Many large software projects go through this lifecycle over and over again. With each pass through the life cycle, a new set of features is added, enhancing the overall application. In fact, that's how you'll write the program that comes with the CD-ROM in this book. In Chapters 2 and 3, you begin building the basic parts of wireless application using a combination of simple programs and throwaway prototypes that demonstrate principles of Wireless Web development. As you proceed further, each of these parts is tested. Then new features are added over the subsequent chapters, working through the life cycle in each chapter.

Let's take a closer look at each of the phases in the iterative life cycle.

Inception

During *inception*, you explain to yourself and others what the program is, and why it's important. This is the make-or-break period where you decide whether or not it's worth the time and effort to write the program in the first place. When you're working with others, you outline what the program does at a high level, find out what you think it costs to write the program, and whether or not the program will repay the cost. (When working on a personal project, you look at the same issues, but your measurements may not be the same. For instance, you can ask yourself,

"Is it worth it for me to spend a month's worth of evenings so I can balance my checkbook on my screen phone?")

One of the best ways to do this is to write a short description of the project. This description should include notes about whom the program is for and what the program will do. You want to keep this description short—less than a page if possible. If you're working with a team, it's important to get everybody involved in this stage to share ideas about what the project will accomplish and what the program will do.

A good outline for the project description is as follows:

1. Problem Description

2. Requirements

3. Risks & Assumptions

In the problem description, you describe the problem you're trying to solve. Then you describe what requirements the application will have: what computers it will run on, how many users the application needs to support, and so on. Finally, you describe the assumptions and risks that impact your ability to succeed.

Once you write the project description, you're better able to ask yourself whether or not you should attempt the project. You can weigh the risks and the size of the project, and look at what you'll achieve by solving the problem you describe.

Elaboration

During *elaboration*, you refine your understanding of what your application does, and what problems you need to solve before finishing your program. Of course, you started this refinement when you wrote your project description, but now you will find you have more questions than answers.

A key part of elaboration is determining how your application works. To answer this question, you can use the technique of use cases described in the preceding section to outline how people will use your application. In turn, these use cases help you understand how you can decompose your problem further, either by creating the functions that implement the use cases, or by determining what kinds of objects can model the behavior your use cases describe. Be careful, though, because you're elaborating, not coding! It's sufficient now to simply give yourself a description of the functions or objects and their responsibilities as you discover them.

But you may actually spend some time programming as you elaborate your project, too. Most of the time, the programs you write at this stage are to determine how something works. In some cases, you write small programs called *prototypes* that simulate different ways your program can work. Some of these prototypes show possible user interfaces; other prototypes enable you to test different ways you might actually build your application. Often, these prototypes are ways to mitigate the risks you uncovered in the project description.

Speaking of risks, you also add to your lists of risks as you spend time in the elaboration phase. You will doubtless come across new risks, and resolve some of the risks you identified earlier. As you do so, you should track these risks, and ask yourself what you can do to keep their likelihood to a minimum.

Construction

Once you have a thorough understanding of your application from elaboration, you begin the *construction* phase. By now, you have a good grasp of how your program works, what functions you need to write, what objects you need to model, and so on. As a result, you actually spend most of your time writing your program in this phase. You also build tests to validate your program, or if you're part of a larger group, you may work with other people responsible for building the tests that validate your program.

Construction itself is best approached in iterations. Start by identifying the core pieces of your application that demonstrate some initial functionality, and construct just those pieces. Once you've built them, you can test and demonstrate your application in limited ways. Not only does this give you a feeling of accomplishment, but also it provides a firm foundation on which to add functionality.

You write more than just your program during construction, however. It's important that you write tests that verify your program at the same time. Some of these tests are called *unit tests*, because they test a specific piece of your application. Other times, your tests exercise your entire application. If you're working with a group, you have other people testing your work, and you need to work with them to determine how best to test your program.

Transition

As you finish writing your program, you enter the *transition* phase, and your program moves from active development to active use. During transition, you teach the people who will use your program how to use it, how to maintain it, and what to do if it needs to be changed. You may be responsible for assisting with the production of manuals, training materials, or other information. You may also simply set the program aside, so you can use it when you work on something else.

As with construction, transition is iterative. You'll probably transition your software several times, after adding set features. Some of these will be formal releases to other organizations such as testers, friends, family, or customers. Others may be informal; you may simply snapshot a working version and set it aside so you can use it as you continue adding features.

Food for Thought

- What kinds of protocols do you follow in daily life? Think about how you exchange information with people in different ways. How would you describe one of these protocols?

- Can you think of other protocols that may be client-server protocols? How are they similar to HTTP? How are they different?

- Use the technique shown in the sidebar on page 16 to eavesdrop on an exchange between a desktop Web client and a Web server. Find out what each header means. (You may want to refer to the Internet Engineering Task Force's documentation on HTTP at `http://www.ietf.org/`.)

- List the markup languages you know—either that you've used to create content, or that you can understand. What do they have in common? What is different?

- If you wanted to create your own programming language, what would it look like? What kind of statements would it have? What kind of operators would it offer?

- Can you think of other areas of your life—your job, your responsibilities at home, or elsewhere—where using the approach in the iterative life cycle would help? Why or why not?

- Draw a use case diagram showing use cases for a common household appliance, such as a VCR, microwave, or toaster oven. Who are the actors? What are the use cases?

- Draw a deployment diagram for the computers on the network in your office.

- Draw a sequence diagram showing what happens when you make a credit card payment.

#### CHAPTER 2

The Wireless Application Protocol and Wireless Markup Language

AT THE HEART OF THE WIRELESS WEB is the Wireless Application Protocol (WAP). WAP builds on the Web's successful technologies (including the HyperText Transport Protocol and Transport Security Layer) and provides a suite of standards for efficient wireless data exchange. The Wireless Web without WAP would be like, well, bacon and ice cream, to paraphrase Lou Reed.

This chapter introduces you to the principles of designing for the Wireless Web, along with how to mark up your content using the Wireless Markup Language (WML). The chapter covers the differences between the Web and the Wireless Web, how to use some of the various tools for creating and testing WML documents, and the Wireless Markup Language itself. Finally, you learn you how to build a prototype of MobileHelper using WML.

The Wireless Web

The Wireless Web is a curious blend of the familiar and the novel, and understanding why this is so will help you understand WAP. More importantly, understanding the differences between the Wireless Web and the Web will help you create better content.

The Wireless Web Is Different

Unless you've actually spent time using one of today's smart phones, you may not be aware that there's a gaping crevasse between the marketing promise of the Wireless Web and the present-day reality. This should not discourage you from

Wireless Web development, but it is an honest assessment of how businesses—today's wireless providers and content developers—build their market share. Over time, technology and content will help bridge the gap, but the fundamental difference will always be the user. Regardless of what wireless providers promise, human interface factors and user expectations of the Wireless Web are far different than for the wired Web.

Before I talk about the typical wireless user, let's look at some of the technology behind the Wireless Web. Today's technologies have several inherent limitations. Smart phones (a term I'll use broadly to refer to anything that has a Wireless Web client, including both true smart phones and devices such as Palm's Palm VII running a WAP client) are wee little beasties, often the size of your fist. Packed inside is a host of electronics, including a radio, computer, screen, keypad, audio hardware, and all the glue that holds these together, along with the batteries that make it go. Not only does the entire package have to be small, it must be cheap: consumers won't pay more than a few hundred dollars for a high-end smart phone. With this small size and constrained cost come a host of limitations, which boil down to four simple consequences:

- Smart phones have limited memory.

- Smart phones have limited computational resources.

- Smart phones have small screens.

- Smart phones have limited throughput.

Smart phones have very little memory when compared to desktop and laptop computers. Cell phone manufacturers generally don't state available memory, but you can bet it will be measured in kilobytes, not megabytes. Even the high-end devices incorporating operating systems such as Symbian or Palm OS have only a few megabytes; until recently, handheld computers offering 4 or 8 megabytes were considered top-of-the-line. Because memory occupies space and is one of the most expensive components in a device, phones get by with as little memory as possible. While you can expect that, over time, phones will be offered with an increasing amount of memory, it's likely that the amount of memory will always be significantly less than you find in other products such as dedicated handheld computers, or their laptop or desktop brethren.

Closely related to constrained memory is constrained processing. Because of the need to keep both purchase prices and energy consumption low, smart phones have fairly slow processors. Consequently, their operating systems and other software, including the client, must be simple. Obviously, simple clients prefer simple content; even if enough memory were available to handle large pages, it would take too long to parse the markup language and present the results.

The screens themselves are constrained, too. Manufacturing costs keep the screen primitive, usually monochrome with a low pixel count. The average screen is on the order of 150 pixels square; while some phones have larger screens, many have screens much smaller than that. Although screen quality will continue to improve, there are fundamental limits. The size of the phone puts an obvious upper limit on how big the screen can be, while the acuity of human vision determines the minimum size a pixel can be. There's no point in making a megapixel display for a 2-inch phone screen; each pixel would be only 2 millionths of an inch across!

Finally, the wireless networks supporting smart phones are slow. Today's wireless networks operate anywhere from 2.4 Kbps to 14.4 Kbps, rates that no self-respecting Web user would tolerate from his or her modem. Data rates will improve over time: the industry's third-generation (commonly called 3G) network initiatives promise data rates comparable to ISDN. This will certainly address much of the current throughput crunch, but rollout of networks supporting 3G won't happen overnight. Critics also point to weaknesses in 3G network design that may lead to significantly lower data rates than promised by manufacturers.

Even postulating order-of-magnitude improvements in these four areas, there's an additional constraint: the Wireless Web user. Wireless Web users aren't like Web users. They're on the go: in meetings, commuting, shopping, driving (frightening, I know), walking, or actively doing *something else in addition to accessing the network*. Compare this to how you use the Web: you sit down, launch a client on a big screen, put one hand on the mouse and another on the keyboard, and surf. Other things you do, such as watch TV, answer e-mail, or even work at your day job, tend to take a back seat in your consciousness. While the bulk of your attention is devoted to your online activities, the same can't be said about your friend on Wireless Web. In a very real way, Wireless Web users suffer from a restriction of cognitive throughput because they can't devote their full attention to the content they're viewing.

For all these reasons—especially the last—the Wireless Web is different than the traditional Web. WAP addresses these differences (see the section, "The Wireless Application Protocol"), making the Wireless Web practical for millions of users.

The Wireless Web User Interface

A key to the success of the Wireless Web is the recognition that the interface to the Wireless Web must be different than the interface to a conventional client. Neither Wireless Web clients nor their users are up to the challenge of viewing content from the conventional Web. WML provides a markup language that's optimized for simple clients to display while providing interface elements that make the most of a smart phone's display for potentially distracted users. Among the differences you should understand from the outset are content size and user-input constraints, graphics, and the new layouts WML affords.

Before I show you these differences, I should point out some of the common-alities. As you view content, you can scroll, select links, and even enter text and make choices (albeit slowly using a 10-key keypad on most devices). When browsing the Wireless Web, you can follow links between decks—the Wireless Web analogue of Web pages—or enter the URL of a deck you'd like to see. You can also bookmark favorite decks, although in most cases, the wireless service provider, rather than the smart phone's client, stores your bookmarks.

> **NOTE** *Some carriers may restrict what decks you can load, limiting subscribers to a "walled garden" of content, rather than any deck at any URL on the Wireless Web. Their justification—that doing so ensures that subscribers see only content of the highest quality—strikes me as dubious at best. When deploying your wireless application, be sure to explore this possibility with your audience's wireless carriers.*

An essential part of designing Wireless Web content is brevity. Your Wireless Web site should contain only information that is absolutely necessary. Wireless Web users are seeking answers, wanting just the facts. Not only will users find poring through a long document on a four-line screen discouraging, but they will quickly turn to sites that show a greater respect for their time.

Keeping a Wireless Web site brief requires a lot of effort. Foremost, you need to hone your content to make every word count. If your site presents frequently updated material such as news stories, brevity is particularly important. Don't rule out hiring a professional editor, especially one with experience meeting time and space requirements.

Your site must be organized differently, too. In fact, WAP recognizes there is no notion of a Web page on the Wireless Web. Wireless Web content is stored in *decks*, consisting of one or more *cards* of content. The difference is crucial: most cards occupy a single page on a smart phone, and links between cards in the same deck don't require the client to turn to the network for additional content. A WML deck is the smallest unit that the server can return to the client. On the server, it's a single file just as an HTML page is a single file. The deck contains one or more cards, each containing content to be displayed. (You can see the syntax of a WML document later in this chapter, in the section "Hello, World".)

> **NOTE** *As you'll see in the next chapter, a deck can actually either be a file or a block of content with one or more cards dynamically created by a PHP script. But the difference doesn't really matter anyway because the block of content, such as script, is equivalent to a single WML deck.*

Each card in a deck should be brief, using a minimum of links and formatting. A good rule of thumb is that a card should contain text, a list of links, or a single form entry. Mixing and matching these items indicates that you're trying to pack too much on to a card, which will make your viewer's navigation more troublesome. The *list of lists* and *mini-sites* are two good strategies. In a *list of lists*, most of your cards are lists of topics, subtopics, and so on, leaving information itself to single cards at the base of the list hierarchy. The *mini-site* concept is similar, except that you don't bother trying to present a unified front with a catalog of topics; you scatter your content among multiple URLs with only minimal cross-linking. As you'll see, links can point to individual cards, so neither of these strategies is terribly burdensome.

You can make links between cards using both a traditional hyperlink mechanism as well as *soft keys*. A soft key is a WML-programmable interface widget that the client must display that connects a label to an action. On some phones, the soft key is labeled on the smart phone's display and the function is mapped to the button below the label; on other phones, soft keys are placed in a menu accessible from a key on the phone. Figure 2-1 shows the implementation of soft keys on two different smart phone emulators. This generality—that a soft key can occupy a menu item or a physical button—is by design. In fact, a client could even link a soft key to yet another interface element, such as a spoken command. You will quickly find when designing your own decks that soft keys take the place of many common links, such as a link to a deck containing help or copyright information, or the **Submit** and **Reset** buttons on a form.

Figure 2-1. Soft Keys on Two Different Smart phones

In terms of forms, you want to avoid making users input information. Smart phone keypads aren't meant for typing. In fact, they're barely adequate for spelling a word or two. If you don't believe me, try typing a short e-mail on your phone's keypad; any touch-tone phone will do. Most smart phones use one of two gimmicks to enable you to enter text: either you can select individual letters from a scrolling menu, or you can use repeated key presses to select one of a series of letters. For example, you may have to scroll down 13 items in order to select the letter L, or you can press the 5 key three times. A few phones may have optimized input schemes, such as Tegic's T-9, which attempts to complete words as you enter text, but even that's too slow to enter more than a few words at a time. Whenever possible, Wireless Web applications should rely on stored user preferences. It's best if the user can set these up using a desktop client *or* the smart phone as he or she first signs on to your site, minimizing the tortuous process of entering information.

Some sites simply must allow user input. A navigation directory providing driving directions, for example, can't anticipate where you want to go. In cases such as this, WML's form input elements give you some additional tools over HTML, including *input validation, events, tasks,* and *variables.*

WML's *input validation* enables you to specify what kinds of input are acceptable. Using input validation enables the client to restrict input to only the characters your application seeks, and to prevent the user from entering syntactically invalid information. For example, if your application seeks a zip code, you can restrict the entry to five numeric digits. In turn, users won't be able to enter text, 20-digit numbers, or punctuation. When designing your application, you should always use the strictest input validation over the input data as you can. Doing so makes input easier for your user, and it also decreases the number of network requests your application has to handle because most erroneous values won't be sent to the server. You should, however, continue to do server-side error checking because there's no guarantee that a bug or malicious user won't find a way around the input validation and cause you grief!

In WML, *events* are things that cause the client to perform a *task.* Selecting an item from a list and pressing a button are examples of events. For each event, you can assign a unique task, such as loading a new URL. Not only can you use tasks to guide user navigation between cards and decks, but you can also use tasks to navigate back and forth between cards in a single deck or submit user input. The WML client defines events for several user actions, including pressing the **Back** key, and for programmable timers that cause an event when a set amount of time elapses.

One kind of task that's especially useful is a task that lets you set *variables.* WML supports *variables* as containers, just as a programming language would. While you can't do anything besides set and display variables, they're still incredibly helpful. Because variables can store user input, you can display user input for confirmation before submitting forms, for example. You can also use variables to track user input and state. Once set, a variable persists until it's deliberately cleared or destroyed using other WML tags, so you can access variables across multiple decks.

Although I spend an entire chapter on the subject of graphics (Chapter 8), it's helpful to make a few comments here about graphics on the Wireless Web. WAP has standards for graphics exchange: the WBMP image format and associated tags in WML to display WBMP images. When applied properly—to convey meaning that can't be conveyed in the same space with the written word—graphics on the Wireless Web are invaluable. They are not, however, appropriate for most of the uses you'd find on the Web, including corporate logos, spacers, advertisements, or cute pictures. The WBMP format is excruciatingly simple: no-frills monochrome images. Because most smart phones have limited displays, and the network is slow anyway, this is as it should be. For now, it's enough for you to know that you can place images in your content, albeit with restraint.

The Wireless Application Protocol

The Wireless Application Protocol Forum (WAP Forum) is a consortium of telephony manufacturers who have joined forces to promulgate and promote data standards for wireless devices. Chief among the WAP Forum's efforts is WAP, which specifies a set of protocols for the exchange and markup of data between wireless devices.

WAP Architecture

Like many other protocols, WAP is actually a stack of individual protocols. Figure 2-2 shows the WAP stack of protocols. One of WAP's primary goals is to span a host of different wireless networks, including the Short Messaging System (SMS), Code Division Multiple Access (CDMA), Cellular Digital Packet Data (CDPD), and various TCP/IP networks. As a result, the WAP stack sits atop many networks, which together are referred to as the *bearer network* because it bears the traffic created by the WAP stack. These bearer networks must meet simple requirements. The bearer network need only use a best-effort delivery mechanism to attempt to send a data packet to its destination. No error checking is required, and the WAP protocols must handle both corrupt data packets and the possibility of lost data packets.

Consequently, above the bearer network WAP provides two protocols for ensuring data security and integrity. The Wireless Transport Layer Security (WTLS) is an adaptation of the Internet's Transport Security Layer, providing authentication and encryption when requested by client and server. The Wireless Transaction Protocol (WTP) adapts the bearer network's best-effort delivery scheme to provide reliable message delivery.

The Wireless Session Protocol (WSP) sits atop these protocols and provides a *session-based* network connection. Unlike the lower-level protocols, WSP simulates a circuit-switched connection between two hosts, making it easy for them to exchange messages longer than a single packet.

Finally, the Wireless Application Environment (WAE) represents any number of applications that uses these protocols, including the WAP client itself. The WAP

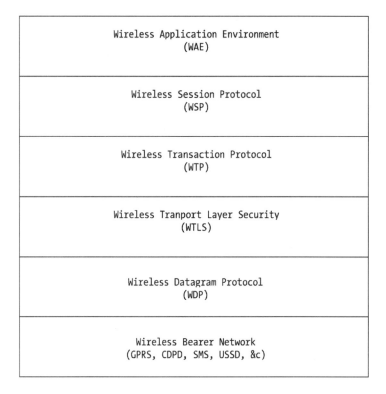

Figure 2-2. The WAP Stack.

client relies on two other standards promoted by the WAP Forum: WML and WMLScript. WML specifies a markup language for representing content format, whereas WMLScript specifies a simple client-side programming language much like JavaScript. (I show you how to write programs using WMLScript in detail in Chapter 4.)

Unlike many previous wireless network initiatives, WAP leverages existing standards and technologies wherever possible. In fact, it's largely built on the technologies and concepts behind the World Wide Web, so most of what you know about the Web is immediately applicable.

Consider how a smart phone requests a wireless page. Figure 2-3 shows a deployment diagram of the typical WAP network. It's a classic client-server network using a gateway. The WAP stack uses a gateway server called the *WAP Gateway* to bridge between the wireless network and the Internet. On the wireless network, clients and servers use the WAP protocols to exchange data. Over the Internet, hosts use Web protocols such as TCP/IP. Figure 2-4 shows the sequence of events that occurs when a smart phone requests a page, say index.wml, from a remote Web server wap.apress.com.

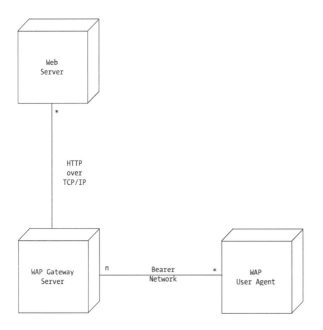

Figure 2-3. The WAP network

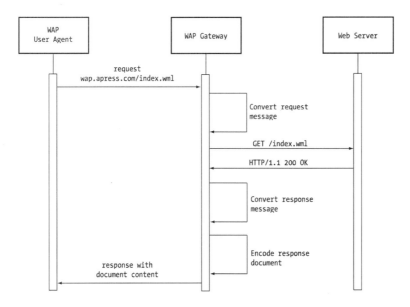

Figure 2-4. WAP client request and server response

In the first step, the client—which you'll often see called the WAP User Agent in the literature—on the phone uses the WSP to make a request of the WAP Gateway for the desired document. In turn, the WAP Gateway converts this request to an HTTP GET request. The WAP Gateway then uses the HTTP GET request to request the desired document from the Web server. The Web server (often called simply the *origin server* because it's where the content originates) processes the HTTP request, and returns the index.wml file to the WAP Gateway. Then, the WAP Gateway translates both the document and the HTTP response, and sends the results back to the client.

As the WAP Gateway converts WAP requests and responses, it synthesizes a number of HTTP headers that Web servers can use to obtain additional information about the client. Listing 2-1 shows headers generated by the WAP gateway Phone.com.

```
01: Accept: application/vnd.wap.wmlc, application/vnd.wap.wmlscriptc, image/
vnd.wap.wbmp, application/vnd.wap.wtls-ca-certificate
02: Accept-Charset: US-ASCII, US-ASCII, ISO-8859-1, ISO-8859-2, ISO-8859-3,
ISO-8859-4,ISO-8859-5, ISO-8859-6, ISO-8859-7, ISO-8859-8, ISO-8859-9, ISO-10646-
UCS-2, latin6, Shift_JIS, EUC-JP,EUC-KR, KS_C_5601-1987, UTF-8, GB2312, Big5,
IBM037, IBM273, IBM280, IBM285, IBM297, windows-1250, windows-1251, windows-1252,
windows-1253, windows-1254, windows-1255, windows-1255, windows-1256, windows-1257
03: Accept-Encoding: 7bit, 8bit, binary
04: Accept-Language: en
05: Host: www.lothlorien.com
06: User-Agent: UP.Client/3.02-MC01 UP.Link/3.2.3.7
07: x-up-devcap-charset: US-ASCII
08: x-up-devcap-immed-alert: 0
09: x-up-devcap-iscolor: 0
10: x-up-devcap-max-pdu: 1492
11: x-up-devcap-numsoftkeys: 2
12: x-up-devcap-screendepth: 1
13: x-up-devcap-screenpixels: 90,24
14: x-up-devcap-smartdialing: 0
15: x-up-devcap-softkeysize: 5
16: x-up-fax-accepts: none
17: x-up-fax-limit: 0
18: x-up-subno: 8315551212_up2.upl.sprintpcs.com
19: x-up-uplink: up2.upl.sprintpcs.com
```

Listing 2-1. HTTP headers returned by the Phone.com WAP Gateway

The first headers, from the first line through the sixth line, are generated by the WAP Gateway based on its knowledge of the WAP client. The remaining headers are HTTP extension headers, offering additional information about the WAP client.

These aren't standard, so your application should not rely on them unless you know you're only working with the Phone.com gateway, or you have fallbacks in case you don't see these headers. However, they're interesting to see, and show some of the information WAP conveys between client and server. From these headers, you can see that the device doesn't have a color display (x-up-devcap-iscolor), how many soft keys the phone has (two, according to the header x-up-devcap-numsoftkeys), the handset's phone number (8315551212, as given by the header x-up-subno), and so forth.

So why does the WAP Gateway have to muck around with the response document? The answer is for efficiency. While the index.wml file is in WML, it's actually much larger than the smart phone needs. WML, like HTML, is a markup language that both people and computers have to read. When a WML document is sent to a client, it's translated into a special binary representation called *compressed WML*. Compressed WML makes the most of every byte of a message, compressing tags and other content to keep wireless transfer times down. You'll never need to deal with compressed WML directly because the WAP Gateway does the translation for you.

The nice thing about WAP is that you don't have to worry about most of these details. As a content provider, all you have to do is place your WML files on a Web server and give your users the URL. The combination of WAP user agent and WAP gateway, together with the Internet, sorts out the rest. Wireless network providers, such as Sprint PCS, AT&T, or British Telecom, typically run WAP gateway servers. You won't need to run one unless you're doing development on their behalf and need hands-on access to the WAP server itself, or you have other stringent requirements. Moreover, it's unusual to need to delve into WAP directly. Most of the time you're working with content, you can simply treat WAP clients as special HTTP clients and ignore the fact that they operate on a totally different network.

First Steps with WML

WML isn't difficult to learn. In fact, if you know HTML, you already know about 80 percent of what you need to know to get started. In general, most people just learning WML have more trouble setting up a development environment in which they can write and test their wireless content than they do actually learning WML itself. In this section, I first walk you through setting up your PC to write and test WML content, and then show you WML itself.

Setting Up the SDK

Many WAP Software Development Kits (SDKs) are available. You will find an SDK on the CD-ROM at the back of this book, the Yospace Smart Phone Emulator Developer Edition (SPEDE). Other SDKs, including Nokia SDK, the Phone.com UP.SDK, and the Ericsson SDK, can be can be obtained from the Web (see Appendix A).

> **TIP** *You can—and should—plan on installing more than one SDK. Despite the WAP Forum's efforts to establish interoperability, different smart phones display your content differently. Rather than buying a bag full of different smart phones and service agreements, you can use the SDKs to preview your content on different platforms. While the SDK simulators might not exactly match a real phone's output, you can get a good idea of what things will look like on different devices.*

Before you begin, you should be sure your computer can access the network. While you don't need network connectivity to use the SDK, having it enables you to use the SDK to view existing Wireless Web content over the Internet. Because network configurations vary so much from site to site, I can only offer these suggestions:

- Test your computer's network configuration using a Web client. If you can get to the Internet with a Web client, things will probably work fine.

- Check the obvious stuff first. Is your modem connected properly? Is your Ethernet cable connected at both your computer's Ethernet port and the network hub? Does the cable work with someone else's computer?

- If you're having problems, determine whether or not you've got domain name server problems or connectivity problems. If you can access a Web site by its IP address (four numbers separated by dots, such as 206.169.23.11), your problem is with DNS, not with connectivity. If you can't, your problem is likely with your network configuration.

When in doubt, scream and shout. If you're doing WAP development as part of your job, your company's system administration staff can help you shake out connectivity problems. If you're doing it on your own time, be prepared to work with your ISP to work out any difficulties.

Next, you'll want to be sure you have the necessary operating system and meet the SDK's other requirements. Most SDK's only support Windows 98, NT, or 2000, although the Yospace SDK is in Java, and runs on Linux, Macintosh, and Windows platforms. Speaking of Java, you'll probably need a Java runtime even if you don't plan on using the Yospace SDK: for example, the Nokia SDK also requires the Java runtime be installed in order for it to operate. (You can find the latest Java tools at `http://www.java.sun.com`.)

Mercifully, you can install most WAP SDKs easily. Smoothing out the wrinkles between your SDK and Web server takes more time. These SDKs usually come packaged as an installer you can double-click. Once you do so, the installer installs several components, chief among them a smart phone *simulator*. This simulator is a program that emulates the behavior of a smart phone, displaying WAP content fetched from your computer's hard disk or over the network. In the case of the Nokia simulator, you'll also find a standalone copy of the Nokia WAP gateway, which the simulator uses to convert WML and WMLScript into their compressed counterparts. Other SDKs, such as the Yospace SDK and the Phone.com UP.SDK, enable you to view content without a gateway by performing the translation from WML and WMLScript to their compressed counterparts internally.

Installing the Yospace SDK

The folks at Yospace have put together an elegant WAP toolkit, the Yospace Smart Phone Emulator. There are actually two versions of the product: the Web Site Edition and the Developer Edition. You can use the Web Edition to demonstrate your Wireless Web applications to your customers using the Web, but what'll really help you in day-to-day use is the Developer Edition, which enables you to test and preview WAP content on your desktop computer.

The Smart Phone Emulator, Developer Edition (SPEDE) is written entirely in Java, and runs without difficulty on most major operating systems that have a Java runtime. To get it running, you need to do the following:

1. If you're going to use SPEDE under Linux, make sure you have a GUI that supports a Java runtime, such as OpenMotif running under X Windows.

2. Download and install a Java runtime, such as Sun's Java runtime (http://www.java.sun.com) or Solaris for Windows, or the Blackdown Java runtime (http://www.blackdown.org) for the various flavors of Linux. (Apple's Mac OS ships with a Java runtime).

3. Launch the SPEDE installer. On a platform with a GUI, you can simply double-click the installer; under UNIX or Linux, simply type **install.bin**.

4. When the installer is finished, you can launch the smart phone emulator by double-clicking its icon or typing **./SmartPhone_Emulator_1.1** in the directory in which the installer placed SPEDE.

As delivered on the CD-ROM that accompanies this book or from Yospace's Web site, SPEDE is an evaluation product. Each time you launch it, you're be prompted to register it. You can use it as often as you like without registering, but each time you run it, it only runs for a handful of minutes. You can purchase a license for a nominal fee from Yospace by going to www.yospace.com. If you're looking for a good WAP SDK, or need the capability to run your SDK on platforms other than Microsoft Windows, SPEDE can't be beat.

Installing the Nokia SDK

Virtually all smart phone manufacturers are providing versions of their SDK for developers. Most, if not all, are free. Two of the best-known free SDKs are the Nokia WAP SDK and the Phone.com SDK. While both have comparable features, the Nokia SDK just seems to suit me better.

The Nokia WAP SDK is relatively large because it includes a slimmed-down version of the Nokia WAP Gateway Server to support the smart phone emulator. It runs on Microsoft Windows 98/2000/NT, but parts of it require Java. To get it running, you'll need to do this:

1. Install a Java runtime, such as Sun's Java Runtime 1.2.2 available from `http://www.java.sun.com`.

2. Launch the Nokia WAP SDK installer by double-clicking it. Answer the questions that follow.

3. When the installer is finished, you can launch the toolkit by double-clicking the **WAP Toolkit** icon.

Unlike SPEDE, the Nokia WAP SDK is a fully featured release out of the box. You don't have to pay a license fee to use the product. On the other hand, it only runs on Microsoft Windows, and it's clearly geared to simulate only Nokia hardware.

At first blush, using any of these tools is just like using a client. For example, Figure 2-5 shows the Yospace Smart Phone Emulator as I enter the URL of a Wireless Web site I'm working on. I can also choose to load a local file from my hard drive. You can write WML using a text editor such as the Notepad, emacs, vi, or Alpha, and then preview it directly in the simulator. In addition to seeing how things work when things go right, you'll have an opportunity to learn about why things go wrong. For example, Figure 2-6 shows an error message the Yospace Smart Phone Emulator displays when it loads a file with invalid WML tags. You can also view the source for a document if it's available, or decompile the binary WML to see what the source looked like. All of these options are available from menu choices within the phone simulator.

The Nokia WAP SDK takes these features further, providing an integrated environment where you can edit your WML, view it in both parsed and rendered forms, and view debugging information such as the variables defined by your WML. In Figure 2-7, you can see how the Nokia WAP SDK gives you a window to edit the WML as well as a smart phone emulator. Through the tabs along the

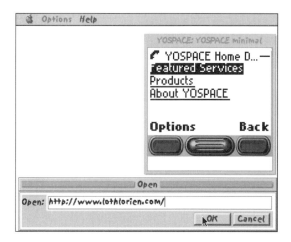

Figure 2-5. The Yospace Smart Phone Emulator Developer Edition

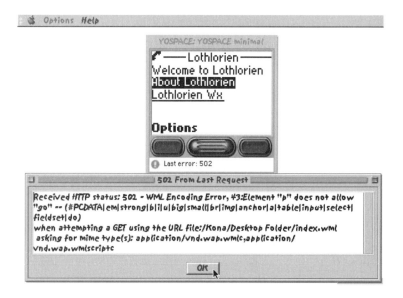

Figure 2-6. The Yospace Smart Phone Emulator Developer Edition displays an error.

bottom of the SDK window, you can select different views of your WML content—
including error messages, a hierarchical display of WML tags, and variables
defined in your WML deck—as you debug your application (as shown in Figure 2-8).

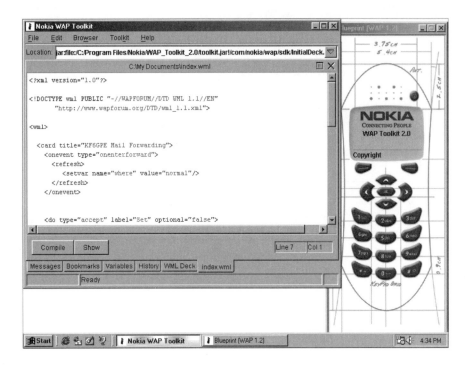

Figure 2-7. The Nokia WAP SDK editing a WML deck

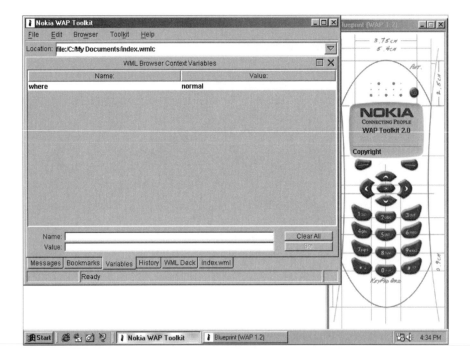

Figure 2-8. The Nokia WAP SDK listing WML variables

Which SDK you choose to use is largely determined by your desktop development platform and personal preference. If you're working on a system running Mac OS or Linux, you'll probably have little choice but to use Yospace's Smart Phone Emulator, Developer Edition. If you have an Intel-based PC running a Microsoft OS, your choices are much broader. All SDKs share the common feature of being able to browse WML, so you can't go too far wrong. The differences are in the details, such as Nokia's support for displaying WML variables. I've found that while the additional features of a more sophisticated SDK can help you get out of the occasional tight spot, the simplicity of Yospace's emulator more than meets my average development needs.

> **TIP** *No matter how good the SDK you choose actually is, it isn't the real thing. It's imperative that you spend some time testing your application with a real device on a real wireless network. SDKs are just that: development tools, simulators that help you assemble your product and get it to market on time. By testing with a real Wireless Web client, you find all kinds of little things that need your attention: minor layout changes, addressing interface changes to compensate for network latency, changes to user input forms, and so on. If you're developing wireless content as part of your business, it behooves you to make the investment and spend time on the Wireless Web testing your application.*

Setting Up the Server

Whether or not you need to run a Web server on your machine depends on a host of factors, such as whether or not you want to share your development effort with multiple machines on your network (or the Internet, for that matter). Of course, you certainly won't use your development workstation as a production-class server for your wireless applications. However, if you're planning on doing any active server development, or simply want to test an end-to-end configuration for your wireless application, you need to have a Web server running to serve content to Wireless Web clients. In fact, if you're going to do anything with PHP, you probably want a server on your development platform so you don't have to spend a lot of time switching between an established Web server computer and your development platform.

Although there are a number of Web servers to choose from, and several that work with PHP (as you'll see in the next chapter), there's really only one good choice: the Apache Web server. Industry studies show that as many as half of the servers on the Web run Apache on a bevy of platforms including Solaris, HP-UX, Linux, and Microsoft Windows. It's proven, reliable, and free: what more can you ask for?

Although choosing a WAP SDK is a largely personal choice, when you install a Web server you may need additional assistance from others in your organization. To install and configure the server correctly, you will probably need to do things on your system that are typically only done by a system administrator. If you're your own system administrator (as is often the case in small development shops), great—you probably know what you're doing anyway. If you're not, don't hesitate to ask for help. Be prepared to explain *why* you need to run your own Web server because many system administrators don't like the idea of random Web servers being run on office machines throughout the network.

> **TIP** *In practice, I've learned two things about organizations with system administration groups: always ask for help, and always be prepared to explain (politely) your needs. Many system administrators are trained to say "no" by reflex because anything that changes their network can risk its operation. But, by the same token, if they understand why you need something for your job, they're more than happy to help you.*

Many of today's operating systems, including Mac OS X, Linux, and various flavors of UNIX come bundled with a version of Apache already. For other operating systems, including Microsoft Windows, you can find precompiled binaries available at `http://www.apache.org`. On the CD-ROM at the back of this book, you'll find a precompiled binary of Apache for Microsoft Windows, along with the sources in case you want to build the server for another operating system.

Installing the Apache Web Server

Ironically, installing the Apache Web server on Windows is easier than installing it on a UNIX box, even though the Apache Web server is primarily targeted at the UNIX marketplace.

On Windows, simply double-click the Apache installer, and off it goes. When you're done with the installation, you can start and stop the Apache Web server manually from the command bar, or launch it as a service so it runs whenever your machine is running.

Under UNIX, it's more of a challenge. If you're using Linux, you can probably find a Red Hat Package Manager file (RPM) of the binary for your system at one of the major sites such as `http://www.redhat.com`. If so, you can log in as root and use the `rpm` command to install the package using the command:

```
# rpm -i <apache package name>
```

If you can't find a precompiled binary in a package, you may be able to find a UNIX tar file with the precompiled binary and use the UNIX tar command to unpack the binary distribution like this:

```
# tar xzf <apache binary tar file name>
```

If all else fails, you can always grab the sources and build it yourself. Building Apache is a bit like magic, so spend time reading the documentation. On my system, a Macintosh G3 PowerBook running LinuxPPC 2000, the spell looked something like this:

```
% tar xzf <apache source tar file name>
% cd <apache directory>
% ./configure -compat
lots of stuff appears here as Apache configures itself.
% cd src
% make
lots more stuff appears here as Apache builds
% su root
Password: <your root password>
# make install
```

If you're paranoid, before you actually assume the root role and install the binary by typing **httpd,** you can test the Apache Web server httpd binary that was built.

A word of warning: if you're doing this on a system with the Apache Web server already installed, if you don't do it correctly, or if you download a version of Apache from a less-than-trustworthy source, you can be in for a world of hurt. At the very least, your computer won't be running a Web server. At worst, you could overwrite a working Web server, destroy important configuration files, or even open your system to potential security risks. You should use the sources on the CD-ROM that accompanies this book or those from http://www.apache.org and read the documentation. If you're not sure you know what you're doing, take time to ask a colleague for help and back up your system.

The installation itself is largely a platform-dependent process. On Microsoft Windows, you can simply double-click the installer (if you want to use the pre-compiled binary). On other systems, you may need to resort to UNIX tools such as tar or the Red Hat Package Manager (RPM) utility to unpack the sources or binary distribution, and then install the resulting binary. If you need to build the sources from scratch, make a point of reading *all* the documentation in the various INSTALL and READ ME files. While building Apache from the sources isn't difficult, it's a lot easier if you read the manual. In either case—building from sources or installing a precompiled binary—you may need to have administrative access on your computer to install the binaries in their appropriate locations and ensure that the server can access the network correctly. This is especially true when you're using one of the various flavors of UNIX or Linux.

> **CAUTION** *If you plan on using the server on your machine to offer content to smart phones on the Wireless Web you **must** work with your organization's system administrator. Many organizations require public Web servers to be placed on a separate network, whereas other organizations need to modify their firewall configuration to permit clients outside the local network to connect to their computer's server. Also, if you don't do things correctly, you can decrease your system's overall security, making it easier for others to accidentally or maliciously mess around with your system. Not only is this a bad idea in theory, but at many places, it's a violation of corporate security policies and your employment agreement. In short, if you're seeking access outside your internal network, seek professional help. Failure to do so can get you in a lot of trouble and potentially cost you your job.*

Once you install the Apache server, you may need to configure it to send the MIME type WML files. To see if you need to set the MIME type for your server, check the MIME type configuration file (usually mime.types in your server's configuration file directory) and look for the line that reads image/vnd.wap.wml wml. If you see one, you're set—if not, just add it to the file and restart your Web server.

Hello, World

With the preliminaries aside, it's time to get to the good stuff: our first WML deck. In Listing 2-2, you can see the now-famous Hello World code in WML. In Figure 2-9, you can see how this deck appears using the Yospace SPEDE; Figure 2-10 shows the same deck in the Nokia WAP SDK 2.0.

> **NOTE** *Subsequent screen shots in the book illustrate the Yospace SPEDE unless I am trying to draw your attention to platform differences between the various WAP clients.*

```
01: <?xml version="1.0"?>
02: <!DOCTYPE wml PUBLIC "-//WAPFORUM//DTD WML 1.1//EN"
03:   "http://www.wapforum.org/DTD/wml_1.1.xml">
04: <wml>
05:   <card title="Hello World">
06:     <p>Hello world!</p>
07:   </card>
08: </wml>
```

Listing 2-2. Hello World in WML

Figure 2-9. Hello World Yospace SPEDE style

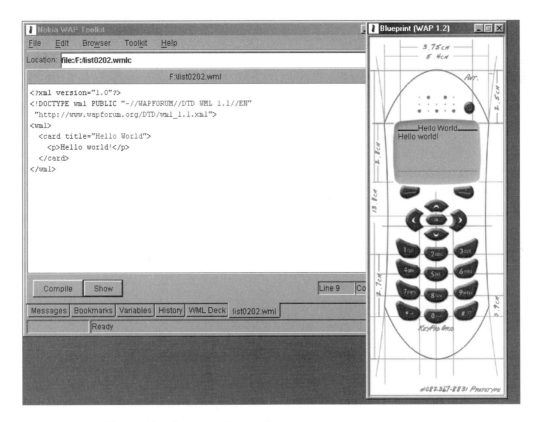

Figure 2-10. Hello World Nokia WAP SDK style

The first three lines of the WML deck aren't WML at all: they're in the eXtensible Markup Language(XML). It just so happens that WML is actually an application of XML, and that you write WML in XML. As you'll see, in practice the distinction is hazy at best; it becomes important only when you're trying to mix and match XML and XML-compliant servers to build large-scale client-independent systems. (I touch on that in more detail in Chapter 9.)

At any rate, the first line tells the world that this file conforms to the syntax set out in XML version 1.0. The second line uses the XML <!DOCTYPE> directive to specify that the file's contents are in WML, as specified by the public Document Type Definition (DTD) located at the URL http://www.wapforum.org/DTD/wml_1.1.xml. These lines are essential for all your WML documents because they tell the WAP gateway what version of XML and WML you expect its clients to support. Without these two lines, a WAP gateway summarily discards your deck as malformed, assuming it's not in WML. Of course, if you're using an earlier or later version of either XML or WML, you should say so in the file by changing either the <xml> tag or the <!DOCTYPE> tag as needed.

Line 4 starts the WML deck using the <wml> tag. Each deck—a file on the Web server—must have at exactly one <wml> tag and its closing counterpart, the </wml> tag. This tag tells the client where the deck itself begins and ends.

Line 5 declares the first (and only) card in the deck using the <card> tag. This tag uses an attribute, the title attribute, to give the card a name. In turn, the WML client can use the name as a title on the WML display, or as a name to show you when you go to bookmark the page. As you can see from Figures 2-9 and 2-10, some clients actually show the title of the card on the display, but not all clients will do this. Most tags have attributes like this one to modify the tag's behavior, or to add additional information about how the client should process the tag. Clients process cards in the deck starting with the first card, so you'll see this card when the deck is loaded.

Line 6 defines a single paragraph of content using the <p> tag. As in HTML, the <p> tag surrounds a paragraph. Unlike early versions of HTML, however, you can't simply insert a paragraph tag using a single <p> tag. In WML, the <p> tag must always be paired with its closing counterpart, the </p> tag. In line 6, the <p> tag encloses the words "Hello world!"

> **NOTE** *You've probably noticed that I use the word "tag" to refer to both a tag pair, such as <p> and </p>, as well as a single tag, such as <p> or </p>. I'll continue to do so wherever it's not necessary to distinguish the difference so you don't have to keep reading ungainly phrases like "tag pair."*

Line 7 ends our card using the </card> tag, while the tag </wml> on line 8 ends the deck itself.

As you can see from this example, WML is quite similar to HTML. Plain text is marked up using tags enclosed in < and > symbols. Each tag can have attributes that control its behavior, as well as enclose content that should be formatted according to the tag's meaning. As with HTML, you can write WML using your favorite text editor, or you can use a commercial software product that supports editing XML or WML to give you additional help such as tag highlighting and syntax checking.

WML Syntax

Speaking of syntax, it's worth the time to take a deeper look at WML's syntax here before you begin using WML to build a prototype of MobileHelper. If you know HTML's syntax, WML's syntax is similar enough that you can read and write simple WML, but a deeper understanding is necessary in order to take advantage of all of WML's tags.

As mentioned earlier in the chapter, WML isn't its own markup language. Rather, it's an example of an XML application—a markup language in XML. Briefly, XML lets software architects design new markup languages with unique tags with a standard grammar that will behave in predictable ways. WML is just one of many XML applications; you will see a couple of others in Chapter 9. Understanding XML's syntax is essential if you want to write correct WML because gateways reject WML that doesn't meet XML's stringent syntax requirements.

XML documents are simply files containing a well-defined *preamble* that declares the file as containing XML, followed by data in the form of tags and content. XML documents may be text or binary files; in practice, you'll find the lion's share to be in a text format. XML supports a number of different character encodings, including ASCII and Unicode. Consequently, there's support for international content with little additional work, although in practice most content developers simply write XML in ASCII using a text editor.

XML tags are words surrounded by ‹ and ›, and come in two flavors: *balanced* tags and *empty* tags. Balanced tags have both an opening and closing tag, and surround the text they're marking. The opening tag is simply the tag itself, while the closing tag uses the same tag name, preceded by a solidus (/). Empty tags, on the other hand, consist of a single tag, which must be closed using the two characters />. The following are examples of balanced tags:

```
01: <p>A paragraph</p>
02: <card>Lots of content for this card here!</card>
03: <SpecialTag>Some content for a very special tag</SpecialTag>
```

And here are some empty tags:

```
01: <BR/>
02: <HR/>
03: <EmptyTag/>
```

In both of these examples, line 3 illustrates a crucial feature of XML I've only hinted at thus far: XML doesn't actually define tags with meaning. It's best if you understand XML as a *grammar* that defines a universe of possible markup languages, each containing their own tags. It's up to markup language designers to come up with the tags themselves. A markup language's tags and the relationship between tags (which tags can contain other tags as content, and so on) is specified by a markup language's *Document Type Definition* (DTD). In Listing 2-2, you saw on lines 2 and 3 how XML specifies what DTD should be used to interpret a particular XML document using the <!DOCTYPE> tag. Markup languages like WML have an associated DTD that computers use to understand the markup language. When a computer can interpret an XML file according to an associated DTD, we say that the document is *well-formed* because it's a syntactically valid file. (Of course, you can easily write well-formed files that don't mean anything, or don't do what you expect them to!)

You've already seen tags that have attributes that modify the meaning of a tag. Like the tags themselves, attributes can be anything; XML enables you to define attributes as you need them. An equals sign (=) connects an attribute with its value, like this:

```
01: <card title="Portfolio"></card>
02: <p align=center mode="nowrap"></p>
```

In line 2, you can see that a tag can have more than one attribute. When you write a tag that has more than one attribute, you can separate the attributes with white space such as spaces, tabs, or line breaks.

I said earlier that both tags and attributes could be anything. That's not quite true. Tags and attributes must follow a simple naming convention:

- The first character must be an uppercase or lowercase letter or underscore.

- The subsequent characters may be uppercase or lowercase letters, numbers, or an underscore.

- You can't use punctuation or white space within the name of a tag or attribute.

Unlike markup languages like HTML, WML is case sensitive. That is, case matters when writing tags and attributes. For instance, if you write <p>, it's not the same as if you write <P>. Most markup languages use only lowercase or only upper-case characters; a few define tags in all lowercase and all uppercase so you can mix and match. WML uses lowercase characters.

XML defines some additional kinds of tags that are reserved for use by the WML parser itself. The tags beginning with the two characters <? and ?> are meta tags used to define what kind of markup language (XML or something else) your file uses. You'll use these tags in two cases: to specify the <?xml?> directive at the beginning of a file, and to specify the beginning and end of a PHP script (see Chapter 3).

The ‹! and › characters surround an XML directive in an XML document. There are a number of these tags, but the only one you're likely to see in WML is the ‹!DOCTYPE› tag, which tells an XML parser which XML-based markup language you're using and how it can verify the syntax of your content. You always need to include the ‹!DOCTYPE› tag because WAP gateways need to know the DTD for the version of WML you're using.

> **TIP** *I keep the initial lines of a WML deck (lines 1, 2, and 3 in Listing 2-2) in an otherwise empty file on my desktop. Whenever I need to create a new deck, I can simply copy those lines and paste them into the deck I'm writing rather than retype them from memory. Because WAP gateways are notoriously picky, even the simplest of mistakes can cause a deck to be seen as invalid. Keeping these lines at hand helps eliminate the time I'd spend tracking down a dumb mistake such as a missing = symbol or a misspelled URL.*

Finally, the ‹!-- and —› tags can be used to distinguish a comment, as in HTML. Comments are for you, not the client, to help you make sense of a particularly complicated or tricky piece of code. In fact, unlike HTML, clients don't ever see comments because the WAP gateway strips out all comments before encoding your deck to send to the client.

Some characters, such as the ‹ and › characters, have special meaning in XML. Because of this, you can't use these characters directly. Instead, you must use *entities* that the client translates to the correct characters. WML defines seven entities, shown in Table 2-1, that enable you to represent characters that have special meaning in WML.

Table 2-1. WML Entities

ENTITY	CHARACTER	NOTE
&amp;	&	Ampersand
&apos;	'	Apostrophe
&lt;	<	Less than symbol
&gt;	>	Greater than symbol
		Non-breaking space
&quote;	"	Quote
&shy;	-	Discretionary (soft) hyphen

This entity notation can be used to construct an entity for any character if you know its numeric equivalent in the character encoding you're using. You can write &#nnn; where *nnn* is the decimal representation for the character in the character encoding scheme, or ꪪ where *aaaa* is the hexadecimal representation for the character in the encoding scheme you're using. For example, the ampersand (&) can be written using any of the entities &, &, or $.

> **NOTE** *Some WAP SDKs don't correctly honor some of the WML entities. When in doubt, test your WML using a real smart phone.*

Going Further with WML

Once you know WML's syntax, learning to use WML is largely a matter of mastering WML's repertoire of tags. You use some of these tags to organize your deck into cards, while other tags dictate how the browser should format the text on a card. Still other tags enable you to control the browser's user interface, assigning tasks to interface elements and timers.

Organizing Decks

As mentioned in the section "The Wireless Web User Interface," you organize your content as a series of cards stored in a deck. Users navigate from card to card; when they jump to a card in a different deck, the client has to fetch the new deck from the phone's cache or from the wireless network. In most cases, you want to group related information in a single deck so that you can minimize how often the client needs to load new material. You can also specify default behavior for all cards in a deck using a card template, a special kind of card you'll encounter later in this section.

Decks, like Web pages, are composed of a heading that specifies handling information about the deck, an optional card template, and cards containing content. A deck—together with its heading and content—hangs on the skeleton shown in Listing 2-3.

```
01: <?xml version="1.0"?>
02: <!DOCTYPE wml PUBLIC "-//WAPFORUM//DTD WML 1.1//EN"
03:    "http://www.wapforum.org/DTD/wml_1.1.xml">
04: <wml>
05:    <head>
06:    </head>
07:    <template>
08:    </template>
09:    <card>
10:    </card>
11: </wml>
```

Listing 2-3: The skeleton of a deck.

The deck itself is contained within the <wml> tag. The deck consists of an optional <head> tag to declare the deck's heading, an optional <template> tag to declare a card template, and one or more <card> tags that define the content for the deck. The <wml> tag may accept a single attribute, the xml:lang attribute. This optional attribute tells the client what natural language (such as English or Spanish) the deck's content is written in. The language codes are those specified in ISO-639, which you can find in Table 1-1 in Chapter 1. Most WAP gateways and clients currently ignore this attribute, so there's little point in including it in your decks for current functionality.

The <head> tag and its contents are completely optional, letting you define a heading for your deck. A deck's heading can contain two bits of information: access control and meta information. You use access control to specify what other decks may link to your deck, while you use meta information to supply additional information such as HTTP headers that should accompany your deck.

There are two reasons why you would want to specify access control. The first is obvious: you may simply want to restrict which sites can link to your content. Using WML's access control, you can avoid *deep linking*, a common practice on the Web where a site points to a page deep within your site, bypassing your main page and other content.

The second reason is more subtle but often more important. As I mentioned earlier in the chapter, WML supports variables, which are named containers for arbitrary values. A deck can set variables to be used later in a deck, or to be used in other decks. If you set variables in one deck and refer to them in another, malicious content developers could provide a phony substitute for the first deck, letting unwary users have variables set to the wrong value and then use those incorrect values with your wireless application.

You specify access control using the `<access/>` tag and its `domain` and `path` attributes. By default, any deck anywhere can link to any card in your deck. By specifying the `<access>` tag, you restrict access to decks within the specific domain, stored at or under the indicated file system path. For example, you can only link to the deck in Listing 2-4 from other decks on the Web server `wap.apress.com` stored under the directory "`/wap-php/`". Thus, the following decks could link to this deck:

- `wap.apress.com/wap-php/demo.wml`

- `wap.apress.com/wap-php/samples/index.wml`

- `wap.apress.com/wap-php/never-worked/broken.wml`

However, none of these decks could link to this deck:

- `wap.apress.com/index.wml`

- `www.apress.com/wap-php/index.wml`

- `www.lothlorien.com/index.wml`

```
01: <?xml version="1.0"?>
02: <!DOCTYPE wml PUBLIC "-//WAPFORUM//DTD WML 1.1//EN"
03:   "http://www.wapforum.org/DTD/wml_1.1.xml">
04: <wml>
05:   <head>
06:     <access domain="wap.apress.com" path="wap-php/"/>
07:   </head>
08:   <card>
09:     <p>
10:       I can only be accessed from decks stored on
11:       the wap.apress.com server under the directory
12:       wap-php.
13:     </p>
14:   </card>
15: </wml>
```

Listing 2-4. Specifying access control

> **TIP** *Most WAP tools enforce the* <access/> *tag. If you try to load or test a deck with access control in one of these tools, you won't be able to because you won't be accessing your deck from the domain and path specified by the* <access/> *tag! To get around this, you have two choices. You can avoid using the* <access/> *tag during development until everything else is done. This is a poor idea because you can't test access control. Consequently, I suggest you use stub* <access/> *tags that enable you to load your content from a test server. When your application moves into transition, you can simply change the* domain *attribute to your production server's domain name. This is especially easy if you're using PHP to generate your decks (see Chapter 3) because you can simply store the domain attribute's value in a PHP variable you change instead of updating each deck.*

The other use for the deck's heading is a catchall for meta information about the deck. Most of this meta information is represented as HTTP headers stored within the body of the deck. You can do this using the <meta/> tag with the http-equiv attribute, which indicates what HTTP header value you'd like to set. You can also set a generic meta using the name attribute. Whichever you choose, you supply the value for the meta in the <meta/> tag's content attribute. Listing 2-5 shows some <meta/> tags.

```
01: <?xml version="1.0"?>
02: <!DOCTYPE wml PUBLIC "-//WAPFORUM//DTD WML 1.1//EN"
03:    "http://www.wapforum.org/DTD/wml_1.1.xml">
04: <wml>
05:   <head>
06:     <meta http-equiv="Cache-Control" content="max-age=60"/>
07:   </head>
08:   <card>
09:     <p>
10:       This deck expires from the cache in one minute.
11:     </p>
12:   </card>
13: </wml>
```

Listing 2-5. Specifying meta data

In Listing 2-5, the <meta/> tag on line 6 will simulate the addition of the HTTP header Cache-Control with a value of 60. This instructs the smart phone how long this deck should remain in the cache.

Before I dive into cache control with the <meta/> tag, it's important to note that different smart phones and WAP toolkits respond to the <meta/> tag differently. For example, the current Nokia products ignore some `<meta/>` tags, notably those containing arbitrary name-value pairs, whereas the Phone.com SDK meets both the WAP standards for supporting the `<meta/>` tag and several Phone.com-specific features. If you're writing content to target a particular device, you should refer to the documentation for that device. Otherwise, it's generally best to avoid using the `<meta/>` tag altogether if you can.

This caveat aside, an important application of the `<meta/>` tag is controlling the smart phone's cache. The phone's cache is an essential part of a wireless application because fetching decks from the local cache is at least an order of magnitude faster than accessing it from a server on the Wireless Web. Consequently, the smart phone attempts to cache content for the user whenever it can.

Unfortunately, some information changes quickly enough that the cached document will be out of date before the phone needs to refresh its cached copy (such as a stock quote). Because you can't predict when a document will be removed from the client's cache, it's hard to know how long such stale data may hang around. For the cases when content changes faster than the contents of the cache expire, you want to specify how long a deck should remain in the client's cache. You do this with the HTTP header `Cache-Control`, which specifies how many seconds the deck should remain in the client's cache. If you don't want to cache the document at all, you may specify the value `no-cache` to tell the client that the deck shouldn't be cached at all. Line 6 in Listing 2-5 says that the deck should be cached for one minute.

> **NOTE** *For static WML, the only way you can specify the* `Cache-Control` *header is with the* `<meta/>` *tag. In the next chapter, you learn how to set HTTP headers directly using PHP, which I recommend when creating dynamic content.*

Creating Cards and Card Templates

Once you finish with the deck's header, you can declare as many cards as you like. You do this using the `<card>` tag, which is the bread and butter of WML. You have already encountered this tag and a few of its attributes in previous Listings.

> **NOTE** *Of course, if you make a habit of declaring more than three or four cards in each deck, you can bet your users won't like you! See "The Wireless Web User Interface" earlier in this chapter.*

While many of your cards will have no attributes, you'll find that the `title` and `id` attributes are fairly common. You've already seen the `title` attribute back in Listing 2-2. The `title` attribute is used to title a card and may be shown at the top of the phone's display, as on Nokia phones, or may just be used in configuration screens, such as when you bookmark a card. The `id` card lets you name a card for navigation; it's similar to an anchor in HTML. With the `id` attribute, a specific card's URL is the URL of the deck, followed by a sharp symbol # followed by the value of the card's `id` attribute. For example, if Listing 2-6 were found at the URL `wap.apress.com/list0206.wml`, you could refer to the first card with the URL `wap.apress.com/list0206.wml#first` and the second card with the URL `wap.apress.com/list0206.wml#next`.

```
01: <?xml version="1.0"?>
02: <!DOCTYPE wml PUBLIC "-//WAPFORUM//DTD WML 1.1//EN"
03:   "http://www.wapforum.org/DTD/wml_1.1.xml">
04: <wml>
05:   <card
06:     id="first"
07:     title="Listing 2-6 - Start"
08:     newcontext="true"
09:     ontimer="#next">
10:     <timer name="Next" value="60"/>
11:     <p>
12:       At first, $$usernav is empty.
13:       This card will set it to "yes"
14:       if you go to the next card using the
15:       soft key, but not if you do nothing.<br/>
16:       $$usernav is $usernav<br/>
17:     </p>
18:     <do
19:       type="accept"
20:       label="Listing 2-6 - Next">
21:       <go href="#next">
22:         <setvar
23:           name="usernav"
24:           value="yes"/>
25:       </go>
26:     </do>
27:   </card>
28:   <card
```

```
29:     id="next"
30:     title="Listing 2-6 - Next">
31:     <p>
32:       $$usernav is $usernav<br/>
33:       $$usernav will be empty if this card
34:       was loaded because the timer elapsed.
35:     </p>
36:     <do
37:       type="accept"
38:       label="Listing 2-7">
39:       <go href="list0207.wml"/>
40:     </do>
41:   </card>
42: </wml>
```

Listing 2-6. Using <card> *attributes*

Listing 2-6 shows not just the id and title attributes but the newcontext and ontimer attributes as well, along with four new tags, <timer/>, <do>, <go>, and <setvar/>. Before diving into how these tags work, you can look at what they do in Figures 2-11 and 2-12.

Figure 2-11 shows the sequence of cards you'll see if you don't press any keys. When the client loads the deck, it shows the first card, which shows an introductory message and waits for six seconds. After six seconds, the client loads the next card, which shows the value of the $usernav variable and lets you load the deck shown in Listing 2-7, using the client's **Accept** key.

On the other hand, while you're viewing the first card, you can press the client's **Accept** key. If you do, the client sets the $usernav variable to "yes" and loads the second card. When you see the second card, the value of $usernav is equal to "yes". You can see this sequence of screens in Figure 2-12.

  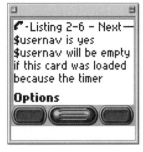

Figure 2-11. Listing 2-6 when no keys are pressed

Figure 2-12. Listing 2-6 when **Accept** *is pressed on the first card*

Because Listing 2-6 is the most complex (and least like HTML) so far, let's walk through it line by line.

After the usual preamble on the first three lines and the beginning of the deck on the fourth line, the first card of my deck starts. I give the card both an `id` and a `title` on lines 6 and 7, although only the title is used (if you display the card or try to bookmark it). Line 8 uses the `<card>` newcontext attribute to tell the client that it should create a new context. A *context* is the space in which the client stores WML variables; by creating a new context, all currently defined WML variables are destroyed.

Line 9 uses the `<card>` ontimer attribute to specify the task the client should perform if the card's timer elapses. The ontimer attribute is shorthand for an event handler with the `<onevent>` tag, which you see in the next section. It specifies the URL of the deck or card to load when the timer event occurs. This attribute points to the card that will be loaded if you don't press the **Accept** key while the card is showing. After this attribute, the attributes for the `<card>` tag end, and the contents of the card begin.

Line 10 declares the timer associated with the card. A WML card may have one timer, which must have a name and a duration stated in tenths of a second. You define a timer using the `<timer/>` tag and its name and value attributes. (Although you have to name a timer, timer names aren't presently used in WML.) Line 10 declares the Next timer, which generates an event after six seconds if this card is still showing. The resulting event is handled by the `<card>` ontimer attribute. (If you navigate to another card while the timer is running, the timer is cancelled and no event occurs.)

Lines 11–17 contain the paragraph the card shows. I display the WML variable `$usernav` on line 16 so you can see it's empty at this point when you view the card. The $ character tells the client that the following word is a variable, so the client displays the contents of the variable rather than the $ and following word. If you want to display a solitary **$**, you write $$, as I did on lines 12 and 16.

Lines 18–26 assign a navigation task—the `<go>` and `<setvar/>` tags—to the client's **Accept** soft key. WML defines a number of custom user interface widgets, including the **Accept** mechanism. Here, I assign the human-readable label

"**Listing 2-6 - Next**" to the soft key and bind the navigation task so that if you press the key, the client executes the `<go>` task after setting the specified variable.

The `<do>` tag assigns a task to an interface widget for the duration of the current card. The custom interface widget can be anything, such as a gesture, jog button, or dial, although it's most often a *soft key* (a key with a programmable label shown on the LCD above the key) or a menu choice. All smart phones conforming to the WML specifications must define interfaces for the interface widget types listed in Table 2-2. Other devices may define additional interface widget types and, of course, the WAP Forum may extend the WML standard in the future to define new kinds of interface widgets.

Table 2-2. WML Interface Widgets and Their Purpose.

WIDGET TYPE	PERFORM A TASK IF THE USER
Accept	Invokes the **Accept** mechanism.
Delete	Invokes the **Delete** mechanism.
Help	Invokes the **Help** mechanism.
Options	Invokes the **Options** mechanism.
Prev	Invokes the **Prev** mechanism.
Reset	Invokes the **Reset** mechanism to reset the client to its default state.

When you assign a task to an interface widget with the `<do>` tag, you must assign the type of widget being assigned using the `type` attribute. You can give the widget a custom name using the `label` attribute, although not all smart phones actually use the this attribute in conjunction with the widget.[1] You can also name the element using the `name` attribute and indicate if the element is optional using the `optional` attribute by setting `optional` to `true`. After describing the interface widget with the `<do>` task, you define the task it should perform within the `<do>` task itself.

---

1. Throughout the text, I often just refer to these interface widgets as either soft keys or keys, unless I want to explicitly remind you that they can be just about anything some crazy hardware engineer can figure out how to manufacture.

> **CAUTION** *The* `<do>` *tag enables you to reassign almost any of the smart phone's customizable user interface widgets. Some of these, like the* **Prev** *soft key, have a well-defined behavior that you learn after reading your phone's manual. While it might seem cool at first to map the* **Help** *soft key's action to the* **Prev** *soft key and vice versa, most of your users aren't going to appreciate the change! When designing your wireless application, you should follow interface precedents and maintain a consistent experience for your users.*

In Listing 2-6, our task is the `<go>` task on lines 21–25. It specifies the destination URL the client should go to if you press **Accept** and uses the `<setvar/>` to set a single variable. This `<go>` tag uses the `href` attribute to specify the task's destination. In this case, the URL is a partial URL simply pointing to the next card in this deck, which has the `id` `"#next"` (on line 28).

Within the `<go>` tag you place one or more `<setvar/>` tags, each with a `name` and a `value` attribute to assign the specified value to the specified variable name. The `<setvar/>` tag on lines 22–24 simply sets the variable `$usernav` to the value `"yes"`. (By contrast, if you don't need to set variables before performing a `<go>` task, you can use the empty tag `<go/>`, which does the same thing in syntactically valid XML.)

The second card, shown on lines 28–41, is similar in form to the first, except that there is no timer, so the user sees this card until he or she presses **Accept** to load the deck shown in Listing 2-7. The `<card>` tag on lines 28–30 sets the current card's `id` to `"next"` and its `title` to the string `"Listing 2-6 - Next"`. After that, it simply shows the value of `$usernav` and a short explanation (lines 31–35) and sets the **Accept** key to navigate to the deck shown in Listing 2-7.

```
01: <?xml version="1.0"?>
02: <!DOCTYPE wml PUBLIC "-//WAPFORUM//DTD WML 1.1//EN"
03:   "http://www.wapforum.org/DTD/wml_1.1.xml">
04: <wml>
05:   <card
06:     id="Only"
07:     title="Listing 2-7 - Only">
08:     <p>
09:       $$usernav is $usernav<br/>
10:       This is because variables persist
11:       across decks.
12:     </p>
```

```
13:      <do
14:        type="accept"
15:        label="Listing 2-6">
16:        <go href="list0206.wml">
17:          <setvar
18:            name="usernav"
19:            value="never seen!"/>
20:        </go>
21:      </do>
22:    </card>
23: </wml>
```

Listing 2-7. Using `<card>` *attributes: variables across decks*

Listing 2-7 is similar to the cards shown in Listing 2-6, so I won't dissect it in detail. Note, however, that when the client loads the deck in Listing 2-7, $usernav is still set because the client is still using the same context created by the first card of the deck in Listing 2-6. Also note that , I set $usernav to the nonsense string "never seen!" before loading Listing 2-6 so you can see the explicit consequences of specifying a card with a newcontext attribute set to true,. If you load the deck in Listing 2-6, then load the deck in Listing 2-7, and then load the deck in Listing 2-6 again, you see that $usernav is, in fact, empty and not "never seen!" as a result of the newcontext attribute on line 8 of Listing 2-6.

As you'll see shortly, you will encounter two other attributes of the `<card>` tag, both shorthand like the ontimer tag. You use the `<card>` onenterfoward attribute to specify a destination URL when the client receives an onenterfoward event, whereas you use the `<card>` onenterbackward URL when the client receives an onenterbackward event. The client creates these events when you navigate to a specific card using a `<go>` task (such as when you choose a link or enter a URL) or a `<prev/>` task (such as when you press the phone's **Prev** key) respectively.

As you can imagine, repeatedly defining events and widget assignments can get tedious quickly, especially if you're overriding several built-in interface widgets such as **Help**, **Prev**, and **Options** across an entire deck of cards. Luck is with the lazy; WML gives you the `<template>` tag, which you can use to specify default onenterforward, onenterbackward, and ontimer attributes as well as any `<do>` tags your deck's cards share. If a deck's template tag defines a `<do>` task you want to replace in a specific card, you can simply provide a `<do>` task within that card with the same name attribute as the `<do>` task in the template.

A common use of the `<template>` tag is to provide a help card from any card in a deck, such as the deck shown in Listing 2-8. This deck is simply a rewritten version of the deck shown in Listing 2-7, showing how you use the `<template>` element to apply the `<do>` element to all cards in a deck. Of course, because only one card needs to use the `ontimer` attribute, I keep that attribute with the card that uses it, rather than moving it to the deck's `<template>` tag.

```
01: <?xml version="1.0"?>
02: <!DOCTYPE wml PUBLIC "-//WAPFORUM//DTD WML 1.1//EN"
03:   "http://www.wapforum.org/DTD/wml_1.1.xml">
04: <wml>
05:   <template>
06:     <do
07:       type="help"
08:       label="Help">
09:       <go href="#help"/>
10:     </do>
11:   </template>
12:   <card
13:     id="first"
14:     title="Listing 2-8 - Start"
15:     newcontext="true"
16:     ontimer="#next">
17:     <timer name="Next" value="60"/>
18:     <p>
19:       $$usernav is $usernav<br/>
20:     </p>
21:     <do
22:       type="accept"
23:       label="Listing 2-8 - Next">
24:       <go href="#next">
25:         <setvar
26:           name="usernav"
27:           value="yes"/>
28:       </go>
29:     </do>
30:   </card>
31:   <card
32:     id="next"
33:     title="Listing 2-8 - Next">
34:     <p>
35:       $$usernav is $usernav<br/>
36:     </p>
37:     <do
38:       type="accept"
39:       label="Listing 2-7">
40:       <go href="list0207.wml"/>
41:     </do>
```

```
42:    </card>
43:    <card
44:      id="help"
45:      title="Listing 2-8 - Help">
46:      <p>
47:        This deck clears all variables, and then
48:        sets the variable $$usernav to "yes" if you
49:        press Accept when viewing the Start card.
50:      </p>
51:      <do
52:        type="Accept"
53:        label="Listing 2-8 - Start">
54:        <go href="#first"/>
55:      </do>
56:    </card>
57: </wml>
```

Listing 2-8. The <template> *tag*

This example doesn't really do the <template> tag justice because I didn't have a help card (or the <do> tags to support a help card) in Listing 2-6. Listing 2-8 is 57 lines, including the help card. (The help card is 13 lines long). By comparison, Listing 2-6 is 42 lines. If I add the help card and the necessary <do> tags to assign the **Help** widget to a <go> task to load the help card, it becomes longer than Listing 2-7. In fact, it grows by almost 20 percent to 65 lines: the original 42 lines plus 13 more lines for the help card, and 5 lines for each <do> task for the help card on each of the original cards. While these savings don't reflect the true savings of a deck's binary representation (because the WAP gateway compresses the deck before sending it to the client) it gives you a warm fuzzy feeling. And who wants to type those extra eight lines anyway?

> **CAUTION**   *For a* <card> *tag's* <do> *tag to override a* <template> *tag's* <do> *tag, both* <do> *tags must have the same name! If you use the* name *attribute, you'll need to be careful.*

Handling Events with Tasks

In the previous section, you saw a preview of how WML lets you define what tasks the client should perform in response to an event. Let's look at the different events that you can use in your content.

The WML standard defines four events the client generates in response to internal changes. These events are the `ontimer` event, the `onenterforward` event, the `onenterbackward` event, and the `onpick` event. Each card in a deck can provide a single task, such as the `<go>` task, to execute for each of these events.

You've already encountered the `ontimer` event, which the client creates when the timer associated with a card's `<timer/>` tag expires. The client creates the `onenterforward` and `onenterbackward` events in response to user navigation. The client creates an `onenterforward` event when you go to a card in a forward direction such as via a bookmark or a link from another deck. The client creates an `onenterbackward` event when you go back to a card, say by pressing the phone's **Prev** key. The client generates the events in response to specific tasks that imply directionality, like the `<go>` task, which implies a forward event and causes the client to generate an `onenterforward` event. Finally, there's the `onpick` event, which the client generates when you pick an item from a list of items delineated by `<option>` tags in a `<select>` tag. You can use this to accept and handle user input within a deck; you'll see more of this in the section "Accepting Input" later in this chapter.

For each of these events, you can define an associated task using the `<onevent>` tag. The `<onevent>` `type` attribute tells the client which event you're assigning a task, while the `<onevent>` tag contains the task itself. The WML standard defines four tasks and their tags: `<go>`, `<prev/>`, `<refresh>`, and `<noop/>`.

The `<go>` tag is the most common task. As you saw in Listings 2-6 and 2-7, it tells the client to go to a card. There's actually two flavors of the `<go>` tag: the `<go>`, which takes content such as `<setvar/>` tags, and the empty `<go/>` tag, which doesn't take any content at all.[2] The `<go>` tag must have a `href` attribute that specifies the card the client will load. This URL can be a partial URL that the client will combine with the current deck's URL to create the full URL of the new card, or a full URL.

The `<go>` tag takes other attributes, too. These attributes change the HTTP headers created by the WAP gateway in response to the client's request for the desired URL. By default, new URLs are requested using the HTTP `GET` method (discussed in the section "Anatomy of a Protocol" in Chapter 1). Sometimes, you want to request a new card using the HTTP `POST` method, such as when you're sending data to a server for it to process. You can specify which HTTP method to use with the `<go>` tag's optional `method` attribute, which should be set to either the value `get` or `post`.

Sometimes, you may want to know what deck has requested that the client load your deck. You can track this using the HTTP header `Referer`, which the client can set to the URL of the deck that linked to your deck. To set this header when loading a card, you use the `<go>` tag's `sendreferer` attribute. When you set this attribute to `true`, the client places the URL of the deck initiating the `<go>` task in

---

2. As you may recall from the section "WML Syntax" earlier in this chapter, in XML languages such as WML, empty tags are written using a closing `/>`, while paired tags with content are written using `<>`.

the HTTP header of the request for the new card. (Of course, for this to work, the deck the client is loading must not be in cache; if it is, the HTTP request doesn't occur because the client simply loads the document from cache.)

You can also override the HTTP header `Accept-Charset` using the `<go>` tag's `accept-charset` attribute. By default, a client requests decks using the same character set as the deck you're currently looking at, but you can specify additional character sets as options using this attribute. If you're writing content in multiple languages and let users change which language they view your content in, you'll use this tag to indicate that you can switch encoding schemes. Otherwise, you probably won't need this attribute.

Similar to the `<go>` tag is the `<prev/>` tag, which instructs the client to go to the previously viewed card. Internally, the browser loads the previous card and removes its URL from the history list, as if you'd pressed the phone's **Prev** key. In conjunction with either a soft key or a timer, `<prev/>` is especially useful when providing information cards such as help information, letting you quickly return from a help card to what you were viewing previously. For example, Listing 2-9 builds on the code in Listing 2-8 to automatically return the user from the help card after 10 seconds.

```
01: <?xml version="1.0"?>
02: <!DOCTYPE wml PUBLIC "-//WAPFORUM//DTD WML 1.1//EN"
03:   "http://www.wapforum.org/DTD/wml_1.1.xml">
04: <wml>
05:   <template>
06:     <do
07:       type="help"
08:       label="Help">
09:       <go href="#help"/>
10:     </do>
11:   </template>
12:   <card
13:     id="first"
14:     title="Listing 2-9 - Start"
15:     newcontext="true"
16:     ontimer="#next">
17:     <timer name="Next" value="60"/>
18:     <p>
19:       $$usernav is $usernav<br/>
20:     </p>
21:     <do
22:       type="accept"
23:       label="Listing 2-9 - Next">
```

```
24:        <go href="#next">
25:          <setvar
26:            name="usernav"
27:            value="yes"/>
28:        </go>
29:      </do>
30:    </card>
31:    <card
32:      id="next"
33:      title="Listing 2-9 - Next">
34:      <p>
35:        $$usernav is $usernav<br/>
36:      </p>
37:    </card>
38:    <card
39:      id="help"
40:      title="Listing 2-9 - Help">
41:      <onevent type="ontimer">
42:        <prev/>
43:      </onevent>
44:      <timer name="timer2" value="100"/>
45:      <p>
46:        This deck clears all variables, and then
47:        sets the variable $$usernav to "yes" if you
48:        press Accept when viewing the Start card.
49:      </p>
50:      <do type="prev" label="Back">
51:        <prev/>
52:      </do>
53:    </card>
54: </wml>
```

Listing 2-9. Using the <prev/> *tag*

The preamble and first two cards (lines 1–37) are familiar to you by now. The help card, on lines 38–54, is similar to the help card on lines 2–9, but there are two important differences. First, I bind the ontimer event to the card's timer on lines 41–44 using the <onevent> tag. I do this with <onevent> instead of the card's ontimer attribute because the <card> ontimer attribute only lets you give a destination URL for the <go> task, not another task such as <prev/>. Here I want the browser to return to the previous card, so I use the <prev/> task instead (line 42).

Lines 50–52 assign the <prev> task to the browser's **Prev** soft key. Figure 2-13 shows the result. Note that on this client, the soft key is labeled with the <do>

tag's `label` attribute. Pressing **Prev** brings you back to the card from which you invoked **Help.**

Having a card simply to display a variable's value after it changes as I do in Listings 2-8 and 2-9 is a waste of space, though. Of course, you could simply go to the same card, but there's an even better way. The ‹refresh› task tag (and its empty tag counterpart ‹refresh/›) tells the browser to redraw the currently visible card after updating any variables. Listing 2-10 shows how you can use this to streamline the previous Listings.

```
01: <?xml version="1.0"?>
02: <!DOCTYPE wml PUBLIC "-//WAPFORUM//DTD WML 1.1//EN"
03:   "http://www.wapforum.org/DTD/wml_1.1.xml">
04: <wml>
05:   <card
06:     id="first"
07:     title="Listing 2-10"
08:     newcontext="true">
09:     <onevent type="timer">
10:       <refresh>
11:         <setvar
12:           name="usernav"
13:           value=""/>
14:       </refresh>
15:     </onevent>
16:     <timer name="Next" value="50"/>
17:     <p>
18:       $$usernav is $usernav<br/>
19:     </p>
20:     <do
21:       type="accept"
22:       label="Refresh">
23:       <refresh>
24:         <setvar
25:           name="usernav"
26:           value="yes"/>
27:       </refresh>
28:     </do>
29:   </card>
30: </wml>
```

Listing 2-10. The ‹refresh› *tag*

For the sake of brevity, I've removed the help card that you saw in the last two examples. This deck has one card, which uses a `timer` event or the **Accept** soft key to cause a ‹refresh› task. If you press the **Accept** soft key, the $usernav variable is set to "yes" and the card is redrawn; if you do nothing, the timer causes an event after five seconds and the $usernav variable is set to an empty string "".

For those times when you really want to do nothing, there's the <noop/> task tag. The first time I came across this tag, I was baffled: in a low-bandwidth, memory-constrained environment like a phone, who wants to waste valuable resources with a tag that does nothing?

It didn't take long for me to realize how wrong I was. In fact, the <noop/> tag comes in quite handy. A common use for <noop/> is to override the default behavior for a key on one card when using the <template> tag in a deck. The admittedly contrived example in Listing 2-11 shows you what I mean.

```
01: <?xml version="1.0"?>
02: <!DOCTYPE wml PUBLIC "-//WAPFORUM//DTD WML 1.1//EN"
03:   "http://www.wapforum.org/DTD/wml_1.1.xml">
04: <wml>
05:   <template>
06:     <do
07:       type="prev"
08:       label="Back">
09:       <prev/>
10:     </do>
11:   </template>
12:   <card>
13:     <p>
14:       Bwahahahaha!<br/>
15:       You can't go back from here!
16:     </p>
17:     <do
18:       type="Accept"
19:       label="Next">
20:       <go href="#card2"/>
21:     </do>
22:     <do
23:       type="prev">
24:       <noop/>
25:     </do>
26:   </card>
27:   <card id="card2">
28:     <p>
29:       To go back, just press Back!
30:     </p>
31:   </card>
32: </wml>
```

Listing 2-11. The <noop/> *tag*

I first define a card template that assigns the ‹prev/› task to the **Prev** key[3] on lines 5–11 of Listing 2-11. In the first card (lines 12–26), though, I don't want the user to be able to go back, so I replace the template's assignment for the **Prev** key with the ‹noop/› tag, using the ‹do› tag on lines 22–25. Thus, you can't go to the previous card from the first card using the **Prev** key on the first card. The second card operates normally, however, inheriting the ‹prev/› tag for the **Prev** key from the template.

Before I close this discussion about tasks and events, I want to revisit the ‹card› attributes ontimer, onenterforward, and onenterbackward in light of what you've learned about tasks and events. As it so happens, these attributes are actually just abbreviations for an ‹onevent› tag containing a ‹go/› tag with a given URL. There's nothing special about these attributes, and under the hood, the browser handles both kinds of task assignment the same way.

Formatting Text

Like HTML, you can use tags in WML to change your content's format. Using these tags, you can ask the browser to make text stand out using bold face or italics or to typeset text in a larger or smaller font. You can also link a block of text to a tag, creating an in-line hyperlink.

The fundamental block of text within a card is a paragraph. You mark paragraphs using the ‹p› tag. Unlike HTML, in which you can get away with placing text outside paragraphs[4], all text within a WML deck must be inside a paragraph. You can't nest paragraphs, either—but then again, you can't do that in traditional writing either, so why would you want to? You've already seen the ‹p› tag in every example in the book, but I've not talked about its attributes.

The ‹p› tag's align attribute instructs the client to center, left-align, or right-align the text. By default, all text is aligned to the left-hand side of the display, as if you'd written ‹p align=left›. On the other hand, you can center a paragraph using ‹p align=center›, or right-justify a paragraph using ‹p align=right›.

By default, clients *word wrap* all paragraphs. If a single paragraph is too long to fit across the display, it's broken up into separate lines at word boundaries, just like this paragraph. Using the ‹p› tag's mode attribute, you can avoid word wrap, and force the browser to display your paragraph as one long line. If you set the mode attribute to nowrap, some clients show the line and provide horizontal scrolling, while others display as much of the line as fits on the display, and then scroll the line, marquee-style. Some clients, however, don't understand this at all, and insist

---

3. I told you this was contrived—by default, the ‹prev/› task *is* assigned to the **Prev** key!

4. You shouldn't do this in HTML, either. You can get away with it in HTML because the browser puts implicit ‹p› tags around such text. Newer versions of HTML, especially XHTML, don't like this sort of thing at all.

on word-wrapping anyway, just as if you'd used a plain vanilla `<p>` tag (or used `<p mode="wrap">`), so it's best to have a good reason to avoid the `mode` tag altogether.

Sometimes, all you want to do is insert a line break. WML has the line break tag `<br/>`, which is the same as HTML's `<br>` tag. You've already seen this in a few places, including Listing 2-6.

WML gives you a handful of text formatting choices, too, although it's up to the client to decide what the resulting card will look like. With the wide variety of devices running WML browsers (handheld computers, palmtops, screen phones, and even the occasional pager), there's a lot of variation in presentation. For example, most smart phones have only one font, so tags that request other font sizes or styles are ignored.

The most widely supported tags enable you to change the style of the current display font. Like HTML, you can set text in bold using the `<b>` or `<strong>` tags. There's also the `<em>` tag to request emphasized text (most platforms set this in bold), the `<i>` tag to request italic text, and the `<u>` tag to request underlined text.

The WML standard calls for three discrete font sizes within the browser. One of these fonts is larger than the standard display font, and the other one is smaller. At present, most browsers simply use the same font size for all three sizes. You can tell the client to set some text in the larger font using `<big>`, or in the smaller font using `<small>`.

Listing 2-12 shows all these tags in use. To give you an idea of how well supported the different tags are, Figure 2-13 shows the resulting cards in three different browsers. As you can see, with the exception of the `<br/>` tag the results are largely unpredictable. The Phone.com SDK—and the versions of its browser you find in today's smart phones—generally does the best with these format tags, but that's not always the case. Moreover, unless you check the type and version of the browser ahead of time, you won't be able to select the right format tags for your viewers. In general, it's best to use the format tags sparingly.

```
01: <?xml version="1.0"?>
02: <!DOCTYPE wml PUBLIC "-//WAPFORUM//DTD WML 1.1//EN"
03:   "http://www.wapforum.org/DTD/wml_1.1.xml">
04: <wml>
05:   <card>
06:     <p mode="nowrap">
07:       Here's a single very long line of text. Whew!
08:     </p>
09:     <p align="center">
10:       <b>Bold</b><br/>
11:       <em>Emphasize</em><br/>
12:       <u>Underline</u><br/>
13:       <big>Bigger</big><br/>
14:       <small>Smaller</small><br/>
15:     </p>
```

```
16:    <p align="right">
17:        Right
18:    </p>
19:  </card>
20: </wml>
```

Listing 2-12. WML text format tags

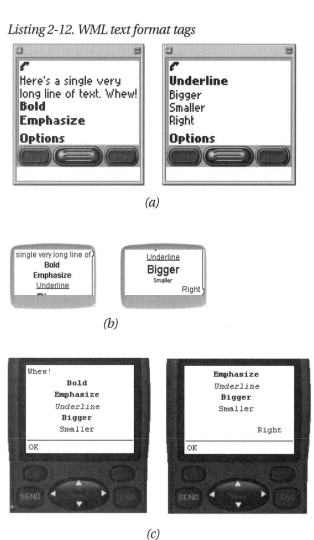

(a)

(b)

(c)

Figure 2-13. Listing 2-12 presented on (a) the Yospace SPEDE, (b) Nokia SDK with WAP 1.2 support, and (c) the Phone.com UP.SDK

Although not a text format tag per se, you should also know about the <anchor> tag and its synonym, <a>. These tags are to text what the <do> tag is to widgets: they enable you to assign a task to a block of text. Similar to HTML's <a> tag that lets you mark a block of text for a hyperlink, they let you assign any of the four tasks, `<go>`, `<prev>`, `<refresh>`, and `<noop/>`, to a block of text. Listing 2-13 shows a simple example.

```
01: <?xml version="1.0"?>
02: <!DOCTYPE wml PUBLIC "-//WAPFORUM//DTD WML 1.1//EN"
03:  "http://www.wapforum.org/DTD/wml_1.1.xml">
04: <wml>
05:   <card>
06:     <p>
07:       Go to
08:       <anchor title="Card 2">
09:         <go href="#card2"/>
10:         the next card
11:       </anchor>
12:     </p>
13:   </card>
14:   <card id="card2">
15:     <p>
16:       Here's card 2!
17:     </p>
18:   </card>
19: </wml>
```

Listing 2-13. The `<anchor>` *tag*

Line 8 starts the `<anchor>` tag, giving the anchor a title for interface widgets using the required `title` attribute. Some browsers may assign anchor titles to soft keys, while others let you navigate through anchors using a cursor and don't show the title anywhere. Line 9 declares the task (a `<go/>` task to the second card) for the anchor. Line 10 contains the text of the anchor, and line 11 completes the anchor with the closing `</anchor>` tag.

Whether to use WML's `<do>` tag with soft keys or the `<anchor>` tag to construct your links is a personal decision largely based on how you want your site to appear. Some browsers, most notably versions of the Phone.com browser, present words in the anchor format in square braces on their own line **[like this]**, making it difficult to read text with a lot of inline anchors. Even when making a list of links, it still looks a little awkward, making other choices such as the `<select>` tag, which I discuss in "Accepting Input" later in this chapter, an easier choice for many readers. However, some authors seem to prefer the `<anchor>` tag, and it's certainly well within acceptable standards to do so.

Making Tables

Some kinds of data, such as financial data or other statistics, aren't presented well in paragraphs. Instead, it's easier for readers if you set this kind of information in a table. Anybody familiar with HTML knows the rich—and potentially confusing— table tags it provides. Mercifully, WML has simpler facilities that are much easier to use.

A WML table is a series of cells, contained in a series of rows. Every row must have the same number of cells, and that number must match the table's declaration that indicates the number of cells per row. You can leave cells empty, but you can't tweak the span of an individual row or column to create multispan table elements.

A table begins with the `<table>` tag. It has two mandatory attributes, `title` and `column`. The `title` attribute should contain a brief caption for the title, in case the client needs to display the table on a separate screen and provide a link to the table. The `column` attribute must contain the number of columns in each row of the table, Of course, you can't set `column` to `0` (zero); you get an error if you do. You can also provide an optional `align` attribute, with one of the values `"left"`, `"center"`, or `"right"`, to tell the client to set the table to the left, in the center, or to the right of the display.

Each line of the table is marked by `<tr>` tags, which take no attributes. Each `<tr>` tag should contain a `<td>` tag for each cell of the table. Within the `<td>` tag, you can place text, images, or anchors. Oddly, when placing text in `<td>` tags, unlike `<card>` tags, you don't put them in paragraphs. Like `<tr>`, `<td>` doesn't take attributes either.

Before you see an example of a WML table, you should know what you should and shouldn't use them for. WML tables are for setting tables of text—multiple narrow columns of figures, tiny icons, or other information. They are not for controlling text flow, simulating multiple columns of multi-paragraph text, aligning input lines with their prompts, coercing the browser to create a specific look and feel, or any of the other heinous uses for tables you may have encountered.

CAUTION *You shouldn't use any tag to coerce the fine details of format such as columns, spacing, fonts, or other minutia. WML tags are requests you make of the client to try to set something a particular way (such as setting text in a font size, in bold, or on this soft key) rather than an imperative. Due to the diverse nature of client devices, you simply can't expect to create a unified look and feel across all Wireless Web devices the way you might with HTML on the Web. Even if you could, you shouldn't; the rapid pace at which new devices are being introduced almost guarantees that as soon as you're done, someone will ship a device that won't render your site correctly. Trust the client's browser and its authors— they know a lot more about the target device than you do.*

Listing 2-14 shows a three-column, three-row table. Line 8 begins the table, giving the table's title and number of columns. The first row, on lines 9–19, are representative of each row of the table. The row begins with the `<tr>` tag and contains three `<td>` tags. Each tag contains text (styled, in the case of the first row, in bold) contained within the `<td>` and matching `</td>` tags. The row closes with a `</tr>`, and the next row begins on line 10 with the next `<tr>` tag. Lines 28–31 show how you can put an anchor in a table cell; this anchor works just like any other anchor would.

```
01: <?xml version="1.0"?>
02: <!DOCTYPE wml PUBLIC "-//WAPFORUM//DTD WML 1.1//EN"
03:   "http://www.wapforum.org/DTD/wml_1.1.xml">
04: <wml>
05:   <card>
06:     <p>
07:     Assignments<br/>
08:       <table title="Assignments" columns="3">
09:         <tr>
10:           <td>
11:             <b>Start</b>
12:           </td>
13:           <td>
14:             <b>Stop</b>
15:           </td>
16:           <td>
17:             <b>Where</b>
18:           </td>
19:         </tr>
20:         <tr>
21:           <td>
22:             1000
23:           </td>
24:           <td>
25:             1200
26:           </td>
27:           <td>
28:             <anchor title="Where">
29:               <go href="#card2"/>
30:               St. Michael's Church
31:             </anchor>
32:           </td>
```

```
33:          </tr>
34:          <tr>
35:            <td>
36:               1400
37:            </td>
38:            <td>
39:               1800
40:            </td>
41:            <td>
42:              <anchor title="Where">
43:                <go href="#card3"/>
44:                Mountain School
45:              </anchor>
46:            </td>
47:          </tr>
48:        </table>
49:      </p>
50:    </card>
51:    <card id="card2">
52:      <p>
53:        St. Michael's Church<br/>
54:        323 Locust Street<br/>
55:        (888) 555-1212
56:      </p>
57:    </card>
58:    <card id="card3">
59:      <p>
60:        Mountain School<br/>
61:        1017 High Street<br/>
62:        (888) 555-1212
63:      </p>
64:    </card>
65: </wml>
```

Listing 2-14. A WML table

Figure 2-14 shows the table on three different WML browsers. As you can see from the figure, different clients format tables very differently. Unfortunately, this makes using tables problematic because it's hard to predict when you'll have line breaks (like those in Figure 2-14(c) within a row, or even within a cell as in Figure 2-14(b). Some clients, such as the Yospace SPEDE in Figure 2-14(a) don't even try to render the table as a table, but instead place each cell on its own line. Consequently, you should follow these guidelines:

- Keep your columns as narrow as possible.

- Present your data using as few columns per table as you can. At most two or three columns is best.

- Abbreviate or eliminate (where meaning is clear) captions for table columns.

Sometimes, you can break a larger table into two or more smaller tables. For example, consider a stock quote report containing a stock's symbol, last trade price, high and low, and volume. On the Web, this information could be kept in one table with four columns: the symbol, last trade, high/low, and volume. On the Wireless Web, it would probably be better to put each piece of information on separate cards, or to make a two-column table, with legends down the first column, and the data down the second.

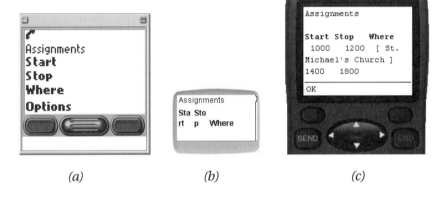

(a)   *(b)*   *(c)*

Figure 2-14. Listing 2-14 presented on (a) the Yospace SPEDE, (b) Nokia SDK with WAP 1.2 support, and (c) the Phone.com UP.SDK

When in doubt, test your layout using different SDKs. While you won't see every possible rendering (and mis-rendering!) of your tables with the different SDKs, you'll quickly see that they all deal with large tables in only a few ways. Predominantly, browsers make tables fit on small screens by either breaking rows onto multiple lines, breaking cells onto multiple lines, truncating data, or placing each cell on its own line. By testing your content before transition, you can avoid the embarrassment of showing tables on these browsers with nonsensical or missing information.

Accepting Input

Although you can create a variety of wireless applications using just the tags I've shown you so far, you're still missing an important element: accepting input from you. Most wireless applications need to collect data from you at least once, to find out what kind of content you want to see. Although it's easy to create decks that accept user input, it's difficult to do so well because of the physical constraints of the device and the likely preoccupation of the user.

As I've noted before, smart phones are small devices with limited input mechanisms. The average device has a numeric keypad; you enter letters by pressing numeric keys repeatedly. For example, to enter the word Apress on my phone, I have to press the sequence of digits **2 7 77 33 7777 7777**, pausing between each group so the cursor advances to the next letter. While some phones have word completion, which tries to guess what word you're entering by the first few letters, the initial difficulty of entering each letter remains. Of course, a few wireless devices—notably handheld computers—may have handwriting recognition, onscreen keyboards, or physical keyboards. Even so, because you often use these devices while standing or moving, the simple fact is it's difficult to enter data on any portable device.

To make matters worse, many times you will be trying to enter data while doing something else, such as walking or having a conversation. Because of this, it's harder for you to accurately enter information. Not only are you distracted, paying less attention to what you're doing, but also the device or your hand wiggles around, making it harder for you to use the device. In both cases, it's difficult for you to enter a lot of data, even if the device has an optimal entry mechanism, which it probably doesn't.

Consequently, your wireless application should make data entry as easy as possible. You should follow these four basic rules:

- Enables users to select an item rather than enter an item whenever possible,

- Create reasonable defaults for both selected and entered data.

- Remember data users enter and make it easy for them to use it again.

- Constrain input to restrict the kinds of mistakes users can make.

Selection, rather than *input,* should be your modus operandi. It's far easier for you to select an item from a list than it is to type the same item on a keyboard. When there are a lot of items, you can organize them in hierarchies so you can navigate hierarchies and keep each list short. For example, if you're prompting for a time of day, you can break the list into the choices "Morning," "Afternoon," "Evening," and "Night." Each of these lists links to another list with only a few hour choices. It's best if each list has no more than six or seven elements because people's short-term memory generally doesn't remember more than seven items at once. Of course, shorter is better if you can manage it because users may be using their short-term memory for other tasks at the same time, such as remembering what they're looking up on their phone in the first place.

Using *reasonable defaults* when a user enters information makes input easier. If you're prompting users to enter their country, for example, you can probably take a pretty good stab at what city they're in by guessing their home city from either client headers (like the client mobile phone number) or other information. If you can only pin it down to a major metropolitan area for the default, that's fine—just don't offer users a guess like Queen Creek if in actuality they could be anywhere in Phoenix, AZ.

Remembering what information your users have already entered likewise makes input easier. Most Wireless Web sites should be personalized so that each user gets a view of the site that's tailored to his or her needs and interests. If you have to enter something, you should only need to once, unless the information is so ephemeral that it's meant to be used and thrown away. Even then, the site can keep a history of the last few entries, letting the user pick from the list. For example, if your application enables users to enter ticker symbols for a stock quote, you can let them pick from symbols on a portfolio or one of the last five symbols entered. This trick—remembering a history of recently entered items—can cut down the need for text entry by up to 80 percent.

Finally, you should *constrain* your users' input as much as possible. If your application accepts zip codes in the United States, for example, there's no reason your users should be able to enter letters, or enter a number with more or less than five digits.[5] WML gives you the capability to restrict input in a variety of ways, and on devices with WMLScript, you can even further validate data on the device with scripts before the deck submits the data to the server. By constraining input to valid values, you reduce the likelihood of data entry mistakes—you simply can't enter a syntactically invalid zip code if you don't let the user enter letters, for example. Of course, your application server must still be able to handle erroneous entry because not all clients support the same input constraints.

Some mobile sites turn to the Web to let their mobile users customize their Wireless Web options for their site. These sites let you log in to their site on the Web and enter preferences using a desktop computer and keyboard. Later, when users return to the site on the Wireless Web, the site can offer them just the information they need. This is a good compromise if you know your users have access to the Web, but consider this: as the number of mobile devices grows, not all Wireless Web users will have access to the Web. Analysts predict that by mid-decade, more users will access the Wireless Web than the traditional Web; if you force your users

---

5. Unless, of course, your application accepts the now-standard five-plus-four zip codes.

to use the Web to configure their options, you'll be leaving behind a significant number of potential users.

Generalities of user input aside, WML provides two kinds of user input: option lists and text input. You use the `<select>` `<option>` and `<optgroup>` tags to define option lists, and you use the `<fieldset>` and `<input/>` tags to define input regions. Both store the data you enter using WML variables so you can display the entries before sending the results to the server or pass the data to WMLScript routines for processing (see Chapter 4).

The `<select>` tag defines an option list containing one or more `<option>` choices from which you can choose items. Each `<option>` tag defines a single option the user can choose. An `<option>` tag may have a `title` attribute, which the browser can assign to a soft key. It may also have an `onclick` attribute, which gives the destination URL the browser should go to when the item is clicked via an implicit `<go/>` task. Most `<option>` tags also have a `value` attribute, which gives the `<select>` value the client will use if the item is selected.

You can group `<option>` choices together within a `<select>` tag to create a hierarchy using the `<optgroup>` tag. This tag simply provides a cue to the browser that the grouped items should be presented as part of a subgroup labeled by the `<optgroup>` tag's `title` attribute. Not all clients support `<optgroup>` to create hierarchies of option lists; many clients simply ignore the tag and lump all the choices together.

The `<select>` tag accepts a dizzying array of attributes, although in practice you use only a subset. Although not required, all `<select>` tags should include a `name` attribute that identifies what WML variable should hold the user's selection. (You might choose to omit the `name` attribute when first mocking up a user-interface prototype, however, if you haven't written anything that will use an entered value.) As the client accepts input from the user, the value of the `<option>` tag selected— that is, whatever the `value` attribute of the `<option>` tag is set to—will be placed in the `name` variable. You should also use the `<select>` tag's `default` attribute to specify the value (again, the value of an `<option>` tag) the client should set before the user picks an item.

Listing 2-15 shows a simple option list that uses the `<select>`, `<optgroup>`, and `<option>` tags. Figure 2-15(a) shows the resulting card, while Figure 2-15(b) shows the option list when you press the **Accept** key with the choice selected. Lines 8–49 define the option list, which stores your choice in the variable `$card`. The list is divided into two groups, one group containing face cards (lines 9–22) and the other group containing number cards (lines 23–48). Each option choice (such as the choice for the option 2 on lines 10–12) sets a `value` for the option and supplies an `onpick` attribute so that the browser loads the card `#card2` after you pick an element. The second card—`#card2`–simply shows the choice you made.

```
01: <?xml version="1.0"?>
02: <!DOCTYPE wml PUBLIC "-//WAPFORUM//DTD WML 1.1//EN"
03:  "http://www.wapforum.org/DTD/wml_1.1.xml">
04: <wml>
05:   <card>
06:     <p>
07:       Pick a card, any card!
08:       <select title="Pick a Card" name="card">
09:         <optgroup title="Number Card">
10:           <option value="2" onpick="#res">
11:             2
12:           </option>
13:           <option value="3" onpick="#res">
14:             3
15:           </option>
16:           <option value="4" onpick="#res">
17:             4
18:           </option>
19:           <option value="5" onpick="#res">
20:             5
21:           </option>
22:           <option value="6" onpick="#res">
23:             6
24:           </option>
25:           <option value="7" onpick="#res">
26:             7
27:           </option>
28:           <option value="8" onpick="#res">
29:             8
30:           </option>
31:           <option value="9" onpick="#res">
32:             9
33:           </option>
34:         </optgroup>
35:         <optgroup title="Face Card">
36:           <option value="jack" onpick="#res">
37:             Jack
38:           </option>
39:           <option value="queen" onpick="#res">
40:             Queen
41:           </option>
42:           <option value="king" onpick="#res">
43:             King
44:           </option>
```

```
45:                <option value="ace" onpick="#res">
46:                  Ace
47:                </option>
48:              </optgroup>
49:            </select>
50:        </p>
51:    </card>
52:    <card id="res">
53:      <p>
54:        You picked the $card!
55:      </p>
56:    </card>
57: </wml>
```

Listing 2-15. An option list using <select>, <optgroup>, *and* <option>

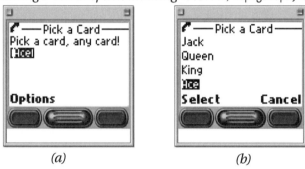

(a)   *(b)*

Figure 2-15. The deck from Listing 2-15: (a) the first card, (b) an option list

Sometimes, it's easier to manage option lists by an item's index (where it sits in the list) than by a value associated with each item. For example, if your application server will use the value of the option a user picks as a number in arithmetic computation, it makes no sense to have the client return a string and then convert the string back to a number at the server before processing the input. In cases such as this, instead of using the <select> tag's name and default attributes, you can use the iname and ivalue options. The iname attribute indicates the name of the variable that will contain the index of the option selected by the user, while the ivalue specifies the index of the default. For example, Listing 2-16 shows the same deck as in Listing 2-15, except I use the iname and ivalue options to find out what you've selected. Lines 8–49 again define the option list, but use iname instead of name. Each option doesn't have to include a value because the list records the index of the selected option in the variable $cardindex. For example, if you choose **2**, $cardindex will be 1 (corresponding to the first item of the option list); if you choose **Ace**, $cardindex will be 12.

```
01: <?xml version="1.0"?>
02: <!DOCTYPE wml PUBLIC "-//WAPFORUM//DTD WML 1.1//EN"
03:   "http://www.wapforum.org/DTD/wml_1.1.xml">
04: <wml>
05:   <card>
06:     <p>
07:       Pick a card, any card!
08:       <select title="Pick a Card" iname="cardindex">
09:         <optgroup title="Number Card">
10:           <option onpick="#res">
11:             2
12:           </option>
13:           <option onpick="#res">
14:             3
15:           </option>
16:           <option onpick="#res">
17:             4
18:           </option>
19:           <option onpick="#res">
20:             5
21:           </option>
22:           <option onpick="#res">
23:             6
24:           </option>
25:           <option onpick="#res">
26:             7
27:           </option>
28:           <option onpick="#res">
29:             8
30:           </option>
31:           <option onpick="#res">
32:             9
33:           </option>
34:         </optgroup>
35:         <optgroup title="Face Card">
36:           <option onpick="#res">
37:             Jack
38:           </option>
39:           <option onpick="#res">
40:             Queen
41:           </option>
```

```
42:            <option onpick="#res">
43:                King
44:            </option>
45:            <option onpick="#res">
46:                Ace
47:            </option>
48:          </optgroup>
49:        </select>
50:      </p>
51:    </card>
52:    <card id="res">
53:      <p>
54:        You picked the item at index $cardindex!
55:      </p>
56:    </card>
57: </wml>
```

Listing 2-16. A selection list using <select> *with* iname *and* ivalue

You can support option lists with multiple selections, too, using the <select> tag's multiple attribute. If more than one item is selected, the value of the variable specified by name will contain a list of all items you select separated by semicolons. If you're using the index attribute iname, the variable specified by iname will contain a list of all the indexes of all the items you select separated by semicolons.

The <select> tag has two more attributes, although these aren't supported by most of today's clients. You can specify an optional title using the title attribute, which the client can assign to a soft key corresponding to the option list. Finally, you can specify how the client presents the list choices to the user using the tabindex attribute.

For times when your application needs free data entry, you can use the <fieldset> and <input/> tags. The <fieldset> tag contains a series of <input/> and <select> tags and other formatted text, each accepting input in a WML variable for your deck to process. Like the option list's <optgroup> tag, it's an optional tag; you don't have to use it, but it helps some clients present the deck in an orderly fashion. (Other clients ignore the <fieldset> tag altogether.) The <fieldset> tag takes the title attribute, which specifies the title for the fields the set contains. You can nest <fieldset> tags to build hierarchies of input, just like you can nest <optgroup> tags, too.

The <input/> tag defines an input region on a card. Cards can contain multiple <input/> tags (or multiple <fieldset> tags containing <input/> tags, for that matter).

Each <input/> tag has a name attribute that identifies the variable that will hold the input data. You can specify the default value for an input field's data by putting the data in the variable specified with the name attribute, or by assigning the data to the default attribute.

While it's not required, you should give each <input/> tag a title using the title attribute and supply its type using the type attribute. The client uses the title when presenting the input field, while it uses the type field to identify the kind of input taking place, either text input or password entry. When type is equal to "text", the browser displays what you enter on the keypad; when type is "password", the browser does not echo what you enter, but shows placeholders like blanks, underlines, or asterisks.

The <input/> tag provides simple entry validation, enabling you to supply hints to the client about what kinds of characters it should accept. Clients may use these hints to optimize user input (say, presenting only a certain kind of input keyboard), or compare the resulting input against the input hints to ensure the input matches the criteria set by the hints. While all clients should use the input hints, the fact is that not all clients do, so your application server should still validate what data users enter before trying to use the data.

You supply these input hints using the <input/> tag's format attribute. The format attribute is a string whose contents describe the kind of characters to accept. The simplest format hints map a single character of input to a single character of the hint; each character entered must fall into one of the sets of characters in the hint string. Table 2-3 shows the hint characters.

For example, the hint string "MxxN" tells the browser that the first character you enter can be anything, the second and third characters must be lowercase letters, and the last character must be a numeric character. Thus, the browser would see the inputs **,zz9** or **Wow0** as valid, whereas the inputs **moO0** (because the third character is uppercase) and **bong** (because the last character is a letter) would be invalid.

Many hint strings have runs of similar kinds of characters. A phone number consists of groups of digits, for example, while a stock ticker symbol consists of a group of letters. Rather than writing "NNNNNNNNNN" for a U.S. phone number with area code, you can use the shorthand "10N", meaning that the following 10 characters should be of type N. Similarly, a stock ticker symbol hint could be "4A".

You can also put characters the client should insert after entry within the hint. While some people write phone numbers as 10 digits, most people find it easier to separate groups of digits with some kind of symbol, such as a dash or period. The hint strings "NNN\-NNN\-NNNN" and "3N\-3N\-4N" both have the same meaning. When the browser encounters an <input/> tag with this format hint, it will automatically insert a dash after the first three digits you enter, and insert a dash after you enter the next three digits.

Table 2-3. Hints for the `<input/>` *Tag* `format` *Attribute*

CHARACTER	ACTION
A	Matches any upper-case alphabetic or punctuation character.
a	Matches any lower-case alphabetic or punctuation character.
N	Matches any numeric character.
X	Matches any upper-case character.
x	Matches any lower-case character.
M	Matches any character.
nf	Matches any n characters of type f.
*f	Matches any number of characters matching f.
\c	Places c in the next position of the input.

Note that if you omit the `format` tag, the client defaults to the value `"*M"`, which matches any sequence of characters.

While the `format` attribute enables you to control what characters the user can enter, it doesn't enable you to control the number of characters that she can enter. The attributes `emptyok` and `maxlength` let you tell the browser how many characters to permit for a particular `<input/>` tag. By default, an `<input/>` tag does not accept an empty string; if you supply an `<input/>` tag with the attribute `emptyok` set to `true`, the client will let the user submit a card with the `<input/>` element empty. The `maxlength` attribute tells the client how many characters can be entered in an `<input/>` element.

Related to `maxlength` is the `<input/>` tag's `size` attribute, which tells the client how many characters wide the visible input prompt should be. If no `size` attribute is set, the client is free to make the interface widget for the `<input/>` tag whatever size it deems best. If you supply a `size` attribute, the client tries to make the interface widget the size you give. Be careful not to confuse the two—you won't get what you expect!

Listing 2-17 shows the deck that implements the login screen in MobileHelper. As you can see from Figure 2-16, it prompts you for your mobile identification number (MIN) and a personal identification number (PIN).

Lines 7–22 use `<fieldset>` to group these inputs on a single card with the title **MIN & PIN**. As you may recall from the section "XML Syntax" earlier in this chapter, & is a reserved character in XML and WML, so you must write & instead to display &.

The `<input>` tag in lines 9–14 defines a single input widget that accepts 10 digits as required by the `format` and `maxlength` attributes. Its `type` attribute is `"text"`, so the client displays the information you enter. Because its `emptyok` attribute is `"false"`, the client won't let you leave it empty. The information you enter will be stored in the WML variable $min.

The second `<input>` tag in lines 16–21 defines a single input widget that accepts six characters. It's a password field, as you can tell by its `type` attribute (equal to `"password"`), so the client won't display what you enter. Like the `<input>` before it, you must give it a value. The value you enter will be stored in the variable `$pin`.

```
01: <?xml version="1.0"?>
02: <!DOCTYPE wml PUBLIC "-//WAPFORUM//DTD WML 1.1//EN"
03:   "http://www.wapforum.org/DTD/wml_1.1.xml">
04: <wml>
05:   <card title="MobileHelper Login">
06:     <p>
07:       <fieldset title="MIN &amp; PIN">
08:         MIN:
09:         <input name="min"
10:           type="text"
11:           format="10N"
12:           emptyok="false"
13:           maxlength="10"
14:           size="10"/>
15:         PIN:
16:         <input name="pin"
17:           type="password"
18:           format="6N"
19:           emptyok="false"
20:           maxlength="6"
21:           size="6"/>
22:       </fieldset>
23:     </p>
24:   </card>
25: </wml>
```

Listing 2-17. The `<input/>` *tag*

Figure 2-16. A deck with `<fieldset>` *and* `<input/>` *tags*

One step is missing from these examples: how does the data you enter get back to the server? When you enter data in a deck, you're doing so with the intention that something's going to do stuff to it, either the back-end server or a WMLScript running on the phone (see Chapter 4).

To pass data back to the server, you use a `<go>` task that includes a `<postfield/>` tag for each variable the server needs. As you'll see in more detail in the next chapter, servers use variables to contain data clients submit. These variables *aren't* the same as the WML variables, however. They exist only on the server, so you need a way to correlate which variables on the client have values that should be stuck in variables on the server. The `<postfield/>` tag bridges that gap.

The `<postfield/>` tag takes two attributes: name and value. The name attribute contains the server variable name, whereas the attribute variable contains the value to assign to the server variable. Because the server variables are completely independent of the WML variables, in theory you can name your server variables anything (as long as you're consistent when you write your server scripts with those variables). In practice, however, it's usually easiest if you use the same names in both places so you can keep track of everything.

Listing 2-18 extends Listing 2-17, using `<postfield/>` to submit the values you enter to the server. The `<do>` task defined on lines 23–28 link the **Accept** soft key to the `<go>` task that submits data to the origin server. On lines 24–27, I use a `<go>` task with the HTTP POST method because that's preferred for handling form input (see the section "Anatomy of a Protocol" in Chapter 1 for more about HTTP methods). Line 25 uses `<postfield/>` to tell the client to send the value of the WML variable $min to the server assigned to the server variable min, while line 26 tells the client to send the value of the WML variable $pin to the server assigned to the server variable pin.

```
01: <?xml version="1.0"?>
02: <!DOCTYPE wml PUBLIC "-//WAPFORUM//DTD WML 1.1//EN"
03:  "http://www.wapforum.org/DTD/wml_1.1.xml">
04: <wml>
05:   <card title="MobileHelper Login">
06:     <p>
07:       <fieldset title="MIN &amp; PIN">
08:         MIN:
09:         <input name="min"
10:           type="text"
11:           format="10N"
12:           emptyok="false"
13:           maxlength="10"
14:           size="10"/>
```

```
15:        PIN:
16:        <input name="pin"
17:           type="password"
18:           format="6*"
19:           emptyok="false"
20:           maxlength="6"
21:           size="6"/>
22:        </fieldset>
23:        <do type="accept" label="Login">
24:           <go href="auth.php" method="post">
25:              <postfield name="min" value="$min"/>
26:              <postfield name="pin" value="$pin"/>
27:           </go>
28:        </do>
29:     </p>
30:   </card>
31: </wml>
```

Listing 2-18. Using `<postfield/>`

WML Within MobileHelper

Whew! I covered a lot of material in the last section. Now, it's time to use it to build a complete wireless application—a prototype of MobileHelper. I'll first show you the use cases that detail what parts of MobileHelper I should prototype, and then actually build the prototype using the WML you've learned in this chapter.

Establishing the Use Cases

Use cases are important even when you're developing a prototype. Although the prototype demonstrates only a small subset of your entire application, defining the use cases before the prototype helps you describe what you're going to do. Equally important, looking at the use cases for your application helps you decide which use cases deserve the attention and effort of a prototype.

Of course, when you're developing a prototype you need to decide *which* use cases you want to implement. Often, it's not necessary to implement all of your use cases, or even implement all of the steps in a particular use case. Moreover, you may find it easier to create several prototypes, each implementing a handful of use cases.

Figure 2-17 shows the Volunteer actor's use cases in MobileHelper. These use cases are at the heart of MobileHelper. Without the Auth use case, for example, you can't log in; without the View Your Tasks use case, you can't see what tasks you need to complete.

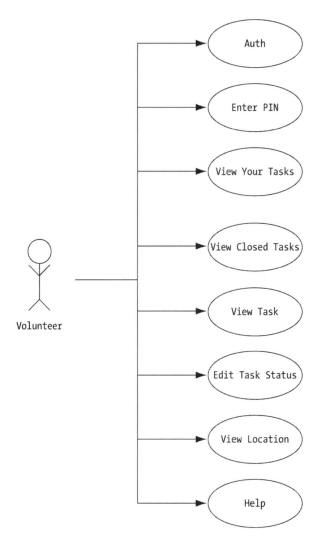

Figure 2-17. Key use cases within MobileHelper

The prototype described in the remainder of this chapter implements elements of the following use cases:

Auth. The Auth use case accepts the user's MIN and PIN and determines whether or not the user can access MobileHelper. Within the prototype, the Auth use case always succeeds, logging in the fictional user "Sandy A."

Enter PIN. Used by the Auth use case, this use case prompts the user for his or her MIN and PIN. This is separate from the Auth use case because it may conceivably be used elsewhere to support a "change user" feature later in development.

View Your Tasks. This use case shows tasks belonging to Sandy A.

View Open Tasks. This use case shows unassigned tasks that may be claimed by any volunteer.

View Closed Tasks. This use case shows tasks closed by Sandy A.

View Task. This use case shows a specific task.

Edit Task Status. This use case enables you to change the current task's status. As you'll see, the prototype enables you to select a new task status, but because the prototype is written using only WML, it will not actually remember the new status.

View Location. This use case shows the details about the location for the current task, including the location's address and phone number.

Help. Each deck implementing a use case includes a help card with rudimentary help information.

Prototyping these use cases helps you refine your application's user interface. As I flesh out each use case for MobileHelper, different pieces of the interface become apparent for the first time. For example, my earliest plans for MobileHelper's login screen didn't include a field for the MIN because, in most cases, the server is able to obtain the client's MIN from the HTTP headers. It wasn't until I identified the Auth use case and recognized that if I were using someone else's device I'd want to be able to enter the MIN. Consequently, the Auth use case now prompts for both the MIN and PIN, but the MIN defaults to the client device's MIN.

The process of prototyping helps determine which use cases are essential features, such as the View Open Tasks use case, and less important features, such as View Closed Tasks or View Location Details. Although all of those use cases are represented in the prototype, they may not be available during the first few iterations of application development. When in doubt, showing the prototype and use cases to prospective users quickly clears up any doubts.

When working from use cases to build a prototype, you need to define a sequence that describes the flow of events through the prototype. Because the prototype—especially a no-script prototype like this one—should have as little logic as is feasible for the purpose of testing the interface and basic concepts, it obviously can't have all the features of the final application. For instance, consider the Auth use case again. The prototype doesn't have any notion of MIN or PIN information besides the format hints in the WML so there's no way the prototype can correctly decide whether or not a given MIN/PIN pair authenticates a client. Defining a sequence to follow when using the prototype (in this case, the script tells us that logging in is always successful) helps us establish our expectations of the prototype. Figure 2-18 shows a sequence diagram for the MobileHelper prototype. As the diagram shows, after following the Auth and View Your Task list, you can follow the use cases in almost any order, unless you log out and return to the Auth use case.

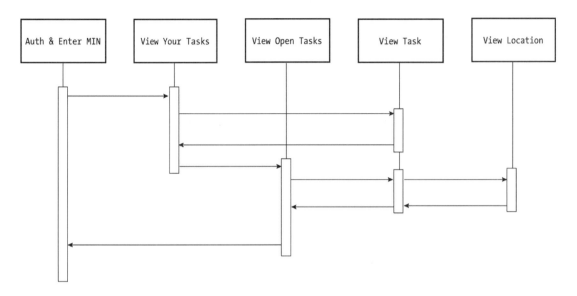

Figure 2-18. MobileHelper prototype use case sequence

Of course, with additional effort, you can extend the script's sequence and the WML to further simulate application logic. By defining additional decks (perhaps using links or soft keys to let me simulate application logic through following additional links), you can create an arbitrarily complex prototype that mimics the behavior of the real application. When you build a prototype with this level of detail, it's called a *smoke-and-mirrors* prototype because it appears to work with magic, rather than bona fide software. With a smoke-and-mirrors prototype, if you follow the sequence carefully, you may be able to convince others that there's actually application logic in place, even when there isn't. Prototyping in this level of detail can be a very powerful tool in getting buy-in from management or customers because it demonstrates that you have a good understanding of their wants and needs. Of course, there's an ethical issue, as well. It's not appropriate to pass off a smoke-and-mirrors prototype as the real thing, although it's been known to happen.

You might think it's odd to build a prototype with no server-side functionality. In fact, prototyping at this level is a great way to start. By building a prototype entirely in WML, you can quickly determine the appropriate look and feel for your wireless application without having to maintain server-side scripting code. More-over, once you finish the prototype and begin working on the server-side scripts, you'll be able to use much of your prototype content as building blocks for the content served by your server-side scripts.

Let's take a detailed look at the WML behind the prototype. I divide the discussion into three segments. In "Authenticating the User," I show you how I prototype the Auth use case. In the following material, "Viewing Task Lists," you see how to simulate the various task view use cases, including View Open Tasks and View Closed Tasks. Finally, in "Viewing Tasks" I tell you about how you can simulate viewing and editing a single task.

Authenticating the User

User authentication is the purview of the Auth use case. The prototype's logic behind the Auth use case is very simple: display a welcome deck, and when you choose the **Login** link, go to a deck with a login form. Once you enter a MIN and PIN, the client loads a deck with a task list.

Like any other Web site, MobileHelper needs a home page. My home page, shown in Listing 2-19, gives a bit of information about MobileHelper, including an About box and the site's current version number.

```
01: <?xml version="1.0"?>
02: <!DOCTYPE wml PUBLIC "-//WAPFORUM//DTD WML 1.1//EN"
03:    "http://www.wapforum.org/DTD/wml_1.1.xml">
04: <wml>
05:    <template>
06:      <do type="help"
07:        label="Help"
08:        name="help">
09:        <go href="#help"/>
10:      </do>
11:      <do type="prev"
12:        label="Back">
13:        <prev/>
14:      </do>
15:    </template>
16:    <card id="MobileHelperHome"
17:      title="MobileHelper"
18:      newcontext="true">
19:      <p align="center">
20:        MobileHelper
21:      </p>
```

```
22:     <p>
23:       Welcome to MobileHelper!
24:       <anchor title="Login">
25:         Login
26:         <go href="login.wml"/>
27:       </anchor><br/>
28:       <anchor title="About">
29:         About
30:         <go href="#MobileHelperAbout"/>
31:       </anchor>
32:     </p>
33:   </card>
34:   <card id="MobileHelperAbout"
35:     title="About MobileHelper">
36:     <p align="center">
37:       <big>MobileHelper</big><br/>
38:       Public Service Deployment Wireless Application<br/>
39:       &#x00A9; 2000-2001 Ray Rischpater<br/>
40:       (Prototype)<br/>
41:       Version 0.0<br/>
42:       (Chapter 2)<br/>
43:     </p>
44:     <p>
45:       This Public Service Deployment Wireless Application
46:       is part of the book
47:       <u>Wireless Applications with PHP</u>
48:       by Ray Rischpater from Apress, LP.
49:     </p>
50:   </card>
51:   <card id="help"
52:     title="MobileHelper Help">
53:     <p>
54:       To use MobileHelper, you must first have a valid
55:       account assigned by your Coordinator and log in
56:       using the Login link.
57:     </p>
58:   </card>
59: </wml>
```

Listing 2-19. MobileHelper's home Page, index.wml

There's little in this Listing that will surprise you. After the obligatory XML and WML header stuff on lines 1–4, the deck begins with a `<template>` tag that links actions to the **Help** and **Prev** soft keys. As you would expect, these take you to a card containing help, or back to the previous card, respectively. Every deck in the prototype contains a `<template>` tag like this.

The first card of this deck (lines16–33) is MobileHelper's home page. This card is simple, containing just a welcome message and links to the deck that lets you log in, and the card describing MobileHelper. This card clears all WML variables using the `<card>` tag's `newcontext` attribute. While I don't need to do this for the prototype, because the prototype doesn't use any variables, it's worth putting it in now so I don't forget it later—forgetting `newcontext` is an easy mistake to make that's hard to track down.

I used the `<anchor>` tag in this first card to make links (lines 24–31), rather than creating an option list with two options containing `onpick` attributes. This decision was largely aesthetic because although the `<select>` tag implies data input, many sites use it for single-choice navigation as well.

The about card (lines 34–50) gives the site's copyright and version information. The WML is straightforward, but the motivation behind this card may not be. Most Web pages place copyright information on every page, with links to a larger disclaimer/acceptable use policy. Rather than burdening every card in each deck with this information, it's easier for both viewers and developers to put that information in a single card. In addition, this card contains a version number. Many sites won't have a version number, but MobileHelper, like other sites providing application services such as messaging, scheduling, and other specific-purpose tasks, will include one. It's especially helpful to include a version number when potential viewers will see different versions, during testing, for example.

The help card (lines 51–58) is straightforward, too, so I won't say anything about it here other than the obvious. It's always best to show your application to both experienced and new users, and watch how they use the application.

You've already seen the authentication deck for MobileHelper in Listing 2-18. It so happens that this Listing isn't adequate for the prototype because it uses the HTTP POST method. Including `<postfield>` tags and the `<go>` tag's `method` attribute will only work if you have a back-end script to accept user input. Because I don't, I need to remove these tags and replace them with a simple `<go/>` task, as shown in Listing 2-20.

```
01: <?xml version="1.0"?>
02: <!DOCTYPE wml PUBLIC "-//WAPFORUM//DTD WML 1.1//EN"
03:  "http://www.wapforum.org/DTD/wml_1.1.xml">
04: <wml>
```

```
05:    <template>
06:      <do type="help"
07:        label="Help"
08:        name="help">
09:        <go href="#help"/>
10:      </do>
11:      <do type="prev"
12:          label="Back">
13:        <prev/>
14:      </do>
15:    </template>
16:    <card title="MobileHelper Login">
17:      <p>
18:        <fieldset title="MIN &amp; PIN">
19:          MIN:
20:          <input name="min"
21:            type="text"
22:            format="NNNNNNNNNN"
23:            value="8885551212"
24:            emptyok="false"
25:            maxlength="10"
26:            size="10"/>
27:          PIN:
28:          <input name="pin"
29:            type="password"
30:            format="6N"
31:            emptyok="false"
32:            maxlength="6"
33:            size="6"/>
34:        </fieldset>
35:        <anchor>
36:          Login
37:          <go href="task.wml"/>
38:        </anchor>
39:      </p>
40:    </card>
41:    <card id="help"
42:      title="Login Help">
43:      <p>
44:        To use MobileHelper, you must first have a valid
45:        account assigned by your Coordinator. Your
46:        Coordinator will give you a four to six digit
47:        Personal Identification Number (PIN).
48:      </p>
```

```
49:     <p>
50:        To log in, please enter your Mobile Identification
51:        Number (MIN) and PIN where requested.
52:     </p>
53:   </card>
54: </wml>
```

Listing 2-20. MobileHelper's login page, login.wml

As in Listing 2-19, the deck begins with a `<template>` tag that links the **Help** and **Prev** soft keys to default actions (the help card and the `<prev/>` task) for the deck. The remainder of the deck is quite similar to Listing 2-18, so I won't discuss it in detail, except to point out the differences.

Line 23 uses the `<input>` tag's value attribute to supply a default MIN. This default tag simulates how MobileHelper will extract the MIN from the client's HTTP headers. Because you can't do this without back-end scripts, however, I just stuff an arbitrary number in the input field for now.

On line 37, you see where I replaced the earlier `<go>` tag with its `<postfield>` contents with the simpler `<go/>` tag for the purpose of the prototype. This line will always load the next page of the prototype, task.wml, simulating a successful user login.

Viewing Task Lists

When you view a list of tasks, you're invoking one of three use cases: View Your Tasks, View Open Tasks, or View Closed Tasks. In addition, you might even exercise the Help use case, if you choose Help from one of these use cases. The prototype uses one deck with three cards to implement these use cases. Listing 2-21 shows this deck.

```
01: <?xml version="1.0"?>
02: <!DOCTYPE wml PUBLIC "-//WAPFORUM//DTD WML 1.1//EN"
03:   "http://www.wapforum.org/DTD/wml_1.1.xml">
04: <wml>
05:   <template>
06:     <do type="help"
07:       label="Help"
08:       name="help">
09:       <go href="#help"/>
10:     </do>
```

```
11:    <do type="prev"
12:        label="Logout"
13:        name="prev">
14:      <go href="index.wml"/>
15:    </do>
16:  </template>
17:  <card id="your"
18:    title="Your Assignments">
19:    <p>
20:    <table title="Your Assignments" columns="2">
21:      <tr>
22:        <td><anchor>11-27-00 1200<go href="20001127.wml"/>
23:        </anchor></td>
24:        <td>
25:          Mountain Fire Dept
26:        </td>
27:      </tr>
28:    </table>
29:    </p>
30:    <p>
31:      <anchor title="Open">
32:        Open assignments.
33:        <go href="#open"/>
34:      </anchor>
35:      <anchor title="Closed">
36:        Closed assignments.
37:        <go href="#closed"/>
38:      </anchor>
39:    </p>
40:  </card>
41:  <card id="open"
42:    title="Open Assignments">
43:    <p>
44:    <table title="Open Assignments" columns="2">
45:      <tr>
46:        <td><anchor>11-28-00 20000<go href="20001128.wml"/>
47:        </anchor></td>
48:        <td>
49:          Valley Church
50:        </td>
51:      </tr>
52:    </table>
53:    </p>
```

```
54:    <do type="prev"
55:       label="Back"
56:       name="prev">
57:       <prev/>
58:    </do>
59: </card>
60: <card id="closed"
61:    title="Closed Assignments">
62:    <p>
63:    <table title="Closed Assignments" columns="2">
64:       <tr>
65:       <td><anchor>11-23-00 0900<go href="20001123.wml"/>
66:       </anchor></td>
67:       <td>
68:          St. Michaels Church
69:       </td>
70:       </tr>
71:    </table>
72:    </p>
73:    <do type="prev"
74:       label="Back"
75:       name="prev">
76:       <prev/>
77:    </do>
78: </card>
79: <card id="help"
80:    title="Assignment Help">
81:    <p>
82:      Select the assignment to view by scrolling to
83:      the assignment and pressing Accept.
84:    </p>
85:    <do type="prev"
86:       label="Back"
87:       name="prev">
88:       <prev/>
89:    </do>
90: </card>
91: </wml>
```

Listing 2-21. MobileHelper task lists, task.wml

Using one deck for all three of these use cases is practical in the prototype, but probably not for the actual application. This is one of the largest decks I've written, and might not even load on some early clients.

The `<template>` in this deck (lines 5–16) is slightly different than in other decks. From this deck, I wanted to give the user a way to log out of the MobileHelper, so two people can use one device, for example. Consequently, the **Prev** soft key default action is a `<go/>` task bringing the user back to the main page for the application so another user can log in.

This deck has one card for each of the three task lists, and a help card. The first card, showing assigned tasks, contains `<anchor>` tags to link the first card to each of the other two cards. These, in turn, use the **Prev** soft key and the `<prev/>` task to return to the assigned task card, overriding the `<template>` tag.

Each of these cards puts tasks in a two-column table, with one table row per task. The first column links to the task's view (see the next section), showing the task date and time, while the second task has the task's location. Getting the format of this table to look right on a wide number of clients was a tremendous challenge because different devices use different strategies for displaying the table. In the end, this layout—two columns, the first holding the short form of the date and time—looked good on a variety of devices, including those that simply draw each cell of a table on its own line. Lines 20–28 show a representative table. Unfortunately, trial and error is the only way to find out what looks good. Figure 2-19 shows this table.

Figure 2-19. Sample MobileHelper task list

This part of the prototype suggested an implementation, which I'll cover in detail in the next chapter. However, it's worth calling out the high points now. The three lists share the same organization: a table of dates and locations. One list, the list of open tasks, has links to the other two tasks, while the other two tasks need only return to the list of open tasks. This implies a generalization: using the same code and interface to create each task list, but using different bits of code to fill out each kind of task list. Each of the three task list use cases use a common use case, List Tasks, which lists a particular task. Figure 2-20 shows this use case diagram.

Reorganizing the task list use cases like this buys us economy of scale: if I were listing every step taken in every use case, I'd only need to list the steps in the List Tasks use case, and then just describe the differences in each of the other use cases.

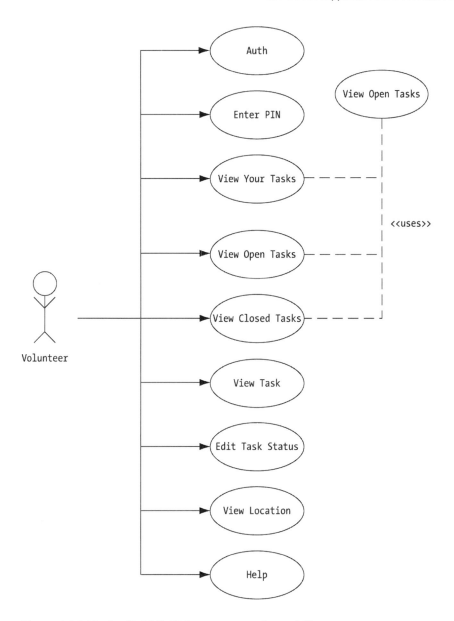

Figure 2-20. Revised MobileHelper use cases for task lists

It also suggests how the underlying program will work—but it doesn't specifically *require* that the program work that way. It's possible (but unlikely in this case) that you might want to implement each use case using a separate module of code, perhaps if the different kinds of tasks were stored in wholly different ways. In practice, however, identifying generalizations in use cases often points to generalizations in the application's implementation.

Viewing Tasks

The last use cases the prototype demonstrates—View Task, Edit Task Status, and View Location—are simulated by a bunch of individual decks.

Each of the tasks you can view from the task lists is in a single deck, named after the date on which the task will occur. For example, the task assigned to Sandy A., our imaginary user, is shown in Listing 2-22 and Figure 2-21.

Figure 2-21. MobileHelper task view deck

```
01: <?xml version="1.0"?>
02: <!DOCTYPE wml PUBLIC "-//WAPFORUM//DTD WML 1.1//EN"
03:   "http://www.wapforum.org/DTD/wml_1.1.xml">
04: <wml>
05:   <template>
06:     <do type="help"
07:       label="Help"
08:       name="help">
09:       <go href="#help"/>
10:     </do>
11:     <do type="prev"
12:         label="Back"
13:         name="prev">
14:       <prev/>
15:     </do>
16:   </template>
17:   <card id="a220001127"
18:     title="11-27-2000 1200">
19:     <p>
20:       11-27-00 1200-1800<br/>
21:       <anchor title="Where">Mountain Fire Dept
22:       <go href="where-mfd.wml"/></anchor>
23:       Assigned to Sandy A.<br/>
24:     </p>
```

```
25:      <p>
26:        Staff communications equipment. Use existing
27:        radio and antenna.
28:      </p>
29:      <p>
30:        <anchor title="Update">Update
31:          <go href="update.wml"/>
32:        </anchor>
33:      </p>
34:    </card>
35:    <card id="help"
36:      title="Assignment Help">
37:      <p>
38:        You may get more information about the
39:        assignment site by selecting it, or update
40:        the status of the assignment by pressing Update.
41:      </p>
42:    </card>
43: </wml>
```

Listing 2-22. MobileHelper task view deck, 20001127.wml

This deck has two cards: the obligatory help card, and the card showing a task. I haven't explicitly defined a structure for task records yet (you'll see that in Chapter 3); in fact, when I first did the prototype, I used the prototype to determine what kinds of information a task contained. After a bit of trial and error, I decided that (in the prototype, anyway), a task would contain the following information:

- The date and time the task starts

- The date and time the task will be completed

- The date and time the task was actually completed

- Where the task occurs

- Who owns the task

- A short description of the task

Listing 2-22 (shown in Figure 2-21) shows all of these items except when the task was actually completed. I chose to use a free-form paragraph (lines 19–28) with strategically placed line breaks rather than a table to hold this information.

My decision to use a paragraph for this information was half laziness and half vision. After spending so much time trying to find a table presentation for the task lists that looked good on more than one device, I wasn't about to do it all over again (probably with less success) for the task view as well. I also recognize that a paragraph with line breaks and the occasional text style (like the anchor linking the task's location to a location description deck) provides an easy framework for extension as new items are added to each task record.

Each task has one required and one optional link to another deck (in addition to the default help card, available from the browser's **Help** soft key). Each task should link to the task's location so you can easily find out where you need to go to fulfill a task. Open tasks and tasks you own should also have a link to the deck that implements the Edit Task Status use case.

The task location detail deck is the simplest deck in the prototype. Listing 2-23 shows the task location deck for Mountain Fire Department, shown in Figure 2-22. One card with one paragraph shows all the information you need. Like tasks, I didn't formally describe the organization of a location record when I built the prototype. In the next chapter, you can see the information a location record stores; for now, you can just think of it as an address.

```
01: <?xml version="1.0"?>
02: <!DOCTYPE wml PUBLIC "-//WAPFORUM//DTD WML 1.1//EN"
03:   "http://www.wapforum.org/DTD/wml_1.1.xml">
04: <wml>
05:   <template>
06:     <do type="prev"
07:         label="Back"
08:         name="prev">
09:       <prev/>
10:     </do>
11:   </template>
12:   <card
13:     title="Mountain Fire Dept">
14:     <p>
15:       Mountain Fire Dept<br/>
16:       7700 East Road<br/>
17:       Hillsdale<br/>
18:       888-555-1212<br/>
19:     </p>
20:   </card>
21: </wml>
```

Listing 2-23. MobileHelper location view, where-mfd.wml

Figure 2-22. MobileHelper location view

The deck shown in Listing 2-24 implements the Edit Task Status use case.
I originally chose to put the Edit Task Status use case in its own deck because I
thought it should show more than it eventually needed to. With the exception of
its help card, there's no reason it can't be in the task view deck.

```
01: <?xml version="1.0"?>
02: <!DOCTYPE wml PUBLIC "-//WAPFORUM//DTD WML 1.1//EN"
03:   "http://www.wapforum.org/DTD/wml_1.1.xml">
04: <wml>
05:   <template>
06:     <do type="help"
07:       label="Help"
08:       name="help">
09:       <go href="#help"/>
10:     </do>
11:     <do type="prev"
12:         label="Back"
13:         name="prev">
14:       <prev/>
15:     </do>
16:   </template>
17:   <card
18:     title="Update">
19:     <onevent type="onpick">
20:       <prev/>
21:     </onevent>
```

```
22:     <p>
23:       <select title="Update Status" multiple="false"
24:         name="status">
25:         <option title="Open"
26:           value="open">Open</option>
27:         <option title="Assigned"
28:           value="assigned">Assigned</option>
29:         <option title="Complete"
30:           value="Complete">Completed</option>
31:       </select>
32:     </p>
33:   </card>
34:   <card id="help"
35:     title="Status Help">
36:     <p>
37:       An assignment can either be <b>open</b>,
38:       <b>assigned</b> or <b>completed</b>.
39:     </p>
40:     <p>
41:       An <b>open</b> assignment is one for which
42:       we're seeking volunteers. If you can accept
43:       this assignment, please mark it as <b>assigned</b>.
44:     </p>
45:     <p>
46:       An <b>assigned</b> assignment is one for
47:       which we have a volunteer. You can only change
48:       the status of a task with this status if the
49:       task has been assigned to you. You may either
50:       return its status to <b>open</b> to indicate that
51:       you can't perform the task, or set its status to
52:       <b>completed</b> when you've completed it.
53:     </p>
54:     <p>
55:       A <b>completed</b> task is one that you've
56:       successfully finished.
57:     </p>
58:   </card>
59: </wml>
```

Listing 2-24. MobileHelper Edit Task Status use case, update.wml

Most of this deck is its help card, which contains a definition for each of a task's possible status values. You can use the deck to pretend to set a task's status using the option list on lines 23–31.

From this organization, it wasn't clear to me yet whether a task's location and the update functionality should be in decks separate from a task, or within the deck of a task. Of course, they can be in either place—the back-end scripts in the application can build decks with any kind of content you want.[6] When I showed the prototype to prospective users, most pointed out that it was annoying to have to wait to load separate decks for both the update and location decks for a particular task. Based on these comments, the Edit Task Status use case will be built into each task's deck, although there is a distinct advantage to leaving the View Location use case content in its own deck.

The advantage to keeping the View Location use case content in its own deck is simplicity. In early versions of the application, for example, location descriptions could be static decks stored in a section of the MobileHelper application server's Web site. The Coordinator can update these decks as needed, writing one deck for each agency volunteers serve. This is admittedly somewhat tedious for the Coordinators because they'll need to know some WML, but it trims a significant portion of the application development time because I can initially skip writing all the scripts that manage location records. In fact, that's exactly what I do—you won't see how I store locations until you start using databases in Chapter 5.

On the CD-ROM

As always, you can find all the listings from this chapter in the chapter directory—chap02—on the CD-ROM.

The applications I discuss—the Yospace SPEDE and the Apache Web server—are also on the CD-ROM. You can find the SPEDE installer, courtesy of Yospace, in the directory Yospace. A version (almost certainly not the current version) of the Apache Web server is in the directory Apache. If you're going to use the Apache server for any length of time, you should take a minute and go to www.apache.org and download the latest version; it's almost certainly newer than what you'll find on the CD-ROM.

---

6. Hey, that's why they call it software, right? Actually, you should remember that in the programs behind the WML, you'll want to carefully organize and separate your data. Those same programs, however, can slice and dice the data in whatever forms make the most sense for your users.

So you don't have to reconstruct the prototype I discuss from each listing, you can find the working prototype in the directory MobileHelper under this chapter's directory. To see the prototype, simply point your favorite WML client at the index.wml file in that directory. Alternately, you can move all the files from that directory up to your Web server, and view the prototype using any WAP-enabled smart phone.

Food for Thought

- Use a WML browser—preferably on a real smart phone, if you have one—to view five or ten WAP sites. A good place to start is with the Cool Wap Site of the Day, `www.coolwapsiteoftheday.com`, or one of the WAP portals. What is it about the decks that you've looked at that you like? What do you dislike?

- View the same sites you've viewed in the previous exercise using a different smart phone or smart phone emulator. How are they similar to what you saw before? How are they different? Can you explain the differences?

- Experiment with using `<select>` and `<anchor>` for navigation. Which do you like better? Which is easier to use on your smart phone?

- Before the Web, the UNIX operating system supported the notion of a user's "home page" via the UNIX command **finger**, which when invoked for a specific user on the system, showed that user's finger file. People often wrote elaborate finger files, providing their resume, research interests, hobbies, and so on. While Web sites are multidimensional, often branching out into photo albums, employer Web pages, favorite sites, and the like, finger files were more personal because the **finger** utility didn't let you link to other content. Home pages in WML are more like finger files than Web home pages because they need to be simpler than a Web home page. Make your own WML home page and post it on your Web site.

- Extend your home page in WML to include links to a few of your favorite WAP sites.

- Display your WML home page in at least three different browsers. What's the same? What's different? Why?

- Make a list of some of the use cases required by the Coordinator actor. Draw a use case diagram to show the relationship between these use cases.

- Prototype in WML some or all of the Coordinator actor's use cases. Be sure to test it using at least two different WML browsers.

- Extend Listing 2-24 to automatically return to the View Task use case deck that invoked the Edit Task Status use case.

#### CHAPTER 3

PHP: HyperText Processor

PERSONALIZATION IS THE FOUNDATION of the Wireless Web. Each user expects his information, on his device, in his preferred format. This requires that your site draw from an array of sources, assembling content for each user. You use active server technology such as PHP: Hypertext Processor (PHP) to automatically create decks containing custom contents from a myriad of sources.

In this chapter, I show you how to create custom content in WML with PHP. Although PHP was originally envisioned to provide a scripting service for HTML and other Web-based technologies, its architecture and implementation make it ideal for building decks for the Wireless Web as well. You'll learn how to organize your thoughts when designing an active Web site, how to set up PHP within your development environment, and how to write scripts using PHP. I close this chapter with an examination of the PHP functions MobileHelper uses to create decks.

Building an Active Web Site

Broadly speaking, any Web site that produces content dynamically in response to a client's request is called an *active* Web site. In contrast, Web servers offering static content are called simply Web servers, traditional Web servers, or flat file Web servers. Many active Web sites mix static and scripted content; in fact, as you'll see later, you can mix static and scripted content within a particular page.

An active server works similarly to a traditional Web server. A Web client requests a script by its URL, rather than a document. In turn, the Web server loads the script, executes it within an environment associated with the Web server, and returns the results to the client. The result can be anything, but is usually Web-formatted content, such as HTML, WML, PDF, or an image.

Active Web servers use *server-side scripting*—the scripts run on the Web server. This is in stark contrast to *client-side scripting* in which the client runs scripts provided by the server. Scripting languages such as JavaScript and WMLScript use client-side scripting, whereas active server technologies such as Microsoft Active Server Pages, Macromedia's Cold Fusion (formerly Allaire's Cold Fusion), and PHP are examples of active Web servers using server-side scripting.

Organizing Your Content

Designing an active Web site is similar to designing a traditional one. A key difference between traditional and active Web sites is the need to define the scripts themselves. Web scripting is an odd mix of software and content development. On the one hand, writing scripts is software development because you're programming the Web server to access and manage your content. On the other hand, many scripts need to manipulate and produce both content and formatting, meaning that you need to think about your content as well. It's unlike traditional software development because you can freely mix content and code; it's unlike Web content development for the same reason. The best strategy is to separate your code and content as much as possible.

To do this, you must define and organize your content carefully. Not only does this help you handle the cognitive dissonance of simultaneously working on scripts and content, but it helps you write better scripts as well. As you'll see in Chapter 5, many sites use a database to store their content. Most of the scripts these sites use are then responsible for searching the database in response to client requests.

From the beginning, you should divide your content into presentation and information. *Presentation* refers to the parts of your site that determine its appearance, such as the markup, corporate look –and feel, and so on. Your *information*, on the other hand, is your reason for being, the content of interest to your viewers. Ideally, your information will have no markup at all because how you mark up your content is driven by decisions about your presentation. On larger projects, it also helps you determine who does what because you don't need to staff your project with content experts that can code (or programmers with a deep knowledge of your content). Instead, you can have a team of content developers and a team of software developers working in tandem to build your site. In Chapter 9, you see one way you can use XML to help keep your presentation and information partitioned using XML.

> **TIP** *Keep your site's presentation and information separate. By doing so, you ensure you can segment your work so that multiple people can contribute.*

For example, MobileHelper's presentation is the WML tags that mark up each of its decks. Broadly, there's presentation information for the lists of tasks (open, pending, and closed), along with MobileHelper's actual presentation of each task. In contrast, MobileHelper's information is the tasks themselves, along with the associated information, such as who is responsible for each task and where each task takes place.

How clearly you separate presentation and information is a matter of degree. For small sites with only a few users and simple content, you may not separate them at all. For medium sites serving many kinds of users or a variety of different kinds of content, you should start to take the division seriously, and ensure that your scripts draw information from one repository and merge it with presentation information in another. The largest—and most expandable sites—have the most well-defined divisions between presentation and information, often using databases to store both information and presentation information, merging them on-the-fly with their server-side scripts.

You need to pay particular attention to the kinds of information your site offers. This is especially true on the Wireless Web, where viewers want small, manageable chunks of information. Because your scripts need to operate on bits and pieces of your information, you need to carefully describe just what those bits and pieces are.

For example, consider again MobileHelper's notion of a task. In the prototype you saw in the last chapter, there's no description of what constitutes a task. For a prototype that's fine, but once you start thinking about how a task is stored, or how a script will format a task, it becomes important to define exactly what goes into a task. MobileHelper's tasks consist of:

- A unique integer, giving a shorthand method to refer to a specific task

- A start time and date

- A stop time and date

- The unique integer—actually the owner's Mobile Information Number (MIN)—associated with an owner, indicating who is responsible for the task

- The unique integer associated with a location, indicating where the task occurs

- A title for the task

- A short description of the task

Similarly, a location consists of:

- A title

- A street address

- A city

- A state

- A postal code

- A phone number

- A short description of the location

Owner records are the shortest records of all, consisting of a user's name, MIN, and PIN. By assigning each task, user, and location a unique integer (often simply called an *identifier* or *ID, or unique identifier, or UID*), records can point to each other without including the entire contents of a record. Moreover, if something about a record changes, only one record needs to be changed because every piece of information is stored in only one place. For example, if a location's phone number changes, MobileHelper need only change one location record, and the tasks depending on the location remain untouched because that location's ID never changes. This is an example of *indirection*—two kinds of data are related indirectly, through an intermediary (the ID, in this case). As you'll see in Chapter 5, MobileHelper stores each of the task, location, and user records in a database.

By breaking up a MobileHelper task into these discrete components, I can write scripts that work with individual pieces. For example, if I want to create a deck that lists the title of all closed tasks with links to each task, I can craft a script that asks the database for all tasks with a stop time and date, and then get the title of each task. Using other scripts responsible for formatting, I can then build a list of those tasks, with each element of the list containing the description of one task and a link to another script that will present the task in its own deck.

Organizing Your Scripts

Of course, you need to organize your scripts, just as you need to organize your content. Like content, some obvious strategies apply to all sites, and others are largely driven by the site itself.

Just as you can divide your content into presentation and information, you can divide your scripts into those responsible for information and those responsible for presentation. In fact, if you're building a small site, this may be all the separation between presentation and information you need. In that case, changing the presentation may be a matter of changing the scripts themselves.

Of course, changing scripts just to change the name or copyright information for your site can get old quickly. Items such as credits, dates, headers, and trailers are best placed in variables, separate files, or a database so they can be changed quickly. At best, placing these kinds of items in their own functions, such as

`OutputFairUseDeck` to output a site's copyright and fair use deck, makes it easy to find and change material later.

There's the larger problem of how you organize the scripts for your site. Conceivably, it's possible for one big script to do everything for your site, drawing on different functions to accept logins, present personalized information, search databases, and so on. If you take this path, your active Web site may operate correctly, but it's a safe bet that it'll be hard to change when you want to add new features or make changes.

You can often find good clues as to how your scripts should be organized by looking at your prototype. Individual files in your prototype often suggest a logical grouping for related functions into a single script that serves related content. For example, the login.wml deck in the MobileHelper prototype from the last chapter suggests that the login and authentication functionality (the Auth use case) should all be contained in a single file.

But what about the scripts to access and verify users? Some of the same information—looking up a user's name from his MIN, for example—is needed elsewhere, such as when a Coordinator updates a Volunteer's information. Many scripts rely on items that belong in separate files. If you're taking an object-oriented approach, the definitions of your classes (the things that each group of objects belongs to) will be in these files; if you're taking a functional approach, you'll have a slew of basic functions that will go in one or more files. For example, MobileHelper has a set of files that perform basic functions, such as accessing the database to manage user, task, and location records, and another file to build WML decks from basic content. You'll see this last file in detail at the end of this chapter.

> **TIP** *Duplication hints at decomposition. If you find yourself putting the same code in multiple places, you probably have an opportunity to replace that with a single instance of the code in a separate file and access it using functions.*

Looking outside the realm of individual scripts and files for a moment, you need to determine how to organize your servers themselves. Low-use sites can often do quite well with a single, fast computer handling Web requests, executing the site's scripts, and storing any databases the site requires. Larger sites need to break the Web server and database apart, keeping each on their own machines. Of course, high-end commercial services need to use multiple databases that are kept synchronized, and multiple Web servers with a mirror image of the service's content to support the thousands of users that simultaneously access the service. In most cases, you're best off sharing your market projections with a professional Web hosting firm, which can provide a good estimate as to the tradeoffs you can make between your site's performance, latency, down time, and hosting costs.

First Steps with PHP

If you've written computer programs using Java, C, or Perl before, you'll find PHP a snap. If you've used other active server technologies, it will be equally simple. Fortunately, even for the complete newcomer, PHP is easy to master.

PHP is a powerful server-side scripting language with extensive support for different content types and integration to databases including MySQL, mSQL, ODBC-compliant databases, PostgreSQL, Sybase, Oracle, and Informix. It has dozens of other interfaces to support network protocols, including the Internet Mail Access Protocol (IMAP), Simple Mail Transfer Protocol (SMTP), Post Office Protocol, version 3 (POP3), Hypertext Transfer Protocol (HTTP) and the Simple Network Management Protocol (SNMP). In addition, there's a bevy of functions that give you access to services including your local file system, sockets, and other services. It's available for UNIX-like operating systems including Linux, BSD, and most other popular dialects of UNIX, as well as Microsoft Windows. The UNIX flavors of PHP are rugged, industrial-quality releases that support millions of sites around the world. There's also a port to Microsoft Windows that you can use when testing and developing your site, or even to build and deploy small sites for a limited number of users.

Rasmus Lerdorf is commonly known as the father of PHP, although since its creation, a number of talented and hard-working individuals have made major contributions. Originally a pool of tools Lerdorf used to monitor his online resume, the first public version of PHP was released in early 1995. Over the last six years, there were four major revisions to the core implementation, along with many follow-on releases. By 1999, PHP was shipping with several industry-strength Web servers such as C2's StrongHold Web server. Today, it's fast becoming one of the most popular of all active server tools.

Setting Up PHP

One of PHP's strengths is that it's free software. You can download it, install it on your servers, get the source code and make changes, and then give it to friends. PHP is protected by the GNU license agreement, which ensures broad freedoms for the users of the software protected by the license agreement.

Before you begin, you need to have a Web server running on your development system. PHP works well with Apache, but can work with other Web servers including Omni HTTPd, Microsoft's Personal Web server, and Microsoft Internet Information Server. You can even configure it as a Common Gateway Interface (CGI) program so, in theory, it's possible to use PHP with any Web server that supports CGI. Thus, before you try to get PHP running on your system, you should have a Web server running on your system. (Chapter 2 reviews some of the important points you need to know about setting up your Web server.)

You can run PHP with your Web server on a server separate from your development machine, and not use a Web server with PHP on your development machine, but I don't recommend it. Developing PHP scripts—especially in the beginning when you're first learning PHP—is an iterative process, and even the small step of connecting to a remote machine to edit or upload your scripts can quickly become tedious. It's far easier to bite the bullet, talk to your system administrator, and install a Web server and PHP on your development system.

> **CAUTION** *I pointed this out in Chapter 2, but it's worth repeating. If you plan on running a Web server on your computer in a corporate setting, talk to your system administrator. Many companies have security policies that may restrict your ability to serve files from your desktop computer. At best, you may run into problems accessing scripts and files from your development workstation; at worst, you might violate corporate policy and lose your job. Seek professional help; this is one of those rare cases in which asking for permission is easier than asking for forgiveness.*

After you install and test your Web server, you install PHP. While the process varies from system to system, the general decisions you make will be the same. If you're using UNIX, first you decide what features of PHP you want to use. Then, you get the source code for PHP from the Internet at `http://www.php.net`.[1] With the source code in hand, you unpack the distribution—generally a compressed tar file—and follow the build instructions, telling the build system what features of PHP you plan to use. If you're going to use PHP on a Windows system, the process is similar, except that you can use the precompiled binary provided by the PHP development team, which includes most of the common PHP features and sets up your Web server for you.

You may encounter two problems when building PHP. First, because PHP has a dizzying array of features, you may not know what you need to select when building PHP. Second, as you build PHP, you may find you're missing other libraries you need, such as a graphics toolkit library for PHP's image creation package.

You can make life easier for yourself by first reviewing what parts of PHP you're likely to need. This is a two-step process: first, list the likely features you know about, such as what databases you may want your scripts to use. Then, review PHP's installation instructions, and decide which of the other features

---

1. For your convenience, a copy of PHP is on the CD-ROM. Given the PHP development team's pace, however, it's almost certain that you'll want to go to the PHP Web site to download the latest and greatest before you begin.

you're likely to want. Out of the box, PHP is configured to include a number of logical defaults, and will generally suffice when you just start out. (In fact, many users begin with the default configuration, and go back and rebuild PHP only when they want to add additional functionality.)

Tackling the second problem is similar, but more annoying. Some features, such as PHP's interface to image functions, require additional libraries. Unfortunately, there's no definitive list of what features rely on external libraries, so you should check PHP's installation instructions and other documentation for additional information. Of course, you'll find out rather quickly when you're missing something because either you won't be able to build PHP, or you won't be able to call the functions you need. Either way, you need to go back, check the PHP manual for the module you're using, and get what's missing.

Once PHP is built and installed, you want to make sure its initialization file, php.ini, is configured correctly for your environment. This file is a set of name-value pairs, separated by an equal sign (=). The default configuration file has met my needs in almost every instance, but you should know that you can change PHP's behavior in several ways, using the following key words in the file:

- The variable `error_reporting` tells PHP how noisy to be about errors in your scripts. This variable contains a set of flags that signals the kinds of errors you want reported.

- The variable `SMTP` should contain either the IP address or host name of your SMTP server when using SMTP with PHP under Windows.

- The variables `debugger.host` and `debugger.port` indicate the IP address (or host name) and port number to which debug messages from PHP's experimental debugger should be sent. The variable `debugger.enabled`, if set to `true`, instructs PHP to actually output debug messages to the desired host's port.

> **NOTE** *As of this writing, the debugger was in an experimental state in PHP3, and not available in PHP4. I hope that by the time you read this, things will have improved somewhat!*

There's a number of other options in the php.ini file, most of which control specific modules, including the interface to a particular database interface such as OBDC. As you start using PHP, it doesn't hurt to skim your configuration file, and make a note of the items that are likely to pertain to your installation.

Once you configure PHP, you need to tell your Web server that it's installed, and what kinds of files contain PHP scripts. While you can configure your Web server to run every file through the PHP parser, it's more efficient to choose files ending in a particular suffix, such as .php. The configuration directives for the Apache Web server are shown in Listing 3-1.

```
01: # Apache PHP configuration
02: AddType application/x-httpd-php .php
03: AddType application/x-httpd-php .phtml
04:
05: # Under Unix, be sure to uncomment the following line and
06: # set the directory to point to where your libphp is.
07: # LoadModule php4_module         /usr/local/php/lib/libphp4.so
08:
09: # Under Windows, be sure to uncomment the following two
10: # lines and set the ScriptAlias to point to your PHP directory
11: # ScriptAlias /php/ "c:/path-to-php-dir/"
12: # Action application/x-httpd-php "/php/php.exe"
```

Listing 3-1. Apache Web server configuration for PHP

Typically, you include the lines shown in Listing 3-1 in your Web server's httpd.conf file. Lines 2 and 3 specify the MIME type and trailing suffix for PHP script files, while Lines 7 and 12 tell the Apache server how to invoke PHP once it has found a PHP script. Line 11, used by Apache running on Windows, links the directory /php/ within the Web server's directory space to the directory on your local disk where you installed the PHP package. Once you've added these lines, you need to stop and restart your Web server, to ensure that it re-reads its configuration correctly.

> **CAUTION** *Warning: In this book, all of the PHP examples assume that PHP ignores the characters* `<? ?>`, *using the long form of PHP's tags* `<?php ?>` *to surround your PHP scripts because WML uses* `<?` *and* `?>` *to contain the initial XML version declaration. If you have problems, be sure to check that the* `short_open_tag` *variable in your php.ini file is equal to* "off".

Installing PHP with the Apache Web Server

Under both LINUX and Windows, installing PHP with the Apache Web server is as easy as the documentation implies. On my LinuxPPC system, I use PHP as a dynamic library within Apache by building it and installing it with the following sequence of commands:

```
$ gunzip -c php-4.0.x.tar.gz | tar xf -
$ cd php-4.0.x
$ ./configure –with-mysql –with-apxs
lots of stuff appears here as PHP configures itself with the default configuration.
$ make
lots more stuff appears here as PHP builds
% su root
Password: <your root password>
# make install
# vi /etc/httpd/httpd.conf
add AddType application/x-httpd-php .php to the httpd.conf file.
# apachectl restart
```

Under Windows if you're using Apache, the process is similar, but slightly more convoluted:

1. Unpack the PHP distribution to an empty directory, such as c:\PHP\.

2. Copy the file php.ini to your %WINDOWS% directory.

3. 3Edit the php.ini file, changing the extension-dir directory to point to the directory where you unpacked PHP.

4. Edit Apache's srm.conf file, adding the following lines:

```
ScriptAlias /php/ "c:/path-to-php-dir/"
AddType application/x-httpd-php .php
AddType application/x-httpd-php .phtml
Action application/x-httpd-php "/php/php.exe"
```

5. Manually stop and restart the Apache Web server.

If you're using a different Web server running on Microsoft Windows, the PHP installer should configure your Web server for you. If it doesn't, you should consult the installation instructions that accompany the installer.

On UNIX systems other than Linux, things can get a little trickier. For example, under Mac OS X, a BSD-based operating system, I could only get PHP and Apache working together by statically linking PHP into Apache. This required that I rebuild both PHP and Apache for Mac OS X.

When in doubt, look at the PHP Web site or drop a note to the PHP mailing list. In most cases, somebody's probably already found a way to get it running on the same flavor of system that you're using, and the particular steps just haven't made it into the documentation yet.

Saying "Hello, World" with PHP

Without further ado, let's reproduce the "Hello World" example from the previous chapter. Listing 3-2 shows one way to do it; the WML this script produces is shown in Listing 3-3.

```
01: <?php
02: // WML Deck HTTP header.
03: header( "Content-type: text/vnd.wap.wml" );
04:
05: // Start of deck. First, the XML prologue
06: echo( "<?xml version=\"1.0\"?>\n" );
07: echo( "<!DOCTYPE wml PUBLIC " );
08: echo( "\"-//WAPFORUM//DTD WML 1.1//EN\" " );
09: echo( "\"http://www.wapforum.org/DTD/wml_1.1.xml\">\n" );
10:
11: // Now, the deck itself
12: echo( "<wml>\n" );
13: echo( "<card title=\"Hello world!\">\n" );
14: echo( "<p>\n" );
15: echo( "Hello world!\n");
16: echo( "</p>\n" );
17: echo( "</card>\n" );
18: echo( "</wml>\n" );
19: ?>
```

Listing 3-2. "Hello World," PHP style

```
01: <?xml version="1.0"?>
02: <!DOCTYPE wml PUBLIC "-//WAPFORUM//DTD WML 1.1//EN"
      "http://www.wapforum.org/DTD/wml_1.1.xml">
03: <wml>
04: <card title="Hello world!">
05: <p>
06: Hello world!
07: </p>
08: </card>
09: </wml>
```

Listing 3-3. The WML produced by Listing 3-2

Because you can freely mix WML content and markup content, all of your PHP scripts must be enclosed in the tags <?php and ?>. In Listing 3-2, I have just one script that begins on the first line of the listing, and finishes on the last line of the listing.

Lines 2, 5, and 11 are comments. Comments in PHP serve the same purpose as comments in WML or HTML. They're simply reminders for the people that maintain the scripts.

Line 3 uses PHP's internal header function to send a HTTP header to the client. I send the Content-type header to the client to specify the MIME type of the data output by the script. In this case, the MIME type is text/vnd.wap.wml, stating that the content is a WML deck stored as text. By default, PHP assumes it's creating HTML and sends an HTTP header asserting that fact by default, so you should always use the header function to specify the MIME type of your script's result data when it's not HTML.

The remainder of the lines (lines 6–9 and lines 12–18) use PHP's echo function to send output to the client. This function takes a series of characters (a string, actually) and sends the string along to the client.

Of course, there's more than one way to skin a cat. Listing 3-4 shows another PHP script that does the same thing, but freely mixes PHP and WML content.

```
01: <?php
02: // WML Deck HTTP header.
03: header( "Content-type: text/vnd.wap.wml" );
04: ?>
05:
```

```
06: <?xml version="1.0"?>
07: <!DOCTYPE wml PUBLIC "-//WAPFORUM//DTD WML 1.1//EN"
    "http://www.wapforum.org/DTD/wml_1.1.xml">
08:
09: <wml>
10: <card title="Hello world!">
11: <p>
12: Hello world!
13: </p>
14: </card>
15: </wml>
```

Listing 3-4. "Hello World," another PHP variant

This PHP script is actually mostly WML, with only a single executable line of PHP on line 3. Line 3, as in the previous PHP script, sends the WML deck's MIME type to the client before sending any of the WML that follows outside the PHP script. Because the remainder of the file falls outside the `<?php>` tag, it's passed directly to the browser.

Deciding whether Listing 3-2 or Listing 3-4 is better is like deciding whether white chocolate tastes better than dark chocolate. It depends a lot on your background, frame of mind, and what else you've eaten that day. There's really no right or wrong, although most purists prefer Listing 3-2 because PHP is directly responsible for generating *all* of the deck's content. On the other hand, Listing 3-4 is nice because you can let content experts freely meddle around with the WML, and tell them not to mess with the stuff inside the `<?php>` tag (or give them tools that ignore the PHP scripts altogether!). Personally, I prefer Listing 3-2, but for a different reason: my poor brain has a hard enough time keeping one language straight; mixing and matching different scripting and markup languages in a single file gives me mental indigestion.

Before I dive into a detailed discussion of PHP's syntax, let's look at just one more way to present a "Hello World" deck. Listing 3-5 shows a script that makes heavy use of functions I show you later in the chapter. These functions enable you to build up a WML deck without directly referring to WML tags. The resulting WML is slightly different, as you can see in Listing 3-6.

```
01: <?php
02: require "wml.php";
03:
04: header( "Content-type: text/vnd.wap.wml" );
05:
06: // Create a deck...
07: $deck = WMLNewDeck();
08:
09: // Home Card...
10: $card = WMLNewCard( "Hello world!" );
11: $para = WMLNewParagraph( "Hello world!" );
12: WMLAddParagraph( $card, $para );
13: WMLAddCard( $deck, $card );
14:
15: WMLEchoDeck( $deck );
16: ?>
```

Listing 3-5. Yet another flavor of "Hello World" in PHP

```
01: <?xml version="1.0"?>
02: <!DOCTYPE wml PUBLIC "-//WAPFORUM//DTD WML 1.1//EN"
        "http://www.wapforum.org/DTD/wml_1.1.xml">
03: <wml>
04: <card title="Hello world!">
05: <p>
06: Hello world!</p>
07: </card>
08: </wml>
```

Listing 3-6. The WML produced by Listing 3-5

You'll see how all these functions work later in this chapter, in the section "Generating WML with PHP." These functions are the backbone of much of MobileHelper, generating WML content on behalf of most of MobileHelper's scripts.

After starting the PHP script on line 1, I use PHP's require function to preload the contents of the file wml.php. When the script executes, PHP replaces line 2 with the contents of the file wml.php, which contains a slew of functions I've defined to manipulate WML content.

Line 4 uses the header function to output the obligatory MIME type.

Line 7 calls the function WMLNewDeck. It, like all the functions beginning with the three letters WML, are functions I defined in the file wml.php. WMLNewDeck returns a blob of data that contains a new WML deck, which the script stores in the variable $deck.

Line 10 uses my `WMLNewCard` function to create an empty card. This function takes an argument, the title for the card it creates. In this case, I give the title `"Hello World!"`. The script stores this card in the variable `$card`.

Line 11 uses my function `WMLNewParagraph` to create a WML paragraph, containing the string `"Hello World"`. The script stores this WML paragraph in the variable `$para`. On line 12, I add this paragraph to the card stored in `$card` using `WMLAddParagraph`, a function that takes a card and the paragraph to append to the card.

On line 13, the script adds the card containing a single paragraph in `$card` to the deck stored in `$deck` using the `WMLAddCard` function. Similar to `WMLAddParagraph`, the `WMLAddCard` function takes a deck and a card (returned by the `WMLNewDeck` and `WMLNewCard` functions) and appends the card to the deck.

The data blobs returned by these functions are *opaque.* That is, their contents are in an internal format, not to be used outside the functions in wml.php. Hiding data between layers of your programs is called *encapsulation*, and it's a very good idea. By encapsulating your data, you restrict the number of places that can access or change your data. Later, when you decide you need to change how something is stored, you don't have to search all over; instead, you need only work with the few functions that know how the data is encapsulated. Although PHP doesn't directly support data hiding, you can simulate it in a variety of ways, as you'll see later in this chapter. Because the deck's structure is opaque, I provide a function, `WMLEchoDeck`, that accepts a deck and sends the contents of the deck to the client using the PHP `echo` function.

The functions in the file wml.php create WML that's syntactically identical but formatted slightly differently than the previous scripts you saw in this section. Listing 3-6 shows the resulting WML. You can see an obvious difference on lines 5 and 6, where the paragraph tag begins on its own line but closes on the same line as the last line of the paragraph's contents. Because the WML content is compiled before being sent to the client, these differences don't matter. In fact, if you use a WML SDK to decompile the WML displayed when running each of these scripts, you see the same WML, even though the scripts formatted them differently.

PHP Syntax

As you've already seen, a PHP script is simply a sequence of instructions contained within special tags. For your convenience, a script can also contain human-readable comments, which are ignored by the PHP interpreter.

You can put PHP scripts in any file the Web server recognizes as having the MIME type `application/x-httpd-php`. By convention, most developers restrict their use of PHP to files whose names end in .php, although there's no reason you can't use another suffix. In fact, some sites freely mix PHP scripts and marked-up content, and set the MIME type of HTML and WML files to `application/x-httpd-php`. By doing this, the casual user can't tell that the site is actually using PHP to generate and process its content.

> **NOTE** *Using the MIME type* application/x-httpd-php *doesn't work with some Web servers, including Microsoft IIS.*

Within a file, you can bracket PHP scripts in a variety of ways. Typically, you should get in the habit of using the `<?php?>` tag to bracket your script because, as you'll see in Chapter 9, this tag is XML-compliant and plays well with almost every Web development tool you're likely to encounter.

Speaking of grief, you can also use the HTML `<script>` tag with the `language` attribute set to `"php"`, although you'll get a cold reception from your peers. Not only is it bad form to mix and match HTML tags within WML content, but many content tools don't understand the `<script>` tag with server-side scripts. You can also use the ASP-style tag bracket `<%%>`, but again, this isn't a good idea unless you're using Microsoft tools elsewhere.

PHP instructions are separated by the semicolon character (;). Like most programming languages, PHP doesn't care where and how you use white space, although your friends and family do. Custom and commonsense both suggest that you restrain yourself to a single instruction per line and use white space to separate logical parts of each instruction. PHP instructions are also called *expressions*, and are built of *operators* that do individual things, and *statements* that affect the execution of an expression.

In addition to white space, you should plan to comment your code liberally as well. Like notes on an architect's blueprints, comments should be written as you work, not saved as an unfortunate task until the very end, when you won't remember what you wanted to comment, and don't have time to do it thoroughly. In larger projects, comments are crucial so that you and others understand the intent of your scripts; without them, it can be nigh impossible to maintain or reuse otherwise perfectly crafted scripts for other purposes.

PHP gives you three ways to comment your code. In the listings you've seen so far, I've used the C++ style single-line comment, which begins with // and continues to the end of the line. When the PHP interpreter encounters the //, it immediately stops attempting to interpret the file as PHP instructions, and skips to the beginning of the next line before looking for another instruction. For those of you familiar with the Bourne and Perl languages, the # character also defines a single-line comment just like //.

There's also the C-style delimiters /* and */, whose contents are ignored by the PHP interpreter. These are good for creating long comment banners, like those you find at the beginning of functions or whole files.

Going Further with PHP

There's a lot more to PHP than just the syntax. If you're familiar with most programming languages, you can quickly puzzle out PHP once you have a handle on its syntax, although it's far easier to learn it by example. Let's have a closer look at how PHP handles the bread and butter of programming, including data types, variables, expressions, control structures, and functions.

Data Types

PHP supports a number of different data types. In the previous examples, you saw one of the most common data types, the *string*. A string is simply a sequence of characters, delimited by single or double quotes, `'like this'` or `"this"`. There's a subtle difference between the two, however.

Strings in single quotes are *literal*; that is, they contain exactly what you see. By comparison, strings in double quotes are interpreted by PHP. In double-quoted strings, you can include variables and special characters, indicated by a preceding \ (solidus) character. (Table 3-1 shows a list of these special characters.) Before doing anything with a string in double quotes, PHP converts variable names to the contents of a variable, and turns special characters into their appropriate counterparts. Listing 3-8 shows the difference between the strings in single and double quotes.

```
01: <?php
02: $kind = "br";
03: $tag = "<$tag/>\n";
04: $oops='<$tag/>\n';
05: ?>
```

Listing 3-8. Single-quoted versus double-quoted strings

Table 3-1. Special Characters in PHP Strings

NEWLINE SEQUENCE	MEANING
\n	linefeed (LF or 0x0A in ASCII)
\r	carriage return (CR or 0x0D in ASCII)
\t	horizontal tab (HT or 0x09 in ASCII)
\\	backslash
\$	dollar sign
\"	double quote

Line 2 assigns the string "br" to the variable $kind. On line 3, I assign the string "<$tag/>\n" to $tag; on line 4, I assign the string '<$tag>\n' to the variable $oops. The difference is subtle: after line 3, $tag contains the characters <br/> and a line break, whereas $oops contains the characters <$tag/>\n, which probably isn't what you want.

Of course, PHP supports numbers, too. You can represent both integers—that is, positive and negative numbers with no fractions—and floating-point numbers. PHP treats any number without a decimal point as an integer, and treats any number with a decimal point as a floating-point number. You can also write integers in octal by including a preceding 0 (zero), or in hexadecimal by including a preceding 0x. For example, PHP treats 23, -127, 020, and 0xff as integers. The last two values have the decimal values 16 and 255, respectively.

Sometimes you want to keep a sequence or list of items. For example, Mobile-Helper often needs to keep a list of tasks (say, the open task list) when building a deck. For this, PHP provides the *array* data type. An array keeps a table of items, called either the *index* or the *key*, and the value associated with each key. Keys can be either integers or strings, letting you create both the *vector* array and *associative* array structures seen in other languages such as Perl. You can create arrays in a variety of ways, but by far the easiest is with the array statement. Listing 3-9 shows two examples.

> **NOTE**   *You'll also hear associative arrays called hashes, especially if you hang around with people who use Perl.*

```php
01: <?php
02: $access = array( "domain" => "www.apress.com",
       "path" => "/wml/" );
03: $open = array( 1272, 1333, 2001 );
04:
05: $path = $access[ "path" ];
06:
07: $nextOpen = $open[ 0 ];
08:
09: $open[] = 2025;
10: ?>
```

Listing 3-9. The array *statement*

On line 2, I create an array with two elements. This array is an *associative* array, associating each string key with a single value. In $access, the key "domain" is associated with the value "www.apress.com", and the key "path" is associated with the value "/wml/". PHP uses the symbol => to separate key and value pairs within the array keyword, while the comma (,) separates each key/value pair. On line 3, I create a *vector* array with the three integer values 1272, 1333, and 2001.

To refer to an element in an array, you write the index of the element you're seeking in brackets after the array. The index can be stored in a variable, so you can walk an entire array's worth of elements if you want. (You'll see examples of how to do that in the section "Control Structures," later in this chapter). Line 5 of Listing 3-9 fetches the value associated with the key "path", setting the variable $path to the string "/wml/". Line 7 sets the variable $nextOpen to the first element of the array $open. (Thanks to the long and convoluted history of mathematicians and computers, the first element of a vector array is referred to using the index 0, rather than the seemingly more natural 1.)

While I'm on the topic of arrays, you might want to know how to add an element to an array. Line 9 shows one way to do it, by assigning a value to the array with no index. This adds a new value to the end of the array, making the array one slot larger than it was previously. You can also use PHP's array_push function, which is a little longer to type but easier for many people to read.

Sometimes, you want to create a variable whose value doesn't change. For example, if you're building the server side of a science news site, you might want to include a scientific calculator that has values for common mathematical constants such as e and π. Of course, you don't just want to assign these to variables; if you make a mistake, you could easily reassign the variable, and end up using the wrong value in a computation someplace. Instead, you can use PHP's define statement to define a constant with the specified value. For example, writing define("PI", 3.1415926536) creates a constant PI whose value is a floating-point approximation for PI. Later, you can simply refer to the constant PI (note that because it's a constant and not a variable, there's no leading $), and PHP substitutes the value of the constant. PHP also includes many built-in constants, some of which you'll encounter as you continue reading this book.

Unlike many programming languages, PHP's handling of types is quite fluid. When you write an expression with different data types, PHP attempts to convert each data type before applying the operations. Thus, you can write something like Listing 3-10, which converts $count from a string to an integer before adding 1 to it.

```
01: <?php
02: $count = "10";
03: $count = $count + 1;
04: ?>
```

Listing 3-10. An example of type conversion

When in doubt, you can use a *cast* to force a value to the type you want. To do this, simply write the name of the type in parentheses before the value. For example, writing (double)10 is the same as writing 10.0; both evaluate to floating-point numbers.

PHP also provides a host of type functions, which are handy when you're debugging scripts that use PHP's type conversion functions. The gettype function returns the type of its argument, while you can set a variable's type explicitly using the settype function. There are also a host of Boolean test functions that return true if the argument is a specific type, such as is_array, is_string, and is_integer.

Variables

In Chapter 1, I hinted that PHP supported variables without explicitly telling you much about them. Since then, you've seen variables in several scripts, but I've not told you more.

Variables are the glue that holds your scripts together. Like WML, a variable holds a datum such as a number, string, or array. PHP variable names begin with a $ and a leading letter or underscore (_) character, followed by letters, numbers, or more underscore characters. Thus, names such as $task, $taskName, $task_name, and $task_1 are valid PHP variable names, whereas $1task isn't.

You've also already seen how to assign values to variables. The = operand assigns the value on the right-hand side of the expression to the variable named on the left-hand side of the expression. For example, on line 2 of Listing 3-10, $count is assigned the value "10". For the sake of consistency, PHP uses = to assign values to array elements, too. Any data type, including an array, can be assigned to a variable.

In later versions of PHP, such as PHP4, you can also assign a *reference* to a variable, which merely points to a variable's value, rather than contains the value of a variable itself. Generally, when you assign a value to a variable, the variable gets a copy of the value. Most of the time, you'd do this only for efficiency's sake, when you're using several variables to refer to a large array. You can also use it when you want to replace a value of a variable, but don't know where else the variable is being used. To obtain a reference value, you use the & operator, as shown in Listing 3-11.

```
01: <?php
02: $owner = 321;
03: $ownerRef = &$owner;
04: $ownerRef = 0;
05: ?>
```

Listing 3-11. PHP variables as references

On line 2, $owner is assigned the value 321. On line 3, the variable $ownerRef is pointed at the variable $owner. When PHP executes line 4, $owner is set to 0. The variable $ownerRef will still point to $owner.

In MobileHelper, I use references with some functions to explicitly change the value of the function's argument. Before I show you how to do this, however, let's look more closely at some of the other building blocks of scripts.

Operations

If variables are the glue that holds your PHP scripts together, then the individual operations in your PHP script and the expressions they comprise are the individual pieces. An operation is merely something that does something to data and creates something else. The arithmetic operations +, −, ×, and ÷ are all examples of operations that have PHP counterparts. In the case of PHP, as with most other programming languages, you express multiplication using the * operator, while you express division with the / operator. Line 3 of Listing 3-10 uses the addition operator to add 1 to the value of $count.

As with arithmetic, operation order is an issue when using different operators. For example, in mathematics, when you write an expression such as $3 \times 5 + 2$, you're saying, "First, multiply 3 by 5, and then add 2." There's no confusion because, by definition, multiplication and division have a higher precedence than addition or subtraction. PHP addresses the issue of precedence as well, defining an order of precedence for operators as well as stating in which direction operators prefer to associate. Table 3-2 shows all of the PHP operators, what they do, and which way they associate. After looking at Table 3-2, you may recognize many of the operators.

PHP defines a series of Boolean operators. This family of operators is divided into two categories: the logical operators and the bitwise operators. Their meaning is quite similar, but their purpose very different. The logical operators look at an entire value and treat that value as either true or false. By definition, any non-empty variable or string is considered true; empty strings or the value 0 are considered false.

In contrast, bitwise operators treat values as integers, and look at each bit in the binary representation of an integer. For example, consider the Boolean operators ! and ~. The ! operator is the logical complement operator: when given a value of true, it returns false, and when given false, returns true. The ~ operator, on the other hand, is the bitwise complement operator: for every bit in the value given, it converts all 1 bits to 0 and vice-versa. For example, !36 is 0, whereas ~36 is 27 (36 in binary is 100100; complementing each bit gives 011011, or 27 decimal).

You want to use bitwise operators when dealing with individual bits (say, when controlling computer hardware via scripts or storing things in a compact manner), while you use logical operators when making logical decisions in conditional statements. The bitwise operators are ~ (complement), & (and), ^ (exclusive or),

and | (bitwise or), while the logical operators are ! (complement), && (and), and ||
(or). PHP also defines the logical operators xor, and, and or, which have a lower
precedence than the && and || operators. When you're working at the level of
individual bits, you can also use the << operator to shift all the bits in an integer
left one bit, or >> to shift all the bits in an integer right one bit. A left shift is the
same as multiplying the number by two and a right shift is the same as dividing a
number by two. Although they're the same, you shouldn't get in the habit of using
shifts when you mean multiplication or division because doing so is not clear to
the reader and not portable between different kinds of computers.

You have already seen the arithmetic operators. In addition to the four arithmetic operators, PHP defines the % operator to perform the modulo (remainder)
operation and the "." operation to concatenate two strings. When working with
variables, PHP also provides the shorthand ++ and -- operations, which increment
and decrement a variable, respectively. Thus, writing $count++; is the same as
writing $count = $count + 1;.

Assignment itself is an operation, denoted using the = operator. PHP also
defines a set of assignment operators, each of which is shorthand for an operation
and simultaneous assignment. The operators +=, -=, *=, /=, %=, ^=, .=, &=, and |=
perform the operation indicated by the first character, followed by an assignment
to the operand's left-hand side. Thus, $count += 1; is yet another way to write
$count = $count + 1;.

Essential to perform most scripted operations, comparison operations return
true or false based on equality, inequality, or ordering. The operator == tests for
equality between the left-hand side and right-hand side, returning true if both are
equal, while the operator != tests for inequality. The < and > operators correspond
to the less than and greater than operations we all learned in grade school, and
the <= and => operators correspond to the grade school operations ≤ (less than or
equals) and ≥ (greater than or equals). As you might expect, these work for both
integers and floating-point numbers. They also work for strings, comparing strings
character-by-character in alphabetical order. For example, "coon" is less than
"dog", but not "cat".

Although PHP provides a rich set of conditional statements that you'll encounter
in the next section, it also defines a shorthand conditional operator ?:. This operator evaluates the first expression (before the ? symbol), and if true, it returns the
second expression (between the ? and :). If the first expression is false, it returns
the third expression (after the :). It's often used as shorthand for an if-else statement when assigning a value to a variable based on the value of another variable.

Internally, casting—forcing a type conversion—is treated as an operation. For
example, writing (double) 3 + 2.5 first converts 3 to the floating-point number 3.0,
and then adds the floating point number 2.5.

You might encounter two more operators. The @ operator tells PHP to suppress
any error messages for the duration of the expression, while the comma operator
(,) tells PHP to discard the value of the left-hand side. The @ operation is useful

when you want to use a function or expression that may fail but you don't necessarily want any debugging output generated by the PHP interpreter itself.[2] Similarly, you may want to perform two actions in one statement, perhaps as part of a loop or conditional.

Table 3-2. Common PHP Operators

OPERATION	ASSOCIATION	PURPOSE
!, ~, ++, –, @, (cast)	Right	Logical complement, binary complement, increment, decrement, disregard error, casting from one type to another
*, /, %	Left	Multiplication, division, and modulo (remainder)
+, -, .	Left	Addition, subtraction, string concatenation
<<, >>	Left	Bitwise left shift, right shift
<, <=, >=, >	Non-associative	less than, less than or equals, greater than, greater than or equals comparisons
==, !=	Non-associative	equivalence, non-equivalence comparisons
&	Left	Bitwise and
^	Left	Bitwise xor
|	Left	Bitwise or
&&	Left	Logical and
||	Left	Logical or
? :	Left	Conditional operation
=, +=, -=, *=, /=, %=, ^=, .=, &=, |=	Left	Assignment
xor	Left	Exclusive logical or
and	Left	Exclusive logical and
or	Left	Exclusive logical or

---

2. Of course, you should only use @ when you're expecting a possible failure. Sprinkling the @ operator around in your code to make your errors go away is begging for disaster!

Control Statements

PHP provides nine *control* statements that govern the flow of execution through a script. Without these statements, execution simply flows from one PHP expression to the next. Using control statements, you can skip some expressions in your script based on whether a particular expression is true or false, or repeat expressions until a predetermined expression is true or false. All of these control statements operate on an individual expression or a group of expressions. You denote a group of expressions using the curly braces { and }.

if-else

The if-else control statement is the simplest of them all. It tells PHP to evaluate an expression and execute the first block *if* the statement is true, and the second block after the optional else if the statement is false. Listing 3-12 shows an if-else control statement with two blocks. On line 2, the if statement evaluates the expression $card["_template"]. If this expression is true—that is, if it's a string with characters or a non-zero number—the first block is executed, setting the variable $tag to the string "template". On the other hand, if the expression is false (an empty string, undefined, or the number 0), the second block is executed, setting the variable $tag to the string "card".

```
01: <?php
02: if ( $card[ "_template" ] )
03: {
04:    $tag = "template";
05: }
06: else
07: {
08:    $tag = "card";
09: }
10: ?>
```

Listing 3-12. An if-else *conditional with two blocks*

You can tack additional if statements on an if-else block, too. You can chain multiple if-else blocks together by writing something like Listing 3-13 using the elseif statement, or by using the switch statement as I do in Listing 3-14.

The switch statement takes a block containing case statements. Execution begins within the block at the first case that matches the expression you give to switch, and continues from there until the end of the block. To keep PHP from executing statements belonging to more than one case, you use the break keyword, which tells PHP to stop executing statements in the current block and hop out to the first statement after the current block. Thus, in Listing 3-14, if $card["_template"] is a string equal to "t", execution within the block begins at line 5, assigning "template" to the variable $tag, and on line 6, skips out to line 12 after encountering the break statement.

```php
01: <?php
02: if ( $card[ "_template" ] == "t" )
03: {
04:    $tag = "template";
05: }
06: elseif ( $card[ "_template" ] == "c" )
07: {
08:    $tag = "card";
09: }
10: ?>
```

Listing 3-13. Chaining if-else *statements with* elseif

switch-case

Another way to represent the if-else relationship is with the switch-case statements, which let you compare the value of an expression against several different values. Although I don't use it in Listing 3-14, the switch keyword permits a special case, which matches anything. The default keyword, used instead of a case, always matches the expression for a switch.

```php
01: <?php
02: switch ( $card[ "_template" ] )
03: {
04:    case "t":
05:       $tag = "template";
06:       break;
07:
08:    case "c":
09:       $tag = "card";
10:       break;
11:  }
12: ?>
```

Listing 3-14. The switch *statement*

for

Sometimes, you don't want to skip instructions, but execute them repeatedly. PHP gives you looping statements such as the for statements to repeatedly execute (or *loop*) a set of instructions.

The for statement is one of the most common loop constructs to repeat a block of statements. The for statement takes three expressions: an initialization expression, a conditional expression, and a loop expression. PHP executes the initialization expression before the block is executed for the first time, giving you a chance to set initial conditions. The for statement executes its block and the loop expression as long as the conditional expression returns true. Listing 3-15 shows an example. This loop looks at every element of the array stored in the "meta" slot of the array $deck, calling the function WMLTagAsString to create WML tags for each element.

```
01: <?php
02: for ( $i = 0; $i < count( $deck[ "meta" ] ); $i++ )
03: {
04:    $result .= "    " . WMLTagAsString( "meta", "",
05:      $deck[ "meta" ][ $i ] ) . "\n";
06: }
07: ?>
```

Listing 3-15. The for *statement in action*

As the loop begins in Listing 3-15 on line 2, the initialization expression of the for statement is evaluated, setting the variable $i to 0. Then, the conditional expression of the for statement is evaluated, checking to see whether $i is less than the value of count($deck["meta"]). If it is, the statement block itself is executed, appending the result of calling WMLTagAsString with a preceding space and trailing newline character to the variable $result on lines 4 and 5. After that, the loop's loop expression is evaluated, adding 1 to the variable $i. Then, the loop executes the conditional expression again and, if it's true, continues to execute the statement block and loop expression until the conditional expression is no longer true.

Recall that you use the { and } to surround a group of statements to make a block. Because the block in Listing 3-16 has only one statement, the { and } surrounding the statement is optional. Personally, I've gotten in the habit of *always* surrounding statement blocks with curly braces, simply because then I don't accidentally forget them when I'm editing a script (say, when I add a statement to a single-statement loop).

Incidentally, Listing 3-15 also shows an example of an array whose elements are another array. On line 4, the expression $deck["meta"][$i] tells PHP to take the "meta" element in the $deck array, and treat it as an array, extracting the element at the location pointed to by the value of the variable $i. You can nest arrays this way as deep as you like, which comes in handy when you're creating larger data structures.

Before I move on, let's look at one more for loop. Unlike Listing 3-15, the loop in Listing 3-16 uses functions rather than arithmetic to determine when the loop should start and stop. This code visits every element in the associative array $attr, but uses PHP functions to determine the key of each element in the array.

```
01: <?php
02: for ( reset( $attr ); $key = key( $attr ); next( $attr ) )
03: {
04:   $value = $attr[ $key ];
05:   if ( $value )
06:   {
07:     $result .=  " $key=\"$value\"";
08:   }
09: }
10: ?>
```

Listing 3-16. Another for *loop*

All associative arrays in PHP keep an internal *cursor* that points to exactly one element in the array. PHP provides several functions that enable you to manipulate this cursor, pushing it along from one element of the array to the next. You can use a function to learn the key of the element to which the cursor points, and from that, determine the value of the element to which the cursor points. This is particularly important when working with associative arrays because with this technique, you don't need to know the keys in an associative array when iterating over all items in the array. The loop in Listing 3-16 does exactly this.

On line 2, the for statement begins. Before anything else happens, PHP executes the expression reset($attr), which tells PHP to set the cursor associated with $attr to point to the first element of the array. Then, PHP executes the expression $key = key($attr), which returns the key of the item the cursor points to. After that, the loop statements in the block on lines 4–8 is executed, saving the value of the key aside and appending the key and value pair to the string in $result if there's both a key and a value for the item.

Once the block completes, the for loop advances the cursor to the next element in the $attr array by calling next($attr). The next function bumps the cursor to the next element in the array, returning false if there are no more elements. When the loop has visited the last element, key won't find the next element and will return false, causing the loop to end and execution to continue on line 10.

foreach

The for statement has a cousin in PHP4 and later versions of PHP, the foreach statement. The foreach statement enables you to iterate over arrays, much as Listing 3-16 does, except that you don't have to explicitly mess around with the reset, key, and next functions. Listing 3-17 is Listing 3-16 rewritten to use foreach.

```php
01: <?php
02: foreach ($attr as $key => $value)
03: {
04:   if ( $value )
05:   {
06:     $result .=  " $key=\"$value\"";
07:   }
08: }
09: ?>
```

Listing 3-17. The foreach *statement*

The foreach statement takes an array, followed by the keyword as and a single variable, which will contain the value of an element of the array each pass through the loop. Alternately, if you need both the item's value and key, you use the expression $key => $value, telling PHP to stuff the key of each item in the variable $key and the value of each item in the variable $value each pass through the loop. Listing 3-17 does just this; for each element in the $attr array, get the element's key and value (storing them in $key and $value, respectively) and then evaluate the statement block. Because foreach uses a copy of the array in its loop, you don't have to worry about the cursor's position in foreach–everything happens behind the scenes.

Because the foreach statement is new in PHP 4.0, you won't see it as often as the for loop construction in Listing 3-16, so it's important you know both. Throughout this book, I use both interchangeably.

while

If for and foreach aren't enough, there's yet another way to write a loop. The while statement is similar to the for statement, except that it's not as compact. For many beginning programmers the while statement is easier to understand: *while* an expression is true, execute the statement block that follows. There's no fooling around with initialization expressions and loop expressions: if you want those, you have to write them explicitly. Take Listing 3-18; it's simply Listing 3-16 written using while instead of for.

```
01: <?php
02: reset( $attr );
03: $continue = current( $attr );
04: while( $continue )
05: {
06:    $key = key( $attr );
07:    $value = $attr[ $key ];
08:    if ( $value )
09:    {
10:      $result .= " $key=\"$value\"";
11:    }
12:    $continue = next( $attr );
13: }
14: ?>
```

Listing 3-18. The while *statement*

The first lines of Listing 3-18 initialize the loop; line 2 resets the $attr cursor, while line 3 calls current to check if there are any elements in $attr. (The current function returns the value of the item pointed at by the array's cursor or false if the cursor doesn't point at anything).

The loop begins on line 4, which tells PHP to execute the following statement block for as long as $continue is true. If there are elements in $attr, the statement block is executed; if current failed to find an element, the block is skipped and execution continues on line 13.

Line 6 extracts the key from the current element of $attr, while line 7 gets the current item's value. As before, the if statement on lines 8–11 simply builds up a string containing key-value pairs, one for each value of $key and $value.

Line 12 moves the cursor for the array $attr to its next value, setting $continue if there's a next value for the loop to examine. Once this occurs, execution continues at line 4, where the loop either executes again if $continue is true, or skips down to line 13.

Despite the while statement's simplicity, it's arguable whether Listing 3-18 is clearer than Listing 3-16, especially once you've been working with PHP for a while. In general, you find that the for statement is used when the initialization, loop, and conditional expressions are all necessary and the loop closely resembles counting. You see while used more often when the loop is a simple one, omitting one or more of those expressions.

Neither for nor while will not execute its statement block unless the conditional expression is true, even on the first pass through the loop. Sometimes, you want to execute the loop statement block the first time regardless of whether or not the conditional is true. This is often the case when your statement block initializes the terms of the conditional expression. You use the do-while statement

for this, writing do, followed by the statement block, followed by the while statement and its conditional expression. You won't see this very often, so I won't
burden you with an example.

With PHP, your loops should *always* exit. If they don't, your loop runs until
your Web server decides it's consumed enough processing time, and kills your
script for you. In the meantime, the client may see nothing, or only some of the
output of your script. You have already seen how you can exit your loops by checking
the conditional statement, but sometimes you need to hop out of a loop's block in
the middle, say because of an error or because you've found what the loop was
searching for. As with the switch statement, you can use the break statement to
stop execution at the current statement and begin it again at the statement after
the loop's block. You can also use the continue statement, which stops executing at
the continue statement and begins execution at the beginning of the loop's block
again. You use the break statement when you want to exit the loop, whereas you
use continue when you want to skip back to the beginning again.

require and include

PHP has two other statements—require and include–that affect flow control,
although they look more like functions than statements. The require statement
replaces itself with the file it names, in essence sucking in the contents of another
file for the PHP interpreter to execute. This replacement happens before the script
is executed, although PHP won't execute the contents of the file unless flow happens
to reach the require statement. On the other hand, the include statement includes
the contents of the current file when the include statement is executed. In either
case, the PHP parser stops looking for PHP instructions and begins looking for
Web content, so if you use these directives to include PHP scripts, your files need
to contain start and ending PHP tags.

I find these statements most useful when breaking scripts up into individual
modules that are responsible for handling specific parts of the site. For example,
MobileHelper uses include to load a set of functions to manage WML from the file
wml.php. That way, I can change how MobileHelper creates its WML by editing
only one file. More importantly, when I develop other PHP-based Wireless Web
sites, I need only include the wml.php file I wrote for MobileHelper, and I'll have
all those functions on which to build.

Functions

Functions enable you to define a part of a script that you can use more than once.
By giving a block of statements a name, you can invoke the block elsewhere in

your scripts. This helps you reuse pieces of your scripts safely because you can reuse scripts without retyping the statements each time.

Listing 3-19 shows a function definition for the function WMLTagAsString. This function takes the name of a tag and its contents, along with an optional array of attributes, and creates a string containing the WML tag. For example, given a tag p with the contents hello world and the attribute align with the value center, it creates a string containing the WML snippet <p align="center">Hello world</p>.

```
01: <?php
02: /********************************************************
03:  * FUNCTION: WMLTagAsString
04:  *
05:  * DESCRIPTION: Generates the WML for a given tag, content
06:  *   and attributes.
07:  *
08:  * RETURNED: String with WML!
09:  ********************************************************/
10: function WMLTagAsString(
11:    $tag, // (in) tag
12:    $content = "", // (in) content of the tag
13:    $attr = array() )
14: {
15:
16: // Open the tag.
17:
18:    $result = "<" . $tag;
19:
20: // Handle the attributes, if any.
21:
22:    for ( reset( $attr );
23:       $key = key( $attr );
24:       next( $attr ) )
25:    {
26:       $value = $attr[ $key ];
27:       if ( $value )
28:          $result .=  " $key=\"$value\"";
29:
30:    }
31:
32: // Handle the contents, if any
```

```
33:
34:    if ( $content )
35:    {
36:      $result .= ">\n$content";
37:    }
38:
39: // Close the tag. If there were no contents,
40: // it's an empty tag.
41:
42:    if ( $content )
43:    {
44:      $result .= "</$tag>";
45:    }
46:    else
47:    {
48:      $result .= "/>";
49:    }
50:
51: // Return the results
52:
53:    return $result;
54: }
55: ?>
```

Listing 3-19. A function definition

The first lines, lines 2–9, are a comment banner that describes this function. While not required by PHP, comment banners are very helpful to you when reading PHP because it's easier to spot the banner than the function declaration. It's an element of good programming style, and I urge you to adopt a similar convention in your own scripts. Exactly what you put in a banner and how you format it is up to you, but you should be sure to include the name of the function and what it does. Regardless of what you choose, keep it simple—banners that take longer than functions to write and keep up-to-date probably won't be high on your list of things to keep current.

Lines 10–14 define the function itself. Line 10 uses the PHP `function` keyword to begin the definition of the function `WMLTagAsString`. This function takes three *arguments*, variables that are defined within the function. The first argument is `$tag`, which contains the type of tag to create. The second and third arguments are *optional* arguments because the script provides *default* values—values to use if no values are supplied when you call the function—for the arguments. The second argument, `$content`, has as its default value an empty string and will contain the content for the tag. Similarly, the third argument, `$attr`, defaults to an empty array, and contains the attributes for the tag.

The script for the function itself is contained within lines 14–55. I explain the function in more detail in the next section, but what it does is build a string containing the WML for the tag, content, and attributes given. It begins by creating the opening tag string and then walks the $attr attributes array to create a list of attributes for the tag. If the caller doesn't provide attributes, the array $attr will be empty, and the script skips this step. Then, if the tag's content in the $content variable is not empty, the tag is closed and the content added. Finally, the tag is closed correctly, either with an ending tag or the empty tag ending with /> if the tag has no content.

Calling a function

To call a function, simply write the name of the function, followed by any arguments in parentheses. In past scripts, I've already called functions defined by PHP and by myself. For example, in Listing 3-15, I called PHP's internal count function, and all the way back in Listing 3-5 I called a number of functions I defined.

If you wanted to call the function WMLTagAsString, you might use WML like that shown in Listing 3-20. This listing shows a function, WMLBreak, which takes no arguments and returns a string containing the WML for a break tag: "<br/>". On line 11, this function takes advantage of WMLTagAsString's optional arguments, letting WMLTagAsString supply defaults for the content and attribute strings.

```
01: <?php
02: /*******************************************************
03:  * FUNCTION: WMLBreak
04:  *
05:  * DESCRIPTION: Creates a WML line break
06:  *
07:  * RETURNED: string containing WML line break
08:  *******************************************************/
09: function WMLBreak()
10: {
11:   return WMLTagAsString( "br" );
12: }
13: ?>
```

Listing 3-20. A function calling a function

When a function executes, it can return a value to the caller of the function. Both of the functions you've seen so far do this using PHP's return statement. In essence, when an expression invokes a function, the function name and arguments are replaced by the return value. If you like, one way to think of a function is as a variable that changes its value based on its arguments. Functions can return data of any type, including strings, numbers, or arrays.

Variable scope

On the topic of variables, it's time you learn a little about variable *scope*. A variable's *scope* determines where the variable can be accessed or changed. In a PHP script, all variables have scope over the current file, as well as any files brought in through `include` or `require` directives. However, when you define a function, a new scope is created so that any variables within the function have unique values outside the function. In other words, you can't directly access variables defined in scripts within functions. In general, this is a Good Thing because it keeps you from accidentally accessing or modifying variables in scripts from within functions.

There *are* times when you want to do so, however. *Global* variables are occasionally used to save state or other information across a module or an entire script, and you may need to access these from within a function. Of course, you can pass the variables you need as arguments, but that's both clumsy and counterintuitive. Arguments generally contain information that changes from function call to function call, so passing a handful of arguments that are simply global variables is a headache.

Instead, you can use PHP's `global` statement from inside your function. This statement provides the PHP interpreter with a list of variables inside your function that should be shared with the global scope. For example, consider the contrived example in Listing 3-21.

```
01: <?php
02: $breakTag = "br";
03:
04: /*******************************************************
05:  * FUNCTION: WMLBreak
06:  *
07:  * DESCRIPTION: Creates a WML line break
08:  *
09:  * RETURNED: string containing WML line break
10:  *******************************************************/
11: function WMLBreak()
12: {
13:   global $breakTag;
14:   return WMLTagAsString( $breakTag );
15: }
16: ?>
```

Listing 3-21. The global *statement*

Here, the function `WMLBreak` relies on the global variable `$breakTag`. The `global` statement on line 13 tells the PHP interpreter that the variable `$breakTag` referred to inside the function `WMLBreak` is really the variable `$breakTag` defined outside the function. Without line 13, the function would refer to its own private version of `$breakTag`, which would be empty—not what I'd intended.

This example is contrived for two reasons. First of all, rather than using a variable to contain a constant such as the name of a WML tag, I'd probably want to use a constant defined using PHP's `define` function. Second, most scripts don't need global variables at all.

A Sampling of Built-In Functions

PHP offers hundreds of functions you can use in your scripts. Rather than list all of the PHP functions, which would substantially increase the size of this book, I think it's better if you look at a handful of the functions you will use more often. Then, at your convenience, you can flip through the PHP manual (which you can find at `http://www.php.net/`) and learn about all the functions at your disposal.

Using functions to manipulate strings

Many of the functions you're likely to need enable you to manipulate strings. With the `.` operator you can concatenate two strings, but what about breaking them apart or searching for material within a string?

The `trim` function takes a string and removes all white space (spaces, tabs, and carriage returns) from the beginning and end of a string. For example, given the string `" Staff communications equipment "`, chop returns `"Staff communications equipment"`. The `trim` function is especially useful when handling input from users because with it you can remove extraneous spaces at the beginning or the end of a string that users may have added accidentally.

The `crypt` function enables you to encrypt a string using the UNIX DES implementation. This is a one-way encryption, suitable for storing information such as passwords, for which you don't want to decrypt the string. In Chapter 5, you will see how I use crypt to store users' PIN information so that if someone accesses the password file, he or she can't immediately see the passwords in cleartext.

Almost all of your scripts will use the `echo` function. The `echo` function returns the string you pass to the browser. Related to `echo`, but more powerful, is the `printf` function. If you've ever programmed with another language, such as C or Perl, you've probably encountered a `printf`-like function. The `printf` function takes a format string, describing how to format the data sent to the client, and the data itself. The format string is text that's copied to the output in conjunction with a series of statements, commonly called *directives* in the PHP documentation, for each item `printf` prints. A directive consists of % followed by five parts, in the following order:

1. An optional character that `printf` will use when padding the datum to the specified size. For example, you can pad decimal numbers with extra zeros by using the character 0.

2. An optional alignment specifying whether the `printf` aligns the character to the left- or right-hand side of the space allotted. You specify + to right-justify the datum, and - to left-justify the datum.

3. An optional number specifying the minimum width for the datum's presentation.

4. An optional number preceded by a . specifying how many decimal points of precision should be shown. This option has no effect for data types other than floating-point numbers.

5. A character stating what type the datum is. With `printf`, you can format numbers in a variety of ways, including hexadecimal (using x for lowercase characters or X for uppercase characters), octal using o, binary using b, and decimal using d. You can format a floating point number using f too. The `printf` function can display a single character using c (interpreting the datum as an integer specifying a character) or s, which shows an entire string. If you just want to show a % in the output, this character can be a %.

For example, the format string `"pi=%4.2f"` contains the plain text `pi=` and a single format directive, `"%4.2f"`. This directive instructs `printf` to print a floating-point number using four characters, with two digits of precision after the decimal point. The statement `printf( "pi=%4.2f", 3.141593)` causes the string `"pi=3.14"` to be sent to the browser.

The `printf` function has a cousin you can use when building up long formatted strings, `sprintf`. The `sprintf` function operates identically to `printf`, except that instead of sending its results to the client, it returns them as a string.

PHP supports a whole bevy of string functions based on the simple string manipulation functions available in the C programming language. For example, the `strstr` function takes two strings and returns the substring containing the first occurrence and remainder of the second string in the first. The `substr` function, on the other hand, enables you to extract a substring from an entire string, given the number of characters into the string and how long a chunk you want to yank out.

Time and date functions

Another thing you'll commonly want to do is manipulate time and date information. Computers store time in time units (often seconds or demiseconds) from a known date called the *epoch*. Unless you're a polymath, this doesn't do you much good; mere mortals think about time and dates in terms of hours and minutes, or months and days. There's a host of functions that enable you to convert to and from different time units and validate dates (especially important if you're going to let people enter times or dates).

The checkdate function does just what its name implies: it tells you whether a given date is valid. The checkdate function returns true if the date is valid or false otherwise; you give it the month, day, and year in question. For example, while you can write 30 February 2001, it's not a valid date—calling checkdate(2, 30, 2001) would yield false.

The time function returns the time from the system clock. PHP keeps time in terms of seconds since the beginning of the UNIX epoch, on 1 January 1970 at 00:00 Greenwich Mean Time. Most often, you'll want to use this value with another function such as date, which returns a formatted string containing the date. You can think of the date function as a time-handling variant of sprintf; given a format string and time, it creates a human-readable string containing the time specified. The format string for date is a sequence of characters, each coding for a particular unit of time. For example, to express the time of day using the traditional 12-hour clock, you can use the format string "h:i A", which instructs date to return a string in the format "hh:mm PM" where hh is the number of hours after noon or midnight, mm is the number of minutes after the hour, and PM is either AM or PM. Table 3-3 shows the format characters supported by date; other characters pass through unchanged.

Table 3-3. date *function format codes.*

CHARACTER	MEANING	EXAMPLE
a	"am" or "pm"	"am"
A	"AM" or "PM"	"AM"
B	Swatch Internet time, a no-frills hour/minute display.	"230"
d	Day of the month (two digits with leading zero)	"02"
D	First three letters of the name of the day of the week	"Sun"
F	Name of the month	"November"
g	12-hour format hour without leading zero	"3"
G	24-hour format hour without leading zero	"15"

Table 3-3. date *function format codes. (Continued)*

CHARACTER	MEANING	EXAMPLE
h	12-hour format hour with leading zero	"03"
H	24-hour format hour with leading zero	"15"
i	Minutes	"30"
I	1 if Daylight Savings Time is in effect, 0 otherwise.	"1"
j	Day of the month without leading zero.	"2"
l	Name of the Day of the week	"Sunday"
L	1 if a leap year, 0 otherwise	"1"
m	Number of the month with leading zero	"05"
M	First three letters of the name of the month	"Nov"
n	Number of the month without leading zero	"5"
s	Seconds	"01"
S	English ordinal suffix for previous unit	"st"
t	Number of days in the given month	"27"
T	Time zone setting of this machine	"PST"
U	Seconds since the epoch	"926470800"
w	Number of the day of the week ("0" is Sunday)	"5"
Y	Year as four digits	"2001"
y	Year as two digits	"01"
z	Day of the year	"308"
Z	Timezone offset in seconds	"28800"

The getdate function returns an associative array containing the date information corresponding to a PHP time. With the associative array, you can quickly determine individual parts of the date, such as the year, weekday, or seconds after the minute. The function mktime is the opposite of getdate; given the year, month, day, hour, minute, and second, it returns a PHP time.

Array functions

You will find that many of your scripts use arrays to keep sets, lists, and complex data structures. It's easy to work with arrays because most of the time you can simply write a loop to work with the elements in an array to do what you want. However, PHP has functions that you can use for most of the common operations on arrays, such as finding an element or sorting an array. These functions are both faster and easier to use than hand-coded alternatives.

You've already seen the `array` call, which lets you create an array. Actually, it's not a function—it's a language statement. The difference is subtle, but important, because you can use the `array` function in places (such as when declaring a function argument's default value) that you can't use a function. The `array` statement returns a PHP array containing the arguments you pass.

The `array_pop` function removes the last item in an array, and returns its value to you. In conjunction with `array_push`, which adds an item to the end of an array, you have a *stack*, a common data structure used in programming. In a stack, the last item you push is the first item you pop, like a spring-loaded cafeteria plate dispenser.

> **NOTE** *The* `array_push` *function is equivalent to writing the array next to empty brackets in an assignment. Thus, the expression* `$array[] = $newValue` *is functionally the same as* `array_push( $array, $newValue )`. *Which you use is largely a matter of preference, although because* `array_push` *is new to PHP4, you will often see the older notation as well.*

The `count` function returns the number of items in an array.

You've seen how to access each item in an array using `reset`, `key`, and `next`. Other functions access an array's cursor as well. The `current` function returns the value of the item the cursor points to, without moving the cursor. The `prev` function moves the cursor to the previous item, just as the `next` function moves the cursor to the next item. Predictably, the `end` function points the cursor at the last element of an array.

The `each` function is a blend of the `key` and `next` functions. It returns a four-value array containing the current key and value, and bumps the cursor forward one element. The elements at indices `0` and `"key"` contain the key of the value pointed at by the cursor, while the elements at indices `1` and `"value"` contain the value of the item pointed at by the cursor.

If you want to know if an item's in an array, you can call the `in_array` function. Given an array and a value, it returns true if the value is found in the array, and false if it isn't.

Often you need to sort an array. PHP has an armada of sorting functions, and it's rare that you will want or need to write your own. The most intuitive functions are the `sort` and `ksort` functions, which sort an array by values and by keys, respectively. There are other functions that sort arrays in reverse order, as well as functions to sort using a function you define, so that you can sort complex data structures by multiple elements.

The best way to learn PHP, as with almost any programming language, is by a combination of example, experimentation, programming, and research. Like so many things in life, this is an iterative process—begin by looking at the examples in this book and on the Web, and then gradually change some of them. You can base your own scripts on what you see, gradually branching out and writing whole scripts from scratch. After that, you should dig into the manual, and skim parts of it that are unfamiliar to you. It's okay if you don't retain everything; the idea is to learn where you'll find what you need to know when you need it. Then you can go back and look at more examples, experiment with new ideas, and repeat the process all over again.

> **TIP** *It's especially helpful to browse the list of functions in the PHP manual on a regular basis. At first, the number and kinds of functions available may overwhelm you. As you gain experience, returning to the list of functions will help you identify functions you missed in prior readings that you can use in scripts. I make a point of leafing through the function reference every six or eight weeks, even if I'm not looking for anything in particular.*

PHP Within MobileHelper

MobileHelper uses PHP under the hood to provide all its content. At this point, you could dig in and look at the finished scripts, or look at just a single script to see how things work.

In this section, I do the latter, looking at the wml.php script that Mobile-Helper uses to build most of its content. This file shows a number of important concepts, including complex data structures built from associative arrays. At the same time, it's a relatively small script, and its single purpose (defining functions to build WML decks) makes it easy to grasp. It's also probably the most immediately useful to you as you learn PHP for WML because you can quickly use it in your own scripts to build WML decks for your own content.

Generating WML with PHP

There are several ways you can generate WML with PHP, but they all boil down to two approaches: use a function like echo to spit out the WML content, or write a bunch of functions to represent a WML deck, one of which uses echo to spit out the WML content. If you're pedantic, these may sound the same, but there's a subtle difference.

When you use echo to generate your WML from many places within your scripts, you have to go back over all of your scripts to find a mistake or make a change. With a small site, especially your first, this doesn't sound so bad. By the time you've designed three or four sites, however, browsing through all your scripts to find the one that forgot to send that missing `</card>` tag can be a royal pain.

By moving all the WML generation into a single script, called a *module*, you don't have to do that. A well-designed module takes care of managing the underlying WML tags, freeing you to build content using its functions. This is known as *abstraction*, replacing a more complex (or cumbersome) concept with a simpler one.

You could simply write a function `WMLEcho` that uses `echo` to emit a tag and its contents. Such a function might take a tag, content, and attributes, and echo the resulting WML. Such a function would be simpler than hand-building the WML because you'd no longer have to make the effort to ensure all of your open and close tags matched.

This approach is better because it helps you prevent one kind of error. Similarly, a more sophisticated WML module might ensure that the `<card>` tag surrounds all `<p>` tags, the `<wml>` tag surrounds all `<card>` tags surrounded by a deck's `<wml>` tag, and so forth. Of course, you can take this to an extreme, where the contents of every tag are judiciously checked to ensure that no tags contain content with tags that aren't allowed (such as text outside of paragraphs).

The wml.php module takes the middle ground, ensuring containment of major tags like cards and paragraphs, but does not ensure that tags contain only valid content. Table 3-4 shows the functions I wrote for wml.php.

Table 3-4. Functions defined by "wml.php".

FUNCTION	ARGUMENTS	PURPOSE
WMLNewDeck	*none*	Creates a hash representing an empty deck.
WMLDeckAsString	$deck	Converts the hash $deck to a string with WML
WMLEchoDeck	$deck	Outputs the hash $deck as a WML deck to the client
WMLSetAccess	$deck, $domain, $path	Sets the `<access/>` tag for the deck in $deck to the specified path and domain
WMLAddMeta	$deck, $name, $content	Adds a `<meta/>` with name $name and content $content to $deck
WMLAddHTTPEquiv	$deck, $name, $content	Adds a `<meta/>` HTTP header with name $name and content $content to $deck
WMLAddCard	$deck, $card	Adds the hash in $card as a card to $deck

Table 3-4. Functions defined by "wml.php". (Continued)

FUNCTION	ARGUMENTS	PURPOSE
WMLNewCard	$title, $id, $ontimer, $onenterforward, $onenterbackward	Creates a new hash containing a card with the given attributes
WMLAddTemplate	$deck, $template	Adds the hash in $template as the template for $deck
WMLNewTemplate	$ontimer, $onenterforward, $onenterbackward	Creates a new hash containing a template with the given attributes
WMLCardAsString	$card	Returns a string with the WML representation of the card.
WMLSetVar	$name, $value	Returns a string with the WML to set the variable $name equal to $value
WMLGo	$href, $content, $method, $sendreferer	Returns a string containing a <go> task with the given attributes
WMLPrev	$content	Returns a string containing a <prev> task with the given content
WMLNoop		Returns a string containing a <noop/> tag.
WMLAddEvent	$card, $type, $content	Adds the event $type with the task $content to $card
WMLAddTimer	$card, $name, $value	Creates a timer named $name with duration $value for $card
WMLAddDo	$card, $type, $content, $label, $name	Adds a <do> binding of $type with $label and task $content to $card
WMLAddParagraph	$card, $para	Adds the hash in $para as a paragraph to $card
WMLNewParagraph	$content, $align, $mode	Creates a new hash representing a paragraph containing $content with $align and $mode attributes
WMLParagraphAsString	$para	Returns a string with the WML representation of the paragraph

Table 3-4. Functions defined by "wml.php". (Continued)

FUNCTION	ARGUMENTS	PURPOSE
WMLAddText	$para, $text	Adds $text to the end of $para's current contents
WMLAddBreak	$para	Adds a tag at the end of $para's current contents
WMLBreak		Returns the string " ", the WML break tag
WMLTagAsString	$tag, $content, $attr	Creates a string containing the WML $tag with attributes enumerated in $attr and $content

This module uses associative arrays to represent decks, cards, and paragraphs, and strings to contain the snippets of WML that make up an individual task, tag, or content within a paragraph. By using associative arrays instead of strings, the data structures are both flexible and legible. A list of attributes is a list, not a string that needs to be edited before adding or removing entries. Although the implementation I show here is simple (you can't easily change attributes of a tag after you create the tag, for example), by using associative arrays it's easy for you to add this capability if you like. Moreover, this module is by no means complete—one of the things you will want to do is add support for tables.

Before I delve into the implementation, let's look at how you'd create a sample deck. Listing 3-22 repeats Listing 3-5, using wml.php to create a simple deck.

```php
01: <?php
02: require "wml.php";
03:
04: header( "Content-type: text/vnd.wap.wml" );
05:
06: // Create a deck…
07: $deck = WMLNewDeck();
08:
09: // Home Card…
10: $card = WMLNewCard( "Hello world!" );
11: $para = WMLNewParagraph( "Hello world!" );
12: WMLAddParagraph( $card, $para );
13: WMLAddCard( $deck, $card );
14:
15: WMLEchoDeck( $deck );
16: ?>
```

Listing 3-22. Using wml.php

Line 2 brings in the whole of the wml.php module, giving this file access to all the functions and variables it defines. Line 4 sends the HTTP MIME header for WML. I spent some time debating whether the wml.php functions or the caller should do this; what settled the issue for me was ease of debugging. By having the caller set the MIME header, you can view content generated by the module using any browser, making it easier to eyeball the generated WML during script development. Then, when you're ready, you can turn to a WML SDK for final polishing. In many cases, these SDKs are a bit more cumbersome than existing Web browsers, making debugging a little easier.

Line 7 creates the deck this script will output and stores it in $deck. This deck is an associative array, although its contents are not of interest to users of wml.php because the module provides all the functions necessary to manipulate the contents of the array. Similarly, lines 10 and 11 use WMLNewCard and WMLNewParagraph respectively to create associative arrays to represent an empty card and paragraph containing the string "Hello World!". (You'll see the elements of these arrays shortly.)

Line 12 uses the function WMLAddParagraph to add the paragraph to the card created on line 10, whereas line 13 uses the function WMLAddCard to add the card with the single paragraph to the deck. Together, these two lines stitch together the elements of the deck the script creates. Then, the script sends the deck itself to the client using WMLEchoDeck on line 15.

Data Structures: The Building Blocks

The wml.php module keeps WML content as an aggregate of strings containing bits of WML and arrays that link these bits together and represent other WML tags. Together, these are called *data structures* because they combine the simple data types in PHP, such as arrays and strings, to form mechanisms that are more complicated to store program data.

The simplest of these data structures is a string, containing a single WML tag. While you can write one and pass it to many of the module's functions, it's safer to create such a string using the function WMLTagAsString, shown in Listing 3-23.

```
01: /*******************************************************
02:  * FUNCTION: WMLTagAsString
03:  *
04:  * DESCRIPTION: Generates the WML for a given tag, content
05:  *  and attributes.
06:  *
07:  * RETURNED: String with WML!
08:  *******************************************************/
09: function WMLTagAsString(
10:   $tag, // (in) tag
11:   $content = "", // (in) content of the tag
12:   $attr = array()  // (in) attributes of the tag
```

```
13: )
14: {
15:
16: // Open the tag.
17:
18:    $result = "<" . $tag;
19:
20: // Handle the attributes, if any.
21:
22:    for ( reset( $attr );
23:      $key = key( $attr );
24:      next( $attr ) )
25:    {
26:      $value = $attr[ $key ];
27:      if ( $value )
28:        $result .=  " $key=\"$value\"";
29:
30:    }
31:
32: // Handle the contents, if any
33:
34:    if ( $content )
35:    {
36:      $result .= ">\n$content";
37:    }
38:
39: // Close the tag.
40: If there were no contents, it's an empty tag.
41:
42:    if ( $content )
43:    {
44:      $result .= "</$tag>";
45:    }
46:    else
47:    {
48:      $result .= "/>";
49:    }
50:
51: // Return the results
52:
53:    return $result;
54: }
55: ?>
```

Listing 3-23. The WMLTagAsString function

This function is straightforward, but because some of the things like differentiating between tags and empty tags are tricky, let's take it one line at a time. Furthermore, let's consider what happens when I call `WMLTagAsString` with the arguments `$tag` equal to `"p"`, `$content` equal to `"Hello world!"` and `$attr` equal to `array( "align" => "center" )`. This generates the two lines of WML shown in Listing 3-24.

```
01: <p align="center">
02: Hello world!</p>
```

Listing 3-24. A simple paragraph made using the `WMLTagAsString` *function*

As with all of the other functions I write, this function has a comment banner on lines 2–8 describing the function and what it returns. If you're working in a corporate setting, it helps to standardize these banners so that everybody on your team provides the same information. To save time, I put a copy of an empty banner like this in a separate file so I can cut and paste it into whatever file I'm working on. Taking the time to type the banner may add a few seconds to the time it takes to write a function, but given the hundreds of times I will scroll through the file looking for a particular function, it ultimately saves me time.

> **TIP** *Intrepid developers using editors such as Emacs can use a macro to prompt you for the various parts of a banner, and then type out the banner itself for you. Macros like this can save a great deal of time and ensure conformity across multiple functions in different files. Not only could your macro spell out the comment banner, but it could write the entire function declaration and braces as well.*

Lines 9 through 13 define the function `WMLTagAsString`. This function has one required and two optional arguments. The first argument, `$tag`, contains the tag to be created. The second argument, `$content`, contains the content for the tag, which may be an empty string for an empty tag. The third argument, `$attr`, is an associative array whose keys are the names of WML attributes and whose values are the values of the WML attributes for the tag. The second and third arguments default to an empty string and an empty array, respectively, so that if you don't name them when you call the function, they'll have default values.

> **NOTE** *When you call a function that specifies default values for its arguments, PHP uses the defaults in order. For example, when calling* WMLTagAsString, *PHP can't use the default value for* $attr *unless you give a value (or use the default) for* $content *as well.*

Given my hypothetical arguments, $tag is equal to "p", $content is equal to "Hello world!" and $attr is equal to array("align" => "center"). None of the defaults are used. If, on the other hand, I'd not specified a value for $attr, writing instead WMLTagAsString("p", "Hello world!"), PHP would set $attr equal to an empty array, that is, one with no keys and no values.

Because WMLTagAsString converts its arguments to a string containing WML, the first line of the function (line 18) creates a new string called $result, setting its value to the open tag mark < and the name of the tag. In this case, $result is set to the string "<p".

Next, I need to collect the tag's attributes from $attr and format them as pairs within the tag being built in $result. I use the for loop on lines 22–30 to do this. You can see that if the array $attr is empty, $key returns false, and the loop never executes. However, in this case, I have one attribute, so $key is set to the string "align".

Then, the function gets the value from $attr corresponding to the value of $key; in this case, this will happen once, and $value is set to "center". If $value is set—that is, if it's a non-empty string—the script appends the attribute name and value, together with = and quotes around the value to $result on line 28. The string I append to $result has a preceding space so that the tag's name and attributes are each separated by a single space. $result now contains the string "<p align="center", and the loop exits.

The script now needs to look at the contents of the tag in $content to determine if the tag is empty, or if it needs to close the tag and place the contents of the tag before creating a matching closing tag. The if statement on line 34 does just this, adding the closing > and a trailing newline along with the tag's content, if necessary. The result $result now contains everything except the closing </p> tag.

It's now time for the function to close the tag. If $content contained anything, the script must create a closing tag. On the other hand, if $content is empty, the script would instead need no closing tag, but would need to close the tag itself with the two characters />. This is the responsibility of the last if statement, on lines 42–49. Here, if $content contained anything, the script constructs a closing tag and appends it to $result. If not, the script appends the trailing /> characters to $result.

Only one task remains—returning the constructed string to the caller. Line 53 uses return to accomplish this.

Many of the functions in wml.php make use of `WMLTagAsString` to create WML as string snippets. Callers build formatted text and tags with `WMLTagAsString`, and other functions use `WMLTagAsString` to build the tags before placing the tags in their internal data structures. For example, let's look at the data structure for a paragraph, created by `WMLNewParagraph`.

```
01: /*******************************************************
02:  * FUNCTION: WMLNewParagraph
03:  *
04:  * DESCRIPTION: Creates an paragraph structure.
05:  *
06:  * RETURNED: Hash containing  paragraph
07:  *******************************************************/
08: function WMLNewParagraph(
09:   $content = "", // (in) what goes in the paragraph
10:   $align = "left", // (in) paragraph aligment.
11:   $mode = "wrap" // (in) whether or not to wrap
12: )
13: {
14:
15: // Minimize bandwidth consumed by removing browser defaults
16:
17:   if ( $align == "left" )
18:     unset( $align );
19:   if ( $mode == "wrap" )
20:     unset( $mode );
21:
22:   return array( "align" => $align, "mode" => $mode,
23:     "_para" => $content );
24: }
```

Listing 3-25. The WMLNewParagraph function

I chose to use an associative array to represent a paragraph, with slots for each of the paragraph's attributes and content, such as the text and <onevent> tags it bears. In `WMLNewParagraph`, the script creates a hash with the slots "`align`", `mode`, and `_para`. I chose to name the content slot with a preceding underscore so that I could easily differentiate between the slots that held WML attributes and those that held WML content.

`WMLNewParagraph` uses a bit of skullduggery to keep the resulting WML small. If the values it gets from its caller are the default values set forth in the WML specifications, it replaces them with empty values. That way, when the paragraph is later converted to text, the WML won't contain a lot of needless attributes like align="left". The function does this with the `if` statements on lines 17–20.

Assembling a Card

I use an associative array to represent a card, too, as you can see from WMLNewCard in Listing 3-26. A card has several slots, some for attributes and some for WML content. As with the paragraph, I use a leading _ character in the key's name to indicate which array slots will contain attributes and which contain WML content. Some array slots, like the slots that hold the paragraphs on the card, are actually arrays as well. By choosing an array for these slots, the script can perform complex manipulations if need be. Although they don't at present, it would be easy to add functions that enable you to change a particular card's event tag, or remove a timer once set.

```
01: /*****************************************************
02:  * FUNCTION: WMLNewCard
03:  *
04:  * DESCRIPTION: Creates an empty card
05:  *
06:  * RETURNED: Returns an empty card hash.
07:  *****************************************************/
08: function WMLNewCard(
09:    $title = "", // (in) Card title
10:    $id = "", // (in) Card ID
11:    $ontimer = "", // (in) ontimer attribute
12:    $onenterforward = "", // (in) onenterforward
13:    $onenterbackward = "" // (in) onenterbackward
14: )
15: {
16:    $card = array(
17:      "title" => $title,
18:      "id" => $id,
19:      "ontimer" => $ontimer,
20:      "onenterforward" => $onenterforward,
21:      "onenterbackward" => $onenterbackward,
22:      "_para" => array(),
23:      "_timer" => "",
24:      "_onevent" => array(),
25:      "_do" => array()
26:    );
27:
28:    return $card;
29: }
```

Listing 3-26. The WMLNewCard function

WMLNewCard specifies default values for all of the card's attributes because more often than not (despite my previous examples) content cards won't have many attributes. With these defaults in hand, WMLNewCard creates a new associative array, with slots for each of these attributes and slots for content such as paragraphs, the timer, events, and <do> tags.

To see how a card hash stores this information, let's look at two more functions, WMLAddTimer and WMLAddDo, shown together in Listing 3-27.

```
01: /*******************************************************
02:  * FUNCTION: WMLAddTimer
03:  *
04:  * DESCRIPTION: Creates a timer tag and adds it to
05:  * the card.
06:  *
07:  * RETURNED: Updated card.
08:  *******************************************************/
09: function WMLAddTimer(
10:    &$card, // (in/out) Card to accept timer
11:    $name, // (in) Timer name
12:    $value // (in) timer duration in demiseconds
13: )
14: {
15: // Only one timer per card, so just
16: // replace any existing timer.
17:
18:    $card[ "_timer" ] = WMLTagAsString( "timer", "",
19:      array( "name" => $name, "value" => $value )
20:    );
21:
22:    return $card;
23: }
24:
25: /*******************************************************
26:  * FUNCTION: WMLAddDo
27:  *
28:  * DESCRIPTION: Adds do binding to the provided card.
29:  *
30:  * RETURNED: Updated card.
31:  *******************************************************/
32: function WMLAddDo(
33:    &$card, // (in/out) what
34:    $type, // (in) event type
35:    $content, // (in) what task to bind to this of element
36:    $label="", // (in) label for the element
37:    $name="" // (in) name for the element
```

```
38: )
39: {
40:   array_push( $card[ "_do" ],
41:     WMLTagAsString( "do", $content,
42:       array(
43:         "type" => $type,
44:         "label" => $label,
45:         "name" => $name )
46:   ) );
47:
48:   return $card;
49: }
```

Listing 3-27. The WMLAddTimer *and* WMLAddDo *functions*

As you'll recall, a card can have no more than one timer. WMLAddTimer calls WMLTagAsString to build a timer with the specified name and value, and tucks it aside in the card's "_timer" slot, overwriting any previous timer set for the card. WMLAddTimer returns the updated card in two ways, using return on line 22 and by modifying the initial value in $card on line 10.

Remember the reference operator & I mentioned in the section "Variables"? In the WMLAddTimer and WMLAddDo functions, I use & to force PHP to pass the actual value of the card array in $card, rather than a copy of that array. Thus, any changes the script makes to $card within these functions change the actual value of $card outside the function itself. This is an example of *pass-by-reference*: the thing being passed points to the value for the function, rather than being a copy of the value itself.

WMLAddDo does the same thing, modifying the card it's given. However, as you can imagine, it changes the card's "_do" slot, pushing a new <do> tag constructed using the function's other arguments and WMLTagAsString. The function WMLAddParagraph operates similarly, pushing a paragraph hash on to the end of the array in the card's "_para" slot.

Before I show you how the module represents decks, let's look quickly at how it handles card templates. The <template> tag is like a simplified <card> tag, stating the elements that are common to all <card> tags for this deck. It has a limited number of attributes and content and no attributes or content that are not in the card tag itself. Thus, because I've already gone to the trouble of writing functions to handle cards, it would be nice if I could re-use that work when handling the <template> tag as well.

Of course, I could simply cut –and paste a bunch of functions such as WMLNewCard, WMLAddCard, and WMLAddEvent and rename them to functions like WMLNewTemplate, WMLAddTemplate, and WMLAddEventTemplate, but this has its drawbacks. First, it's ugly and time-consuming. More importantly, it's error-prone. Not only could I make mistakes copying and editing each of these functions, but if I have to change the logic that handles a card, I'll probably have to do it for a template as well. Because the code is in two different places, it's more likely I'll make a mistake, perhaps one I won't find until long after working on the code.

Instead, I use a card as a template, but give that card an extra slot so that the script knows it's a template when it's time to output the deck. The WMLNewTemplate function in Listing 3-28 shows how I do this.

```
01: /*******************************************************
02:  * FUNCTION: WMLNewTemplate
03:  *
04:  * DESCRIPTION: Creates an empty template
05:  *
06:  * RETURNED: Returns an empty template card hash
07:  *******************************************************/
08: function WMLNewTemplate(
09:   $ontimer = "", // (in) ontimer attribute
10:   $onenterforward = "", // (in) onenterforward attribute
11:   $onenterbackward = "" // (in) onenterbackward attribute
12: )
13: {
14:
15: // A template's an ordinary card with a few restrictions.
16:
17:   $template = WMLNewCard( "", "",
18:     $ontimer, $onenterfoward, $onenterbackward );
19:   $template[ "_template" ] = 1;
20:
21:   return $template;
22: }
```

Listing 3-28. The WMLNewTemplate *function*

On lines 17–18, I use the WMLNewCard to create a card with the template's attributes. On line 19, I set the slot "_template" in the template card to 1. Later, as you'll see when I discuss WMLDeckAsString, I use this flag to create the WML for a template, rather than a card, when examining this card.

Creating the Deck

Like cards and paragraphs, the deck is an associative array. It's somewhat special though because while most cards have a few paragraphs and decks may have more than one card, it's highly unlikely that any script will want to create more than one deck.

When I first set out to write wml.php, the fact that any script is unlikely to create more than one deck tempted me to make the deck a global variable containing an associative array within wml.php. Doing so would make writing some functions easier because you wouldn't need to pass around the deck to the functions that manage the deck itself, such as `WMLAddCard` and `WMLAddTemplate`.

After some consideration, I decided not to, for two reasons: quality and extensibility. If I stored the deck globally, there'd be no way for me to be sure that a calling script wouldn't use the same name somewhere. Of course, I could name it something obscure, like `_WMLDeckOfCards` or `CartesAJouer`, if I knew nobody speaking French would use my scripts. Obscurity isn't security, however, and this still might cause problems. It was better to let the caller manage the deck variable, and be done with it. On the topic of extensibility, letting the caller handle the array makes it easier to extend the module as well. If I need more space to store things that pertain to the deck, I can simply stick them in the array, rather than adding new global variables (which may break callers' scripts). Consequently, letting the caller keep the deck array on behalf of the WML functions seems the best solution.

> **NOTE**   *Remember that global variables in PHP exist only across a given Web client's request. Thus, I would not have had any problems if I'd chosen to use a global to hold the deck, and more than one script was presently running to create decks for different clients, because each script would get its own copy of the variable holding the deck. This is a fundamental difference between Web scripting and application development. You can think of a specific Web script running on behalf of a Web client as an application unto itself; it does not share memory or variables with other copies of the same script running on behalf of other clients.*

The empty WML deck array is created by the `WMLNewDeck` function in Listing 3-29. As `WMLNewCard` and `WMLNewParagraph` before it, it uses the `array` statement to initialize an empty associative array.

```
01: /******************************************************
02:  * FUNCTION: WMLNewDeck
03:  *
04:  * DESCRIPTION: Creates a new (empty) deck hash.
05:  *
06:  * RETURNED: The hash representing the deck.
07:  ******************************************************/
```

```
08: function WMLNewDeck()
09: {
10:    $result = array(
11:       "access" => array(),
12:       "meta" => array(),
13:       "template" => "",
14:       "card" => array()
15:    );
16:
17:    return $result;
18: }
```

Listing 3-29. The WMLNewDeck function

The resulting array has slots to hold a deck's <access> and <meta> information as well as a <template> and list of cards. These slots are managed by functions like WMLSetAccess and WMLAddMeta, which stuff name-value pairs for the <access/> and <meta/> tags in the "access" and "meta" slots respectively. Because these operate similarly to functions such as WMLAddTimer and WMLAddDo, I won't take up space showing them here.

Converting the Deck to WML

Because the deck and its cards are stored as associative arrays, I need functions to convert each of these to strings. This is the responsibility of the functions WMLParagraphAsString, WMLCardAsString, and WMLDeckAsString, the first of which is shown in Listing 3-30. Their operation is straightforward, but not necessarily simple.

```
01: /*******************************************************
02:  * FUNCTION: WMLDeckAsString
03:  *
04:  * DESCRIPTION: Converts deck given to a string
05:  *
06:  * RETURNED: String containing WML for indicated deck
07:  *******************************************************/
08: function WMLDeckAsString(
09:    $deck // (in) deck to convert to string
10: )
11: {
12:    $result = "<?xml version=\"1.0\"?>\n" .
13:          "<!DOCTYPE wml PUBLIC " .
14:    "\"-//WAPFORUM//DTD WML 1.1//EN\" " .
```

```
15:     "\"http://www.wapforum.org/DTD/wml_1.1.xml\">\n";
16:
17: // Opening WML tag
18:
19:     $result .= "<wml>\n";
20:
21: // WML Heading. We only output this if there's
22: // an access or meta
23:
24:     if ( count( $deck[ "access" ] ) ||
25:       count( $deck[ "meta" ] ) )
26:     {
27:
28:       $result .= "  <head>\n";
29:
30: // <access>
31:
32:       if ( count( $deck[ "access" ] ) )
33:       {
34:
35:         $result .= "    " . WMLTagAsString( "access", "",
36:           $deck[ "access" ] ) . "\n";
37:       }
38:
39: // <meta>
40:
41:       if ( count ( $deck[ "meta" ] ) )
42:       {
43:         for ( $i = 0; $i < count( $deck[ "meta" ] ); $i++ )
44:         {
45:           $result .= "    " . WMLTagAsString( "meta", "",
46:             $deck[ "meta" ][ $i ] ) . "\n";
47:         }
48:       }
49:
50: // Close heading
51:
52:       $result .= "  </head>\n";
53:     }
54:
55: // Template
56:
57:     if ( $deck[ "template" ] )
58:       $result .= WMLCardAsString( $deck[ "template" ] )
```

```
59:        . "\n";
60:
61: // Cards: Loop across all cards, one at a time.
62:
63:    for ( $i=0; $i < count( $deck[ "card" ] ); $i++ )
64:    {
65:      $result .= WMLCardAsString( $deck[ "card" ][ $i ] )
66:      . "\n";
67:    }
68:
69: // Closing WML tag
70:
71:    $result .= "</wml>\n";
72:
73:    return $result;
74: }
```

Listing 3-30. The WMLDeckAsString *function*

If you look at their operation from the point of view of building a deck, WMLDeckAsString walks across each of its slots, building a WML heading and body as needed based on the contents of its slots. In turn, as it creates the body, it uses WMLCardAsString to create the template and cards. WMLCardAsString looks at each of its slots, generating WML by calling WMLTagAsString and WMLParagraphAsString as needed. At the lowest level, an individual tag is built up using WMLTagAsString; WMLParagraphAsString does this when creating the WML for each paragraph. Like WMLTagAsString, these functions use string concatenation for the lion's share of the work.

Looking at Listing 3-30, on line 12 WMLDeckAsString begins by storing the XML preamble for the deck in the string $result. On line 19, the function continues by appending an opening <wml> tag to start the deck.

Next, the function determines whether it needs to create a WML heading. If the deck contains any of the heading tags (<access/> or <meta/>), it needs to create both a heading using the WML <head> tag and the tags included in the deck. The script makes this determination on lines 24 and 25; if either the "access" or the "meta" slots of the deck contain data, the script converts them to tags and adds them to the $result string after surrounding them with a <head> tag. Note that while the "access" slot is simple because a deck can have only one <access/> tag, the "meta" slot requires a loop because decks can have more than one <meta/> tag. I chose a simple counting loop, rather than using the reset, key, and next statements because it's more intuitive for a simple list like that stored in the deck's "meta" slot.

NOTE   *I could have just as easily used* foreach *for this loop. I decided not to, however, because* foreach *copies the array before iterating over each element. Because I don't need a copy of the array, the loop I use is slightly more efficient than one written with* foreach.

After the WML heading is created (lines 26–53), the script appends the template card's contents to the deck (if one exists) on lines 57–59. Because the scripts treat a template card and regular cards the same way, WMLCardAsString needs to decide whether the card is a template or regular card. (More about that in a moment.) Continuing onward (lines 63–67), the function loops through all cards in the deck's "card" slot, converting each to a string with WMLCardAsString and appending the string to the $result array.

Finally, the function appends a closing </wml> tag and returns the string to the caller on lines 69–73.

Listing 3-31 shows WMLCardAsString, which operates similarly, walking through each of its slots in turn and using their content to build up a string representation in WML of the card.

```
01: /*****************************************************
02:  * FUNCTION: WMLCardAsString
03:  *
04:  * DESCRIPTION: Converts a card to its WML representation
05:  *
06:  * RETURNED: String containing WML for card
07:  *****************************************************/
08: function WMLCardAsString(
09:   $card // (in) card to convert
10: )
11: {
12:   $content = "";
13:
14: // Generalization: handle both cards and templates here.
15:
16:   if ( $card[ "_template" ] )
17:   {
18:     $tag = "template";
19:   }
20:   else
21:   {
22:     $tag = "card";
23:   }
24:
```

```
25: // Build content for card from internal representation
26:
27: // do tags
28:
29:    for ( $i = 0; $i < count( $card[ "_do" ] ); $i++ )
30:    {
31:      $content .= $card[ "_do" ][ $i ] . "\n";
32:    }
33:
34: // timer
35:    if ( $card["_timer"] )
36:      $content .= $card["_timer"] . "\n";
37:
38: // Content
39:
40:    for ( $i = 0; $i < count( $card[ "_para" ] ); $i++ )
41:    {
42:      $content .= $card[ "_para" ][ $i ] . "\n";
43:    }
44:
45: // onevent tags
46:
47:    for ( $i = 0; $i < count( $card[ "_onevent" ] ); $i++ )
48:    {
49:      $content .= $card[ "_onevent" ][ $i ] . "\n";
50:    }
51:
52:
53: // Produce the card
54:
55:    $str = WMLTagAsString( $tag, $content, array(
56:      "title" => $card[ "title" ],
57:      "id" => $card[ "id" ],
58:      "ontimer" => $card[ "ontimer" ],
59:      "onenterforward" => $card[ "onenterforward" ],
60:      "onenterbackward" => $card[ "onenterbackward" ]
61:    ) );
62:
63:    return $str;
64: }
```

Listing 3-31. The WMLCardAsString *function*

Unlike the creation of a deck, WMLCardAsString uses the WMLTagAsString function to convert a block of content—the card's content—to a single <card> tag in a string. This way, WMLCardAsString doesn't have to know how to handle a WML tag's attributes.

After initializing the variable $content to an empty string[3] WMLCardAsString begins on line 16 by ascertaining whether the card is a true card or a template by checking for a "_template" slot. If the card is really a template, then the function should build up the WML using the template tag; otherwise it should use the card tag (lines 16–23).

Next, on lines 29–32 the function loops through the <do> tags for the card, appending each one to the card's content. These <do> tags are stored as WML snippets in the card's "do" slot, as appended by WMLAddDo, which you saw previously. Similarly, the function adds the <timer/> tag if the card had one stored in its "timer" slot (lines 34–36).

After handling the <do> and <timer/> tags, the function continues by assembling each of the paragraphs—stored as text by WMLAddParagraph–and the <onevent> tags for the card. Again I use for loops to iterate over all of the tags in the arrays stored in the "_para" and "onevent" slots for these cards (lines 38–50).

Finally, the function has built all of the content for the <card> tag, and it uses this content in conjunction with the card's attributes, such as the "title" and "id" slots, to build the actual string representation using WMLTagAsString.

A paragraph's content is handled similarly, except that the card stores each paragraph as a string containing WML from the get-go in the "_para" slot of the card hash. When you add a paragraph to a card using WMLAddParagraph, it calls WMLParagraphAsString, pushing its result on to the end of the array in the "_para" slot. WMLParagraphAsString, shown in Listing 3-32, is simple: it's just a wrapper around WMLTagAsString, specifying the <p> tag and paragraph attributes.

```
01: /*******************************************************
02:  * FUNCTION: WMLParagraphAsString
03:  *
04:  * DESCRIPTION: Converts paragraph structure to WML String
05:  *
06:  * RETURNED: String containing WMl
07:  *******************************************************/
08: function WMLParagraphAsString(
09:   $para // (in) paragraph to convert
10: )
11: {
```

---

3. This is stylistically good but syntactically unnecessary because PHP automatically sets new variables to an empty value.

```
12:    return WMLTagAsString( "p", $para[ "_para" ], array(
13:      "align" => $para[ "align" ],
14:      "mode" => $para[ "mode" ] )
15:    );
16: }
```

Listing 3-32. The WMLParagraphAsString *function*

If WMLAddParagraph only calls WMLParagraphAsString, and all WMLParagraphString does is call WMLTagAsString, why bother making WMLAddParagraph a separate function? As you might guess, the answer is simplicity. It's easier to tell what a function named WMLParagraphAsString does than a specific call to WMLTagAsString with the paragraph tag buried as one of its arguments. Moreover, there are three data structures used by wml.php, one each for the deck, card, and paragraph structures. Writing one conversion function for each of these leaves the code clearer because the reader won't wonder how and when a paragraph hash is converted to a string containing WML.

On the CD-ROM

You will find the source and Windows binary for the PHP interpreter on the CD-ROM in the directory PHP. In addition, a version (almost certainly not the current version) of the Apache Web server is in the directory Apache. If you're going to use PHP or the Apache server for any length of time, you should take a minute and go to their respective Web sites and download the latest version. It's almost certainly newer than what you'll find on the CD-ROM.

As always, you can find all the listings from this chapter in the chapter directory—chap03—on the CD-ROM. The file wml.php is in the chap03 directory of the CD-ROM. You can use it in your own PHP-based WML development, or simply look it over as you write your own PHP scripts.

Food for Thought

- What happens if your PHP script generates WML and you leave out the header function? What if you put the header function after your output? Try both of these using both a WML browser and your Web browser.

- Write a set of PHP scripts that use PHP's type conversion to convert strings to numbers and vice versa. How does PHP interpret a string as a number?

- Mathematicians define the *factorial* function as $x! = x\,(x\text{-}1) \times (x\text{-}2) \times \ldots \times 1$. Explore the differences between the `for`, `while`, and `do-while` statements by writing a loop that evaluates the factorial function with each of these statements. Which is easiest for you to write? To debug? To read? Which is the hardest?

- The wml.php module has only limited error checking. For example, in `WMLAddParagraph`, the function does not check to be sure that the hash passed in `$para` is a hash representing a paragraph, or that it's even a hash. While adequate for our purposes, this style lacks *defensive coding*, in that the functions don't protect against many kinds of errors. How would you extend the wml.php module so that each function checks the type of its arguments.

- How would you extend the wml.php module to provide functions for tables? Hint: Would arrays or multidimensional arrays help?

#### CHAPTER 4

WMLScript

ON THE WEB, client-side scripting languages such as JavaScript play an important role. Many sites use JavaScript for input validation, animation, custom formatting, and other dynamic behavior, all without interacting with the server. On the Wireless Web, client-side scripting becomes even more important. Because of the high latency of wireless networks, your content needs to access the server as little as possible. WMLScript, the client-side Wireless Web scripting language, enables you to build dynamic content that executes solely on the client.

In this chapter, you will learn how to write WMLScript scripts for your Wireless Web sites. You'll learn what client-side scripting is and why it's important for your Wireless Web content, while examining the limitations inherent in today's implementation of WMLScript. This chapter also introduces to you a calculator written in WMLScript and shows how MobileHelper uses WMLScript to validate user input.

Client-Side Scripting

You're probably familiar—at least in principle—with client-side scripting because for many Web developers experience with client-side scripting predates experience with active-server scripting. Client-side scripting is an area owned by Web developers, and software developers, doing other server work, own server-side scripting.

With client-side scripting, you create scripts that are downloaded by the Web client and executed locally on the client device. The most familiar application of this is JavaScript, based on the ECMAScript standard. Languages such as Java are also popular for client-side scripting on the Web.

On the Web, client-side scripts are used for lots of things, including input validation, input completion, animation, and popup windows with tailored content. As with virtually all things wireless, the applications of client-side scripting aren't very broad because the factors that limit the Wireless Web constrain scripting, too. A device with a small screen and a paucity of memory simply cannot handle a complex scripting language.

As a result, WMLScript, the scripting language advanced by the WAP forum, entered the Web scene. WMLScript is designed to fit in the limited processing and memory capacity of wireless terminals while providing a modicum of functionality. With syntax and concepts similar to JavaScript, it's easy for Web developers to learn. It has flow control and loop statements, so you can write real programs using the language.

It's not as powerful as JavaScript, however. Notably, you can't directly manipulate browser content or interact with the browser except in limited ways such as telling it to load a URL when a script completes. Access to the screen is limited to drawing text-only dialogs and input prompts, and you probably won't use those, preferring instead WML decks with variables manipulated in WMLScript.

To make matters worse, WMLScript isn't available on all wireless clients. At the time of this book's writing, only two phones among the dozens of Wireless-Web-enabled phones in the United States support WMLScript. But the situation is better in Europe, where WAP adoption leads the United States; significantly more models of phones there support WMLScript. Of course, over time this will change as more phones domestically are sold with WMLScript. However, it's unlikely that consumers will replace a phone simply to upgrade their browser. Consequently, sites that require WMLScript won't be available to the largest possible audience for quite some time.

While this limits accessibility, it does not nullify WMLScript's utility. WMLScript shines in the key market of vertical applications, where a specific wireless application is sold to a client in conjunction with server and client hardware. In the vertical marketplace, software developers have more freedom to dictate hardware requirements and to assist their customers in choosing handsets with WMLScript support. Sales force automation and field service dispatch are just two areas where WMLScript can help build a winning wireless application.

Another key WMLScript market is in device-specific control. Some products have WMLScript functions in packages called *libraries* that you use to control specific hardware functions. Again, you have to be sure your customers can use the device, but often, the presence of these functions produces a market for additional software, such as device control or entertainment. For example, the Yospace Smart Phone Emulator Developer Edition has a WMLScript library that enables you to debug WML and WMLScript content on your desktop before you make it available to wireless clients.

Other applications of WMLScript can augment existing Wireless Web features, adding value for WMLScript-enabled clients without restricting access to those without WMLScript. You can use WMLScript to validate input on the client side, while leaving input validation in place on the back end for clients without WMLScript. Doing so catches errors made by all users, as quickly as possible, for those clients with WMLScript, while not handicapping those users without. Other sites, such as sites offering games or other entertainment, can use server-side scripts to provide the same functionality with lower performance or offer two tiers of service—one tier for users with WMLScript and the other for those without.

First Steps with WMLScript

Writing WMLScript is easy—fire up your favorite text editor and dig in. When you're ready, you can load your scripts using virtually any of the Wireless Web SDKs available (including the two on the CD-ROM accompanying this book) for testing. When you're ready, you move the scripts to your production Web server, and voila! you have client-side dynamic content.

Unfortunately, it's not quite *that* easy. Server configuration work must be done and if your content requires WMLScript, you need to use PHP or another mechanism to look at the HTTP `Accept` header to ensure that only clients supporting WMLScript get WMLScript content. Let's take a closer look.

Setting up the Server and Client

Server configuration is simple: just match your WMLScript suffix with the MIME type for WMLScript. By convention, most Web sites use the four-letter suffix .wmls to denote WMLScript files. Assuming you've configured your Web server as described in Chapters 2 and 3, this is as easy as adding the MIME type `text/vnd.wap.wmlscript` for whatever extension your WMLScript files use. For example, with Apache, you can just add the line `AddType text/vnd.wap.wmlscript .wmls` to the appropriate configuration file such as httpd.conf. Other Web servers probably have a similar configuration file or a GUI interface where you can add this information.

If you *don't* add the MIME type for your WMLScript files, different things can happen depending on the client. Most clients reject the WMLScript files because the gateway server doesn't recognize the plain text of WMLScript as something that it can compile into a WMLScript binary. A few clients will attempt to compile the text into WMLScript, but it's not wise to rely on that behavior, because many clients don't.

In general, you don't have to do anything to set up your client to accept WMLScript: either it will or it won't. Almost all of the SDK's and many of the PDA-based browsers support WMLScript, but as mentioned in the previous section, many wireless terminals do not. Consequently, you need to either ensure that only WMLScript-compatible terminals access your site or serve different content to those terminals that do and do not support WMLScript.

You can do this by using PHP to check the HTTP `Accept` header and serve content tailored to devices with and without WMLScript. Listing 4-1 shows `WMLClientHasWMLScript`, a simple function added to the wml.php module shown in Chapter 3 to determine whether or not the client can execute WMLScript.

```
01: <?php
02: /****************************************************
```

```
03:  * FUNCTION: WMLClientHasWMLScript
04:  *
05:  * DESCRIPTION: WMLClientHasWMLScript checks the
06:  * $HTTP_ACCEPT to see if the client accepts WMLScript.
07:  *
08:  * RETURNED: true if client accepts WMLScript
09:  ******************************************************/
10: function WMLClientHasWMLScript()
11: {
12:   global $HTTP_ACCEPT;
13:   return strstr( $HTTP_ACCEPT, "text/vnd.wap.wmlscript" );
14: }
15: ?>
```

Listing 4-1. The WMLClientHasWMLScript *function*

In Chapter 1, you learned that the HTTP Accept header contains a comma-delimited list of MIME types the client can accept. PHP automatically sets the reserved variable $HTTP_ACCEPT to the value of this header. The function WMLClientHasWMLScript simply checks this string for an occurrence of the WML-Script MIME type using the function strstr; if the client accepts WMLScript, this variable will contain the MIME type, and strstr returns true. (Actually, strstr returns the rest of the value of $HTTP_ACCEPT after the WMLScript MIME type, which is evaluated as true.)

Listing 4-2 shows a simple PHP script that uses this function at a site's opening page to accept or reject a client based on its support for WMLScript.

```
01: <?php
02: require "wml.php";
03:
04: if ( WMLClientHasWMLScript() )
05: {
06:   readfile("index.wml")
07: }
08: else
09: {
10:   readfile("no-wmlscript-error.wml");
11: }
12: ?>
```

Listing 4-2. Using WMLClientHasWMLScript

This function calls `WMLClientHasWMLScript`, and then uses the PHP function `readfile` to read one of two decks and send that deck to the client. If `WMLClientHasWML` returns true, the script sends the deck index.wml to the client. If the client doesn't support WMLScript, `WMLClientHasWML` returns false and the script returns the deck no-wmlscript-error to the client.

Listing 4-2 is a simple example of how to filter server responses based on the client type. In Chapter 9, you'll see more sophisticated ways of doing the same thing.

Saying Hello, World with WMLScript

In the previous two chapters, you were introduced to several ways to say "Hello world!" Listing 4-3 shows another way, using WMLScript, while Listing 4-4 shows a WML file that uses this WMLScript.

```
01: /*****************************************************
02:  * FUNCTION: HelloWorld
03:  *
04:  * DESCRIPTION: Presents a Hello World Dialog
05:  *
06:  *
07:  * RETURNED: nothing
08:  *****************************************************/
09: extern function HelloWorld()
10: {
11:     Dialogs.alert("Hello World!");
12: }
```

Listing 4-3. "Hello World" WMLScript

```
01: <?xml version="1.0"?>
02: <!DOCTYPE wml PUBLIC "-//WAPFORUM//DTD WML 1.1//EN"
03:   "http://www.wapforum.org/DTD/wml_1.1.xml">
04: <wml>
05:   <card title="Go to Hello World">
06:     <p>
07:       Press Accept to see Hello World in WMLScript.
08:     </p>
09:     <do type="accept" label="Accept">
10:       <go href="hello.wmls#HelloWorld()"/>
11:     </do>
12:   </card>
13: </wml>
```

Listing 4-4. WML Deck to invoke `HelloWorld` *WMLScript*

Listing 4-3 defines a single WMLScript function, named HelloWorld on lines 9–12. The function is defined by using the extern keyword, which means that it can be called from a WML deck. This script does one thing: call the function Dialogs.alert with the single argument "Hello World!" (line 11). In turn, this function clears the client's display, showing the message **Hello World!**.

Actually, the function HelloWorld calls the alert function, which is part of the Dialogs library. WMLScript supports the notion of a *library*, a bundle of code on the device that your scripts can invoke. The WAP Forum defines several standard libraries, including the Dialogs library that enables you to draw a simple dialog on the screen.

If used alone, the code in Listing 4-3 does nothing. In order to use the script, you need to call it from a WML deck. Listing 4-4 shows a WML deck that invokes the HelloWorld function. This deck binds a <go> task to the accept button that launches the WMLScript (line 10).

The syntax to call a WMLScript from WML is decidedly odd until you get used to it. To invoke a WMLScript, you use a navigation task such as <go> to navigate to the script's URL, followed by an anchor naming the function. The function's name *must* be followed by parentheses, informing the client that the URL is a WMLScript to execute.

> **CAUTION**   *Don't forget the parentheses in the script's URL! This is an easy thing to do and very challenging to find after the fact because the URL looks fine. If you forget the parentheses, many clients will download the script, not execute anything, and not give you an error message, so you won't know what's wrong.*

Once the WMLScript executes, the client returns to the card and deck that called the script, unless a specific WMLScript function call has told the client to do otherwise (such as navigating to a new deck).

A Simple Calculator with WMLScript

The example in Listing 4-3 and 4-4 was simple, but it really didn't do much. Let's look at a more complex application—a client-side calculator written using WMLScript and WML.[1] This calculator uses WMLScript to perform addition, subtraction, multiplication, division, exponentiation, square roots, and factorials using WMLScript. To

---

1. This example was initially presented in my book *Wireless Web Development*, which is also available from Apress. Even if you are familiar with it from that book, you may want to continue reading this section because I've added some new things of interest to you.

make things a little simpler (see the sidebar "What Is Reverse Polish Notation"), this calculator only accepts mathematical expressions in Reverse Polish Notation.

What Is Reverse Polish Notation?

Polish Notation is a formal logic system that enables mathematical expressions to be specified without parentheses by placing operations symbols before (prefix notation) or after (postfix notation) the operands. For example the expression

$(3 + 2) * 5$

could be expressed in postfix Polish notation as

$3\ 2 + 5\ *$

In the 1920s, the Polish mathematician Jan Lukasiewicz developed this notation system, which came to be known as Polish Notation in honor of its inventor. (Presumably, no one outside of Poland could reliably spell or pronounce his name!) Over time, postfix Polish notation became known as Reverse Polish Notation.

When Hewlett-Packard introduced the HP-35 calculator, competing calculators could provide only partial interpretation of algebraic order. Hewlett-Packard recognized that RPN would enable it to design a calculator meeting its cost constraints that could evaluate expressions without needing parentheses while respecting algebraic order of operations.

Today, RPN persists due to the wide user base of Hewlett-Packard computing products developed over the last thirty years. Those familiar with RPN tend to see it as the "natural" way to use a calculator, demonstrating that it is both faster and less error-prone than the traditional alternatives.

Figure 4-1 shows a screen shot of the calculator application in action. To use it, enter each of the two numbers, followed by the operation. The first time you enter an expression, your phone needs to fetch the WMLScript calc.wmls; after that it should be in your phone's cache, and you can continue to calculate without needing to use the network.

> **NOTE** *Depending on the phone's browser and amount of free memory, the script may or may not be cached between invocations of Listing 4-5. When writing your WMLScript applications, you should always bear in mind that you can't rely on a particular script being available in the cache because phones may not have enough room to cache the script.*

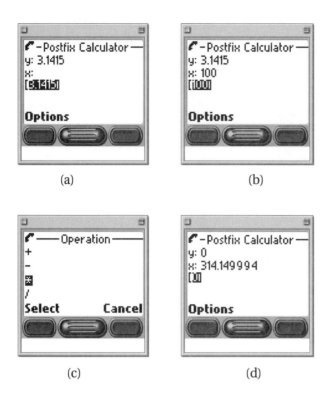

(a)   (b)

(c)   (d)

Figure 4-3. The calculator application

Listing 4-5 shows the WML deck displayed in Figure 4-1. The first card on lines 10–20 produces the display shown in Figure 4-1(a), and the second card on lines 21–31 produces the display shown in Figure 4-1(b). Once you enter both of the operands, the third card (lines 32–52) lists the operations, shown in Figure 4-1(c). These three cards are all basic input cards; the first two cards use a single `<input>` tag to obtain each of the operands (lines 14–35 and lines 25–26), and the third card uses a `<select>` list to present a list of operations.

```
01: <?xml version="1.0"?>
02: <!DOCTYPE wml PUBLIC "-//WAPFORUM//DTD WML 1.1//EN"
03:    "http://www.wapforum.org/DTD/wml_1.1.xml">
04: <wml>
05:   <template>
06:     <do type="help" label="Help">
07:       <go href="rpn.wml"/>
08:     </do>
09:   </template>
10:   <card id="y" title="Postfix Calculator">
```

```
11:      <p>
12:        <b>y: </b>$y<br/>
13:        <b>x: </b>$x<br/>
14:        <input name="y" type="text"
15:          value="0" emptyok="false"/><br/>
16:      </p>
17:      <do type="accept" label="Accept">
18:        <go href="#x"/>
19:      </do>
20:    </card>
21:    <card id="x" title="Postfix Calculator">
22:      <p>
23:        <b>y: </b>$y<br/>
24:        <b>x: </b>$x<br/>
25:        <input name="x" type="text"
26:          value="0" emptyok="false"/><br/>
27:      </p>
28:      <do type="accept" label="Accept">
29:        <go href="#op"/>
30:      </do>
31:    </card>
32:    <card id="op" title="Postfix Calculator">
33:      <p>
34:        <b>operation</b>
35:        <select  title="Operation" name="op">
36:          <option value="+" onpick="calc.wmls#calculate()">
37:            +</option>
38:          <option value="-" onpick="calc.wmls#calculate()">
39:            -</option>
40:          <option value="*" onpick="calc.wmls#calculate()">
41:            *</option>
42:          <option value="/" onpick="calc.wmls#calculate()">
43:            /</option>
44:          <option value="^" onpick="calc.wmls#calculate()">
45:            ^</option>
46:          <option value="!" onpick="calc.wmls#calculate()">
47:            !</option>
48:          <option value="v" onpick="calc.wmls#calculate()">
49:            Square Root</option>
50:        </select>
51:      </p>
52:  </card>
53: </wml>
```

Listing 4-5. The calc.wml deck

Once you select an operation, the <option> tags on the third card navigate to the calculation script, named calculate in the WMLScript file calc.wmls. This script performs your chosen operation and refreshes the browser display, showing the first card again with the result, as Figure 4-1(d) shows. Listing 4-6 shows the calculate function invoked by each of the <option> tags.

```
01: /********************************************************
02:  * FUNCTION: calculate
03:  *
04:  * DESCRIPTION: Given WML variables x, y, and op,
05:  * performs the operation given by op on x and y.
06:  * Returns the result in the WML variable result.
07:  *
08:  * RETURNED: nothing
09:  ********************************************************/
10: extern function calculate()
11: {
12:   var x, y, op, result;
13:
14: // Retrieve arguments from WAP Context
15:
16:   x = WMLBrowser.getVar( "x" );
17:   y = WMLBrowser.getVar( "y" );
18:   op = WMLBrowser.getVar( "op" );
19:
20: // Validate arguments
21:
22:   if ( x == invalid || y == invalid ||
23:        !Lang.isFloat(x) || !Lang.isFloat(y) )
24:   {
25:     Dialogs.alert("x and y must be numbers!");
26:
27: // Set better defaults for invalid registers
28:
29:     if ( x == invalid || !Lang.isFloat(x) )
30:     {
31:       WMLBrowser.setVar( "x", "0" );
32:     }
33:     if ( y == invalid || !Lang.isFloat(y) )
34:     {
35:       WMLBrowser.setVar( "y", "0" );
36:     }
37:     Lang.exit("");
38:   }
39:
```

```
40: // Convert registers to floating point numbers for our use
41:
42:   x = Lang.parseFloat( x );
43:   y = Lang.parseFloat( y );
44:
45: // Determine type of operation
46:
47:   if ( op == "+" )
48:   {
49:     result = y + x;
50:   }
51:   else if ( op == "-" )
52:   {
53:     result = y - x;
54:   }
55:   else if ( op == "*" )
56:   {
57:     result = y * x;
58:   }
59:   else if ( op == "/" )
60:   {
61:     result = y / x;
62:   }
63:   else if ( op == "^" )
64:   {
65:     result = Float.pow( y, x );
66:   }
67:   else if ( op == "v" )
68:   {
69:     result = Float.sqrt( x );
70:   }
71:   else if ( op == "!" )
72:   {
73:     result = _fact( x );
74:   }
75:   else
76:   {
77:     Dialogs.alert("An invalid operation was chosen!");
78:     WMLBrowser.setVar( "op", "+" );
79:     Lang.exit("");
80:   }
81:
82: // Clean up result for display
83:
```

```
84:   result = String.format( "%10f", result );
85:
86: // Set registers to resulting value for next calculation
87:
88:   WMLBrowser.setVar( "x", result );
89:
90: // don't mess with the y register for the
91: // ! and square root operators
92:
93:   if ( op != "v" && op != "^" )
94:   {
95:     WMLBrowser.setVar( "y", 0 );
96:   }
97:
98: // Return the browser to the first page for
99: // another calculation
100:
101:   WMLBrowser.go("#y");
102: }
```

Listing 4-6. The calculate function

This function gets the values of the user's input and performs the desired operation. At a high level, it obtains the values of each of the inputs and a string containing the name of the operation, determines which operation to perform in WMLScript, formats the result, and then gives the result values back to the WML Browser.

The function definition itself begins on line 10. This function, such as HelloWorld before it, is defined as an extern function, so that it can be called from the browser. (By comparison, the _fact function, discussed in the following section, is available only to the other functions within the file calc.wmls.)

The function uses four variables internally: x, y, op, and result. You have to tell the WMLScript interpreter that you're going to use these variables before using them for the first time when using the var statement as on line 12. In turn, the interpreter allocates space for the variables. (If you don't define the name of a variable before first using it, the client would show an error when it tried to run the script.) As with PHP, WMLScript is loosely typed; variables can hold any data type, such as a string, integer, or a floating-point number.

WML variables aren't the same as WMLScript variables. Consequently, the function retrieves the numeric values and operand you keyed in the browser using the WMLBrowser library's getVar function. This function takes the name of a variable currently defined in the WML browser and returns its value.

Lines 22–23 use an if statement to determine whether or not the x and y variables contain valid floating-point numbers. On line 22, the function tests x

CAUTION *You can happily mix and match variable names between WML and WMLScript because the browser and the script interpreter are in different worlds called contexts. That is, a variable x in WML isn't the same as a variable x in WMLScript. When sharing variables between these contexts, you should give them the same name so you can keep the purpose of each variable straight. Also, consistent naming ensures you only have to remember one variable for a given value in both contexts.*

and y to see if they're equal to the WMLScript keyword invalid, which is a special value returned by functions such as WMLBrowser.getVar to signal an error condition. Line 23 uses the Lang library's isFloating-point number function to determine if x or y is not a floating-point number. If anything is amiss, the block on lines 24–58 is executed. This block first displays a message warning the user of the mistake on line 25, using the alert function of the Dialogs library that you encountered in the previous sample.

This block also attempts to correct the wayward user's entry by stuffing a zero (0) in the incorrectly entered WML variable. For each of x and y, this block first tests the variable independently, and if it's invalid, stores the string "0" in the appropriate WML variable using the WMLBrowser.setVar function. As you might imagine, this function is the counterpart to WMLBrowser.getVar: given a WML variable name and value, it assigns the value to the WML variable. You use this function when a WMLScript generates a value you want to give back to the WML browser. Finally, this block returns control to the WML browser by calling the Lang library's exit function. The exit function takes a value such as an error code or string, which clients can use in platform-specific ways to notify the user of an error.

Assuming x and y both hold valid floating-point numbers as strings from WMLBrowser.getVar, none of this happens and execution continues on lines 42 and 43. Here, the strings in x and y are actually converted to floating-point numbers, so that the script can use them in mathematical expressions. This isn't strictly necessary because WMLScript attempts to convert data types for you, but it makes the code clearer.

On lines 47–74, the function examines the string stored in the op variables to determine what operation it should perform. The resulting expressions are obvious: add, subtract, multiply, or divide the two numbers, or apply one of the exponentiation, root, or factorial functions, respectively. WMLScript can perform basic arithmetic on floating-point numbers, but advanced functions such as square root and exponentiation require the Floating-point number library, which is available on most clients. Line 73 uses our _fact function (shown later in this section) to calculate the factorial of x if required.

There's a bit more error checking, too. On lines 76–80, if you requested an operation that can't be performed, the script shows you an error message, selects the addition operation +, and returns control to the browser so you can try again. Of course, the deck doesn't enable you to select an invalid operator—but that's no excuse for being lazy and not validating the value of op. Because you could make a mistake in writing the WML that uses this function, it's important that you check the values in the WMLScript, so that your viewers won't encounter strange and frustrating errors in your wireless application.

> **TIP** *Be paranoid. Check the value of arguments passed to your WMLScript functions, especially at the boundary between WML and WMLScript. (Heck, do the same in PHP too!) Often, causal testing won't find simple mistakes that these checks can catch. Including these kinds of checks—called defensive programming—makes for a more fault-tolerant application. In turn, fault-tolerant applications keep customers happy.*

Each of the blocks associated with the if statements on lines 47–74 store the result of the computation in the variable result. This value is a floating-point number, but the script uses a WMLScript function to convert it to a formatted string containing the number. On line 84, the script uses the format function of the String library—similar to PHP's printf function—to convert the floating-point number back to a string, keeping ten digits of precision.

On line 88, the script stores the result of the computation in the WML variable result, again using the WMLBrowser library's setVar function.

Lines 93–96 do some cleanup on the value of the y variable. By convention, the operands in an RPN calculator are often called *registers*. When the calculation performs a two-operand operation such as addition, the value is returned in one register, and the other register is cleared, so that the calculator is ready for the next variable. However, if a one-operand function (such as taking a square root) is performed, only one register changes; the other remains untouched. That way, you can evaluate an expression such as 2×5 by entering 2 5 ×.[2] If the script computed the values of either of the two-operand functions (+, -, ×, ÷, and exponentiation, also written as y^x or ^), it stuffs the value 0 in the y variable.

Finally, the function instructs the browser to return to the first page of the deck and exits on lines 101–102. The go function of the WMLBrowser library tells the browser to navigate to a specific URL; by going to the URL "#y", the browser returns to the first card of calc.wml after the script exits, showing the new values of the WML variables x and y.

---

2. If the subtleties of this point escape you, don't worry. This has absolutely no bearing on WML, WMLScript, or the Wireless Web; it's simply a nice feature of RPN calculators that you wouldn't want to be without.

While lengthy, this script typifies the kinds of work you do in a WMLScript and the steps you'll follow such as taking some variables from the WML browser, doing something with those variables, and then returning control to the browser. Sometimes you'll set the value of WML variables from within your script, or go to a different URL depending on decisions made by the script. Most of the time you'll only need the basic statements you see here, or the occasional for loop. Listing 4-7 shows the for loop used by the calc.wmls _fact function.

```
01: /********************************************************
02:  * FUNCTION: _fact
03:  *
04:  * DESCRIPTION: Calculates x!
05:  *
06:  * RETURNED: the value of x!
07:  ********************************************************/
08: function _fact(
09:   x // (in) value to take factorial
10: )
11: {
12:   var i, result;
13:
14:   result = 1;
15:
16:   for ( i = x; i > 1; i- )
17:   {
18:     result *= i;
19:   }
20:
21:   return result;
22: }
```

Listing 4-7. The _fact function

In WMLScript, the for statement's syntax is the same as in PHP. The for statement receives an initial expression executed as the loop starts, a conditional expression evaluated each pass through the loop to determine whether or not it should execute again, and a loop expression executed each pass through the loop, along with the loop statement block.

In Listing 4-7, the function keyword defines the _fact function, which you can call only within the confines of calc.wmls. This function uses two variables: i, used by the loop, and result, used to determine the value of $x!$. (You'll recall from the previous chapter that $x!=x \ (x-1) \times (x-2) \times \ldots \times 1$.) The function initially assigns the value 1 to result, and then sets result to result times each of the integers between x and 1 in the loop on lines 16–19. When the loop exits, the value of result is returned to the caller.

Although strict rules don't exist regarding function naming, I have a habit of naming my extern functions using conventional names, and starting the names of other functions with _ so I can quickly recognize that they can't be called from WML.

WMLScript Syntax

Mercifully, WMLScript's syntax is almost identical to PHP's syntax. Once you've learned PHP, you can pick up WMLScript in less than a day, making it easy to build wireless sites using a combination of PHP and WMLScript.

WMLScript files are text files that are compiled into a compact binary representation by the wireless provider's gateway before being sent to the client. These files must have the MIME type text/vnd.wap.wmlscript so that the gateway recognizes them as WMLScript files. You can name a WMLScript file anything you like, but be sure that your server maps between your naming scheme and this MIME type (see "Setting Up the Server and Client," earlier in this chapter).

Within your WMLScript file, you can define one or more functions, but ensure that at least one of these functions is externally accessible using the extern keyword or else you won't be able to call any of the functions in the file.

Functions are defined exactly as they are in PHP, using the function statement. After the function statement, you write the name of the function and any arguments it takes in parentheses, followed by a block containing the statements that constitute the function definition. This block of statements may define local variables using the var statement and may return a value to the function caller using the return statement, as the _fact function does in Listing 4-6. Function arguments and return values only exist within the scope of WMLScript, however. As you saw in the previous section, passing values between the browser and the WMLScript interpreter requires functions offered by the interpreter's WMLBrowser library.

Semicolons separate individual statements in WMLScript, just as they are in PHP. Unlike PHP, however, statements must be contained within a function—the *only* way to execute a WMLScript statement is by executing its containing function. Of course, white space is both optional and strongly encouraged. There's little point in writing cramped code because the gateway server strips out all but WML-Script statements anyway.

WMLScript isn't quite as flexible as PHP, accepting only the C++ style comments demarcated by /* */ and //. As with PHP, comments beginning with // continue to the end of the current line.

Going Further with WMLScript

In many ways, writing WMLScript feels as if you're writing a script using a watered-down dialect of PHP or JavaScript. The statements are the same, data types and variables are similar, and the syntax is almost identical. In this section, you learn the nitty-gritty details of WMLScript by comparing it to PHP, which you learned in the last chapter.

Data Types

WMLScript has four basic data types: *integers, floating-point numbers, strings,* and *Booleans.* As with PHP, WMLScript is loosely typed: variables can hold data of any type, and WMLScript attempts to make type conversions on your behalf.

The first three of these data types are very similar to PHP's data types. Integers store positive or negative whole numbers; floating-point numbers hold decimal numbers; and strings hold groups of characters. Not all clients support floating-point numbers, though; some clients produce errors when you attempt to assign floating-point values to variables or do arithmetic with them. You can test for floating-point support on a device without generating an error by calling the function `Lang.float`, which returns true if the device supports floating-point numbers.

WMLScript strings are written between single or double quote marks, `"such as this"` or `'this.'` Also just as with PHP, a set of special characters enables you to represent characters that you can't type directly. Table 4-1 shows a list of these characters. Unlike PHP, you can't evaluate variables inside WMLScript using the $ symbol—you'll need to build strings with variable values using concatenation, discussed in the "Operations" section later in this chapter.

Table 4-1. Special Characters in WMLScript Strings

NEWLINE SEQUENCE	MEANING
\'	single quote
\"	double quote
\n	linefeed (LF or 0x0A in ASCII)
\r	carriage return (CR or 0x0D in ASCII)
\t	horizontal tab (HT or 0x09 in ASCII)
\\	backslash

A *Boolean* is a type that explicitly represents the Boolean values `true` and `false`. When converting between types, WMLScript treats anything not an empty string and not equal to the number zero to a Boolean with the value `true`; anything else gets converted to `false`.

Finally, there's the special value `invalid`, which many WML library functions use to represent an error condition. You can test a variable of any type for equivalence with `invalid` to look for an error condition, or use `invalid` in your code to represent errors.

Unlike PHP, WMLScript has no support for arrays. This affliction can be mildly painful to fatal, depending on what you're trying to achieve. Later in the chapter, you will see how a string holds a set of data that would have been better kept in an array, if only WMLScript supported arrays.

Variables

You've already seen WML variables in action. They're conceptually equivalent to PHP variables: they relate a name (the variable's name) to a value (what's in the variable). Variables can hold a datum of any type.

WMLScript variable names may begin with a leading letter or underscore _ character, followed by letters, numbers, or more underscore characters. There's no leading $ symbol, however.

Also just as with PHP, the WMLScript = operation assigns the value on the right-hand side of the expression to the variable named on the left-hand side of the expression. For example on line 16 of Listing 4-6, x is assigned the value returned by the function `WMLBrowser.getVar`.

Unlike PHP, WMLScript has no notion of references.

Operations

WMLScript supports a subset of the operations present in PHP, shown in Table 4-2. These operators behave the same as they do in PHP.

Table 4-2. Common WMLScript Operators

OPERATION	ASSOCIATION	PURPOSE
!, ~, ++, −, isvalid, typeof	Right	Logical complement, binary complement, increment, decrement, complement equivalence to isvalid, returns type
*, ÷, %	Left	Multiplication, division, and modulo (remainder)

Table 4-2. Common WMLScript Operators (Continued)

OPERATION	ASSOCIATION	PURPOSE
+, -	Left	Addition, subtraction, string concatenation
<<, >>	Left	Bitwise left shift, right shift
<, ≤, ≥, >	Non-associative	less than, less than or equals, greater than, greater than or equals comparisons
==, !=	Non-associative	equivalence, non-equivalence comparisons
&	Left	Bitwise and
^	Left	Bitwise xor
|	Left	Bitwise or
&&	Left	Logical and
||	Left	Logical or
? :	Left	Conditional operation
=, +=, -=, *=, ÷=, div=, %=, ^=, .=, &=, |=	Left	Assignment

Unlike PHP, there is no string concatenation operation. Instead, the + operation concatenates two strings.

One operator not found in PHP is isvalid. The isvalid operator is equal to comparing against invalid and complementing the result; it returns true if its operand is not equal to invalid. The typeof operation, similar to PHP's typeof function, returns an integer corresponding to the type of the argument: 0 for integer, 1 for floating-point, 2 for string, 3 for Boolean, and 4 for the special value invalid.

Control Statements

WMLScript offers the same basic control statements as PHP, including conditional execution and loops. Unlike PHP, however, there aren't as many control statements to choose from, although those offered by PHP are functionally equivalent. In essence, you can say the same things, but you can't choose your words.

Your scripts can make conditional decisions using WMLScript's if-else construction. My calculate function in Listing 4-6 uses a set of if-else statements to select a specific operation based on the value of the variable op. Unlike PHP, however, there's no switch-case statement. Had one been available, it could have used instead of chaining multiple if statements together.

WMLScript supports looping with a single while statement and a for statement. As with PHP, they're functionally equivalent: anything you can write using while you can also write using for, but sometimes it's more readable to use one instead of the other. Listing 4-7 used a for function to calculate *x!*. The while statement could have been used to do the same, such as in Listing 4-8. There is no do-while in WMLScript; all while statements must begin with their conditional expressions.

```
01: /*******************************************************
02: * FUNCTION: _fact
03: *
04: * DESCRIPTION: Calculates x!
05: *
06: * RETURNED: the value of x!
07: *******************************************************/
08: function _fact(
09:   x // (in) value to take factorial
10: )
11: {
12:   var result;
13:
14:   result = 1;
15:
16:   while ( x > 1 )
17:   {
18:     result *= x;
19:     x = x - 1;
20:   }
21:
22:   return result;
23: }
```

Listing 4-8. The _fact *function using* while

WMLScript also offers the break and continue statements, enabling you to transfer control to the first statement after a loop or continue a loop's execution, respectively.

Functions

Without functions, WMLScript would be useless. This isn't hyperbole: every WMLScript statement must be written in a WMLScript function.

WMLScript has two kinds of functions: those with scope only within the WMLScript file, and those with external scope that may be called from WML decks. You define both kinds of functions using the `function` statement, using the `extern` statement before a function definition to make it externally accessible. Listing 4-8 shows the function definition for the `_fact` function, available only within the file that contains it. Listing 4-6 shows the `calculate` function, which you can call from any WML deck.

Libraries

WMLScript gives you functions in *libraries,* in addition to the functions that you define. Some packages, such as the `Lang` package, are available on all devices. Other packages, such as the `Float` package are only available on some devices. Finally, vendors can add additional packages of libraries to specific devices to add features such as access to device databases or graphics. There are six libraries defined by the WAP Forum.

- The `Lang` library provides functions that are features of the WMLScript language. These functions enable you to convert types, obtain random numbers, determine whether the device has floating-point support, and obtain the minimum and maximum values for integers.

- The `Float` library provides functions for simple floating-point operations, including exponentiation and extracting square roots. (This library does not provide trigonometric functions, however.)

- The `String` library provides a set of primitive string functions, including a `printf`-style string formatter and functions to treat a string as a list of elements separated by a known character.

- The `URL` library provides routines for extracting the various parts of a URL to obtain the host, protocol, and port. While you could do this using the string functions, it's not as easy as it sounds without the `URL` library.

- The `WMLBrowser` library provides routines for accessing and controlling the WML browser on the device.

- The `Dialog` library provides routines for creating simple text dialogs on the phone's screen.

Tables 4-3 through 4-8 detail the standard WMLScript libraries and functions available todevelopers.

Table 4-3. Functions in the WMLScript Lang *Library*

FUNCTION	ARGUMENTS	RETURNS	PURPOSE
abort	string		Causes the interpretation of the WMLScript to abort and returns control to the caller of the WMLScript interpreter with the given string describing the error.
abs	number	number or invalid	Computes the absolute value of the given number
characterSet	string		Returns an integer code indicating the character set supported by the WMLScript interpreter.
exit	value		Causes the interpretation of the WMLScript to terminate and returns control to the caller of the WMLScript interpreter with the given value.
float	*none*	boolean	Returns true if the platform supports floating-point arithmetic, false otherwise
isInt	string	boolean	Returns true if string can be interpreted as an integer, false otherwise
isFloat	number	boolean	Returns true if string can be interpreted as a float, false otherwise
min	n1, n2	number or invalid	Computes the minimum of two given numbers

Table 4-3. Functions in the WMLScript Lang *Library (Continued)*

FUNCTION	ARGUMENTS	RETURNS	PURPOSE
minInt		number	The minimum integer value supported.
max	n1, n2	number	Computes the maximum of two given numbers
maxInit		number	The maximum integer value supported.
parseInt	string	integer or invalid	Returns an integer corresponding to an interpretation of the string, or invalid if the string could not be interpreted as an integer
parseFloat	string	float or invalid	Returns a floating-point number corresponding to an interpretation of the string, or invalid if the string could not be interpreted as a floating-point number
random	integer	integer	Returns a random integer between 0 and the value passed, or invalid if value is less than zero or not a number
seed	value	string	Initializes the random number sequence and returns an empty string.

TABLE 4-4. FUNCTIONS IN THE WMLSCRIPT Float **LIBRARY**

FUNCTION	ARGUMENTS	RETURNS	PURPOSE
ceil	number	number	Returns the smallest integer value that is not less than the given number
int	number	number	Returns the integer part of the given number
floor	number	number	Returns the greatest integer value that is not greater than the given number
maxFloat		number	Returns the maximum supported floating-point number
minFloat		number	Returns the minimum supported floating-point number.
pow	y, x	number	Returns an implementation-dependent approximation of the result of computing y^x
round	number	number	Returns the integer that is closest to number.
sqrt	number	number	Returns an implementation-dependent approximation of the square root of number

Table 4-5. Functions in the WMLScript String *Library*

FUNCTION	ARGUMENTS	RETURNS	PURPOSE
charAt	string, index	string	Returns a new string with one character containing the character in string at position index.
compare	string1, string2	integer	Indicates whether string1 is less than, equal to, or greater than string2 based on the character codes of the native character set.
elements	string, sep	integer or invalid	Returns the number of elements in string that are separated by sep
elementAt	string, index, sep	string	Returns the index'th element of string as separated by sep
find	string, sub	value	Returns the index of sub in string or invalid
format	format, value	string	Uses the printf-style format string to format the value
insertAt	string, new, elem, index	string	Returns a new string where new is inserted at the index'th element of string separated by sep
isEmpty	string	boolean	Returns true if the string length is zero or false otherwise
length	string	number	Returns the number of characters in string
replace	string, old, new	string	Returns a new string resulting from the replacement of all occurrences of the string old by new in string

Table 4-5. Functions in the WMLScript String *Library (Continued)*

FUNCTION	ARGUMENTS	RETURNS	PURPOSE
removeAt	string, index, sep	string	Returns a new string where element and sep at index have been removed from string.
replaceAt	string, new, elem, index	string	Returns a new string where the index'th element of string separated by sep has been replaced by new.
squeeze	string	string	Returns a string where all consecutive white spaces are reduced to single spaces
subString	string, start, length	string	Returns a new string consisting of the characters in string from start and extending length characters.
toString	value	string	Returns a string representation of value.
trim	string	string	Retuns string where all leading and trailing white space has been removed.

Table 4-6. Functions in the WMLScript URL *Library*

FUNCTION	ARGUMENTS	RETURNS	PURPOSE
escape-String	string	string	Computes a new string where special characters have been escaped to create a valid URL.
getBase	string	string	Returns an absolute URL of the current WMLScript file.
getFragment	url	string	Returns the fragment in url.

Table 4-6. Functions in the WMLScript URL *Library (Continued)*

FUNCTION	ARGUMENTS	RETURNS	PURPOSE
getHost	url	string	Returns the host in url.
getPath	url	string	Returns the path in url.
get-Parameters	url	string	Returns parameters in the last path segment of url.
getPort	url	string	Returns the port number specified in url.
getQuery	url	string	Returns the query part specified in url.
getReferer		string	Returns the smallest URL relative to the base URL of the current WMLScript file.
getScheme	url	string	Returns the protocol (scheme) in url.
isValid	url	boolean	Returns true if url is a valid URL.
loadString	string, type	string, integer, or invalid	Returns the content denoted by the given absolute URL and the given content type.
resolve	base, embedded	Returns an absolute URL created from the given base and embedded URL strings.	
unescape-String	string	string	Computes a new string where URL escaped characters are returned to their normal values.

* Note: Relative URLs are not resolved in these functions.

Table 4-7. Functions in the WMLScript WMLBrowser *Library*

FUNCTION	ARGUMENTS	RETURNS	PURPOSE
getVar	name	string	Returns the value of the WML variable name.
go	string	string or invalid	Tells browser to load the deck at the URL string when script exits.
getCurrent-Card		string	Returns the smallest relative URL (relative to the script) specifying the card being displayed by the browser.
newContext			Clears all variables and the history of the browser.
prev		string or invalid	Signals the browser to go to the previous card.
refresh		Signals the browser to update its UI based on the current context.	Signals the browser to update its UI based on the current context.
setVar	name, value	string	Sets WML variable name to value.

Table 4-8: Functions in the WMLScript Dialogs *Library*

FUNCTION	ARGUMENTS	RETURNS	PURPOSE
alert	message		Displays the message to the user and waits for user confirmation.

Table 4-8: Functions in the WMLScript `Dialogs` *Library*

FUNCTION	ARGUMENTS	RETURNS	PURPOSE
`confirm`	`message, ok, cancel`	boolean	Displays message and two reply alternatives. Waits for the user to select a reply and returns true for `ok` and false for the `cancel` alternative.
`prompt`	`message, default`	string	Displays `message` and prompts for user input. Returns the user input.

WMLScript Within MobileHelper

MobileHelper uses WMLScript for input validation. While the `<input/>` tag's `format` attribute provides crude input validation, WMLScript gives finer control. Dates and times are difficult to exhaustively validate using WML because, while you can ensure numeric entry, you can't check that input is bounded. For example, verifying that the user entered a valid month number requires computation, which must be done in a script or on the server side of the network.

Server validation plays an important role in any wireless application, but WMLScript can help improve a user's experience. Server validation should be seen as a defense of last resort: you don't want your server-side script to store inappropriate data, crash, or return an invalid result as a result of user error. On the other hand, you don't want the server to have to check all of a user's input because, if it does, a user is forced to wait for a wireless transaction to complete before being notified of an error. It's akin to calling your credit card company to check your account balance, being put on hold for five minutes, and being told you called the wrong number and that you should try again. While not fatal, it's unprofessional and annoying. WMLScript enables you to avoid doing this to your customers—or avoids enabling your customers to do this to themselves, depending on your perspective.

MobileHelper uses functions in the file dateCheck.wmls to verify that dates and times entered are correct. These validation functions are somewhat primitive, but catch most common user mistakes, including entering an invalid month or day number. The script checks dates to ensure that the day of the month is valid, that the month number is valid, and that the date occurs sometime after Mobile-Helper was written (implying that it was a correctly entered date). Similarly, the script checks the hour and minute value for times, flagging questionable results. Also, this script looks for correct separators—a colon (:) for times and / for dates—helping ensure that you correctly keyed a time or date.

Validating Times

MobileHelper enables you to enter times in two key places: when a Volunteer marks a task as completed and when a Coordinator enters new times. In each of these places, MobileHelper prompts you for a time in twenty-four hour format, using the <input/> format value "NN:NN" to ensure that the value you enter consists of four numeric digits, separated by a single colon. This entry is passed to the WMLScript function IfTimeValidGo, defined in dateCheck.wmls. Listing 4-9 shows this function and the functions it uses in dateCheck.wmls to validate time entries.

```
01: /*******************************************************
02:  * FUNCTION: IfTimeValidGo
03:  *
04:  * DESCRIPTION: Checks WML variable time. If it contains
05:  * a valid time ("hh:mm", 24-hour clock), navigates to the
06:  * URL in the WML variable validTimeURL. Otherwise,
07:  * navigates user agent to URL in WML variable
08:  * invalidTimeURL.
09:  *
10:  * RETURNED: nothing
11:  *******************************************************/
12: extern function IfTimeValidGo()
13: {
14:   var time, validTimeURL, invalidTimeURL;
15:
16:   time = WMLBrowser.getVar( "time" );
17:   validTimeURL = WMLBrowser.getVar( "validTimeURL" );
18:   invalidTimeURL = WMLBrowser.getVar( "invalidTimeURL" );
19:
20:   if ( URL.isValid( validTimeURL ) &&
21:     URL.isValid( invalidTimeURL ) )
22:   {
23:
24: // Check the time
25:
26:     if ( _checkTime( time ) )
27:     {
28:
29: // It's good; continue to the next URL.
30:
31:       WMLBrowser.go( validTimeURL );
32:
33:     }
34:     else
```

```
35:    {
36:
37: // It's bad: tell the user.
38:
39:       WMLBrowser.go( invalidTimeURL );
40:
41:    }
42:  }
43:  else
44:  {
45:
46: // One or the other of the URLs is bad. Say so now.
47:
48:    if ( URL.isValid( validTimeURL ) )
49:    {
50:     Dialogs.alert( "IfTimeValidGo given invalid URL " +
51:        "for invalidTime" );
52:    }
53:    else
54:    {
55:     Dialogs.alert( "IfTimeValidGo given invalid URL  " +
56:        "for validTime" );
57:
58:    }
59:  }
60: }
61:
62:
63: /********************************************************
64:  * FUNCTION: _checkTime
65:  *
66:  * DESCRIPTION: Examines the first argument to see if it
67:  *  is a valid time. If so, returns true; otherwise,
68:  *  returns false.
69:  *
70:  * RETURNED: true or false
71:  ********************************************************/
72: function _checkTime(
73:   time  // (in) time to validate
74: )
75: {
76:   var hour, minute;
77:   var result;
78:
```

```
79: // Assume the worst: an invalid time.
80:
81:    result = false;
82:
83: // Divider must be a : with two components.
84: // There must be an hour segment and a minute segment.
85:
86:    if ( String.elements( time, ":" ) == 2 )
87:    {
88:
89: // Extract hour and minute.
90:
91:       hour = Lang.parseInt(
92:         String.elementAt( time, 0, ":" )
93:       );
94:       minute = Lang.parseInt(
95:         String.elementAt( time, 1,  ":" )
96:       );
97:
98: // Validate hour and minute
99:       if ( isvalid( hour ) && isvalid ( minute ) &&
100:          ( hour >= 0 && hour <= 23 ) &&
101:          ( minute >= 0 && minute <= 59 ) )
102:       {
103:         result = true;
104:       }
105:
106: // Validate minute
107:
108:    }
109:    return result;
110: }
```

Listing 4-9. Portions of dateCheck.wmls that validate times

Personally, it's always bothered me that WML has variables, but it doesn't have conditional evaluation in some form. Arguably, there's no historical precedent in other markup languages for the Web, but other markup languages such as TeX have similar features. You can fake (as I did) a similar behavior for IfTimeValidGo, by crafting a function that brings the browser to one of two URLs based on whether the time it examined was a valid time or not. Moreover, by enabling callers to supply IfTimeValidGo with their own URLs, you could reuse the code in Mobile-Helper and elsewhere.

The function `IfTimeValidGo` takes three arguments. (Although you can't pass arguments to WMLScript functions from WML, the idea of passing values in WML variables and getting them in the WMLScript function is similar, so I'm going to use the term *argument* to refer to the data passed from WML to WMLScript.) You pass the first argument, the time the function validates, in the WML variable `time`. The second and third arguments are URLs, passed in the WML variables `validTimeURL` and `invalidTimeURL`. If `time` contains a string that the `IfTimeValidGo` interprets as a valid time, the browser navigates to the URL in `validtimeURL`; otherwise, the browser navigates to the URL in `invalidTimeURL`.

On line 12, `IfTimeValidGo` is defined as an `extern` function, so that it can be called from MobileHelper's WML. The function uses three variables to store the WML variables it obtains from the browser: `time`, `validTimeURL`, and `invalidTimeURL`. The function fetches the WML values for these variables on lines 16–18.

The rest of the function is almost entirely error handling. This is common with `extern` functions: you don't ever want one to be called in a state that can cause an error because it generates error messages better left unseen in the eyes of your viewers. The script first validates the URLs using `URL.isValid` on lines 20 and 21. The `URL.isValid` function checks its argument to see if it's a syntactically correct URL. It can't tell you whether there's good content at a particular URL, but it at least helps you avoid silly mistakes such as incorrectly entering a protocol in your source code. If both URLs check out, `IfTimeValidGo` uses the `_checkTime` function (defined on lines 60–110) to select which URL goes on lines 26–42. The `WMLBrowser.go` function called on lines 31 and 39 simply queues its given URL with the browser, so that when the script exits, the browser loads the deck at the given URL.

If either of the URLs is invalid, the function uses `URL.isValid` to determine which is invalid and display an alert dialog with `Dialogs.alert` on lines 43 through 60. Ideally, passing a bad URL to `IfTimeValidGo` should never happen when your site is in production, but if it does, you'll catch it quickly this way. Alternately, you could rework `IfTimeValidGo` to pass control to a server-side PHP script using `WMLBrowser.go` if either URL was invalid. Such a script could e-mail the Webmaster with a bug report, delay error checking, or do whatever damage control is appropriate.

The `_checkTime` function performs the actual entry validation. This function accepts a string (presumably in `"hh:mm"` format in twenty-four hour time) and returns `true` if it's a valid time, or `false` otherwise. (I could have chosen to have it return either `true` or `invalid` instead; there's no difference.) `_checkTime` works by looking at the string to find the colon separating the hours and minutes, and then extracting each of the hours and minutes values. It then inspects each of these values to be sure that both are within valid ranges (0–23 for hours, 0–59 for minutes).

The function defines three variables on lines 76–77. The function uses the first two, `hour` and `minute`, to store the individual pieces of the time. The other, `result`, is assigned the value `false` in anticipation of an invalid date. The variable `result` is assigned the value `true` only if everything is okay for both `hour` and `minute`.

Then the function looks for the hours and minutes components of the time, first by determining how many components of the string are found separated by : (colon) and then by actually collecting the values if there are only two of them (lines 86–96). The String library functions elements and elementAt treat their first argument as a list, separated by the character specified by the second element. Thus, the if statement on line 86 counts the number of elements in a list whose elements are separated by colons. In the case of the time, a single colon separates the two elements. The value of hour is the first element in the list and the value of minute is the second element. As with arrays in PHP, elementAt counts starting from zero, not one. Thus, on line 91, writing String.elementAt(time, 0, ":") extracts the first element of the string in time.

Lines 91 and 95 use the Lang.parseInt function on the resulting hour and minute values to ensure they're really integers. This is overkill given the <input/> format, which is "NN:NN"; a user can't enter a value that's not an integer. However, it's a good idea to use this anyway, because there's no guarantee from the perspective of the WMLScript code that the values _checkTime obtains are really from an <input/> value with this format: the WMLScript doesn't know which WML decks call its functions. Thus, choosing to err on the side of paranoia, check to ensure that both hour and minute are integers before continuing to deal with them.

This test—whether hour and minute are integers—actually takes place on line 99. The if statement on lines 99–101 is probably the most complex in the book, so it's worth looking at closely. This statement first checks to ensure that hour and minute are integers. If they are, it checks to ensure that hour is between the values 0 and 23, and that minute is between the values 0 and 59. If—and only if—they are, then result is set to true. Otherwise, result remains false.

Validating Dates

Validating a date is conceptually the same as validating a time: take the incoming string, break it into three pieces and then ensure that each piece is valid.

The interface to IfDateValidGo is the same as IfTimeValidGo. You pass a date the function examines and URLs for both the valid and invalid date cases. If the URLs look valid, the script attempts to validate the date using a separate function, _checkDate, and jumps to the appropriate URL depending on whether the date is valid or not. Listing 4-10 shows the IfDateValidGo and _checkDate functions.

```
01: /*********************************************************
02: * FUNCTION: IfDateValidGo
03: *
04: * DESCRIPTION: Checks WML variable date. If it contains
05: * a valid date ("mm/dd/yyyy"), navigates to the
06: * URL in the WML variable validDate. Otherwise, navigates
```

```
07:  * user agent to URL in WML variable invalidDate.
08:  *
09:  *
10:  * RETURNED: nothing
11:  ******************************************************/
12: extern function IfDateValidGo()
13: {
14:    var date, validDateURL, invalidDateURL;
15:
16:
17:    date = WMLBrowser.getVar( "date" );
18:    validDateURL = WMLBrowser.getVar( "validDateURL" );
19:    invalidDateURL = WMLBrowser.getVar( "invalidDateURL" );
20:
21:    if ( URL.isValid( validDateURL ) &&
22:      URL.isValid( invalidDateURL ) )
23:    {
24:
25: // Check the date
26:
27:      if ( _checkDate( date ) )
28:      {
29:
30: // It's good; continue to the next URL.
31:
32:        WMLBrowser.go( validDateURL );
33:
34:      }
35:      else
36:      {
37:
38: // It's bad: tell the user.
39:
40:        WMLBrowser.go( invalidDateURL );
41:
42:      }
43:    }
44:    else
45:    {
46:
47: // One or the other of the URLs is bad. Say so now.
48:
49:      if ( URL.isValid( validDateURL ) )
50:      {
```

```
51:        Dialogs.alert( "IfDateValidGo given invalid URL " +
52:          "for invalidDate" );
53:      }
54:    else
55:    {
56:        Dialogs.alert( "IfDateValidGo given invalid URL " +
57:          "for validDate" );
58:
59:    }
60:  }
61: }
62:
63:
64:
65: /*********************************************************
66: * FUNCTION: _checkDate
67: *
68: * DESCRIPTION: Examines the first argument to see if it
69: *   is a valid date. If so, returns true; otherwise,
70: *   returns false.
71: *
72: * RETURNED: true or false
73: *********************************************************/
74: function _checkDate(
75:   date  // (in) date to validate
76: )
77: {
78:   var month, day, year;
79:   var result;
80:   var dom = "31/28/31/30/31/30/31/31/30/31/30/31";
81:   var numDay;
82:
83: // Assume the worst: an invalid date.
84:   result = false;
85:
86: // Divider must be a / with three components.
87: // There must be elements for month, day, and year.
88:
```

```
 89:   if ( String.elements( date, "/" ) == 3 )
 90:   {
 91:
 92: // Extract day, month, and year
 93:
 94:     month = Lang.parseInt(
 95:       String.elementAt( date, 0,  "/" )
 96:     );
 97:     day = Lang.parseInt(
 98:       String.elementAt( date, 1,  "/" )
 99:     );
100:     year = Lang.parseInt(
101:       String.elementAt( date, 2,  "/" )
102:     );
103:
104: // Were these each valid integers?
105:     if ( isvalid( month ) &&
106:          isvalid( day ) &&
107:          isvalid( year ) )
108:     {
109:
110: // Check year: Just see if it's after 2000.
111: // If it's between 00 and 99, assume it's
112: // really 2000-2099.
113:
114:       if ( year > 0 && year < 99 )
115:       {
116:         year += 2000;
117:       }
118:       if ( year > 2000 )
119:       {
120:         result = true;
121:       }
122:
123: // Check month - should be in the range 1-12.
124:
125:       if ( result )
126:       {
127:         if ( month < 1 || month > 12 )
128:         {
129:           result = false;
130:         }
131:       }
132:
```

```
133: // Check day
134:
135:     if ( result )
136:     {
137:
138: // Fetch number of days in current month.
139:
140:         numDay = Lang.parseInt(
141:         String.elementAt( dom, month - 1,  "/" )
142:         );
143:
144: // Correct February's date count if it's a leap year.
145:
146:         if ( month == 2 && _isLeapYear( year ) )
147:         {
148:           numDay = numDay + 1;
149:         }
150:
151: // Is the day within the number of days in the month?
152:
153:         if ( day < 1 || day > numDay )
154:         {
155:           result = false;
156:         }
157:       }
158:     }
159:   }
160:
161:   return result;
162:
163: }
164:
165: /*****************************************************
166:  * FUNCTION: _isLeapYear
167:  *
168:  * DESCRIPTION: Returns true if the given year is a leap
169:  *  year, false otherwise.
170:  *
171:  * RETURNED: true or false
172:  *****************************************************/
```

```
173: function _isLeapYear(
174:   year  // (in) date to validate
175: )
176: {
177:
178: // Leap years are divisible by 400 or 4, but not 100.
179:
180:   if ( year % 400 == 0 )
181:   {
182:     return true;
183:   }
184:   if ( year % 100 == 0 )
185:   {
186:     return false;
187:   }
188:   if ( year % 4 == 0 )
189:   {
190:     return true;
191:   }
192:   return false;
193: }
```

Listing 4-10. Portions of dateCheck.wmls that validate dates

While checking date validity is conceptually the same as checking time validity, in practice the problem is more complex because you have to know how many days are in each month if you're going to validate the suspect date completely. While you could assume that all months have thirty-one days and catch many errors, you'd miss subtle errors such as 6/31/2002. Worse yet, the number of days in February changes from year to year depending on whether or not it's a leap year, so in order to check the day component of a date, you need to know about both the month and the year of the date in question.

Leap years are handled by the simple function _isLeapYear. Given a leap year, this function returns true if it thinks the year is a leap year. By definition, our calendar has a leap year every fourth year (every year evenly divisible by four), except every hundredth year, unless that year is a four hundredth year. (Y2K aficionados will recall that this—the fact that 2000 was actually a leap year—was a second subtle Y2K bug largely dealt with when squeezing space for the century digits in software). _isLeapYear uses the WMLScript remainder (modulo) operator % to obtain the remainder from dividing the year in question by each of the three values 4, 100, and 400, returning the appropriate true or false value at each point. Note that the function has to make the tests in the order it does because returning true if a year is divisible by 4 would indicate that 2200 is a leap year, and it isn't.

The _checkDate function uses isLeapYear when determining how many days are in the month of February. For each month, _checkDate has a corresponding element of a list in a variable named dom (short for *day of month*), which is equal to the value "31/28/31/30/31/30/31/31/30/31/30/31". After performing initial counting checks and breaking the incoming date into three parts stored in month, day, and year, _checkDate uses the dom array to verify the value of day.

Before it does so, however, it performs a bit of underhanded business with the value of the year. On lines 110–121, you can see that if _checkDate receives a year between 0 and 99, it assumes that the user actually entered a two-digit year, and that the user presumably intended a date in the range 2000–2099. Given MobileHelper's <input/> format of "NN/NN/NNNN", that's not likely to happen, but it's quite possible that you may find yourself using a format of "NN/NN/NN". This trickery runs counter to the generality urged in the previous note because the function no longer works for years in the first century of our calendar.

Which is correct? They both are—as long as the code is clearly documented so you know what it's doing. The three comments on lines 110–112 call out exactly what we're doing and why. It's far more likely that my clients will bemoan needing to enter "20" for the next hundred years than this module will be used with dates nineteen hundred years old. Any date routines that work that far back in time need to be converted between the Julian calendar and the Gregorian calendar, for instance. When in doubt, comment your code because nobody else can explain it to you later.

Going back to our problem with validating the value of day, the solution is actually quite simple. After extracting and validating the value of month, the script uses it as an index into the string in dom on line 140. Recall that indices count from zero, not one; the script must first subtract one from the date before finding the appropriate element in dom on line 140. This is converted to an integer, so that the variable numDay now contains the number of days in the month of the date in question.

If the month is February and it's a leap year (lines 146–149), the script increments numDay, denoting that February has 29 days in a leap year instead of 28. The script then uses the value of numDay to verify the day field of the date in question.

After verifying the month, day, and year, the function returns the value result. As with _checkTime, result is initially false as the script expects the worst. To make our `if` statements a little clearer, the function assumes the date is valid if the year is valid, and later reverses its decision if either the month or the day is invalid.

On the CD-ROM

Both of the SDKs on the CD-ROM support WMLScript, so you're ready to begin programming the minute you open the book.

Of course, you can find all the listings from this chapter in the chapter directory— chap04—on the CD-ROM. The files dateCheck.wmls and calc.wmls are also in the chap04 directory of the CD-ROM.

Food for Thought

- Today, many people find postfix notation either quaint or incomprehensible, depending on their experience. How would you modify calc.wml and calc.wmls to provide a more conventional, in-fix interface? Make your suggested changes and try it. Which is easier for you to use?

- Write WMLScripts to validate input for input types such as street addresses, ZIP codes, or postal codes in your country. How do the scripts compare with the `<input/>` tag's `format` attribute? How would you use these scripts in conjunction with PHP to support clients without WMLScript?

- Extend the scripts in dateCheck.wmls to provide more robust time and date support, including twelve-hour clocks and European (day/month/year) date validation.

- Extend the scripts in dateCheck.wmls to provide more robust handling of incorrectly formed URLs by navigating to a server-side script to log and resolve incorrectly typed URLs.

- Can you think of a better interface to `IsTimeValidGo` and `IsDateValidGo`? Write functions that implement your new interfaces and see if they're easier for you to use.

CHAPTER 5
MySQL

IN THE LAST TWO CHAPTERS, you saw how to create dynamic content with PHP and WMLScript. While the combination of PHP and WMLScript is flexible, most Wireless Web sites need an additional component: a database. With a database, Wireless Web sites can store data such as news stories, stock quotes, appointments, or user preferences. PHP provides a host of functions to interface to different databases, including the freely available MySQL database management system (DBMS).

In this chapter, you learn how to use MySQL with PHP to create Wireless Web sites that draw their content directly from a database. I begin by reviewing some basic concepts about databases. Then I show the Structured Query Language (SQL), used to access the majority of today's high-end database systems, MySQL. This chapter closes with the first fully functional version of MobileHelper, building on what you've learned over the previous four chapters.

Database Fundamentals

Almost everyone who has used a computer is familiar with the notion of a database. Many of the things you do on the Web—including logging into a personalized Web site, buying a product from an e-commerce site, or searching for your dream house—require databases, whether you're aware of the databases or not. Closer to home, your computer has database programs installed, such as a special-purpose database like a contact manager or the general-purpose database provided by the operating system to store an application's preferences and other data, such as the Microsoft Windows registry or the Apple Macintosh NetInfo database.

Most Web sites—including Wireless Web sites—make use of a database to store information. For example, an e-commerce site database would have information about the site's products and users, organized so that a user could quickly find and order a product of interest. MobileHelper's database stores information about volunteers, the tasks they carry out, and where they carry out those tasks.

Choosing a Database

As you start to design your application, one of the first questions you face is which database you should use. In fact, if you're not familiar with databases in general, you may even wonder why you need one to begin with. After all, PHP has a bevy of file functions, so if you like, you can store all of your server-side data in files on the server with these functions.

For most Wireless Web applications, however, databases are far superior to flat files for several reasons. They are simpler to use: when using a database you can think in terms of your data's representation, rather than files and file formats. They are reliable because somebody else (the folks that wrote the database) spent the time and effort validating the database code. They are more efficient, providing features you can only emulate with flat files. Most databases provide *locks*, ensuring that while part of the database is being updated, no one else can change the same data (or read it halfway through an update). More sophisticated databases also provide *transactions*, enabling you to group a sequence of changes so that either they all will happen, or none will happen, ensuring that no data is lost when the system goes down. In general, flat files within a PHP script are best used only in the simplest of applications such as bare-bones prototypes; any PHP script requiring data storage on the server is better off with a database.

The major factors that determine which database you choose are scale and cost. Of course, these factors are often directly related: most commercial databases like those from companies such as Oracle or Sybase scale well across orders of magnitude in performance and use, and you'll pay for their scalability in software license fees and hardware costs. For large-scale sites, you may have little choice because, with your content in a database, you need the performance of one of these products or it's possible the database won't keep up with the site's requests for data. Of course with these products, in return you get peace of mind and the support of a major company; depending on what you pay, you may be able to outsource your database development to your database vendor or one of their partners.

Recently, open source products like MySQL and PostgreSQL have become attractive alternatives to commercial databases for medium-scale Web development. MySQL, featured in this book, is a freely available server that's being successfully used with hundreds of Web sites. PostgreSQL has grown from an academic experiment to a successful high-performance database capable of taking on its commercial rivals.

All of these products have similar features. Most are relational databases supporting SQL, so you can apply fundamental concepts in database development as you move from one database to another. All are capable of storing different kinds of information, and let you interface your database to your Web server.

At the smallest scale, PHP even has support for a simple key-value database using successors to the Berkeley DBM library, a simple database system that's been around for over a decade. The DBM module gives you a simple way to store key-value pairs, such as login names and their passwords, or pages and how many times they've been hit. With a bit of time and effort, you can use this module to prototype systems that, in practice, would use a larger database.

Understanding Database Terminology

Let's begin by looking at how MobileHelper uses a database to store volunteer information. For each volunteer, MobileHelper must store three pieces of information:

- The user's name

- The user's Mobile Information Number (MIN), a unique number that the wireless network uses to identify the handset

- The user's Personal Identification Number (PIN), a simple password that the user uses when logging in to MobileHelper

Together, these items constitute a *record*. Figure 5-1 shows records for several volunteers that use MobileHelper; together, these people are called users. As you can see from the figure, these records form a *table*. In each row is a single record, while the columns contain the fields for a given record. For example, the name column contains each

user

name	min	pin
Jarod	8885553333	3141
Rachel	8885552222	2718
Ray	8885557777	0000

Figure 5-1. The user *table*

of the user's names, while the min field contains each of the user's MINs. Similarly, a second table—the location table—stores the details of each location Mobile-Helper volunteers might need to visit.

There's a third table, too, to store events. This table, the event table, has columns for each field of a record. Each row of this table contains an event's scheduled start and stop times, along with the times at which the event actually started and stopped, the event's name and a note about the event. But how does a row in the event table keep information about an event's location and owner?

MobileHelper could track this relationship in two ways. The simplest would be for each row in the event table to have all of the information about its owner and location. While simple, there's an obvious drawback: if you need to change something about either a user or a location, you're going to have to change it in multiple places, in every row containing the information for that user or location.

Instead, each event refers to a user using the user's MIN, and to a location using a unique identifier for that location. Thus, I link the event table to the user table using the user table's min field, and link the event and location tables using the id column of the location table. For example, if you want to see who is responsible for supporting the first Communications task, you read across that event's row in the event table until you find the min column, and then find the user with that MIN in the user column. Similarly, you can find where the First Night party is by reading across its row to the location column, and then looking for the location with that id in the location table. Figure 5-2 demonstrates this relationship.

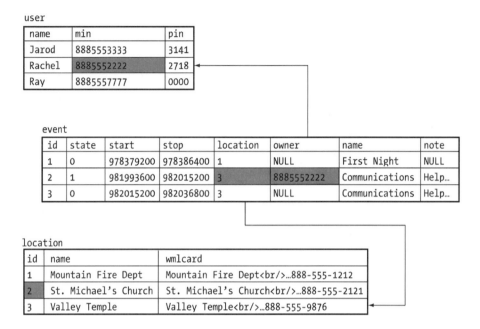

Figure 5-2. Links between the event, user, *and* location *tables*

At this point, you're either thinking this is a clever trick or a stupid idea. It seems clever because each datum occurs in only one place, making it easy to find information and update the database. It also seems stupid because it appears unnecessarily complex. To help sort out this complexity, database designers use *schema* diagrams to show the columns in each table and the relationships between tables. Figure 5-3 shows a schema of the MobileHelper tables I've already discussed.

ISchemas help you visualize the relationship between tables, but they also tell you the structure of each table's columns. In the user table, for example, the min field is a 20-character field, while name is a field of type tinytext (a string of characters between 0 and 255 characters). In a later section, you learn the meanings of each of these type identifiers; for now, it's enough to recognize that the schema tells you how tables are related as well the kind of data in each column of a table.

Many, but not all, databases use this notion of storing records as rows in tables. These databases are called *relational* databases. A relational database has two key features:

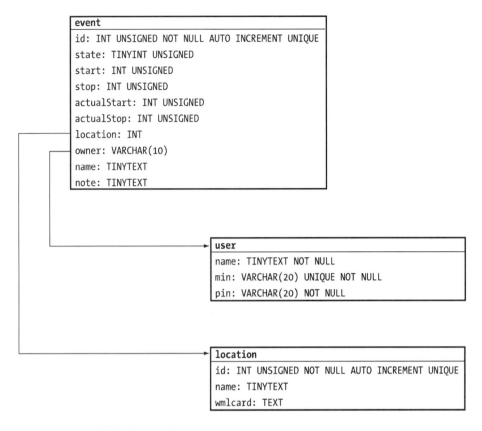

```
event
id: INT UNSIGNED NOT NULL AUTO INCREMENT UNIQUE
state: TINYINT UNSIGNED
start: INT UNSIGNED
stop: INT UNSIGNED
actualStart: INT UNSIGNED
actualStop: INT UNSIGNED
location: INT
owner: VARCHAR(10)
name: TINYTEXT
note: TINYTEXT
```

```
user
name: TINYTEXT NOT NULL
min: VARCHAR(20) UNIQUE NOT NULL
pin: VARCHAR(20) NOT NULL
```

```
location
id: INT UNSIGNED NOT NULL AUTO INCREMENT UNIQUE
name: TINYTEXT
wmlcard: TEXT
```

Figure 5-3. MobileHelper schema

- Records in the database are stored as rows in a table. For example, a single user's record is simply a row in the user table.

- The result of any operation on data within the database is itself another table. Thus, when I ask the database for information corresponding to the user MIN 8885554444 from the user table, the database gives me a table containing a single row—the record with the MIN 8885554444.

Most of the large-scale databases you'll encounter are relational databases because relational databases have a number of properties that lend themselves to mathematical analysis. In fact, the name "relational" draws from the mathematical notion of relations, which can be represented as tables of values. A relation correlates values in a one-to-one relationship, which can be represented using a table of rows, one row for each value. The theory of relational databases plays an important role in formal database systems engineering and design. While important when designing large-scale systems, it's not necessary at this stage that you have a grasp of it, and in general, I prefer a simpler, from-your-gut approach to designing a database's organization and contents.

> **NOTE**   *Despite the casual attitude I take in this chapter toward database design, formal database analysis has an important place in Web development. If you find yourself designing a complex database for a large system, or just spending an inordinate amount of time puzzling out database issues, then it's worth your time to learn more about the formal theory of databases. When building a small system, it's often easy to iterate your database development and learn as you go; when you build a mission-critical system, you won't have that luxury. If you're working in the latter category, a course in database design or a look at a book such as C. J. Date's An Introduction to Database Systems will save you tremendous agony.*

Designing the Database

At first, designing the database behind your Wireless Web application can be daunting. As with all things software, there is no single recipe, but some general guidelines can help:

1. Identify the kinds of data your database must contain.

2. Identify what information belongs in each table.

3. Determine what belongs in each column of each table.

4. Assign names and data types to each column of each table.

Of course, the first step is to identify what data your database must store. It's best if you do this in rough strokes, gradually expanding detail as you go. During your initial inception, you can make a high-level list. Often, you find the data you need to store early during this phase, as you bandy about words like "customer," "invoice," "inventory," "story," "account," and "preferences." For example, during inception it was clear that MobileHelper needed to store event information, including where events occur and who is responsible for each event.

How you organize the database—what tables it contains and what columns are in each table—is a topic to explore during elaboration. Once again, you can look toward the keywords describing your data for hints. If you're replacing or augmenting an existing system, there are other places to look, including any paper forms or other online interfaces, and so on. These will suggest the kinds of data your database will store, and often hint at relationships between each kind of data. Of course, you *shouldn't* look to these for user interface ideas; as I point out in Chapter 2, when you design an interface for a Wireless Web application you need to respect the input and display constraints common to all mobile users.

Often, the list of data types—events, customers, preferences, and what have you—shows you what tables your database will contain. By probing further and listing the kinds of information about each datum, you can identify the columns in a particular table. For example, an event describes something that takes place at a particular time, so it's reasonable to expect that an event table will contain start and stop times for the event, as well as an event description. Sometimes it helps to actually look at a specific datum, such as an actual appointment, customer record, or whatever your application stores.

As you list the columns in each table, note what kind of data is in each column. Times, for example, can be stored as times using PHP functions (if PHP is the predominant mechanism for accessing the database) or using the database's native time fields. Strings will be just that: strings, although it's helpful to have an idea of how long a particular string may be. Most databases are faster when you can be specific about the types and sizes of each column, such as how many characters are in a string, or whether a number is an integer or a floating-point number.

Expect to iterate over this process of defining tables and columns several times, especially if you're new to software development. It helps to start on paper, using a sheet of paper for each table to describe your schema. As you do so, work to eliminate redundancy and nonsensical dependencies in your tables. Each datum should occur in only one place; if it's needed elsewhere, a relationship between tables should link the datum to the rows of interest. In addition, each piece of information should be identified with a key (in MobileHelper, for example, the user table uses the min as a key) so you can link between tables.

> **TIP** *If every table in your database doesn't have at least one column whose contents are unique from row to row, you're probably not done with your design.*

At the same time, keep another sheet of paper to list the kinds of queries your users will make. These queries can be in English, but it helps if their syntax approximates SQL, so you can see how your database schema and requests interact. You'll find that by reworking some of your schema, your queries will be simpler, or that you need to rework your schema to include columns you'd initially forgotten.

As you go through this process, you reach a point where your schema and queries stabilize. At this point, you can build the database in the computer, populating it with a handful of sample records in each table. You can then refine your queries, phrasing them in SQL and trying them with your sample data. Even now, you may find you need to change a table, altering a column or changing a data type. That's okay because it's easier to do that now, rather than later when you have to work through your PHP to find the bits and pieces of SQL that need to be changed—or worse yet, rework a database running in a production environment.

You should expect to spend more effort defining your database when your database is complex, contains many records, or when you will have a large number of users accessing you database. A small system like MobileHelper can use an informal, less-than-optimal database organization because it contains relatively little information for only a few users. Even in mid-use it's possible to bring MobileHelper down to change the database schema to meet changing requirements (or an oversight on the part of the author!). That's simply not possible for larger sites. Iterating over your database design throughout your elaboration will help you avoid costly mistakes.

Interacting with the Database

There are at least as many ways to interact with a database as there are databases. Many database systems have multiple interfaces: a command-line interface where you can directly interact with data as well as programming interfaces for a variety of programming languages like C, Perl, and PHP. You'll find that different interfaces play a role at different points of your development cycle. For example, when first building a new database, you spend time experimenting with a command-line or graphical tool designing the database. Once your ideas solidify and you start constructing your system, you spend more time using a software interface, called an Application Programming Interface (API), that enables you to talk to the database using function calls in whatever programming language you use.

Regardless of the interface you use, all have the notion of a *query*, a request you (or your application) makes of the database. Some queries are obvious, such as "tell me the user whose MIN is 8885554444" or "show me all of the events that occur on 31 Dec 2000". Other requests, such as "change the name field of the record whose MIN is 8885554444 to read 'Raymond,'" are queries, too, although they might not seem so to you because you're interested in what the request does (change a field) rather than the results (the changed field).

The Structured Query Language (SQL) is a standard way to express these queries. It's supported by many large databases, including those from Oracle, Sybase, and Microsoft, and open-source database systems like MySQL and PostgreSQL. Queries in SQL have a well-defined syntax that resembles English. When working with a database interface, you build queries in SQL graphically or type them in, and the database produces the results. Similarly, when using an API to a database that supports SQL, you imbed SQL within your application, and the API shuttles your

SQL statements to the database and gives you access to the database's responses. Listing 5-1 shows three queries to give you the flavor of SQL; I show you a great deal more in subsequent sections.

```
01: INSERT INTO user VALUES ('Frank','8885551111','1111');
02: SELECT name FROM event WHERE id = 2;
03: SELECT event.start, event.stop, event.name, user.name
  FROM event
  LEFT JOIN user ON event.owner = user.min;
```

Listing 5-1. Three simple SQL queries

The first query, on line 1, inserts a row into the user table. This row corresponds to a user with the name "Frank," MIN "888-555-1111," and PIN "1111."

The second query, on line 2, looks up the record in the name table whose id field is equal to 2. More formally, this query requests a new table containing one column, which will contain the name fields of all records that match the WHERE clause of the request. The new table has one row for each row in the event table where the row's id column is equal to 2.

The query on line 3 joins two tables, the event and user tables, creating a new table with elements of each. The new table has four columns, containing the start, stop, and name fields of the event table with the name field of the user field, matching the name of the user owning a specific task. The capability to join different tables in SQL is a crucial feature because it not only lets you create complex reports from data in diverse tables, but also resolve links between tables. The query I show here returns a list of tasks and their owners, just as if you'd issued a query for tasks and then iterated over each task, looking up the owner's name for each task.

As you might imagine, under the hood a database is a complex beast. Although as a developer you spend most of your time worrying about how to represent your data as tables, behind the scenes the database does a lot to map your tables to a storage medium that's fast, efficient, and reliable. Most database systems store data in multiple files across different directories on your hard drive; the largest databases do this across multiple drives, or even multiple computers on a closed network. Administering a system like this can become a full-time task.

In installations with large databases, you often encounter a division of responsibilities between contributors:

- One person is responsible for *database administration*, that is, the nuts-and-bolts of the database system and software. This person maintains the hardware and software and is responsible for backing up data (and restoring it when the unthinkable happens).

- Another person is responsible for database programs. She works with content experts to devise the tables, queries, and applications that users work with when interacting with the database.

- A third individual or group is responsible for the database content. He spends his time entering or examining data. In the sections that follow, I show you what you need to know about these responsibilities from the perspective of the database developer.

> **NOTE** *Database administration is a lot like systems administration. As a database administrator, you have a number of responsibilities far different than that of a software developer, including hardware and software maintenance. Consequently, the tools and concepts can be very different than those you'd encounter when using a database as a developer or a user. If you need to administer your own databases, be sure to read the documentation that came with your database system (such as the MySQL manual). It will show you how to create new databases, remove unwanted ones, back up and restore data, and keep the system operating in optimum condition.*

Integrating with the Database

Your database plays an essential role in your wireless application. In essence, it becomes the core of your content. Around this core are SQL statements and server-side scripts, which operate as valets for your users with wireless clients. Figure 5-4 revisits the deployment diagram for a typical Wireless Web site. In this figure, the database, rather than the server's local file system using Apache, is responsible for storing the site's content.

On small sites, your Web server and database server can operate on the same machine. This works especially well during development and early testing because you can minimize your investment in hardware and hardware support. As your site grows, however, you can offload database responsibility to a separate machine so that the Web server uses separate resources.

At the software level, you use APIs within your active server tools to access the database. PHP sports APIs for different database systems from a variety of vendors. Listing 5-2 shows a typical script using the MySQL interface from MobileHelper.

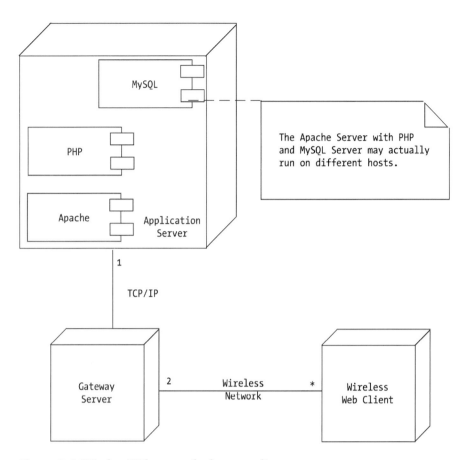

Figure 5-4. Wireless Web server deployment diagram

```
01: /*******************************************************
02: * FUNCTION: DBGetOpenTasks( )
03: *
04: * DESCRIPTION: Returns an array of open assignments.
05: *
06: * RETURNED: array of event hashes or 0
07: *******************************************************/
08: function DBGetOpenTasks()
09: {
10:
11: // Do the query, return the record or null
12:
13:   $dbqr = mysql_query(
14:     "SELECT * FROM event " .
15:     "WHERE state=" . DBTASKOPEN . " " .
16:     "ORDER BY start ASC"
17:   );
18:
```

```
19: // Validate
20:
21:  if ( !$dbqr )
22:    return 0;
23:
24: // We've got something… create a result array and return
25:
26:  $result = array();
27:
28:  while( $row = mysql_fetch_array( $dbqr ) )
29:  {
30:    array_push( $result, $row );
31:  }
32:
33:  return $result;
34: }
```

Listing 5-2. Typical use of SQL within PHP

Listing 5-2 shows the function DBGetOpenTasks, which returns an array of open tasks for MobileHelper. This script follows a familiar recipe: make a request of the database, check to see if the results are valid, and then do something with the request. On line 13, the function calls the mysql_query function, a PHP API that passes an SQL query from the PHP script to the database. In return, the function returns true (non-zero) if the query succeeded, or false (zero) otherwise. Note that mysql_query doesn't tell you anything about the results of the query, just whether or not it succeeded.

To get the results of the query, the script uses the mysql_fetch_array function. This function returns an array for each row in the table that was created by the last mysql_query call. Thus, to build a list of all of the rows in the result table, DBGetOpenTasks iterates over mysql_fetch_array on lines 28–31, taking each row from the result table and appending it to the array $result. Eventually, mysql_fetch_array will run out of rows, and the loop terminates, letting the function return the array $result on line 33.

First Steps with MySQL

It's time to actually work with a database, instead of talking about one. In this section and the remainder of the book, I show you how to use MySQL, a freely available relational database that runs on various flavors of UNIX and Microsoft Windows.

MySQL is a great database for many small- to medium-sized Web and Wireless Web sites. It's affordable (generally it's free, unless you want to buy technical support), fast, and has a robust feature set. MySQL is a relational database that supports SQL, so you won't need to learn a lot of MySQL-specific information that won't help you when you use another database. It supports multiple users with separate access information for each user so you can control which users have access to different tables and databases. Like most other open-source software, a vibrant developer community contributes to MySQL, ensuring that you can find support, additions, and bug fixes when you need them.

A more abstract benefit of MySQL is that it's quite similar to other SQL databases, both internally and in relation to PHP. Consequently, even if you don't plan on using MySQL in your application, learning about MySQL and how MySQL and PHP work together will help you understand how you can access the database of your choice from within PHP.

Of course, MySQL isn't perfect for all uses. It doesn't have some of the high-end features you might need when building an e-commerce system, such as support for transactions. It also doesn't support very high loads (say, more than 15 or 20 hits a second on moderate hardware) or commercial databases or PostgreSQL. Odds are good, though, that unless you have a pressing reason to use another database, you'll find that MySQL is up to the task for your site.

> **NOTE** *MySQL is a largely SQL-compliant database management system. Throughout the remainder of this chapter, I show you various parts of MySQL, and call your attention to both features of MySQL and features found in all database systems that offer SQL. I use the name MySQL when describing specific features of MySQL, and SQL when describing features of MySQL that are shared with other databases that implement SQL.*

Setting up MySQL

MySQL isn't a single program. Rather, it's a database *system*, comprised of the database server, a command-line database client you use to interact with the server, and a host of utilities to help maintain databases kept by the database server. Consequently, installing MySQL is a little more time-consuming than simply installing a WAP SDK or even the Apache server. Unless you've worked with MySQL before or have special requirements, you'll want to get a copy of a binary distribution so you won't have to sort through the various parts yourself. (See the sidebar for more about how to install MySQL.)

Within MySQL, the database server **mysqld** maintains databases themselves. This server is analogous to the HTTP server, listening on a specific network port for requests from other programs. Instead of requests for Web content, however, **mysqld** listens for database queries from other MySQL tools and your applications.

As it receives requests from clients, it interprets the requests, performs various operations on the files containing the databases, and returns the result to the application over the network connection. Fortunately, most of the time you don't need to know what files MySQL works with or how they're formatted, unless you're backing up the server's contents or restoring server data.

One benefit of this client-server approach is that the server need not run on the same machine as its clients. In a large setting you might have one fast computer dedicated to running the **mysqld** program, providing database services to two Web servers (one for the Web and one for the Wireless Web) and a bunch of desktop clients responsible for entering and maintaining data. It also makes it easy to integrate MySQL functionality into your own applications because you can take a client library containing code that knows how to talk to MySQL and integrate it into an application written in another language like C, C++, Perl, or Java. In fact, that's how PHP works with MySQL behind the scenes: PHP uses the MySQL client library, giving you PHP functions that in turn call MySQL client library functions.

Many of the other tools in the MySQL system perform overlapping functions— you create a database with several different tools, for example. These tools include:

- The **mysqld** program. Your computer should always have a copy of this running, so that the database will be available to clients when they need it.(The trailing d is short for daemon, a program that runs continuously to provide a service.)

- The **mysql** program (also called the monitor). This program lets you interact directly with the database server by entering SQL statements and viewing the results of database queries.

- The **mysqladmin** program, which lets you perform administrative functions such as adding new databases and tables or flushing tables to disk. Some of these functions, such as adding new databases and tables, can also be done directly within **mysql**.

- The **mysqldump** program, which lets you dump the structure and contents of a database either as SQL statements or a tab-delimited text file. You use **mysqldump** to create images of the database to load on other computers for backup or archival purposes.

- The **mysqlimport** program, which lets you import a text file into a database table. It's functionally equivalent to a command you can issue in **mysql**, but often it's easier to use this program when automating data imports.

- The **mysqlshow** program, which gives you information about the databases, tables, and indexes maintained by a server. You can also get this information using **mysql**.

- The **myisamchk** program, which lets you validate, repair, and optimize tables in the event of a system failure.

Before you can use any of these programs, you need a username and password for MySQL. By default, MySQL comes with a single user, "root." This user is akin to the root or administration login on your workstation; it has permission to make changes anywhere. Generally, you don't want to use the root user for daily activity (either on your workstation or within your database) because there's no guarantee that a mistake won't destroy or alter valuable data. Moreover, if your database is going to be accessible by several people, it's more useful to have a separate account for each person. On my server, I have an account for each user, with permission to access the databases they need, along with a special user php that PHP scripts use when they need to access a database.

If you're running your own MySQL server, you can create a new user by running **mysql** and entering the command **GRANT ALL ON * TO name IDENTIFIED by "password"** where **name** is your username and **password** is your password. (Don't worry about what this means right now; I get to it in the section "Statements," later in this chapter). If, on the other hand, you're using someone else's server, talk to the administrator for that server and ask them to give you an account and create your database.

With your MySQL login name and password in hand, you're ready to try using the **mysql** program to work with a simple database. You do this by typing **mysql -u name -p** (where **name** is your MySQL user name) at a prompt near you. (If your login name is the same as your MySQL username, you can generally leave out the **-u name** clause. You can also configure MySQL to automatically know who you are; see the documentation for details.) Assuming everything's set up correctly, you'll be asked for your password. Supply your password, and you'll be met with a message like that shown in Listing 5-3 on lines 3–8. You can now enter MySQL commands, including SQL queries.

```
01: [localhost:~/public_html] dove% mysql -u dove -p
02: Enter password:
03: Welcome to the MySQL monitor. Commands end with ; or \g.
04: Your MySQL connection id is 4 to server version: 3.23.28-gamma
05:
06: Type 'help;' or '\h' for help. Type '\c' to clear the buffer
07:
08: mysql>
```

*Listing 5-3. Beginning a **mysql** session*

Installing MySQL

Unlike the other programs discussed in this book, which are included on the CD-ROM, MySQL is not, so you'll want to visit `http://www.mysql.com` to download a copy of MySQL for your operating system. These instructions describe basic installation steps; be sure to read the documentation that comes with the version you download.

If you're using Microsoft Windows, simply unzip the binary archive in an empty directory and run the Setup.exe installer program. By default, MySQL will be installed in c:\mysql, which is almost always where you want it. (You can change its location using the installer, however.) To start the MySQL server, type

```
c:\>c:\mysql\bin\mysqld
```

at a command-line prompt, or add this line to your system's startup sequence. Alternately, there's a version of MySQL that you can install as a service, so you don't need to start the MySQL server every time you reboot your system.

Under UNIX, you have more choices. If you're using Linux, you can find a Red Hat Package Manager file (RPM) of the binary for your system at the MySQL Web site at `http://www.mysql.com`. Log in as root and use the **rpm** command to install the package using the command:

```
# rpm -i <package name>
```

At the MySQL Web site you will also find precompiled binaries for a number of UNIX platforms. Download the precompiled binary for your system, log in as root and, to install the binaries and documentation, use the **tar** command:

```
# tar xzf <binary tar file name>
```

After unpacking either the package or the tar file, you'll have to do some additional work to configure the server.

Of course, if all else fails, you can grab the sources and build it yourself. MySQL has been around long enough that it's been ported to almost every imaginable flavor of UNIX, so building it is straightforward, although you need to spend time customizing the build process so it knows how to build MySQL for your operating system. First, as root, create a user and group identifier for MySQL:

```
# groupadd mysql
# useradd -g mysql mysql
```

Then you need to unpack the distribution and configure it for your platform:

```
# tar -xzvf <archive name>
# cd mysql-VERSION
# ./configure –prefix=/usr/local/mysql
```

Next, you build and install the MySQL server and client applications, along with various utilities:

```
# make
# make install
# scripts/mysql_install_db
```

Finally, you set ownership for the files you've just installed, and start the server so you can test it.

```
# chown -R mysql /usr/local/mysql
# chgrp -R mysql /usr/local/mysql
# /usr/local/mysql/bin/safe_mysqld –user=mysql &
```

You probably also want to set your system so that it automatically starts MySQL whenever it boots. To do this, you can add an entry to your system's boot script, typically /etc/rc.d/rc.local:

`/usr/local/bin/mysqlctl start`

As you build MySQL, things may not go as you expect. That's okay; often it's something somebody else has seen. Take a deep breath (or jump up and down and scream, if that helps), and read the MySQL documentation, especially the INSTALL-SOURCE file. If all else fails, check out the MySQL Web page and mailing lists for advice.

A Simple Database

In the section "Understanding Database Terminology," I showed the schema for the MobileHelper database, concentrating on the user table. To get a feel for using **mysql**, let's create a simple database with one table, the user table. This table will have three columns: the user's name, MIN, and PIN.

Creating a database

Listing 5-4 shows how to create the database with **mysql**.

```
01: [localhost:~] dove% mysql -u dove -p
02: Enter password:
03: Welcome to the MySQL monitor. Commands end with ; or \g.
04: Your MySQL connection id is 7 to server version: 3.23.28-gamma
05:
06: Type 'help;' or '\h' for help. Type '\c' to clear the buffer
07:
08: mysql> SHOW DATABASES;
09: +——————+
10: | Database  |
11: +——————+
12: | mysql     |
13: | test      |
14: +——————+
15: 2 rows in set (0.00 sec)
16:
17: mysql> CREATE DATABASE MobileHelper;
18: Query OK, 1 row affected (0.01 sec)
19:
20: mysql> Bye
```

Listing 5-4. Creating a database

After connecting to the database server with **mysql** on the first line, I issue the SHOW DATABASES query on line 8. This isn't strictly necessary; MySQL won't let me clobber a database by creating another one with the same name. It is illustrative, however, because it shows you a simple database query.

A query is a sequence of statements terminated by a semicolon and the **Return** key. In response to a query, the server returns either a table or an error; the table may be empty, indicating that no data satisfied the query. In Listing 5-4, the table responding to our first query is shown on lines 9–16, along with the table summary on line 15 showing that the table contained two rows and that it took an infinitesimal amount of time to process the query. It's worth noting that queries are not case-sensitive, although by long convention, SQL statements are written in capital letters while arguments such as table or column names are written in lowercase.

> **NOTE** *Using the* SHOW DATABASES *query in* **mysql** *is the same as using the* **mysqlshow** *utility. In fact, almost everything you can do with the utilities you can do with* **mysql** *queries, so in the following discussion I stick with showing you how to do things just using* **mysql**.

After getting a list of databases, I ask the server to create a new database on line 17 with the CREATE DATABASE statement. This statement takes an argument, naming the database. This time, the server doesn't return a table but lets me know that the query succeeded on line 18. After that, I exit the monitor. (I don't have to exit **mysql** between creating the database and creating the table, but doing so keeps the listings in the book to a manageable length.)

Creating a table

Now that the database is created, I can create a new table within the database, as Listing 5-5 shows.

```
01: [localhost:~] dove% mysql -u dove -p
02: Enter password:
03: Welcome to the MySQL monitor. Commands end with ; or \g.
04: Your MySQL connection id is 7 to server version: 3.23.28-gamma
05:
06: Type 'help;' or '\h' for help. Type '\c' to clear the buffer
07:
08: mysql> USE MobileHelper;
09: Database changed
10:
11: mysql> CREATE TABLE user (
12:    -> name TINYTEXT,
13:    -> min VARCHAR(10) UNIQUE,
14:    -> pin VARCHAR(10)
15:    -> );
16: Query OK, 0 rows affected (0.04 sec)
17:
18: mysql> SHOW TABLES;
19: +-----------------------+
20: | Tables_in_MoblieHelper |
21: +-----------------------+
22: | user                  |
23: +-----------------------+
24: 1 row in set (0.01 sec)
25:
```

```
26: mysql> SHOW COLUMNS FROM user;
27: +————-+————-+———+———+———————+——
    +———————————+
28: | Field | Type    | Null | Key | Default | Extra
    | Privileges          |
29: +————-+————-+———+———+———————+——
    +———————————+
30: | name | tinytext  | YES |     | NULL  |
    | select,insert,update,references |
31: | min  | varchar(10) | YES | UNI | NULL  |
    | select,insert,update,references |
32: | pin  | varchar(10) | YES |     | NULL  |
    | select,insert,update,references |
33: +————-+————-+———+———+———————+——
    +———————————+
34: 3 rows in set (0.00 sec)
35:
36: mysql> Bye
```

Listing 5-5. Creating a new table

Before you can directly access a database's contents, you must tell MySQL which database you're talking about using the USE statement, shown on line 8 of Listing 5-5. The USE statement is shorthand—without it, every table reference would need to include the name of the database containing the table as well.

You're now ready to create the table. When creating a table, you give MySQL two pieces of information for each column: the column's name and its type. Unlike the programming languages you encountered in previous chapters, MySQL is very picky about data types. This is partially out of respect for the existing SQL standard, and partially because it's more efficient to store large volumes of data if the computer doesn't have to guess what kind of data it's storing.

MySQL has a number of data types, which I explain in the section "Data Types" later in this chapter. For simplicity's sake, let's make all three columns in the user table strings. The first column, name, will contain the user's name, which is a variable-length string. Because you don't know how long the longest user name is, simply use the MySQL TINYTEXT type, which is big enough to hold almost any name. (In fact, a TINYTEXT holds between 0 and 255 characters.) The second and third fields will hold the MIN and PIN values. You can take a stab at how big these are—a MIN consists of a handset's area code and phone number, or 10 characters, while the PIN has a similar upper bound. The min column has another interesting property: it's unique. No two handsets will ever have the same MIN, so you can use a user's MIN as a key into the user table. I tell the database this as well when I create the table, so that if I accidentally try to create two records with the same MIN, I receive an error.

On lines 11–16 I create the user table using the CREATE TABLE statement. This statement spans several lines for readability; I could have just as easily written it all on one line. The CREATE TABLE statement takes the name of the table to create and a list of its columns in parentheses. Each column contains the name of the column, its type, and any modifiers to its type. You separate each column in the list with commas.

I define the first column, name, on line 12. The **mysql** program provided the leading indent and the -> prompt, while I typed the column description. The name column is a TINYTEXT field with no special attributes. On line 13, I define the second column to be a unique 10-character string called min using the type VARCHAR(10) UNIQUE. Finally, I define the last column, pin, as another 10-character string using VARCHAR(10).

You can see the names of the tables in the database. That's helpful if you're working on an existing database and don't have your schema handy. You do this with the SHOW TABLES statement, as I do on line 18. Similarly, you get a table of the columns in a specific table using the SHOW COLUMNS FROM statement. Shown on lines 27–33, this statement demonstrates one of the drawbacks of using the **mysql** monitor: its output is frequently hard to read. The **mysql** command doesn't have any of the niceties such as word-wrapping, so reading long tables is often an exercise in sliding your finger along the screen or a printout hoping to see what you want. Fortunately, once you create your tables and nail out the specifics of your queries, you can spend most of your time looking at output obtained via PHP in a Web browser or WAP SDK. At any rate, this table shows not just each column's name and type, but also whether it can hold empty entries, whether or not each column is a key, what its default value is, and what permissions I have as a user to access or modify a specific column.

> **NOTE** *You may or may not see the permissions column, depending on whether you follow the instructions exactly in this section, or use the version of the MobileHelper database provided on the CD-ROM that accompanies this book.*

Inserting, updating, and deleting rows

Speaking of queries, let's add some rows to my new table so I can try a few simple queries. Adding rows is easy: use the INSERT INTO statement, as Listing 5-6 shows. The INSERT INTO statement takes the name of the table and a list of values, specified by the keyword VALUE and a list of values in parentheses. In Listing 5-6, I insert three rows, corresponding to records for the volunteers Rachel, Jarod, and myself, on lines 11–12, 15–16, and 19–20.

```
01: [localhost:~] dove% mysql -u dove -p
02: Enter password:
03: Welcome to the MySQL monitor. Commands end with ; or \g.
04: Your MySQL connection id is 7 to server version: 3.23.28-gamma
05:
06: Type 'help;' or '\h' for help. Type '\c' to clear the buffer
07:
08: mysql> USE MobileHelper;
09: Database changed
10:
11: mysql> INSERT INTO user
12:    -> VALUES ('Rachel','8885552222','2718');
13: Query OK, 1 row affected (0.00 sec)
14:
15: mysql> INSERT INTO user
16:    -> VALUES ('Jarod','8885553333','3141');
17: Query OK, 1 row affected (0.00 sec)
18:
19: mysql> INSERT INTO user
20:    -> VALUES ('Ray','8885554444','0000');
21: Query OK, 1 row affected (0.00 sec)
22:
23: mysql> Bye
```

Listing 5-6. The INSERT INTO *statement*

You can change column values for a row or group of rows, too. Listing 5-7 shows an erroneous INSERT INTO statement and a corresponding UPDATE SET statement to correct the mistake.

```
01: [localhost:~] dove% mysql -u dove -p
02: Enter password:
03: Welcome to the MySQL monitor. Commands end with ; or \g.
04: Your MySQL connection id is 7 to server version: 3.23.28-gamma
05:
06: Type 'help;' or '\h' for help. Type '\c' to clear the buffer
07:
08: mysql> USE MobileHelper;
09: Database changed
10:
```

```
11: mysql> INSERT INTO user
12:    -> VALUES ('Sherwin','888888','1357');
13: Query OK, 1 row affected (0.02 sec)
14:
15: mysql> UPDATE user
16:    -> SET min = "8885558888"
17:    -> WHERE min = "888888";
18: Query OK, 1 row affected (0.06 sec)
19: Rows matched: 1 Changed: 1 Warnings: 0
20:
21: mysql> Bye
```

Listing 5-7. The UPDATE SET *statement*

Similarly, you can delete rows from a table. At some point, Jarod's going to go to college and won't be in the area to help. When he does, I can issue the DELETE FROM statement shown in Listing 5-8 to delete his record.

```
01: [localhost:~] dove% mysql -u dove -p
02: Enter password:
03: Welcome to the MySQL monitor. Commands end with ; or \g.
04: Your MySQL connection id is 7 to server version: 3.23.28-gamma
05:
06: Type 'help;' or '\h' for help. Type '\c' to clear the buffer
07:
08: mysql> USE MobileHelper;
09: Database changed
10:
11: mysql> DELETE FROM user
12:    -> WHERE min = "8885553333";
13: Query OK, 1 row affected (0.01 sec)
14:
15: mysql> Bye
```

Listing 5-8. The DELETE FROM *statement*

Of course, the WHERE clause can be more complex. In fact, the WHERE clause of SQL is responsible for most of the work when searching the database for virtually all other commands. The WHERE clause accepts comparisons for equality, inequality, and ordering between columns in the same table, different tables, and computed values as well as the simple scalar comparisons shown here. You'll see examples of this throughout this chapter.

Selecting rows

If this were all you could do with a database, it wouldn't be terribly useful. The SELECT FROM statement lets you get data out of a database. The SELECT FROM statement takes a list of columns (or the asterisk (*) to show all columns in a particular table) along optional clauses specifying which rows to show and how to sort the resulting table. Listing 5-9 shows a simple SELECT FROM statement on line 11 that returns all the rows in the user table of database, followed by a second SELECT FROM on line 21 that returns only the MIN and name of each user.

```
01: [localhost:~] dove% mysql -u dove -p
02: Enter password:
03: Welcome to the MySQL monitor. Commands end with ; or \g.
04: Your MySQL connection id is 7 to server version: 3.23.28-gamma
05:
06: Type 'help;' or '\h' for help. Type '\c' to clear the buffer
07:
08: mysql> USE MobileHelper;
09: Database changed
10:
11: mysql> SELECT * FROM user;
12: +--------+------------+------+
13: | name   | min        | pin  |
14: +--------+------------+------+
15: | Rachel | 8885552222 | 2718 |
16: | Ray    | 8885554444 | 0000 |
17: | Sherwin| 8885558888 | 1357 |
18: +--------+------------+------+
19: 3 rows in set (0.01 sec)
20:
21: mysql> SELECT min, name FROM user;
22: +------------+---------+
23: | min        | name    |
24: +------------+---------+
25: | 8885552222 | Rachel  |
26: | 8885554444 | Ray     |
27: | 8885558888 | Sherwin |
28: +------------+---------+
29: 3 rows in set (0.02 sec)
30:
31: mysql> Bye
```

Listing 5-9. Simple SELECT FROM *statements*

Of course, you can pick which rows are included in a SELECT FROM query, too. Let's say you're interested in seeing the information for Rachel. You can do this in a number of ways: asking SELECT FROM to match only rows in which the name column contains "Rachel", or, if you know Rachel's MIN, by matching only the row with her MIN. The two approaches are shown in Listing 5-10. As with the UPDATE SET statement, you can specify which rows to select using a WHERE clause.

```
01: [localhost:~] dove% mysql -u dove -p
02: Enter password:
03: Welcome to the MySQL monitor. Commands end with ; or \g.
04: Your MySQL connection id is 7 to server version: 3.23.28-gamma
05:
06: Type 'help;' or '\h' for help. Type '\c' to clear the buffer
07:
08: mysql> USE MobileHelper;
09: Database changed
10:
11: mysql> SELECT * FROM user
12:    -> WHERE name = "Rachel";
13: +--------+------------+------+
14: | name   | min        | pin  |
15: +--------+------------+------+
16: | Rachel | 8885552222 | 2718 |
17: +--------+------------+------+
18: 1 row in set (0.01 sec)
19:
20:
21: mysql> SELECT * FROM user
22:    -> WHERE min = "8885552222";
23: +--------+------------+------+
24: | name   | min        | pin  |
25: +--------+------------+------+
26: | Rachel | 8885552222 | 2718 |
27: +--------+------------+------+
28: 1 row in set (0.01 sec)
29:
30: Empty set (0.00 sec)
31:
32: mysql> Bye
```

Listing 5-10. SELECT FROM *statements using a* WHERE *clause*

As I show later in the chapter, you can mold your WHERE clauses to find virtually anything in the database. For example, consider again finding information about the user Rachel. Given that I know that the Mountain Neighbor Network spans a small area and that most users have the same area code and prefix, there's little reason for me to type in those bits of a MIN when searching for someone. In fact, I might just remember that Rachel's MIN ends in 2222.

I can use a WHERE clause with a *wildcard* to find all phone numbers matching a partial string, as shown on lines 11–18 of Listing 5-11. The clause WHERE min LIKE "%2222" tells MySQL to find all rows with a min column containing any combination of characters followed by the string "2222". The leading % asks MySQL to match any set of characters, while the LIKE keyword says that the next string contains a wild-card instead of a %.

Of course, there's the chance that somebody else's number ends in 2222 as well. To restrict the results of my SELECT FROM to include only Rachel's information, I can be more specific and include her name as well. In the second query, on lines 20–27, you can see that you can combine several conditions within a single WHERE clause. Here, I tell MySQL to return only columns with a name field containing the string "Rachel" and the desired MIN.

While the % wildcard matches zero or more characters, MySQL also provides the _ character to match a single character. In the last query on lines 29–31, I show you the _ wildcard. This *won't* match Rachel's MIN: it will only match five-character strings such as 1222 or a2222.

```
01: [localhost:~] dove% mysql -u dove -p
02: Enter password:
03: Welcome to the MySQL monitor. Commands end with ; or \g.
04: Your MySQL connection id is 7 to server version: 3.23.28-gamma
05:
06: Type 'help;' or '\h' for help. Type '\c' to clear the buffer
07:
08: mysql> USE MobileHelper;
09: Database changed
10:
11: mysql> SELECT * FROM user
12:     -> WHERE min LIKE "%2222";
13: +--------+------------+------+
14: | name   | min        | pin  |
15: +--------+------------+------+
16: | Rachel | 8885552222 | 2718 |
17: +--------+------------+------+
18: 1 row in set (0.05 sec)
19:
```

```
20: mysql> SELECT * FROM user
21:    -> WHERE name = "Rachel" AND min LIKE "%2222";
22: +--------+------------+------+
23: | name   | min        | pin  |
24: +--------+------------+------+
25: | Rachel | 8885552222 | 2718 |
26: +--------+------------+------+
27: 1 row in set (0.01 sec)
28:
29: mysql> SELECT * FROM user
30:    -> WHERE min LIKE "_2222";
31: Empty set (0.00 sec)
32:
33: mysql> Bye
```

Listing 5-11. More uses of the WHERE *clause in* SELECT FROM *statements*

Joining columns from different tables

You can select columns from different tables, too. Skipping ahead to where the entire MobileHelper database has been defined (which you will see in the section "MySQL Within MobileHelper," later in this chapter), let's say you want to know the names of the people responsible for each of the tasks in the database.

Listing 5-12 shows a query that answers this question. On the first line of the query (line 11) I ask for the name column of the user table and the name column of the event table. This . notation is used between table names and column names. In fact, you can refer to a particular column of a particular table in a specific database using the notation database.table.column, if you need to access data in a different database as part of a statement. On line 12, I instruct MySQL to walk each row of the event table when performing the SELECT FROM. Line 13 tells MySQL to merge each row of the event table with the row in the user table where event.owner is equal to user.min.

```
01: [localhost:~] dove% mysql -u dove -p
02: Enter password:
03: Welcome to the MySQL monitor. Commands end with ; or \g.
04: Your MySQL connection id is 7 to server version: 3.23.28-gamma
05:
06: Type 'help;' or '\h' for help. Type '\c' to clear the buffer
07:
08: mysql> USE MobileHelper;
09: Database changed
10:
```

```
11: mysql> SELECT user.name, event.name
12:    -> FROM event
13:    -> LEFT JOIN user ON event.owner = user.min;
14: +———————+———————————————+
15: | name  | name          |
16: +———————+———————————————+
17: | Ray   | First Night    |
18: | NULL  | Communications |
19: | NULL  | Communications |
20: +———————+———————————————+
21: 3 rows in set (0.03 sec)
22:
23: mysql> Bye
```

Listing 5-12. Joining two tables with SELECT FROM

An operation such as this involving more than one table is called a *join* operation because it joins columns from different tables to make a new table. The join is a crucial operation because you can use it to combine elements from different tables and resolve links between tables in a single step.

There are two kinds of joins, the *left join* and the *full join*. The query in Listing 5-12 is a left join that iterates over each row of the first table, producing a new row in the result table for each row in the first table. The full join, on the other hand, iterates across each row of the first table combined with each row of the second table and returns only those rows that match the conditions you state.

> **NOTE** *In many texts, especially those with a formal tone, you also see references to a third kind of join, the trivial join. The trivial join is simply a join in which only one table is named. While calling it a trivial join is justified when you're thinking about the relationships between tables from a mathematical perspective, it's often confusing when first learning SQL, and I prefer to avoid it.*

Another way to think of a join is in terms of other language's foreach statements. Although MySQL doesn't have a foreach statement, the notion of a left join is the same: for each element in the first table, visit the row, perform the comparison that's indicated by the ON clause, and return a new row based on the SELECT clause. In contrast, a full join's foreach statement visits not just each row of the first table, but all possible rows created by combining each row of the first and second tables.

In practice, joins don't visit every possible row in each table. If they did, operations on large databases would be near impossible: a full join on two tables containing just one thousand entries apiece would require the creation of a million rows. Instead, the database uses a number of mathematical tricks to build a smaller subset of rows that might match the other parts of the SELECT FROM statement and then computes the result.

Dropping database contents

Occasionally you find a table or database has outlived its utility. Perhaps you are prototyping a new table, or maybe you're moving a database to a new host and want to make sure you don't waste space with the old copy. MySQL provides the DROP TABLE and DROP DATABASE statements. As you might surmise, the former removes a table from the database, while the latter removes an entire database. Listing 5-13 shows an example of each.

```
01: [localhost:~] dove% mysql -u dove -p
02: Enter password:
03: Welcome to the MySQL monitor. Commands end with ; or \g.
04: Your MySQL connection id is 7 to server version: 3.23.28-gamma
05:
06: Type 'help;' or '\h' for help. Type '\c' to clear the buffer
07:
08: mysql> USE MobileHelper;
09: Database changed
10:
11: mysql> show tables;
12: +-----------------------+
13: | Tables_in_MobileHelper |
14: +-----------------------+
15: | user                  |
16: +-----------------------+
17: 1 row in set (0.01 sec)
18:
19: mysql> DROP TABLE user;
20: Query OK, 0 rows affected (0.02 sec)
21:
22: mysql> DROP DATABASE MobileHelper;
23: Query OK, 1 row affected (0.01 sec)
24:
25: mysql> Bye
```

Listing 5-13. The DROP TABLE *and* DROP DATABASE *statements*

> **CAUTION**   *There's no undo for any of the SQL statements you saw in this section (or the other SQL statements, for that matter!). Inadvertently dropping other people's tables or databases makes you very unpopular around the office!*

MySQL Syntax

SQL's syntax—and that of MySQL as well—is unlike anything you've encountered in this book. SQL's syntax was developed in a period of computing history when many scholars believed that the simplest computer languages for people to learn had syntax reminiscent of natural languages like English.

MySQL isn't a programming language *per se*. Rather, it's a query language and query languages have subtle but important differences from programming languages. You don't write a lot of SQL for your Web application. Rather, you write the SQL that describes the database, which is run once when the database is built, and write SQL queries your application uses to access the database.

You build each of these queries using a SQL *statement* such as INSERT INTO or SELECT FROM, along with *clauses* that describe how MySQL should perform the statement. In turn, clauses may contain *expressions* that tell MySQL to perform computations as it evaluates the query. When using the **mysql** monitor, you need to terminate each SQL query using a semicolon, but you don't have to do that when invoking MySQL from PHP or another programming language because you'll issue each MySQL query separately. (More on how that works in the section "Accessing MySQL from PHP" later in this chapter.)

Identifiers, used to name tables and columns, are alphanumeric strings that may include the _ underscore character as well as digits. Case—whether a word is in capitals or not—is a tricky thing in MySQL. Within MySQL queries, case doesn't matter: SELECT FROM is the same as Select from, for example. Similarly, MySQL ignores case when referring to column names, so I could write MIN instead of min when referring to a column in the user table. Database and table names, on the other hand, may or may not be case-sensitive because MySQL uses a local file system to store databases and tables. Consequently, the name of a database or table may be insensitive to case on one system, but when you move your database and queries to another system, errors crop up as case sensitivity becomes an issue. One way to avoid this problem is to be in the habit of pretending that MySQL statements are case-sensitive. It's easiest to use the convention that SQL statements and operations are in capitals, and database, column, and table names are all lowercase. This is the approach I take, except that at times I use mixed case for names made from more than one word, like "MobileHelper." Even then, I am sure to capitalize consistently so moving the database to different computers doesn't become a problem. In short, adopt a convention for capitalization and stick with it.

MySQL is far more tolerant of white space, however. You can use spaces, tabs, and line breaks wherever you want, as long as they don't break apart key words like statement or function names.

Although it's not terribly common to do so, you can comment MySQL statements. Often you do this when you're writing a set of MySQL statements to create a new database, or insert a lot of data. There are two ways to write comments: C-style comments surrounded by /* and */, and Bourne shell style comments using a # character. When using C-style comments, anything between the /* and */ is ignored by the MySQL interpreter. The # comment character, on the other hand, instructs the MySQL interpreter to ignore everything from that point through the end of the line. You can also use two hyphens, like this - -, to begin a comment that spans a whole line. Listing 5-14, an excerpt from the MobileHelper.dump file on the CD-ROM that will create a new MobileHelper database with some sample data, shows the typical use of comments. (This particular listing was generated by MySQL itself using the **mysqldump** utility.)

```
01: # MySQL dump 8.11
02: #
03: # Host: localhost Database: MobileHelper
04: #————————————
05: # Server version 3.23.28-gamma
06:
07: #
08: # Table structure for table 'event'
09: #
10:
11: CREATE TABLE event (
12:   id int(10) unsigned NOT NULL auto_increment,
13:   state tinyint(4),
14:   start int(10) unsigned,
15:   stop int(10) unsigned,
16:   actualStart int(10) unsigned,
17:   actualStop int(10) unsigned,
18:   location int(11),
19:   owner varchar(10),
20:   name tinytext,
21:   note tinytext,
22:   PRIMARY KEY (id)
23: );
24:
```

```
25: #
26: # Dumping data for table 'event'
27: #
28:
29: INSERT INTO event VALUES (1,0,978379200,978386400,
30:   NULL,NULL,1,NULL,'First Night',NULL);
31: INSERT INTO event VALUES (2,0,981993600,982015200,
32:   NULL,NULL,3,NULL,'Communications',
33:   'Provide back-up radio communications');
34: INSERT INTO event VALUES (3,0,982015200,982036800,
35:   NULL,NULL,3,NULL,'Communications',
36:   'Provide back-up radio communications');
37:
38: #
39: # Lots more of this stuff would follow...
40: #
```

Listing 5-14. Comments in MySQL

Going Further with MySQL

Of tools in this book you'll probably find it easiest to learn MySQL by experimenting with it, rather than digging through a lot of documentation. There are two
reasons for this: interactivity and simple syntax.

First, you can work with MySQL interactively. Once you're over the hassle of
installing MySQL, it's incredibly easy to plink away at the **mysql** monitor and see
how different queries work. You don't have run an SDK, edit text files, or post content
to a server. Typing a query and immediately seeing the response helps you quickly
learn how different SQL statements work.

Second, MySQL's syntax is easy to learn. It's easy to think of SELECT FROM as getting
records from a database. While you may find yourself stumbling over the keywords ("Was it SHOW TABLES IN MobileHelper, or SHOW TABLES FROM MobileHelper?")
your fingers will quickly learn the difference.

Let's take a more in-depth look at the various pieces of MySQL. (And, yes, it
was SHOW TABLES FROM MobileHelper.)

Data Types

Columns are the building blocks of the tables that contain your data. As you
define each column, you tell MySQL what type of data a column will contain. In

doing so, you specify both the column's data type and attributes that refine the description of what kind of data the column will store.

Like the other languages you've seen, SQL distinguishes between two fundamental data types: numbers and character strings. Unlike other languages, SQL requires you to pay special attention to the size of individual data types, such as how many characters a string will hold, or what the range of a numeric value will be. This is important for two reasons: database space and performance. By selecting the smallest possible data type for each datum, MySQL can save disk space when storing tables. Moreover, when you use small data types, MySQL spends less time manipulating data, speeding database operations.

SQL offers five data types: integers, floating-point numbers, strings, temporal values (dates and times) and a special value of its own type called NULL. In addition, SQL provides alternate names for several data types, enabling you to create more abstract column types. Table 5-1 shows the data types.

Table 5-1. MySQL Types

TYPE NAME	DATA TYPE	RANGE/NOTE
TINYINT	Signed integer	-128 to 127
	Unsigned integer	0 to 255
SMALLINT	Signed integer	-32768 to 32767
	Unsigned integer	0 to 65535
MEDIUMINT	Signed integer	-8388608 to 8388607
	Unsigned integer	0 to 16777215
INT	Signed integer	-2147683648 to 2147683647
	Unsigned integer	0 to 4294967295
BIGINT	Signed integer	-9223372036854775808 to 9223372036854775807
	Unsigned integer	0 to 18446744073709551615
FLOAT	Floating-point number	$\pm 1.175494351 \times 10^{-38}$ to $\pm 3.402823466 \times 10^{38}$
DOUBLE	Floating-point number	$\pm 2.2250738585072014 \times 10^{-308}$ to $\pm 1.7976931348623157 \times 10^{308}$
CHAR(n)	Fixed-length character string	n characters
VARCHAR(n)	Variable-length character string	No more than n characters

Table 5-1. MySQL Types (Continued)

TYPE NAME	DATA TYPE	RANGE/NOTE
TINYTEXT	Variable-length character string	No more than 255 characters; same as VARCHAR(255)
TEXT	Variable-length string	No more than 65535 characters; same as VARCHAR(65535)
MEDIUMTEXT	Variable-length string	No more than 16777215 characters; same as VARCHAR(255)
LONGTEXT	Variable-length string	No more than 4294967295 characters; same as VARCHAR(4294967295)
TINYBLOB	Variable-length byte string	No more than 255 characters
BLOB	Variable-length byte string	No more than 65535 characters
MEDIUMBLOB	Variable-length byte string	No more than 16777215 characters
LONGBLOB	Variable-length byte string	No more than 4294967295 characters
ENUM	Individual strings	65535 distinct strings
SET	Individual elements of a set	64 distinct elements
DATE	Temporal date	OS dependent; date in YYYY-MM-DD format
TIME	Temporal time	-838:59:59 – 838:59:59; time in hh:mm:ss format
DATETIME	Temporal date and time	OS dependent; in YYYY-MM-DD hh:mm:ss format
TIMESTAMP	Temporal date and time	OS dependent; in YYYYMMDDhhmmss format
YEAR	Temporal year	0000, 1901–2155; year in year in YYYY format

Most of these types are self-explanatory. An INT, for example, holds a single integer between –2147683648 and 2147683647. You've already seen a VARCHAR, in the user table shown in previous sections.

The CHAR and VARCHAR types differ only in that CHAR strings are always the same size. Thus, if you define a column as having the type CHAR(10), all strings will consume 10 characters' worth of memory, even if you never store more than one character in the column. The various TEXT types (TINYTEXT, MEDIUMTEXT, and LONGTEXT, as well as TEXT) are similar to VARCHAR types of the same size, but more readable when you're creating a database and thinking in the context of things like names, descriptions, or stories. You can write strings in either single or double quotes. There's no notion of variable expansion with $ as there is in PHP and WMLScript, but you can use the solidus (\) character to include special characters such as quote marks in a string. Table 5-2 lists these special characters.

> **NOTE** *Actually, the various* TEXT *types are the same as the various* BLOB *types of a given length. The key differences are that* TEXT *columns, like* BLOB *columns, can't have default values, and strings with trailing spaces inserted into* TEXT *columns keep the trailing spaces, while they lose the trailing spaces in a* VARCHAR *column.*

Table 5-2. Special Characters in MySQL Strings

NEWLINE SEQUENCE	MEANING
\n	Linefeed (LF or 0x0A in ASCII)
\r	Carriage return (CR or 0x0D in ASCII)
\t	Horizontal tab (HT or 0x09 in ASCII)
\\	Backslash
\'	Single quote
\"	Double quote

The BLOB types are also character data, but MySQL treats them a little differently. When comparing or sorting values in a column, MySQL treats TEXT types as case-insensitive, while in BLOB types, MySQL distinguishes between uppercase and lowercase characters. Generally, you use the BLOB types to hold binary data, such as images or sounds.

The ENUM and SET types are special string types for which you must specify values when you define the column. You use the ENUM type to define an enumeration, whose values are mutually exclusive, such as what kind of pizza crust you want on a pizza ("thin" or "pan," for example). The SET type enables you to define a set of multiple choices from a list of values, such as pizza toppings (pepperoni and sausage, anyone?). For both, you specify the values after the data type in parentheses. For example, consider the hypothetical table in Listing 5-15, which will contain pizza orders for our local pizza parlor.

```
01: mysql> CREATE TABLE orders (
02:     -> size ENUM( "S", "M", "L", "XL" ),
03:     -> crust ENUM( "thin", "pan" ),
04:     -> topping SET( "pepperoni", "sausage",
05:     ->         "anchovy", "Canadian bacon",
06:     ->         "mushroom", "olive", "onion",
07:     ->         "pineapple" ),
08:     -> where ENUM( "here", "to go",
09:     ->         "safe delivery", "unsafe delivery" ),
10:     -> custId INT,
11:     -> comment TINYTEXT
12:     -> );
```

Listing 5-15. Using the ENUM *and* SET *types*

Here I use the ENUM type to represent a pizza's type and crust type, along with how a pizza will be delivered, because for these items, the customer can make only one choice. You can't have a thin pan-crust pizza, for example, or get your pie both here and to go. Toppings, however, are elements of a set: the Carnivore's Special drips the grease from pepperoni, sausage, anchovies, and Canadian bacon.

Before I discuss the temporal types, a digression is in order. The ENUM and SET types are best suited for values that don't change very often. If my pizza parlor adds ground beef to its list of toppings, I'll have to add "beef" to the topping column definition, and quite possibly rework not just my SQL but some of the code behind the database. If I store toppings in a separate table and refer to them using links, however, I can add new toppings just by adding a new item to a topping table.

Unlike PHP, in which time is simply represented as some number of seconds past a known date, MySQL gives you specific data types to store times and dates. These data types make it easier to search for records meeting time criteria because you can just write a date instead of shuffling between dates, times, and seconds after a known date. The DATE and TIME types enable you to store just a date or time, while the DATETIME and TIMESTAMP types store both a date and time in one of two formats. Finally, the YEAR type enables you to store a single year.

You don't have to use MySQL's temporal types, however. If you're building a database to interact with another language like PHP that has a robust set of date and time format functions, it's often easier to simply store that platform's date and time information in the database. For example, as you'll see later in this chapter, MobileHelper stores an event's start and stop time as integers, rather than MySQL dates. By using integers to store the times I can easily use PHP's functions to format output in any format I'd like, rather than the restricted formats offered by MySQL.

There's one last special type, NULL. NULL is a value of its own type, indicating that a column has no value. You use NULL when you want to store the fact that a value isn't known in the database, denoting an empty row value for that column.

As you describe a table, you provide both the data type (one of the types in Table 5-1) as well as optional attributes that modify how the type behaves. The first option you provide is the display width of the field, used by the **mysql** monitor when it displays a value of a column. This, like the width of a character string, is simply a number in parentheses. Looking back at Listing 5-14, you see that every column type is followed by a number in parentheses, such as state TINYINT(4). The (4) after TINYINT tells MySQL that when this column is displayed, it should be four characters wide. In practice you won't use field widths much except when defining text fields because most of your users won't use **mysql** to interact with your data. Instead, you use another language like PHP to obtain information from the database and format it for your users.

The UNIQUE attribute applies to a string or numeric column and indicates that a particular value can appear in, at most, one row of the table. If you try to insert two rows with the same value in a column marked UNIQUE, MySQL returns an error. The UNIQUE attribute is vital when creating IDs to link tables, or when tracking other values such as item serial numbers that can't be duplicated.

The NOT NULL attribute tells MySQL that a column must have a value when you insert a row. MobileHelper uses the NOT NULL attribute in the user table to ensure that every user has a MIN. There's also the NULL attribute, which tells MySQL that it's okay for a column to hold a NULL value, but since that's the default, you seldom see it as an attribute.

The UNSIGNED and AUTO_INCREMENT attributes apply to integers. An UNSIGNED integer column is one that will hold only zero and positive integers. You can use unsigned integers whenever your data won't assume a negative value, such as when counting items. The AUTO_INCREMENT attribute tells MySQL to automatically number rows sequentially when they're inserted into the table, giving you an easy way to create identification numbers when linking rows of different tables.

One attribute you probably won't use right away but will see often is the PRIMARY KEY attribute. It popped up in Listing 5-14, for example, having been automatically generated by MySQL when I created the event table. The PRIMARY KEY attribute tells MySQL that a particular column will have an index. Like the index at the back of this book, a database index helps you find information quickly. To help overall performance and speed database queries, MySQL automatically creates indices for table columns when certain criteria are met. Each table can have one column marked as the PRIMARY KEY, speeding searches against that column.

Operations and Functions

Although you won't write applications in SQL *per se*, operations and functions play an important role in many of the queries you write. SQL operations include common arithmetic operations and comparisons, and SQL offers a number of mathematical functions you can use when making queries. These functions and operations can be applied to the criteria for selecting table rows—a statement's WHERE clause—as well as the designator for a query table's result columns. Thus, you can perform computations such as computing the difference between two tables.

You've already seen examples of the comparison operator = in many of the SELECT FROM statements throughout this chapter. SQL gives you the typical comparison operators as well, including <=, >=, <, >, and !=, corresponding to the mathematical operations ≤, ≥, <, >, and ≠. You can use these anywhere you need to express a comparison, or in mathematical expressions. In a mathematical expression, these operations return 1 if the expression is true, 0 (zero) otherwise.

You can combine these comparison operations logically using SQL's AND and OR operations, as well as the logical complement NOT. Thus, the expressions 3 != 2 and NOT 3 = 2 are equivalent.

MySQL has arithmetic operations, too. You can use them as parts of queries to refine search criteria, or to specify a computation to perform on a result column. These arithmetic operations include +, -, /, *, and %, corresponding to the arithmetic +, −, × and ÷ as well as the *mod* remainder operation. Precedence for these operations follows the usual mathematical rules: multiplication, division, and modulo have precedence over addition and subtraction. Finally, the arithmetic operations have precedence over any of the comparison operations. Table 5-3 shows the MySQL operations sorted by precedence.

Table 5-3. MySQL Operations Sorted By Precedence

OPERATION	ASSOCIATION	PURPOSE
NOT, !	Left	Logical complement
-	Left	Arithmetic negation
*, /, %	Left	Multiplication, division, and modulo (remainder)
+, -	Left	Addition, subtraction, string concatenation
<<, >>	Left	Bitwise left shift, right shift
&	Left	Bitwise and
|	Left	Bitwise or
<, <=, >=, >, ==, !=	Non-associative	Less than, less than or equals, greater than, greater than or equals comparisons, equivalence, non-equivalence comparisons
AND, &&	Left	Logical and
OR, ||	Left	Logical or

Consider for a moment crafting a query to determine how many staff-hours Mountain Neighbors Network will have to volunteer this year. Given the schema shown previously, you know that the database stores each task's start and stop times as PHP times, (which are expressed as the number of seconds after the start of the epoch). Armed with this information, the query on line 11 of Listing 5-16 determines how many seconds each task in the database spans.

```
01: [localhost:~] dove% mysql -u dove -p
02: Enter password:
03: Welcome to the MySQL monitor. Commands end with ; or \g.
04: Your MySQL connection id is 7 to server version: 3.23.28-gamma
05:
06: Type 'help;' or '\h' for help. Type '\c' to clear the buffer
07:
08: mysql> USE MobileHelper;
09: Database changed
10:
11: mysql> SELECT stop-start FROM event;
12: +————————+
13: | stop-start |
14: +————————+
15: |    7200    |
16: |   21600    |
17: |   21600    |
18: +————————+
19: 3 rows in set (0.01 sec)
20:
21: mysql> SELECT (stop-start)/(60 * 60) FROM event;
22: +————————————+
23: | (stop-start)/(60 * 60) |
24: +————————————+
25: |          2.00          |
26: |          6.00          |
27: |          6.00          |
28: +————————————+
29: 3 rows in set (0.02 sec)
30:
31: mysql> SELECT SUM((stop-start)/(60 * 60)) FROM event;
32: +———————————————+
33: | SUM((stop-start)/(60 * 60)) |
34: +———————————————+
35: |            14.00            |
36: +———————————————+
37: 1 row in set (0.09 sec)
38:
39: mysql> Bye
```

Listing 5-16. SELECT *using an arithmetic expression*

This query simply returns a table containing a single column, the difference between the stop and start times for each appointment. With a bit more arithmetic, you can convert each of these time durations in seconds to hours, as the second query does on line 21. Of course, you still have to sum up each row to determine how many staff-hours everyone will work.

The third query on line 31 uses an SQL function to eliminate the need to sum across rows. SQL has functions that operate on a single row value, like the trigonometric functions SIN, COS, and TAN. More useful in most cases, however, are functions that compute a value based on a table's entire column. The SUM function in the query on line 31 is one of these. As its name indicates, it calculates the arithmetic sum of a column of values. You can find a full list of the SQL functions MySQL supports in the MySQL documentation.

Whether to use MySQL's operations and functions or to use those in the language from which you invoke MySQL can be a challenging decision with no clear answer. In many cases you can accomplish the same purpose using a query in MySQL, or a chunk of code in a scripting language like PHP. From the perspective of performance, it's best to do as much with your data in MySQL as possible. By doing so, your data remains in its native representation in the database, and the server won't need to shuffle data back and forth between MySQL and your application just for your application to perform computation. This is especially important as the size of you data grows because it's likely that your application needs to do additional work to process the additional elements. A valid counterargument is that at times it may be clearer to manipulate your data in another language. This is especially true when you first learn SQL, or when you're working on a prototype and focus your attention on your application, rather than the database. In these cases, it's perfectly reasonable to use a bit of extra code to keep SQL queries simple.

Statements

In the section "A Simple Database" earlier in this chapter, you saw the SQL statements you're most likely to use during your software development. You will find that several others will come in handy, however, so I'll touch on them briefly.

The ALTER TABLE statement enables you to change a database table once you've defined it. With ALTER TABLE, you can rename a column or change its type, as well as change the attributes associated with a table. The ALTER TABLE statement accepts one of the following clauses:

- The ADD clause enables you to add a column by including the type of the column to add, such as in the query ALTER TABLE user ADD type SET("Volunteer", "Coordinator") NOT NULL.

- The CHANGE clause enables you to change the type, name, or attributes of an existing column. When writing the CHANGE clause, you must always include the column's new name—so to change the type of a column, simply write the column's name twice, like this: ALTER TABLE user CHANGE name name TINYTEXT.

- The DROP clause enables you to drop a column from a table: ALTER TABLE user DROP type. Be careful—there's no undo!

The ALTER statement is invaluable during elaboration as you tweak your database schema, although you should take care when using it because altering the type of an existing column can, in some cases, cause MySQL to drop rows from your table, such as when making a column's value UNIQUE.

You've already seen the CREATE DATABASE, CREATE TABLE, DROP DATABASE, and DROP TABLE statements, so I won't discuss them again here. (See "A Simple Database" for details about these statements.)

You've also seen the DELETE FROM and UPDATE statements, which let you delete or change the value of rows from a specific table. Most of the time you'll probably want to use the WHERE clause to restrict changes to a specific set of rows, such as a row matching a given ID, or all rows with a date before a certain time. If you omit the WHERE clause, MySQL deletes or changes *all* rows in the table.

The GRANT statement grants privileges to a user to access or change parts of a database. Each user may have privileges to use the ALTER, CREATE, DELETE, DROP, INSERT, SELECT, or UPDATE statements, as well as privileges to perform administrative commands, such as shutting down the server. The GRANT statement consists of the GRANT keyword, the clause listing the privileges to grant to the user, the ON clause listing the database or table name to which the privileges apply, and the name of the user. For example, GRANT ALL ON * TO dove@localhost gives the user dove on the local machine the ability to do anything with every database. Typically, you'll want to be more restrictive, using a query such as GRANT ALL ON MobileHelper TO php@% to give the user php on any host the ability to do anything with the Mobile-Helper table. The GRANT statement also enables you to assign passwords to users, important when you first create a user. To set a password, include the IDENTIFIED BY clause with the user's password.

The opposite of the GRANT statement is the REVOKE statement, which revokes the privileges from the specified user. Its syntax is identical to GRANT. For example, to remove the privileges I gave to dove, I issue the query REVOKE ALL ON * FROM dove.

Two statements enable you to control whether or not clients can read or write to a specific table. When you're making several requests that change a table, you may want to be sure that no other clients can see the table while it's being changed (say, when updating an inventory database). To prevent other clients from reading or changing a table, you can *lock* the table. Correspondingly, once you're done making your changes, you need to be sure to *unlock* the table so that other clients can use it again. While you keep a table locked, other clients will wait to access the table so it's important you keep a table locked for only as long as you need it. The LOCK TABLES statement takes a list of the tables to lock, and keeps them locked until an UNLOCK TABLES statement unlocks them, or another LOCK TABLES statement specifies a different list of tables to lock. When you lock a table, you specify whether other clients can read, but not write, to the table, or whether other clients should be denied both the ability to read and write from a table.

You've seen the SELECT FROM statement in several queries. It's arguably one of the most complex SQL statements, letting you join tables from multiple sources, select individual rows from different tables, and sort results. You can even use SELECT to evaluate an expression by simply writing SELECT followed by the expression, like this: SELECT 2+2.

Most of the time, however, you use SELECT in conjunction with the FROM keyword to specify table columns. Each column must be named unambiguously, so it's common to see columns named by both the table containing the column and the table name itself, separated by a period (.) character, like this: event.stop.

The SELECT statement enables you to select from different tables using the FROM clause. By default when you list tables in the FROM clause, the rows will be drawn from a full join, iterating across all rows of the listed tables, You can constrain the SELECT statement to draw only from rows in the first table by using the LEFT JOIN statement.

When constructing a SELECT statement, you usually want to select specific rows in a table. You describe these rows using a WHERE clause that contains an expression describing the rows of interest to you. An expression can be simple, such as a test for equality using =, or complex with many parts combined using the AND and OR logical operations. For each row under consideration, the SELECT statement includes the row only if the expression in the WHERE clause is true (non-zero).

Finally, you can sort the results of a SELECT statement by including an ORDER BY clause. The ORDER BY clause contains a list of column names to use when sorting the resulting rows. By default, MySQL sorts these rows in ascending order, but you can specify ascending order using the keyword ASC or descending order using the keyword DESC. For example, to see a list of all rows in MobileHelper's event table sorted by start time, you write SELECT * FROM event ORDER BY start ASC.

There are other SQL statements that you won't commonly encounter. Because I don't use them in this book, I suggest you consult the MySQL manual to become familiar with the entire suite of SQL statements as you continue working with MySQL.

Using MySQL with PHP

Using MySQL with PHP is a two-step process: first ensure that MySQL and PHP can talk to each other on your server, and then write the PHP scripts that send SQL requests to the MySQL server.

Integrating MySQL with PHP

Before you can use MySQL with PHP, you need to be sure that MySQL's client support is enabled. Of course, if you built PHP yourself, you can go back and check your build notes (see the sidebar). If you're running on someone else's system, the easiest way to check is using the PHP function phpinfo. Listing 5-17 shows a simple PHP file containing this function.

```
01: <?php
02: phpinfo();
03: ?>
```

Listing 5-17. The phpinfo *function*

The phpinfo function returns to the browser an HTML page containing a great deal of information about how PHP is configured on the server, as you can see in Figure 5-5. Among other things, the second line of the table in the resulting page shows what options you built PHP with. If that line contains the phrase **–with-mysql**, you're in business. If not, you'll need to rebuild PHP (see the sidebar "Installing PHP with the Apache Web Server" in Chapter 3) with MySQL support enabled (discussed in the sidebar in this section).

> **NOTE** *If you're using PHP under Microsoft Windows, you won't see the configuration with which PHP is built with the* phpinfo *function. Instead, you should scroll down the page until you see the table that describes MySQL support. By default, the versions of PHP available from* www.php.net *include MySQL client support.*

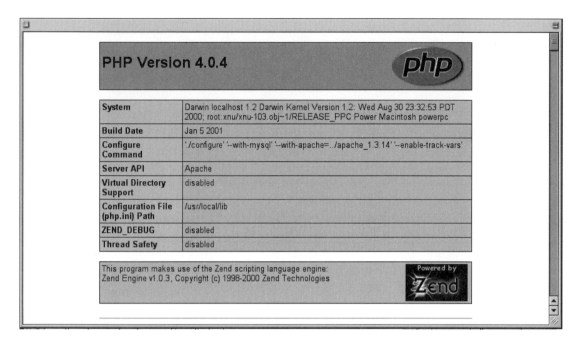

Figure 5-5. Output from `phpinfo`

MySQL and PHP

Because MySQL is a client-server database, PHP needs to include some of MySQL's code when it's built in order to be able to access MySQL databases. Generally, that's not a problem, unless you built PHP yourself before installing MySQL, or if you installed MySQL in a non-standard location. If you're running MySQL for Windows, odds are that it has MySQL support built in, and you can go back to reading the rest of this section now.

If you built MySQL on your own, however, you should be sure that you included the **–with-mysql** option to MySQL's **configure** build script. Moreover, if you built MySQL and put it someplace other than where it would normally install itself, you need to be sure to tell MySQL where it is using **configure** as well.

When in doubt, you can check for MySQL support using the PHP function `phpinfo`. If it's not there you can rebuild PHP with MySQL support by including the **–with-mysql** argument when running the configure build script. Don't forget that you need to either re-install the resulting PHP module in Apache (if you're using Apache's support for dynamic modules) or rebuild your Apache server including the new PHP library (if you're including PHP as a static module).

Accessing MySQL from PHP

Your scripts access MySQL through a set of functions that enable you to send SQL queries to the MySQL server and obtain response data in PHP arrays.

Typically, you use these functions the same way you use the MySQL monitor. First, you connect to the MySQL server, specifying the server's host name along with your account name and password. Next, you tell MySQL which database you want to use and then you issue SQL queries using the connection you established. For each query, you can access the resulting table row-by-row, with PHP storing each table row in an array.

To connect to the MySQL server, you can use either the `mysql_connect` or `mysql_pconnect` functions. When executing either function, MySQL creates a link to the specified server using the login name and password provided. If a link already exists, PHP uses an existing link, saving the overhead of creating multiple network connections between PHP and the server. Unlike `mysql_pconnect`, PHP closes MySQL connections created with `mysql_connect` once the script exits, or when you call `mysql_close`. By comparison, PHP doesn't close connections your script opens with `mysql_pconnect` until the server itself terminates. It's best to use `mysql_pconnect` when you're frequently accessing the same server because it saves the overhead of repeatedly opening and closing connections to the database server.

You tell PHP which database you want to use with the `mysql_selectdb` function. This function is similar to the SQL USE statement; it sets the current database and returns a value you can use with subsequent calls to the MySQL functions to access that database. You don't have to use this return value, however, because by default, subsequent calls to the MySQL API assume that this is the connection you want to use.

All of these functions can fail—`mysql_connect` might fail because it can't find the database server, for example, and `mysql_selectdb` fails if MySQL doesn't have the database you name. Consequently, you need to be sure that you include error-checking code in your PHP scripts in case these functions don't succeed.

Once you establish a connection and select your database, you issue queries using the `mysql_query` function. This function takes a string containing the SQL query PHP will send to MySQL, and returns an opaque result structure. You can't look directly at the results of `mysql_query`, except to see whether or not the request succeeded. If the returned result is 0 (zero), an error occurred: either MySQL couldn't understand your SQL query, or something happened between PHP and the server (such as a connection failure). A non-zero result indicates that the query succeeded, but doesn't tell you anything about the number of rows in the result.

There are a number of ways you can access the results of your query, but by far the easiest is to use the `mysql_fetch_array` function. With `mysql_fetch_array` you pass the result from a call to `mysql_query`, and you receive an associative array containing the next row in the result table, or false if there are no more rows. Repeated calls to mysql_fetch_array iterate over rows in the result table, so to obtain an entire result table, you can simply use a while loop with mysql_fetch_array. PHP also has the mysql_fetch_row function, which returns a conventional array, where the *i*'th column in the result table corresponds to the *i*'th element in the array. It's easier to use mysql_fetch_array, however, because you can use column names to refer to individual columns of a row in the result of a database query.

Sometimes you may only be interested in knowing how many rows a query has changed, or how many rows were returned in a result. PHP also has the mysql_affected_rows function, which returns an integer telling you how many rows were affected by a query, and mysql_num_rows, which returns the number of rows in the result.

In the event of an error, such as a problem with your SQL or when PHP is unable to complete the query, MySQL provides an error message, as if you were using the monitor. If you need to see the error message, call mysql_error, which returns a string containing an error message. If you want to handle errors programmatically, it's often easier to do so by examining an error number. To determine the numeric code identifying a particular kind of failure, call mysql_errno. Typically, you use mysql_error while debugging your code—you can print the results as part of your WML or HTML output and see what's going wrong. You probably won't want to include such messages in your production application, however, because most of your users won't give a hoot about the kinds of SQL errors that occur. Instead, you can call mysql_errno and use the result to display a specific user-friendly error message, or simply tell the user nicely that an error has occurred and what they can do about it (request the deck again, send mail to an administrator, or what have you).

Listing 5-18 puts all these functions together. Drawing from MobileHelper's db.php file, which I discuss at length in the next section, it shows the sequence of connection, selection, query, and response operations from PHP with a MySQL database.

```
01: <?php
02:
03: define( "DBHOST", "localhost" );
04: define( "DBUSER", "php" );
05: define( "DBPASS", "secret" );
06:
07: // We open the link once for each page as this file is
08: // loaded.
09: // We use a persistent connection, so PHP will cache
10: // the connection and really only open as many
11: // connections as are needed (not one per page using
12: // this file)
13:
```

```
14: $dbLink = @mysql_pconnect( DBHOST, DBUSER, DBPASS )
15:  or exit();
16: @mysql_selectdb( "MobileHelper" ) or exit();
17:
18: /*********************************************************
19: * FUNCTION: DBGetOpenTasks( )
20: *
21: * DESCRIPTION: Returns an array of open assignments.
22: *
23: * RETURNED: array of event hashes or 0
24: *********************************************************/
25: function DBGetOpenTasks()
26: {
27: // Do the query, return the record or null
28:
29:  $dbqr = mysql_query(
30:    "SELECT * FROM event " .
31:    "WHERE state=" . DBTASKOPEN . " " .
32:    "ORDER BY start ASC"
33:  );
34:
35: // Validate
36:
37:  if ( !$dbqr )
38:    return 0;
39:
40: // We've got something… create a result array and return
41:
42:  $result = array();
43:
44:  while( $row = mysql_fetch_array( $dbqr ) )
45:  {
46:   array_push( $result, $row );
47:  }
48:
49:  return $result;
50: }
50: ?>
```

Listing 5-18. Accessing MySQL from PHP

You wouldn't access the PHP in Listing 5-18 directly; rather, you `include` Listing 5-18 at the beginning of another PHP file that generates content for a client. On line 14, I attempt to establish a connection to the MySQL server using mysql_pconnect. This script uses mysql_pconnect to establish the connection because one connection to MySQL will suffice for all clients accessing MobileHelper. The leading @ before mysql_pconnect tells PHP that if an error occurs, it should not send the error information to the Web client. If I hadn't included the @ and an error occurred, PHP would send the results to the client, disrupting the WML that the script should send. Instead, in the event of an error, the PHP process silently exits using the exit function on line 15. This isn't ideal—in fact, it's only appropriate at the early stages of development because, if an error occurs, the user won't see anything. A better solution (see "Food for Thought" later in this chapter) would be to send a canned deck prompting the user to try back later. Line 16 selects the MobileHelper database, again exiting with no output in case of an error.

By including lines 14–16 in the file, I ensure that the database connection will always be open before you can ever call DBGetOpenTasks because if the database doesn't open, the DBGetOpenTasks function won't be defined. This significantly increases the likelihood that DBGetOpenTasks will succeed because odds are that unless I've written the SQL wrong in DBGetOpenTasks nothing can go wrong.

The DBGetOpenTasks function issues a single query to MySQL and creates an array with one entry for each row of the result table. Each entry in the resulting array is itself an associative array, containing the individual fields of that row. On line 29, I call mysql_query, passing an SQL SELECT statement to pull all rows corresponding to open events from the event table sorted by start time. If the query succeeds, the while loop on lines 44–47 pushes each row from the query into the array $result, using the mysql_fetch_array function.

MySQL Within MobileHelper

MobileHelper stores all of its persistent data in four tables using MySQL. After an initial WML deck that prompts the user for her PIN and MIN, PHP generates all MobileHelper content the client displays. Let's look first at MobileHelper's database schema, and then how MobileHelper uses PHP and MySQL to handle login, store open and pending tasks, and close tasks.

MobileHelper's Schema

In Figure 5-3, you saw a schema of MobileHelper's database showing the user, event, and location tables. Figure 5-6 shows MobileHelper's full schema.

Tasks are at the heart of MobileHelper. MobileHelper stores each task as a row of an event table with links to both the user and location table. A task has start and stop times (both scheduled and actual times, stored in the columns start, stop, actualStart, and actualStop), a name and note (stored in the columns name and

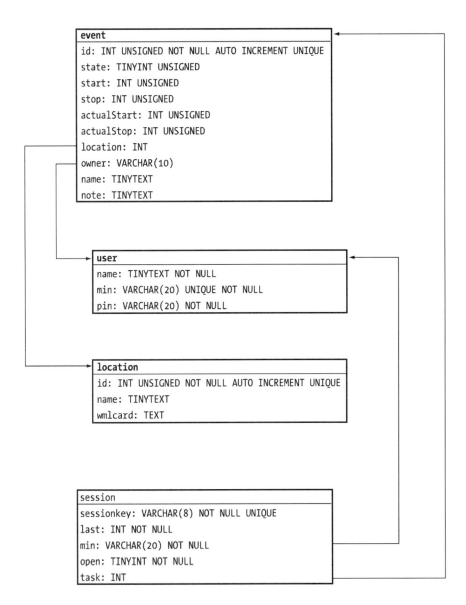

Figure 5-6. MobileHelper database schema

note) and a state. The task's state indicates whether it's open (unassigned), assigned
to a specific user, or completed. While you can figure this out using clever tricks
such as looking at the owner field (if the owner field is NULL, the task isn't linked to a
user, and therefore must be unassigned), the addition of a state column makes
coding queries for the event table easier. The state field is a TINYINT, but I could
have just as easily made it an ENUM because an event can be in only one state.
Making state an integer, however, makes the PHP scripts slightly faster because
it's faster to manipulate integers than strings.

The user table contains simply the name, min, and pin columns. A user record consists of the user's name, MIN, and PIN. While illustrative, this table is neither complete nor secure for a real-world application, for three reasons.

First, many applications need to be able to separate parts of a person's name. Stashing an entire name in a single column is okay for a prototype or example, but is a problem when you need to sort by last name instead of first or store people's middle initials. In your applications, you should store the first name, middle name (or initial), and surname as separate fields.

Second, the user's PIN is stored in clear text in the VARCHAR field PIN. This is a blatant security risk: anyone with access (authorized or not) can simply get a list of account MIN and PIN information and then access MobileHelper as any user. A better solution is to store a password that's been subject to a function that irreversibly computes a new value. When a user tries to log in, MobileHelper can apply the same function (called a *one-way* function because you can't take the results of the function and determine the original value) to the entered password; if the results match, MobileHelper safely assumes that the entered password was correct. At the same time, however, because the entries in the user table are the results of a one-way function, casual browsing of the user table reveals nothing about a person's password. UNIX systems store password data this way: not as passwords, but as their encrypted counterparts.

Finally, the table contains minimal information about a particular user. It's quite likely that the Coordinator will want to store additional information, such as whether a user is a Volunteer or Coordinator, contact information, skills, and so on, along with notes about the user.

Despite these limitations, however, the user table is adequate for my purposes in illustrating MySQL in MobileHelper throughout this book. You should take a look at the section "Food for Thought" at the end of this chapter to see ways to extend the user (and other) tables to better meet the needs of a real-world application.

The location table is absurdly simple but adequate for my needs. This table has three columns: a location's id, name, and the wmlcard column containing WML that describes the location. Scripts use the event table with the location table's id column to determine the location's name. Similarly, the database uses the wmlcard column to store other information about the location, including its address. By stashing all the information about the location in a single column containing WML, displaying a location's information is easy, although updating bits of a location's information becomes difficult because you need to edit the WML for the location and update the single field. In addition, you really can't get more than two views of the location table: a list of locations and the WML associated with a list of locations. If you wanted to extract location addresses (say, to draw them on a map) you'd be stuck doing it by hand.

The session table keeps the persistent variables that scripts use during each client session. As you know, PHP destroys script variables after the execution of a script. Thus, wireless applications like MobileHelper needs a persistent store for script variables between client requests. This store keeps data, such as which task you are viewing. There are two places a script can stash the value of variables so they are available between different scripts.

The first is to give the variable values to the client itself, either as a cookie or as variable values for an HTTP GET or POST request. Cookies, used to store bits of data for a server on the client, aren't currently supported in WAP. This makes sense because your viewers don't want to waste precious bandwidth and memory on data that your server can store. Similarly, embedding script variable values in WAP content is inappropriate: it increases the size of each deck the client receives, which in turn slows both wireless delivery and display processing.

The second alternative is to store the variable values on the server. Because MobileHelper uses MySQL, it's easy to just add another table to the MobileHelper database in MySQL and use a row in the table for each client currently connected to the server.

As you can see from the schema, the session table tracks five items for each user. Two of these items are used to administer the session table: the session key and the last request time. The client's session key, stored in the sessionkey column, uniquely identifies each client to MobileHelper, and is sent by the client as part of each request. In essence, the session key is a client-side variable stored in the WML deck; MobileHelper uses this relatively small key to obtain all of the other variables a PHP script needs. The last request time, stored in the last field, is a PHP time indicating the last time the client made a request. As new clients make requests, a PHP function uses this field to purge old idle clients from the database, increasing both security and performance. The remainder of the columns min, open, and task, correspond to PHP variables in the scripts I discuss in the following sections.

Login and Authentication

You log into MobileHelper by loading the main page at index.wml, shown in Figure 5-7. This static page greets you and provides the obligatory "about" and copyright information. In addition, it has a timer that automatically loads the login deck for you at login.wml, shown in Figure 5-8.

Both index.wml and login.wml are similar to the decks of the same name written for the prototype in Chapter 2, with two key differences. First, each deck has both anchor links and soft key assignments for actions like **About** and **Login** because some clients bury soft key assignments in a menu. By including anchors as well as soft key references, the decks work well on most browsers. Second, the index.wml deck's first card uses a timer to bring you to the login screen if you don't explicitly select an action. Listing 5-19 shows the index.wml deck.

Figure 5-7. MobileHelper's main screen

Figure 5-8. MobileHelper's login screen

```
01: <?xml version="1.0"?>
02: <!DOCTYPE wml PUBLIC "-//WAPFORUM//DTD WML 1.1//EN"
03: "http://www.wapforum.org/DTD/wml_1.1.xml">
04: <wml>
05:  <card id="MobileHelperHome"
06:   title="MobileHelper"
07:   ontimer="login.wml">
08:   <timer name="login" value="100"/>
09:   <do type="accept" label="Login">
10:    <go href="login.wml"/>
11:   </do>
12:   <p align="center">
13:    MobileHelper
14:   </p>
15:   <p>
```

```
16:    Welcome to MobileHelper!<br/>
17:    <anchor title="Login">
18:    Login
19:    <go href="login.wml"/>
20:    </anchor>
21:    <anchor title="About">
22:    About
23:    <go href="#MobileHelperAbout"/>
24:    </anchor>
25:    </p>
26: </card>
27: <card id="MobileHelperAbout"
28:   title="About MobileHelper">
29:   <p align="center">
30:   <big>MobileHelper</big><br/>
31:   Public Service Deployment Wireless Application<br/>
32:   &#x00A9; 2000-2001 Ray Rischpater<br/>
33:   <br/>
34:   Version 1.0<br/>
35:   (Chapter 5)<br/>
36:   </p>
37:   <p>
38:   This Public Service Deployment Wireless
39:   Application is part of the book
40:   <u>Wireless Applications with PHP</u>
41:   by Ray Rischpater from Apress, LP.
42:   </p>
43: </card>
44: </wml>
```

Listing 5-19. The index.wml deck

On line 8, you see the timer that automatically loads the login.wml deck after 10 seconds of inactivity, while on lines 9–11 the script assigns the navigation task to load the login.wml deck to the **Accept** key. The deck includes the same navigation task as an anchor on lines 17–20, so if you're using a client that makes soft keys harder to access, you can still log in easily. Another way to address different soft key interfaces would be to detect the client type using HTTP headers and send different WML. (You'll see how to do this in Chapter 9.)

The login.wml deck, shown in Listing 5-20, now uses the HTTP POST method to send the user-entered MIN and PIN data back to the server for authentication by the auth.php script (lines 24–38). Note again that this deck uses both a soft key and an anchor reference for easy navigation on different clients.

```
01: <?xml version="1.0"?>
02: <!DOCTYPE wml PUBLIC "-//WAPFORUM//DTD WML 1.1//EN"
03: "http://www.wapforum.org/DTD/wml_1.1.xml">
04: <wml>
05:  <card newcontext="true"
06:  title="MobileHelper Login" id="login">
07:   <p>
08:    <fieldset title="MIN &amp; PIN">
09:     MIN:
10:     <input name="min"
11:      type="text"
12:      format="NNNNNNNNNN"
13:      emptyok="false"
14:      maxlength="10"
15:      size="10"/>
16:     PIN:
17:     <input name="pin"
18:      type="password"
19:      format="*N"
20:      emptyok="false"
21:      maxlength="6"
22:    size="6"/>
23:    </fieldset>
24:    <anchor>
25:     Login
26:     <go href="auth.php" method="post">
27:      <postfield name="min" value="$min"/>
28:      <postfield name="pin" value="$pin"/>
29:     </go>
30:    </anchor>
31:    <do type="accept"
32:     label="Login"
33:     name="Login">
34:     <go href="auth.php" method="post">
35:      <postfield name="min" value="$min"/>
36:      <postfield name="pin" value="$pin"/>
37:     </go>
38:    </do>
39:   </p>
40:  </card>
41: </wml>
```

Listing 5-20. The login.wml deck

The auth.php script performs three tasks: it verifies that you are who you say you are, sets up a new row in the session table for the session key, and returns a deck with the list of your assigned tasks. It does this using the db.php script to access the user and session tables of the database. Listing 5-21 shows the auth.php script.

```
01: <?php
02: /*******************************************************
03: * auth.php
04: *
05: * This module validates the user and brings them to the
06: * first deck.
07: *******************************************************/
08: include "db.php";
09:
10: // On entry, $min should be set to the user's MIN and
11: // $pin to the user's PIN.
12:
13: // First, look up the user's record and see if the
14: // login is valid.
15: $user = DBGetUserByMIN( $min );
16:
17: if ( $user[ "min" ] == $min && $user[ "pin" ] == $pin )
18: {
19: // Valid user. Hand control off to an appropriate deck.
20:   $key = DBSetUserSession( $min );
21:   include "tasklist.php";
22:   exit();
23: }
24: else
25: {
26:   include "logininvalid.php";
27:   exit();
28: }
29: ?>
```

Listing 5-21. The auth.php script

On line 8, auth.php first loads db.php, which opens the database and defines a bunch of database functions, including DBGetUserByMin and DBSetUserSession. Then the script calls DBGetUserByMIN to obtain your user record on line 15.

On lines 17–28, the script compares the MIN and PIN you enter with the values found in the database. If they match, a new session key is created using the DBSetUserSession function, and the script includes "tasklist.php", which shows a list of open tasks for the user. Otherwise, the script includes `"logininvalid.php"`, which returns a deck informing the user that his login attempt was invalid.

Listing 5-22 shows `DBGetUserByMIN` as well as the initial setup code in db.php. (Rather than show all the code for db.php at once and leave you flipping back and forth throughout the remainder of the chapter, I show you the beginning of db.php here, and relevant functions from db.php as I use them throughout the remaining sections.)

```php
01: <?php
02: /********************************************************
03: * db.php
04: *
05: * This module contains functions to access MobileHelper
06: * databases.
07: *******************************************************/
08:
09: if ( !$dbDefined ) {
10:
11: $dbDefined++;
12:
13: // Database access info.
14:
15: define( "DBHOST", "localhost" );
16: define( "DBUSER", "php" );
17: define( "DBPASS", "secret" );
18:
19: // Timeout for session authentication in seconds
20:
21: define( "DBSESSIONTIMEOUT", 10 * 60 );
22:
23: // Task states
24: define( "DBTASKOPEN", 0 );
25: define( "DBTASKPEND", 1 );
26: define( "DBTASKCLOSE", 2 );
27:
28: // We open the link once for each page as this file loads.
29: // We use a persistent connection, so PHP will cache the
30: // connection and really only open as many connections
31: // as are needed (not one per page using this file)
32:
```

```
33: $dbLink = @mysql_pconnect( DBHOST, DBUSER, DBPASS )
34:  or exit();
35: mysql_selectdb( "MobileHelper" )
36:  or exit();
37:
38: /********************************************************
39: * FUNCTION: DBGetUserByMIN()
40: *
41: * DESCRIPTION: Loads the specified user's record from the
42: * database
43: *
44: * RETURNED: hash containing info for desired user or NULL
45: ********************************************************/
46: function DBGetUserByMIN(
47:  $min // (min) id of user to load
48: )
49: {
50: // Do the query, return the record or null
51:
52:  $record = mysql_query(
53:   "SELECT * FROM user WHERE min='$min'"
54:  );
55:
56: // Validate—and since there's only one per MIN,
57: // return if found.
58:
59:  if ( $record )
60:   return mysql_fetch_array( $record );
61:  else
62:   return array();
63: }
64:
65: // The rest of db.php follows…
66: ?>
```

Listing 5-22. Setup code in db.php and the DBGetUserByMIN *function*

The db.php script begins by looking for the variable $dbDefined, which it uses to keep track of whether or not the db.php script has already been included. This is necessary because if db.php executes more than once, errors occurring as functions are redefined. Unfortunately, just this situation occurs in auth.php when it includes tasklist.php.

> **NOTE** *I could have included db.php using the* include_once *statement in both auth.php and tasklist.php to avoid this situation. Many other languages don't have this feature, however, so the trick of defining and testing a constant may come in handy for you in the future.*

You've already seen pieces of the code in lines 15–36 of Listing 5-22 back in Listing 5-18. The script begins by defining a bunch of manifest constants, including the MySQL database access information (lines 15–17), how long a client can remain inactive before losing his session key (line 21), and the states for a task (lines 24–26). Finally, the database opens a persistent connection to the database and selects the MobileHelper database on lines 33–36. Note that by defining the event states as constants, you could easily change the event table's state column to an ENUM by issuing an ALTER TABLE statement in the monitor and changing the value of the three constants on lines 24–26.

The DBGetUserByMIN function on lines 38–63 makes a single SQL query. Functions such as this are often called *wrappers* because they encapsulate a bit of code with an interface more suited to other parts of an application. While I could just as easily have scattered bits of SQL like the query found on line 52 all over my PHP scripts, by putting it in a wrapper function it's easy to find if I need to change parts of the database schema.

The function begins on line 52 by making a MySQL query to find any rows matching the MIN you pass to the function in $min. Because the min column of the user table is unique, MySQL returns either one row or none. On lines 59–62, the script returns the result, either an associative array containing the row with the given MIN or an empty array in case of an error.

Session Management

Four functions in db.php are responsible for MobileHelper's session management. Together, these functions create a new session key, store persistent script variables between client requests, and age rows in the session table so that out-of-date session keys don't waste space.

Starting a new session

A session begins when auth.php calls `DBSetUserSession` with a user's
MIN. `DBSetUserSession`, shown in lines 35–74 of Listing 5-23, first removes
expired session keys from the database and then creates a new session key for
the client with the specified MIN.

```php
01: <?php
02: // exerpt from db.php
03:
04:
05: /*****************************************************
06: * FUNCTION: DBNewSessionKey()
07: *
08: * DESCRIPTION: Creates a session key.
09: *
10: * RETURNED: integer containing session key
11: *****************************************************/
12: function DBNewSessionKey()
13: {
14:
15: // Some characters to draw from to make the session key
16:
17:  $pool = "ABCDEFGHIJKLMNOPQRSTUVWXYZ" .
18:   "abcdefghijklmnopqrstuvwxyz" .
19:   "01234567890";
20:
21: // Seed the random number generator
22:
23:  srand( time() );
24:
25:
26: // Build an eight-character session key randomly.
27:
28:  for ( $i = 0; $i < 8; $i++ )
29:   $sessionkey .= substr( $pool,
30:   rand() % strlen( $pool ), 1 );
31:
32:  return $sessionkey;
33: }
34:
```

```
35: /********************************************************
36: * FUNCTION: DBSetUserSession()
37: *
38: * DESCRIPTION: Marks the user authenticated for this
39: * session.
40: *
41: * RETURNED: session key for posterity
42: ********************************************************/
43: function DBSetUserSession(
44:  $min // (in) id of user
45: )
46: {
47:
48: // Pick a key
49:
50:  $key = DBNewSessionKey();
51:
52: // Get our user's time
53:
54:  $now = time();
55:
56: // Flush old junk from the database
57:
58:  $result = mysql_query(
59:   "DELETE FROM session WHERE last < " .
60:   ($now - DBSESSIONTIMEOUT ) );
61:
62: // Store the session info for this user.
63:
64:  $result = mysql_query(
65:   "INSERT INTO session " .
66:   "VALUES( '$key', $now, '$min', 0, 0 )" );
67:
68: // If it succeeded, return the expiry; otherwise bail.
69:
70:  if ( $result )
71:   return $key;
72:  else
73:   return 0;
74: }
75:
76:
```

```
 77: /********************************************************
 78: * FUNCTION: DBCheckUserSession()
 79: *
 80: * DESCRIPTION: Checks the user's session key.
 81: *
 82: * RETURNED: hash with session variables
 83: ********************************************************/
 84: function DBCheckUserSession(
 85:  $key // (in) key returned by user to validate
 86: )
 87: {
 88:
 89: // Get the session record for this key
 90:
 91:  $record = mysql_query(
 92:   "SELECT * FROM session WHERE sessionkey='$key'" );
 93:
 94:  if ( $record )
 95:   return mysql_fetch_array( $record );
 96:  else
 97:   return array();
 98: }
 99:
100: /********************************************************
101: * FUNCTION: DBUpdateUserSession()
102: *
103: * DESCRIPTION: Updates the user's session variables
104: *
105: * RETURNED: nothing
106: ********************************************************/
107: function DBUpdateUserSession(
108:  &$session // (in/out) hash of session variables
109: )
110: {
111:
112: // Update the last query time.
113:
114:  $session[ "last" ] = time();
115:
116: // Store the revised session data for this key.
117: // DO NOT CHANGE THE MIN OR THE SESSION INFO!!
118:
```

```
119:  $key = $session[ "sessionkey" ];
120:  $last = $session[ "last" ];
121:  $open = $session[ "open" ];
122:  $task = $session[ "task" ];
123:
124: // Update the table
125:
126:  $result = mysql_query(
127:    "UPDATE session " .
128:    "SET last=$last, open=$open, task=$task " .
129:    "WHERE sessionkey='$key'"
130:    );
131:
132: }
133: ?>
```

Listing 5-23. Session management functions in db.php

DBSetUserSession begins by creating a new session key using the DBNewSessionKey function (defined on lines 12–33). DBNewSessionKey uses the PHP random number generator to create an eight-character random string from the set of all uppercase and lowercase letters and numbers in the string $pool. DBNewSessionKey begins by resetting the random number generator to a new starting point with the srand function, and then loops eight times. Each pass through the loop on lines 28–30, DBNewSessionKey selects a random character in the string $pool, appending the selected random character to $sessionkey. It's highly unlikely that two session keys will be the same (the odds are roughly one in two hundred trillion), but if it happens, the subsequent SQL query inserting the new session record into the session table will fail because the sessionkey column is declared UNIQUE.

Once DBSetUserSession has created a session key, it finds the current time using the PHP time function on line 54. The script uses the current system time for two things: to delete out-of-date session records, and to provide a timestamp for the new session record. On lines 58–60, the script queries the server with the SQL statement DELETE FROM session WHERE last < nnnn, which deletes all rows of the session table with timestamps older than nnnn. By setting *nnnn* to the current time less the constant DBSESSIONTIMEOUT, the query deletes all records DBSESSIONTIMEOUT seconds in the past, ensuring that old records don't stick around and fill the session table. It also keeps old session keys from being used to illicitly access the database; otherwise someone could snoop on the network, steal a session key, and use the stolen session key to gain access to the other PHP scripts later.

Removing old sessions

Once the old session keys are deleted from the `session` table, `DBSetUserSession` inserts a new session record with the query on line 64–66. Then the script unlocks the `session` table and returns the new session key. The new session key is handed to clients, which return the session key with subsequent requests so that other scripts can access session variables using the function `DBCheckUserSession`. `DBCheckUserSession`, shown on lines 84–98, is identical in form to `DBGetUserByMin`. It queries the database (lines 91–92) and returns an associative array or empty array depending on whether the query succeeded or failed (lines 94–97) respectively.

Maintaining session variables

Scripts such as tasklist.php need to update the session table when their global variables change. To do this, they call `DBUpdateUserSession`, defined on lines 107–133. This function takes a hash with the session variables, saving the session variables to the database after updating the last request timestamp in the `last` column of the `session` table. It first updates the time (on line 114) of the last request, extracts the variables (lines 119–122), and issues the update request using an SQL `UPDATE` statement (on lines 137–141). To make things simple, `DBUpdateUserSession` can take the same hash returned by `DBCheckUserSession`. Scripts, such as tasklist.php, that use these functions get the current values of session variables using `DBCheckUserSession`, update relevant slots in the returned array, and then promptly save the result using `DBUpdateUserSession`.

The client must send a session key to the server with each request. There are two ways the client can do this: as a variable defined at the end of an HTTP `GET` request, or as a form variable as part of an HTTP `POST` request. The `GET` request has the advantage of being simple, at the expense of cluttering up every request URL. The `POST` request has the advantage of legible URLs, but requires additional complexity in each deck because subsequent URLs must be requested using the HTTP `POST` method, posting whatever WML variable the browser uses to store the session client. Despite the added complexity, `MobileHelper` uses the `POST` technique to pass the session key to the server because it gives me the opportunity to show you an oft-needed but seldom-documented trick.

Recall that WML variables are set using a `<setvar/>` tag. This tag is *only* valid inside another navigation tag, such as `<go>` or `<prev>`. You can't simply define a WML variable inside the context of a paragraph; you'll get an error. To get around this, you can make the first card of your deck empty except for an `oneventforward` event that sets your WML variables appropriately and then opens the desired card using a `<go>` task. Listing 5-24 shows a copy of the WML generated by tasklist.php that does just this.

```
01: <?xml version="1.0"?>
02: <!DOCTYPE wml PUBLIC "-//WAPFORUM//DTD WML 1.1//EN"
03: "http://www.wapforum.org/DTD/wml_1.1.xml">
04: <wml>
05:  <head>
06:   <meta http-equiv="Cache-Control" content="no-cache"/>
07:  </head>
08:  <card>
09:   <onevent type="onenterforward">
10:    <go href="#your">
11:     <setvar name="key" value="i0tZP2I4"/>
12:    </go>
13:   </onevent>
14:   <onevent type="onenterbackward">
15:    <prev/>
16:   </onevent>
17:  </card>
18:  <card title="Your Tasks" id="your">
19:   <do type="accept" label="View" name="view">
20:    <go href="taskview.php" method="post">
21:     <postfield name="key" value="$key"/>
22:     <postfield name="task" value="$task"/>
23:    </go>
24:   </do>
25:   <do type="cancel" label="Open" name="open">
26:    <go href="tasklist.php" method="post">
27:     <postfield name="key" value="$key"/>
28:     <postfield name="open" value="1"/>
29:    </go>
30:   </do>
31:   <p mode="nowrap">
32:    <select title="Open Tasks" name="task">
33:     <option value="2">
34:      2-12-01 0800:Communications
35:     </option>
36:    </select>
37:   </p>
38:  </card>
39: </wml>
```

Listing 5-24. Task listing with empty first card

The "hidden card" is on lines 8–17. It has no content aside from two <onevent> tags that make sure the browser never stays on this card. The first <onevent> tag, of type "onenterforward", sets the WML variable key to the session key for this session, " i0tZP2I4", and promptly goes to the second card, named "your". (This card is the remainder of the deck, spanning lines 18–38). The second ‹onevent› tag, which catches ‹prev› tasks such as the user pressing **Prev** from the "your" card, simply navigates to the card before the hidden card itself. Thus, when the browser loads this deck, it loads the first card, triggers an onenterforward event, sets the WML variable key to the string " i0tZP2I4", and loads the "your" card, showing the list of open events. This is slightly slower than if the session key were part of the URL, but not noticeably so.

To facilitate setting the session key in a hidden card, the wml.php file now has an additional function, WMLAddDeckVar. This function takes a deck, a variable name, and variable's value, and sets aside the variable and value names in the same way that the WMLAddHT TPEquiv function does. When generating the deck with WMLDeckAsString, WMLDeckAsString looks for any deck variables, and creates a hidden card containing their values if needed. (See "Food for Thought," later in this chapter.)

Open and Pending Task Lists

After creating a new session, auth.php uses include to execute the script tasklist.php. This script shows a list of either open (see Figure 5-9) or pending tasks, depending on the value of the persistent variable $open in the session row for the current session. Both lists are shown using the same format, a ‹select› list with one ‹option› per task. Listing 5-25 shows tasklist.php.

Figure 5-9. MobileHelper task list

```
01: <?php
02: /********************************************************
03: * tasklist.php
04: *
05: * This script builds a list of tasks in WML for the
06: * current user.
07: ********************************************************/
08:
09: include "db.php";
10:
11: // Is the user's session valid?
12:
13: $session = DBCheckUserSession( $key );
14:
```

```
15: if ( !is_array( $session ) || count( $session ) == 0 )
16: {
17:  include "logintimeout.php";
18:  exit();
19: }
20:
21: // Update the session variables
22:
23: if ( isset( $open ) )
24: {
25:  $session[ "open" ] = $open;
26: }
27: if ( isset( $task ) )
28: {
29:  $session[ "task" ] = $task;
30: }
31: DBUpdateUserSession( $session );
32: $open = $session[ "open" ];
33: $task = $session[ "task" ];
34:
35: // Get a list of the tasks.
36: // The following will fetch either open or pending tasks.
37:
38: if ( $open )
39: {
40:  $taskList = DBGetOpenTasks(  );
41: }
42: else
43: {
44:  $taskList = DBGetPendingTasksForUser(
45:   $session[ "min" ]
46:  );
47: }
48:
49: // Build the response deck.
50:
51: header( "Content-type: text/vnd.wap.wml" );
52:
53: include "wml.php";
54: $deck = WMLNewDeck();
55:
56: // Start with the session key.
57:
```

```
58: WMLAddDeckVar( $deck, "key", $key );
59: WMLAddHTTPEquiv( $deck, "Cache-Control", "no-cache" );
60:
61: // Build the table of tasks
62:
63: if ( $taskList && count( $taskList ) > 0 )
64: {
65:  $table = "<select title=\"". ( $open ? "Open" : "Pending" ) .
66:    " Tasks\" name=\"task\">\n";
67:  for ( $i = 0; $i < count( $taskList) ; $i++ )
68:  {
69:    $table .= "<option value=\"" .
70:    $taskList[ $i ][ "id" ] .
71:    "\">" .
72:    date( "n-d-y Hi", $taskList[ $i ][ "start" ] ) .
73:    ":" . $taskList[ $i ][ "name" ] .
74:    "</option>\n";
75:  }
76:  $table .= "</select>\n";
77: }
78: else
79: {
80:  $table = "No " .
81:    ( $open ? "open" : "pending" ) .
82:    " tasks.";
83: }
84:
85:
86: // Card listing pending assignments
87:
88: $card = WMLNewCard( $open ? "Open Tasks" : "Your Tasks",
89:  $open ? "open" : "your" );
90:
91: // Add the table into its own paragraph.
92:
93: $para = WMLNewParagraph( $table, "", "nowrap" );
94: WMLAddParagraph( $card, $para );
95:
96: // Add the selection event handler.
97:
```

```
 98: $taskAcceptAction =
 99:  "<postfield name=\"key\" value=\"\$key\"/>\n" .
100:  "<postfield name=\"task\" value=\"\$task\"/>\n";
101: $taskAccept = WMLGo( "taskview.php",
102:  $taskAcceptAction, "post" );
103: WMLAddDo( $card, "accept", $taskAccept, "View", "view" );
104:
105: $notopen = $open == 1 ? 0 : 1;
106:
107: // Add the pending list event handler
108:
109: $taskCancelAction =
110:  "<postfield name=\"key\" value=\"\$key\"/>\n" .
111:  "<postfield name=\"open\" value=\"$notopen\"/>\n";
112: $taskCancel = WMLGo( "tasklist.php",
113:  $taskCancelAction, "post" );
114: WMLAddDo( $card, "cancel", $taskCancel,
115:  $notopen ? "Open" : "Pend" ,
116:  $notopen ? "open" : "pend" );
117:
118: // Add the card to the deck
119:
120: WMLAddCard( $deck, $card );
121:
122: // Return the deck
123:
124: WMLEchoDeck( $deck );
126: ?>
```

Listing 5-25. The tasklist.php script.

Listing 5-25 begins with a block of code, common to all MobileHelper scripts, that loads your session from the session table using DBCheckUserSession. On lines 13–19, the script uses your session key $key to load the session variables. When first loaded by auth.php immediately after you log in, $key is set; subsequent execution of tasklist.php sets $key using the HTTP POST variable of the same name.

If the session key is bad—either because you attempted to access the page using a forged session key or because the session key is too old—tasklist.php includes the logintimeout.php script and exits. The logintimeout.php script simply creates a WML deck that informs you that your session is invalid and invites you to log in again.

After fetching the current session, tasklist.php updates the session information with the value of the $open and $task variables on lines 23–30. The first time tasklist.php executes, these variables are set to default values by DBSetUserSession, selecting a list of pending tasks. As you navigate tasklist.php, however, you have an opportunity to set $open to select either a list of open or pending tasks. Once the script updates these variables, their values are flushed to the database using DBUpdateUserSession on line 31, and their true values extracted on lines 32 and 33 for the script to use.

With these preliminaries aside, tasklist.php gets a list of the pending or open tasks, depending on whether $open is zero or non-zero. To do this, it uses the database functions DBGetOpenTasks and DBGetPendingTasksForUser (shown in Listing 5-26), both of which return an array of tasks. Each task is an associative array with a field for each column in the event table.

After getting the list of tasks to display, tasklist.php then builds the response deck by creating the deck and iterating over the list of tasks. This deck creation occurs on lines 53–59, first including the wml.php file to add support for WML deck creation (described in Chapter 3) and then stashing the session key in the deck using the hidden card trick described in the last section.

On line 59, tasklist.php explicitly deactivates caching for this deck, so that as the event table is updated when you accept and close tasks, the client always downloads a new list from the server.

Lines 63–83 build the actual task, creating different content depending on whether there are tasks to list or no tasks. If there are tasks to list, PHP executes the loop on lines 67–74, adding an <option> tag for each task. If not, the script adds an empty task list message on lines 79–83.

Unlike the prototype I show in Chapter 2, the task list is an option list, facilitating selection of individual items. My testing on a variety of clients shows that the <select> tag is easier to navigate than a table with a number of anchors. Using the <select> tag results in a smaller deck, too, speeding delivery and display for the user.

Each <option> contains the task's date and time (formatted using the PHP date function) as well as the task's name, and has a selection value equal to the task ID. Thus, selecting a task returns the task ID, which MobileHelper uses to fetch the task to show. The script places the selection list in its own card on lines 86–94. The script first creates a card (named either "Open Tasks" or "Your Tasks" on line 88), and then creates an unwrapped paragraph to contain the list.

The task list enables you to toggle between views of open or pending tasks or view a specific task. These actions are mapped to the client's **Accept** and **Cancel** keys on lines 96–116. When you accept a task, the client gives the server both the task's id and the current session key via a POST request. Similarly, when you choose either the open or pending list, the client provides the session key and either 0 (zero) or 1, representing the open or pending task list.

On lines 98–103, the script uses the wml.php functions to assign the **Accept** key. This key is set to perform an HTTP POST to the client, sending the value of the HTTP POST variables key and task. The key variable contains the session key, and the task variable contains the ID of the task selected by the user. These are returned to the server as the $key and $task variables when taskview.php executes.

Lines 105–116 operate similarly to set the **Cancel** key action, except that the button label and caption must read either **Open** or **Pend** depending on whether the choice you select represents a list of open or pending tasks. To accomplish this, I simply determine ahead of time which list the script would create if you select the **Cancel** key. The script does this by calculating the complement of $open on line 105. With $notopen, I can use the ?: construct to select the appropriate strings, either "Open" or "Pend," for the button label and caption on lines 114–116.

The script tasklist.php uses two functions in db.php, DBGetPendingTasksForUser and DBGetOpenTasks. These are shown in Listing 5-26.

```php
01: <?php
02: // exerpt from db.php
03:
04: /*******************************************************
05: * FUNCTION: DBGetPendingTasksForUser( )
06: *
07: * DESCRIPTION: Returns an array of pending assignments
08: * for the specified user.
09: *
10: * RETURNED: array of event hashes or 0
11: *******************************************************/
12: function DBGetPendingTasksForUser(
13:   $min // (min) id of user
14: )
15: {
16: // Do the query, return the record or null
17:
18:   $dbqr = mysql_query(
19:     "SELECT * FROM event " .
20:     "WHERE owner='$min' AND state=" . DBTASKPEND . " " .
21:     "ORDER BY start ASC"
22:   );
23:
24: // Validate
25:
26:   if ( !$dbqr )
27:     return 0;
28:
29: // We've got something... create a result array and return
30:
31:   $result = array();
32:
```

```
33:  while( $row = mysql_fetch_array( $dbqr ) )
34:  {
35:   array_push( $result, $row );
36:  }
37:
38:  return $result;
39: }
40:
41: /*******************************************************
42: * FUNCTION: DBGetOpenTasks( )
43: *
44: * DESCRIPTION: Returns an array of open assignments.
45: *
46: * RETURNED: array of event hashes or 0
47: *******************************************************/
48: function DBGetOpenTasks()
49: {
50: // Do the query, return the record or null
51:
52:  $dbqr = mysql_query(
53:    "SELECT * FROM event " .
54:    "WHERE state=" . DBTASKOPEN . " " .
55:    "ORDER BY start ASC"
56:  );
57:
58: // Validate
59:
60:  if ( !$dbqr )
61:    return 0;
62:
63: // We've got something... create a result array and return
64:
65:  $result = array();
66:
67:  while( $row = mysql_fetch_array( $dbqr ) )
68:  {
69:   array_push( $result, $row );
70:  }
71:
72:  return $result;
73: }
74: ?>
```

Listing 5-26. Database functions used by tasklist.php in db.php

DBGetPendingTasksForUser and DBGetOpenTasks work the same way. Each executes a query, validates the result of that query, and then iterates over the resulting table, adding each row of the resulting table to an array. You saw the general technique in Listing 5-18, so I'll focus on the SQL statements here.

DBGetPendingTaskForUser uses the SELECT FROM statement SELECT * FROM event WHERE owner=$min AND state=DBTASKPEND ORDER BY start ASC, where PHP expands $min to the current user's MIN (supplied as the only argument to DBGetPendingTaskForUser) and DBTASKPEND is the constant you use to denote pending tasks. This SELECT FROM statement returns all rows in the event table that the user with the Mobile Identification Number equal to $min owns that are currently pending, sorting the results by the event's scheduled start time. In contrast, DBGetOpenTasks uses the simpler SELECT * FROM event WHERE state=DBTASKOPEN ORDER BY start ASC, selecting all open tasks and sorting the results by scheduled start time.

Task View

When you select a task from the task list, you see a deck containing the details about the task (see Figure 5-10). This view of a task includes not just information from the event table, but information about the task's owner and location from the event and location tables as well. The PHP script taskview.php, shown in Listing 5-27, builds a task view given a task's ID.

Figure 5-10. MobileHelper task view

```
01: <?php
02: /*******************************************************
03: * taskview.php
04: *
05: * This script shows a selected task in WML for the
06: * current user (indicated by $min and $task).
07: *******************************************************/
08:
09: include "db.php";
10:
11: // Is the user's session valid?
12:
13: $session = DBCheckUserSession( $key );
14:
```

```
15: if ( !is_array( $session ) || count( $session ) == 0 )
16: {
17:  include "logintimeout.php";
18:  exit();
19: }
20:
21: // Update the session variables
22:
23: if ( isset( $open ) )
24: {
25:  $session[ "open" ] = $open;
26: }
27: if ( isset( $task ) )
28: {
29:  $session[ "task" ] = $task;
30: }
31: DBUpdateUserSession( $session );
32: $open = $session[ "open" ];
33: $task = $session[ "task" ];
34: $min = $session[ "min" ];
35:
36: // Get details of this task
37:
38: $taskDesc = DBGetTaskDetail( $task );
39:
40: // Build the response deck.
41:
42: header( "Content-type: text/vnd.wap.wml" );
43:
44: include "wml.php";
45: $deck = WMLNewDeck();
46:
47: WMLAddHTTPEquiv( $deck, "Cache-Control", "no-cache" );
    48:
49: // Show the task
50:
51: if ( $taskDesc && count ( $taskDesc ) > 0 )
52: {
53:
54: // When is it in 1-01-01 2000-22000
55:
```

```
56:  $content = date( "m-d-y H:i",
57:    $taskDesc[ "start" ] ) . "-" .
58:    date( "H:i", $taskDesc[ "stop" ] ) .
59:    WMLBreak() . "\n";
60:
61: // What is it
62:
63:  $content .= $taskDesc[ "taskName" ] .
64:    WMLBreak() . "\n";
65:
66: // Where is it
67:
68:  if ( $taskDesc[ "locationName" ] )
69:  {
70:
71: // Forge a link to the location deck
72:
73:    $lid = $taskDesc[ "locationId" ];
74:    $pf = "<postfield name=\"key\" value=\"\$key\"/>\n" .
75:      "<postfield name=\"location\" value=\"$lid\"/>\n";
76:    $go = WMLGo( "location.php", $pf, "post" );
77:
78: // Add the link & name to the content
79:
80:    $content .= "<anchor title=\"Where\">" . $go .
81:      $taskDesc[ "locationName" ] . "</anchor>" .
82:      WMLBreak() . "\n";
83:
84:  }
85:  else
86:  {
87:    $content .= "No location." . WMLBreak() . "\n";
88:  }
89:
90: // Who owns it
91:
92:  $content .= ( $taskDesc[ "ownerName" ] ?
93:    $taskDesc[ "ownerName" ] : "Not assigned" ) .
94:    WMLBreak() . "\n";
95: // Notes
96:
97:  $content .= ( $taskDesc[ "taskNote" ] ?
98:    $taskDesc[ "taskNote" ] . WMLBreak() . "\n" : "" ) ;
99: }
```

```
100: else
101: {
102:  $content = "No task matches the given data.";
103: }
104:
105:
106: // Card showing the task
107:
108: $card = WMLNewCard( date( "m-d-y Hi",
109:  $taskDesc[ "start" ] ) );
110:
111: // Place the task into its own paragraph.
112:
113: $para = WMLNewParagraph( $content );
114: WMLAddParagraph( $card, $para );
115:
116: // Add the accept event handler.
117:
118: if ( $taskDesc[ "state" ] == DBTASKOPEN )
119: {
120:
121: // Add this task to current user's queue
122:
123:  $taskAcceptAction =
124:   "<postfield name=\"key\" value=\"\$key\"/>\n";
125:  $taskAccept = WMLGo( "taskassign.php",
126:   $taskAcceptAction, "post" );
127:   "Accept", "accept" );
128: }
129: else if ( ( $taskDesc[ "state" ] == DBTASKPEND ) &&
130:  ( $taskDesc[ "owner" ] == $min ) )
131: {
132:
133: // Close this task
134:
135:  $taskAcceptAction =
136:   "<postfield name=\"key\" value=\"\$key\"/>\n";
137:  $taskAccept = WMLGo( "taskcloseinput.php",
138:   $taskAcceptAction, "post" );
139: WMLAddDo( $card, "accept", $taskAccept,
140:   "Close", "accept" );
141: }
```

```
142: else
143: {
144:
145: // Just go back to the current list
146:
147:  $taskAcceptAction =
148:   "<postfield name=\"key\" value=\"\$key\"/>\n";
149:  $taskAccept = WMLGo( "tasklist.php",
150:   $taskAcceptAction, "post" );
151:  WMLAddDo( $card, "accept", $taskAccept, "OK", "prev" );
152: }
153:
154: // Add the card to the deck
155:
156: WMLAddCard( $deck, $card );
157:
158: // Return the deck
159:
160: WMLEchoDeck( $deck );
161: ?>
```

Listing 5-27. The taskview.php script

The taskview.php script is long because it displays both open and assigned tasks, with links to accept or close a task. Let's look at it line-by-line to see how it works.

The first lines—up to line 36—are similar to the lines in tasklist.php. These check the session key, obtain session variables, and update the session key record. They are similar enough, in fact, that I could separate them into their own file, and need only write them once. I chose not to for two reasons: the two files use different persistent variables (taskview.php uses $min, for example, whereas tasklist.php does not), and I have a personal distaste for include files that set global variables (such as $open, $task, and $min). However, there's no reason why you couldn't wrap this code up in a tidy package (say, MobileHelperCommon.php) and share all this material between the files tasklist.php, taskview.php, taskassign.php, taskcloseinput.php, taskclosedo.php, and location.php.

On line 38, taskview.php uses DBGetTaskDetail to get a full description for the task with the indicated ID. This ID, stored in $task, originates with the client when you select a task from the <select> list in the task list deck. DBGetTaskDetail returns a hash containing the task description, with the following fields:

- The "start" slot contains the task's scheduled start time (the database's event.start column for the task).

- The "stop" slot contains the task's scheduled end time (the database's event.stop column for the task).

- The "taskName" slot contains the task's name (the database's event.name column for the task).

- The "taskNote" slot contains the task's note (the database's event.note column for the task).

- The "state" slot contains the task's state (the database's event.state column for the task).

- The "owner" slot contains the task's owner MIN (the database's event.owner column for the task).

- The "locationId" slot contains the ID of the location where the task occurs (the task.location column for the task).

- The "ownerName" slot contains the name of the task's owner (the database's user.name column for the row in the user table linked to this task).

- The "locationName" slot contains the name of the location where the task occurs (the database's location.name column for the row in the location table linked to this task).

If none of these fields exist in the array DBGetTaskDetail returns, the function did not find desired record.

The rest of taskview.php is responsible for formatting the resulting deck. On lines 40–56, the script creates the new deck and turns caching off for the deck. Unlike tasklist.php, taskview.php doesn't need to explicitly set the session key in the browser using WMLAddDeckVar. This is because tasklist.php sets the session key to the WML variable key, and this variable will persist across all decks you view until you visit a card the newcontext attribute set to "true".

Lines 56–59 format the task's scheduled start and stop time for the first line of the task display, storing the result in the variable $content. The resulting date looks something like **11-05-02 18:00-19:00**. The code on lines 56–59 demonstrates why I chose to keep times in the database as PHP times: PHP has a number of flexible functions for formatting time and date information. While SQL has similar functions, they're neither as easy to use nor as intuitive as PHP's date function.

On lines 63 and 64, the script appends the name of the task to the dates previously stored in $content.

The code on lines 68–88 creates a navigation task taking you to a deck containing information about the task's location, as well as the task location's name, when you select the anchor. The PHP script location.php displays a location in detail given the location ID; lines 73–76 create a navigation task that requests location.php with the key and location variables set in the HTTP POST body. Lines 80–82, in turn, actually append the location's name within the anchor to the content.

Lines 92–94 append the task owner's name to the content, while lines 97–98 append the task's note to the content.

All of the content is packaged in a single paragraph on lines 113–114.

Lines 118–152 define the actions you can take when viewing a task and depend on whether the task is unassigned (open), pending and owned by you, or otherwise. If the task is open, anyone may accept the task. Otherwise, you can close tasks you have open, but only view tasks that belong to other people. If, on the other hand, you're viewing a task for any other reason, you may look at the task but not make changes to its state. The three-condition if-else if on lines 118, 129, and 142 covers each of these cases.

The first possibility—that a task is open and may be accepted—spans lines 118-128. On these lines, the script maps the **Accept** soft key to a navigation task that takes you to the taskaccept.php script with the session key and task ID for the displayed task. The taskaccept.php script, discussed in the next section, updates the task in the database, setting its state to pending and its owner to your MIN, and linking the task to your user record. The second possibility—that a task is pending and belongs to you—is on lines 129–141. These lines map the **Accept** soft key to a navigation task that takes you to the taskcloseinput.php script, which prompts you to input the actual start and stop times for the task. Finally, if you can't change the task because it has been assigned to someone else, the script assigns the **Accept** soft key to return to the list on lines 143–152. Each of these assignments uses a WML <go> task with an HTTP POST field containing the session key.

The taskview.php script uses the DBGetTaskDetail function, defined in db.php, and shown in Listing 5-28. This function uses a SELECT statement with two LEFT JOIN clauses to find the desired task's owner and location information.

```
01: <?php
02: // exerpt from db.php
03:
04: /*********************************************************
05: * FUNCTION: DBGetTaskDetail( )
06: *
07: * DESCRIPTION: Returns a task hash with details of the
08: * task
09: *
10: * RETURNED: task hash
```

```
11: *****************************************************/
12: function DBGetTaskDetail(
13:  $taskId // (in) ID of task to get
14: )
15: {
16: // Do the query, return the record or null
17:
18:  $dbqr = mysql_query(
19:    "SELECT event.start, event.stop, " .
20:    "event.name, user.name, " .
21:    "event.note, location.name, " .
22:    "location.id, event.state, " .
23:    "event.owner " .
24:    "FROM event " .
25:    "LEFT JOIN user ON event.owner = user.min " .
26:    "LEFT JOIN location ON event.id = location.id " .
27:    "WHERE event.id=$taskId"
28:  );
29:
30: // Validate
31:
32:  if ( !$dbqr )
33:    return 0;
34:
35: // We've got something... create a result array and return
36:
37:  $record = mysql_fetch_row( $dbqr );
38:
39:  return array(
40:    "start" => $record[ 0 ],
41:    "stop" => $record[ 1 ],
42:    "taskName" => $record[ 2 ],
43:    "ownerName" => $record[ 3 ],
44:    "taskNote" => $record[ 4 ],
45:    "locationName" => $record[ 5 ],
46:    "locationId" => $record[ 6 ],
47:    "state" => $record[ 7 ],
48:    "owner" => $record[ 8 ]
49:  );
50: }
51: ?>
```

Listing 5-28. The DBGetTaskDetail *function from db.php*

Unlike other queries, DBGetTaskDetail collects its results, using numeric indices, from the array mysql_fetch_row returns, rather an array from mysql_fetch_array indexed by associative names, because the names of the columns containing the event's name, location name, and username are the same. When this happens, PHP creates only a single column for all columns with the same name in arrays returned by mysql_fetch_array containing the value of the last column with the same name.

To access the other columns, you need to use the numeric indices with the array mysql_fetch_row returns. Each numeric index corresponds to a column value. Thus, the element in slot 0 of the result array corresponds to the event's start time, the element in slot 1 of the result array corresponds to the event's stop time, and so on.

Task Management

When you press **Accept** while viewing a task, two things can happen: MobileHelper assigns the task to you if the task is unassigned, or closes the task if it belongs to you. In each case, the steps the scripts take are essentially the same: making a database query and returning the appropriate content.

Assigning a task

Task assignment is straightforward: Figure 5-11 shows the result of accepting a task, while Listing 5-29 shows the taskassign.php script.

Figure 5-11. MobileHelper accept task deck

```
01: <?php
02: /*******************************************************
03: * taskassign.php
04: *
05: * This script assigns the current task to the
06: * current user.
07: *******************************************************/
08:
09: define( "ASSIGNPREVTIMER", "100" );
10:
11: include "db.php";
12:
13: // Is the user's session valid?
14:
15: $session = DBCheckUserSession( $key );
16:
17: if ( !is_array( $session ) || count( $session ) == 0 )
18: {
19:   include "logintimeout.php";
20:   exit();
21: }
22:
23: // Update the session variables
24:
25: if ( isset( $task ) )
26: {
27:   $session[ "task" ] = $task;
28: }
29: DBUpdateUserSession( $session );
30: $task = $session[ "task" ];
31: $min = $session[ "min" ];
32:
33: // Do the assignment and show the results…
34:
35: if ( DBAssignUserTask( $min, $task ) )
36: {
37:
38: // Ahhh… success!!
39:
40:   $content = "This task has been added to your queue.";
41: }
```

```
42: else
43: {
44:
45: // Don't give a lot of details when we fail.
46:
47:  $content = "An error occurred. This task could not " .
48:  "be added to your queue. If this persists, please " .
49:  "contact your Coordinator.";
50: }
51:
52: // Build the response deck.
53: header( "Content-type: text/vnd.wap.wml" );
54:
55: include "wml.php";
56: $deck = WMLNewDeck();
57:
58: WMLAddHTTPEquiv( $deck, "Cache-Control", "no-cache" );
59:
60: // Card showing result
61:
62: $card = WMLNewCard( "Assigning Task", "a$min-$task" );
63:
64: // Place the description into its own paragraph.
65:
66: $para = WMLNewParagraph( $content );
67: WMLAddParagraph( $card, $para );
68:
69: // Add the accept event handler.
70:
71: $taskAcceptAction =
72:  "<postfield name=\"key\" value=\"\$key\"/>\n";
73: $taskAccept = WMLGo( "taskview.php",
74:  $taskAcceptAction, "post" );
75: WMLAddDo( $card, "accept",
76:  $taskAccept, "OK", "accept" );
77:
78: // Add a timer to make life easier for the user.
79:
80: WMLAddTimer( $card, "prev", ASSIGNPREVTIMER );
81: WMLAddEvent( $card, "ontimer", $taskAccept );
82:
83: // Add the card to the deck
84:
```

```
85: WMLAddCard( $deck, $card );
86:
87: // Return the deck
88:
89: WMLEchoDeck( $deck );
90:
91: ?>
```

Listing 5-29. The taskassign.php script

By now, most of this should look familiar to you. In taskassign.php, the call to DBAssignUserTask on line 35 links a task to a user. Both the task's ID and user's MIN are already known from the session key record; the MIN was set during the initial login and authentication phase, while the task ID was set when you selected a task from the list of tasks. (In addition, if a script links to taskassign.php with a new task ID in $task, the code on lines 25–28 ensures that the supplied task ID takes precedence over the session table.)

After the script calls DBAssignUserTask, it constructs a result deck that reports success or failure on lines 62–85. The failure message is explicitly vague because most users won't care whether the problem is with the scripts, the database, or anything else.

The script uses a timer to aid navigation on lines 80–81. This timer forces a <prev> after it elapses so that you see the deck containing the task view again after accepting a task. Because the taskview.php script creates a deck that is marked as not being cacheable, your browser reloads the deck, showing you as the task's owner and providing additional confirmation.

The DBAssignUserTask function is shown in Listing 5-30.

```
01: <?php
02: // exerpt from db.php
03:
04: /*****************************************************
05: * FUNCTION: DBAssignUserTask()
06: *
07: * DESCRIPTION: Assigns the unassigned task $task to $user
08: *
09: * RETURNED: nonzero on success; zero on failure
10: *****************************************************/
11: function DBAssignUserTask(
12:   $min, // (in) min of user
13:   $task // (in) id of task
14: )
15: {
16:
```

```
17: // Lock the event table so no one else gets this task
18:
19:  mysql_query( "LOCK TABLES event WRITE" );
20:
21: // Get the task
22:
23:  $taskRecord = DBGetTaskDetail( $task );
24:
25:  if ( !is_array( $taskRecord ) ||
26:    count( $taskRecord ) == 0 )
27:  {
28:    mysql_query( "UNLOCK TABLES" );
29:    return 0;
30:  }
31:
32: // Is it open?
33:
34:  if ( $taskRecord[ "state" ] != DBTASKOPEN )
35:  {
36:    mysql_query( "UNLOCK TABLES" );
37:    return 0;
38:  }
39:
40: // Yes. Set its state and its owner.
41:
42:  $result = mysql_query(
43:    "UPDATE event " .
44:    "SET state=" . DBTASKPEND . ",owner='$min' " .
45:    "WHERE id='$task'"
46:    );
47:  $success = $result && mysql_affected_rows();
48:
49:  mysql_query( "UNLOCK TABLES" );
50:
51:  return $success;
52: }
53: ?>
```

Listing 5-30. The DBAssignUserTask *function defined in db.php*

This function first locks the event table in the database on line 19. If the script didn't lock the event table, it would be possible (albeit unlikely) for another user to accept the task between the time the function calls DBGetTaskDetail and the next mysql_update call.

The script then fetches the record of the task using DBGetTaskDetail, and checks to make sure that the task ID the caller provides is valid. If it is, and if the task is currently unassigned, the script issues an UPDATE query to the database on lines 43–46, setting the state to DBTASKPEND and the owner to the desired MIN.

On line 47, the script establishes whether it succeeded by determining the number of rows that were affected by the query. If $result is non-zero, the query succeeded but may not have updated any rows. Calling mysql_affected_rows and checking to see that at least one row was changed in addition to being sure that $result is non-zero determines success conclusively.

Regardless of success or failure, the script unlocks the event table on line 49. (It also does so if an error occurs and the function exits before updating the event table on lines 28 and 36, to be sure that the table isn't left locked in case of an error.) It then returns indicating its success or failure on line 51.

Closing a task

Closing a task is more complex than accepting a task because you must first enter the task's actual start and stop times before closing the task. Figure 5-12 shows a deck generated by taskcloseinput.php, which is shown in Listing 5-31. Cards taskcloseinput.php include default start and stop times (drawn from the scheduled start and stop times for the task) in their input fields so that in the vast majority of cases, you need only accept the defaults entered by the server.

Figure 5-12. MobileHelper close task deck (first of four cards)

```
01: <?php
02: /******************************************************
03: * taskcloseinput
04: *
05: * This script prompts the user for the information
06: * needed to close a particular task.
07: ******************************************************/
08:
09: include "db.php";
10:
11: // Is the user's session valid?
12:
13: $session = DBCheckUserSession( $key );
14:
15: if ( !is_array( $session ) || count( $session ) == 0 )
16: {
17:   include "logintimeout.php";
18:   exit();
19: }
20:
21: header( "Content-type: text/vnd.wap.wml" );
22:
23: // Update the session variables
24:
25: if ( isset( $task ) )
26: {
27:   $session[ "task" ] = $task;
28: }
29: DBUpdateUserSession( $session );
30: $task = $session[ "task" ];
31:
32: // Get details of this task
33:
34: $taskDesc = DBGetTaskDetail( $task );
35:
36: // Set the default start and stop times for the task.
37:
38: $dstartdate = date( "m/d/Y", $taskDesc[ "start" ] );
39: $dstarttime = date( "H:i", $taskDesc[ "start" ] );
40: $dstopdate = date( "m/d/Y", $taskDesc[ "stop" ] );
41: $dstoptime = date( "H:i", $taskDesc[ "stop" ] );
42:
43: // Build the response deck.
44:
```

```
45: include "wml.php";
46: $deck = WMLNewDeck();
47:
48: WMLAddHTTPEquiv( $deck, "Cache-Control", "no-cache" );
49:
50: // Start date input card
51:
52: $card = WMLNewCard( "Close Task: Start", "sd" );
53: $content = '<fieldset title="Close Task: Start">' .
54:   'Actual start date:' .
55:   '<input name="startdate" type="text" ' .
56:   'format="NN/NN/NNNN" emptyok="false" ' .
57:   "value=\"$dstartdate\" " .
58:   ' maxlength="10" size="10"/></fieldset>';
59: $para = WMLNewParagraph( $content );
60: WMLAddParagraph( $card, $para );
61:
62: $task = WMLGo( "#st");
63: WMLAddDo( $card, "accept", $task, "OK", "accept" );
64:
65: WMLAddCard( $deck, $card );
66:
67: // Start time input card
68:
69: $card = WMLNewCard( "Close Task: Start", "st" );
70: $content = '<fieldset title="Close Task: Start">' .
71:   'Actual start time:' .
72:   '<input name="starttime" type="text" ' .
73:   'format="NN:NN" emptyok="false" ' .
74:   "value=\"$dstarttime\" ".
75:   'maxlength="5" size="5"/></fieldset>';
76: $para = WMLNewParagraph( $content );
77: WMLAddParagraph( $card, $para );
78:
79: $task = WMLGo( "#ed");
80: WMLAddDo( $card, "accept", $task, "OK", "accept" );
81:
82: WMLAddCard( $deck, $card );
83:
84: // Stop date input card
85:
```

```
86: $card = WMLNewCard( "Close Task: Stop", "ed" );
87: $content = '<fieldset title="Close Task: Stop">' .
88:   'Actual stop date:' .
89:   '<input name="stopdate" type="text" ' .
90:   'format="NN/NN/NNNN" emptyok="false" ' .
91:   "value=\"$dstopdate\" " .
92:   'maxlength="10" size="10"/></fieldset>';
93: $para = WMLNewParagraph( $content );
94: WMLAddParagraph( $card, $para );
95:
96: $task = WMLGo( "#et");
97: WMLAddDo( $card, "accept", $task, "OK", "accept" );
98:
99: WMLAddCard( $deck, $card );
100:
101: // Stop time input card
102:
103: $card = WMLNewCard( "Close Task: Stop", "et" );
104: $content = '<fieldset title="Close Task: Stop">' .
105:   'Actual stop time:' .
106:   '<input name="stoptime" type="text" ' .
107:   'format="NN:NN" emptyok="false" ' .
108:   "value=\"$dstoptime\" " .
109:   'maxlength="5" size="5"/></fieldset>';
110: $para = WMLNewParagraph( $content );
111: WMLAddParagraph( $card, $para );
112:
113: $task = WMLGo( "#submit");
114: WMLAddDo( $card, "accept", $task,
115:   "OK", "accept" );
116:
117: WMLAddCard( $deck, $card );
118:
119: // Submit card
120:
121: $card = WMLNewCard( "Submit", "submit" );
122: $taskAction =
123:   "<postfield name=\"key\" " .
124:   "value=\"\$key\"/>\n" .
125:   "<postfield name=\"startdate\" " .
126:   "value=\"\$startdate\"/>\n" .
127:   "<postfield name=\"starttime\" " .
128:   "value=\"\$starttime\"/>\n" .
129:   "<postfield name=\"stopdate\" " .
```

```
130:    "value=\"\$stopdate\"/>\n" .
131:    "<postfield name=\"stoptime\" " .
132:    "value=\"\$stoptime\"/>\n" ;
133: $task = WMLGo( "taskclosedo.php",
134:    $taskAction, "post" );
135: WMLAddEvent( $card, "onenterforward", $task );
136:
137: WMLAddCard( $deck, $card );
138:
139: // Return the deck
140:
141: WMLEchoDeck( $deck );
143: ?>
```

Listing 5-31. The taskcloseinput.php script

This lengthy script builds a deck with four cards, one corresponding to each of the actual start date and time and stop date and time. Let's look closely at how the script establishes default values for each of these inputs, and how it builds one card.

On line 34, taskcloseinput.php uses DBGetTaskDetail to get the scheduled start and stop times for the task you're closing. These values are used in lines 38–41, where the four variables $dstartdate, $dstarttime, $dstopdate, and $dstoptime are set to formatted versions of their scheduled counterparts using the date function. The script uses these variables when setting the value attribute of each <input> field on each of the four cards. The format that the date function uses for each of these values must match the format attribute of the <input> field, however, or the client won't accept the default data for the <input> tag.

The script's creation of the first card spans lines 52–66. These lines are largely pure WML mashed into PHP strings because the wml.php functions don't directly support building <input> tags (although you could use the WMLTagAsString function) as a separate entity. This card contains a single <fieldset> with a single field, the WML <input> element named startdate that accepts the actual start date you enter. This field uses the format attribute to validate your input and the default attribute to supply the predetermined default $dstartdate, containing the scheduled start date for the task.

> **NOTE** *I could have set the default values using the hidden card trick I showed you in the section "Session Management," by setting the four WML variables* startdate, starttime, stopdate, *and* stoptime. *I prefer using the WML* <input> *tag's* value *attribute because it's a standard part of WML, although in practice it doesn't save much space or download time. Which you use is largely a matter of personal taste.*

The three remaining cards on lines 67–117 are similar, each defining a
`<fieldset>` with a single `<input>` tag to accept one of the start time, stop date, and
stop time values. If you split the input across four cards, it's easy for you to integrate WMLScript validation of entered dates and times (see the previous chapter
and "Food for Thought" at the end of this chapter) if you choose.

The last card must also submit the session key and entered values to the
server to update the task. The script creates a `<go>` task with the appropriate
`<postfield/>` tags on lines 122–134. When the user finishes entering the value on
the fourth card, the browser requests the taskclosedo.php script, shown in Listing
5-32.

```php
01: <?php
02: /*********************************************************
03: * taskclosedo.php
04: *
05: * This script closes the current task
06: *
07: *********************************************************/
08:
09: include "db.php";
10:   define( "ASSIGNPREVTIMER", "100" );
11: // Is the user's session valid?
12:
13: $session = DBCheckUserSession( $key );
14:
15: if ( !is_array( $session ) || count( $session ) == 0 )
16: {
17:   include "logintimeout.php";
18:   exit();
19: }
20:
21: // Update the session variables
22:
23: if ( isset( $task ) )
24: {
25:   $session[ "task" ] = $task;
26: }
27: DBUpdateUserSession( $session );
28: $task = $session[ "task" ];
29:
30: // Convert incoming date and time stuff...
31:
```

```
32: $actualStart = DateTimeToPHPTime( $startdate, $starttime );
33: $actualStop = DateTimeToPHPTime( $stopdate, $stoptime );
34:
35: // Do the assignment and show the results...
36:
37: if ( $actualStart > 0 && $actualStop > 0 &&
38:  $actualStart < $actualStop )
39: {
40:  if ( DBCloseTask( $task, $actualStart, $actualStop ) )
41:  {
42:   $content = "This task has been closed.";
43:  }
44:  else
45:  {
46:   $content = "An error occurred. This task " .
47:    "could not be closed. If this persists, " .
48:    "please contact your Coordinator.";
49:  }
50: }
51: else
52: {
53:  $content = "Either the " .
54:   ( $actualStart < 0 ? "start " : "stop " ) .
55:   "date or " .
56:   ( $actualStart < 0 ? "start " : "stop " ) .
57:   "time was not entered correctly.";
58:  $invalid = 1;
59: }
60:
61: // Build the response deck.
62:
63: header( "Content-type: text/vnd.wap.wml" );
64:
65: include "wml.php";
66: $deck = WMLNewDeck();
67:
68: WMLAddHTTPEquiv( $deck, "Cache-Control", "no-cache" );
69:
70: // Card showing result
71:
72: $card = WMLNewCard( "Closing Task", "cl$min-$task" );
73:
74: // Place the description into its own paragraph.
75:
```

```
76: $para = WMLNewParagraph( $content );
77: WMLAddParagraph( $card, $para );
78:
79: // Add the accept event handler.
80:
81: $taskAcceptAction =
82:  "<postfield name=\"key\" value=\"\$key\"/>\n";
83: $taskAccept = WMLGo( "taskview.php",
84:  $taskAcceptAction, "post" );
85: WMLAddDo( $card, "accept", $taskAccept, "OK", "accept" );
86:
87: // Add the prev event handler.
88:
89: $taskPrevAction =
90:  "<postfield name=\"key\" value=\"\$key\"/>\n";
91: $taskPrev = WMLGo( "taskview.php",
92:  $taskPrevAction, "post" );
93: WMLAddDo( $card, "prev", $taskPrev, "Back", "prev" );
94:
95: // Add a timer to make life easier for the user.
96:
97: WMLAddTimer( $card, "prev", ASSIGNPREVTIMER );
98: WMLAddEvent( $card, "ontimer", $taskPrev );
99:
100: // Add the card to the deck
101:
102: WMLAddCard( $deck, $card );
103:
104: // Return the deck
105:
106: WMLEchoDeck( $deck );
107: ?>
```

Listing 5-32. The taskclosedo.php script

After the session management code, lines 32 and 33 convert the PHP variables (supplied by the incoming HTTP POST request) $startdate, $starttime, $stopdate, and $stoptime to PHP dates and times using the function DateTimeToPHPTime, defined in db.php. DateTimeToPHPTime validates the incoming date and time arguments, returning either the time in seconds after the epoch or -1 if it could not parse either the date or time correctly.

On lines 37 and 38, the script checks to be sure that both the $actualStart and $actualStop variables contain valid times, and that the start time is before the stop time. If both contain valid times in the proper order, the script calls DBCloseTask to update the task with the actual times and mark the task as closed on lines 40–49; otherwise, the script creates an error message telling you which time isn't correct. The remainder of the script creates the deck containing the status message and sends the resulting deck back to the client. As when you initially accept a task, the deck produced by taskclosedo.php uses a timer (lines 97–98) to show you the closed event after 10 seconds.

The taskclosedo.php script uses two functions in db.php: DateTimeToPHPTime and DBCloseTask. Listing 5-33 shows these functions.

```php
01: <?php
02: // exerpt from db.php
03:
04: /*******************************************************
05: * FUNCTION: DateTimeToPHPTime
06: *
07: * DESCRIPTION: Given a string with a date and a string
08: * with a time (mm/dd/yyyy and hh:mm in 24-hour format),
09: * returns an integer with the PHP (UNIX) time.
10: *
11: * RETURNED: positive integer or -1 for error
12: *******************************************************/
13: function DateTimeToPHPTime(
14:   $date, // (in) date as "mm/dd/yyyy"
15:   $time  // (in) time as "hh:mm"
16: )
17: {
18:   $result = -1;
19:
20: // get date components
21:
22:   $mo = strtok( $date, "/" );
23:   $dy = strtok( "/" );
24:   $yr = strtok( "/" );
25:
26:   if ( !checkdate( $mo, $dy, $yr ) )
27:     return $result;
28:
29: // get time components
30:
31:   $hr = strtok( $time, ":" );
32:   $mi = strtok( ":" );
33:
```

```
34:   if ( $hr < 0 || $hr > 23 ) return $result;
35:   if ( $mi < 0 || $mi > 59 ) return $result;
36:
37: // Convert to date and time...
38:
39:   $result = mktime( $hr, $mi, 0, $mo, $dy, $yr );
40:
41:   return $result;
42: }
43:
44: /*******************************************************
45: * FUNCTION: DBCloseTask()
46: *
47: * DESCRIPTION: Closes the task
48: *
49: * RETURNED: nonzero on success; zero on failure
50: *******************************************************/
51: function DBCloseTask(
52:   $task, // (in) id of task
53:   $start, // (in) actual start time
54:   $stop // (in) actual stop time
55: )
56: {
57: // Lock the table
58:
59:   mysql_query( "LOCK TABLES event WRITE" );
60:
61: // Get the task
62:
63:   $taskRecord = DBGetTaskDetail( $task );
64:
65: // Is it defined and pending?
66:
67:   if ( !is_array( $taskRecord )
68:     || count( $taskRecord ) == 0
69:     || $taskRecord[ "state" ] != DBTASKPEND )
70:   {
71:     mysql_query( "UNLOCK TABLES" );
72:     return 0;
73:   }
74:
75: // Yes. Set its state and its times.
76:
```

```
77:  $result = mysql_query(
78:    "UPDATE event " .
79:    "SET state=" . DBTASKCLOSE .
80:    ",actualStart='$start',actualStop='$stop' " .
81:    "WHERE id='$task'"
82:    );
83:
84:  $success = $result && mysql_affected_rows();
85:
86: // Unlock the table
87:
88:  mysql_query( "UNLOCK TABLES" );
89:
90: // Return
91:
92:  return $success;
93: }
94: ?>
```

Listing 5-33. The DateTimeToPHPTime *and* DBCloseTask *functions in db.php*

The DateTimeToPHPTime function uses the PHP function strtok to interpret the date and time strings, a nifty function originally found in the standard library for the C programming language. The strtok function returns successive pieces of a string separated by *tokens*, invariant characters separating parts of the string known ahead of time. The first time you call strtok, you pass the original string and a string containing the tokens that separate the first part of the string from the second. In subsequent calls to strtok, you pass only the tokens separating subsequent parts of the string. Each return value from the string is the next substring between the given tokens; thus, the first call to strtok returns the first substring up to the first token, the second call returns the second substring between the first and second tokens, and so on. When you're done with strtok and want to begin working with another string, simply pass the new string and first token and the process begins anew.

DateTimeToPHPTime is pessimistic, initially assuming that the given date or time is invalid and setting $result to -1 on line 18. It then extracts the month, day, and year (which must each be separated by a single / character) using three calls to strtok on lines 22–24. The resulting segments are stored in the variables $mo, $dy, and $yr, and may contain anything—a valid date, a mostly valid date, or complete and utter nonsense. To determine whether the given date is valid, DateTimeToPHPTime uses the PHP function checkdate on line 26. The checkdate function runs through a number of tests, including making sure that all three components of the dates are numeric, that the month number is a valid number, that the number of days in the month doesn't exceed the specified month, and so on. If all these tests pass, checkdate returns true; otherwise, it returns false. If it returns false on line 26, the function exits returning -1.

The script then uses strtok on the time to extract the hours and minutes and store the results in $hr and $mi on lines 31–32. There's no handy PHP function to check the entered time, but you can do so pretty easily by ensuring that both the hours and minutes values are within logical ranges. Line 34 validates the hours field stored in $hr, while line 35 validates the minutes range stored in $mi.

If and only if the time and date are valid, they are converted to a valid PHP time in seconds before the epoch using the PHP function mktime on line 39.

The DBCloseTask function, shown on lines 44–93 of Listing 5-33, closely resembles the DBAssignUserTask function you saw in Listing 5-30. The function begins by locking the event table, although it's highly unlikely that another client might change the state of the desired task while DBCloseTask is closing the task.

> **NOTE** *Locking the table before checking the state of the* event *row in* DBCloseTask *and* DBAssignUserTask *protects against accidental mid-changes of state not just from multiple PHP clients, but from administrative action using the* **mysql** *monitor as well. When developing your wireless application, be sure to consider not just possible interference between clients but between clients and administrative tools as well.*

After locking the event table on line 59, the function gets the indicated task on line 63. With the task in hand, the function checks to be sure it's valid and in the DBTASKPEND state on lines 67 before issuing the UPDATE request on line 77. If it's not valid, the event table is unlocked and the function exits. Once the UPDATE request takes place on lines 77–82, the function computes a return value, unlocks the event table, and exits.

There's actually a simpler way to write both DBCloseTask and DBAssignUserTask, one that does not require table locking and unlocking. Do you see it? Here's a hint: *you only need to lock the event table if you're issuing multiple queries that must be executed as a group.*

Consider Listing 5-34, an alternate version of DBCloseTask.

```
01: <?php
02: // exerpt from db.php
03:
04: /*******************************************************
05: * FUNCTION: DBCloseTask()
06: *
07: * DESCRIPTION: Closes the task
08: *
09: * RETURNED: nonzero on success; zero on failure
10: *******************************************************/
11: function DBCloseTask(
12: $task, // (in) id of task
13: $start, // (in) actual start time
14: $stop // (in) actual stop time
15: )
16: {
17:
18: // Set its state and and times
19:
20: $result = mysql_query(
21:   "UPDATE event " .
22:   "SET state=" . DBTASKCLOSE .
23:   ",actualStart='$start',actualStop='$stop' " .
24:   "WHERE id='$task' AND state=" . DBTASKPEND
25:   );
26:
27: $success = $result && mysql_affected_rows();
28:
29: return $success;
30: }
31: ?>
```

Listing 5-34. A better `DBCloseTask`

Listing 5-34 shows a `DBCloseTask` function that updates the database using a single query. Because MySQL provides row-level locking, you are assured that only one MySQL client can attempt to change the record for the event at a time. Moreover—and here's the kicker—because the query checks both the record's `id` and `state` columns, the query ensures that the event is in the right state.

The approach used in Listing 5-34 is better for three reasons.

- The event table is never locked, so other clients don't have to wait while DBCloseTask executes.

- DBCloseTask is shorter and issues fewer queries to the MySQL server so it executes more quickly.

- There's no way an error can occur that accidentally leaves the table locked, preventing other clients from accessing it.

For these reasons, both DBCloseTask and DBAssignUserTask appear with this technique on the CD-ROM that accompanies this book in db.php.

Location View

From a task view, you can select the task's location to see more information about where the task occurs. MobileHelper uses the location.php script to generate this deck. Figure 5-13 shows a location deck generated by location.php.

Figure 5-13. MobileHelper location view

The script location.php builds the location view deck using the location table of the MobileHelper database, pulling the WML content in the wml-card column for a specific record into its own card. Listing 5-35 shows location.php.

```
01: <?php
02: /*******************************************************
03: * location.php
04: *
05: * This script shows a selected location in WML
06: * (using variables $min, $location, and $task).
07: *******************************************************/
08:
09: include "db.php";
10:
```

```
11: $session = DBCheckUserSession( $key );
12:
13: if ( !is_array( $session ) || count( $session ) == 0 )
14: {
15:  include "logintimeout.php";
16:  exit();
17: }
18:
19: // Get the location details
20:
21: $location = DBGetLocationDetail( $location );
22:
23: // Build the response deck.
24: header( "Content-type: text/vnd.wap.wml" );
25:
26: include "wml.php";
27: $deck = WMLNewDeck();
28: WMLAddHTTPEquiv( $deck, "Cache-Control", "300" );
29:
30: // Show the location
31:
32: if ( $location && count ( $location ) > 0 )
33: {
34:  $content = $location[ "wmlcard" ];
35: }
36: else
37: {
38:  $content = "No data for this location.";
39: }
40:
41:
42: // Card showing location data
43:
44: $card = WMLNewCard( $location[ "name" ],
45:  "l" . $location[ "id" ] );
46:
47: // Place the description into its own paragraph.
48:
49: $para = WMLNewParagraph( $content );
50: WMLAddParagraph( $card, $para );
51:
52: // Add the card to the deck
53:
```

```
54: WMLAddCard( $deck, $card );
55:
56: // Return the deck
57:
58: WMLEchoDeck( $deck );
59: ?>
```

Listing 5-35. The location.php script

Clients always invoke the location.php script with an HTTP POST variable location, corresponding to the PHP variable $location. On line 21, location.php calls the DBGetLocationDetail function with the value of $location, which predictably returns an associative array consisting of a row in the location table. The script then creates a new deck, setting the cache timeout appropriately (line 28) and placing the contents of the wmlcard column for the specified location (lines 32–39) on an empty card. The script then returns the card to the browser.

The DBGetLocationDetail function, shown in Listing 5-36, uses a single SELECT FROM to obtain a location record given its ID. It's the same as the other DBGet... functions you've seen throughout the chapter.

```
01: <?php
02: // exerpt from db.php
03:
04: /********************************************************
05: * FUNCTION: DBGetLocationDetail( )
06: *
07: * DESCRIPTION: Returns a location hash with details of
08: * the given location
09: *
10: * RETURNED: location hash
11: ********************************************************/
12: function DBGetLocationDetail(
13:   $id // (in) ID of location to get
14: )
15: {
16: // Do the query, return the record or null
17:
18:   $dbqr = mysql_query(
19:     "SELECT * FROM location WHERE id=$id"
20:   );
21:
22: // Validate
23:
```

```
24:  if ( !$dbqr )
25:    return 0;
26:
27: // We've got something... create a result array and return
28:
29:  $record = mysql_fetch_array( $dbqr );
30:
31:    return $record;
32: }
33: ?>
```

Listing 5-36. The DBGetLocationDetail *function from db.php*

On the CD-ROM

Because of the fast pace of MySQL development, you *won't* find MySQL on the CD-ROM. Rather, you should download a copy from the MySQL Web site at http://www.mysql.com and install it on your system.

You will, however, find the PHP and WML for the version of MobileHelper described in this chapter in the directory chap02 on the CD-ROM. If you want to actually install these on a system running MySQL and PHP, you need to add a database named "MobileHelper" and seed the database with some new tables. To do this, connect to the server using the **mysql** utility and issue the command:

```
mysql> CREATE DATABASE MobileHelper;
```

Now you can seed the new database using the **mysql** command using

```
% mysql -u root < MobileHelper.dump
```

or enter the **mysql** monitor and type

```
mysql> source MobileHelper.dump
```

This will seed the database with the tables used by MobileHelper as well as a handful of tasks and volunteers.

If you just want to peek at a listing or two, don't forget that all of the listings are on the CD-ROM as well.

Food for Thought

- MobileHelper lacks help cards. Is it easier for you to add help content to each deck, or create a separate script (say, help.php) that returns a help deck for a particular feature? What are the pros and cons of integrating help within each deck versus having a separate help script that produces help decks for each of the other scripts?

- What kinds of error reporting are appropriate for MobileHelper? For your application? How would you extend db.php to tell users of errors when connecting to MySQL, selecting a database, or handling specific queries?

- How would you extend MobileHelper's user table to store first and last names as well as middle initials, and store whether a given user is a Volunteer or a Coordinator? Modify the PHP scripts to reflect these changes when showing a user's name.

- How would you address MobileHelper's security risks in the user table? (Hint: Look at the PHP documentation for the crypt function.)

- How would you modify wml.php to support the notion of deck-level variable assignments as described in the section "Session Management"? Give it a go and compare your results with the wml.php file for this chapter on the CD-ROM.

- The table for locations is simplistic: it doesn't store a location's address or telephone number in separate columns, for example. How would you extend the location table to be more useful? How would you modify MobileHelper's database and scripts to include these new fields?

- If you accept a task, and choose to accept another task with a time that overlaps the first, you are responsible for both tasks, even if they require you to be in two places at once! How would you fix this?

- MobileHelper currently doesn't show completed tasks anywhere. It might be helpful to do so—consider a Volunteer at a meeting reviewing assignments with her Coordinator, for example. Extend tasklist.php to provide three views into the event table, one each for open tasks, pending tasks, and closed tasks.

- MobileHelper's implementation allows only one volunteer per task. If a task needs multiple contributors, you'd need to enter multiple copies of the task because the task-volunteer relationship is maintained through the user column of the event table. How would you reorganize MobileHelper's tables to support multiple volunteers for a given task? (Hint: Think about adding another table.)

#### CHAPTER 6

Content Delivery: To Pull or Push?

IN SOME CASES, your applications can't wait for users to fetch your content. Service dispatch applications, e-mail, and wireless chat are all applications where the server must push content to the client rather than waiting for you to refresh a page.

WAP defines the Push Access Protocol (PAP) that your applications can use to push content to smart phones. In this chapter, you learn about how the network pushes content to clients and how to use PAP. You'll also be introduced to some of the ethical challenges behind pushed content.

Push Fundamentals

Web browsing traditionally has been a *client-pull* application, in which the client user agent requests content from the server. While progress has been made towards supporting content push on the traditional Web, most users are still far more familiar with making requests of Web servers, rather than having new content from a server appear on their desktop computer.

In the Wireless Web, however, things are different. Just as you expect your telephone to ring when someone calls you, your smart phone is capable of operating as a pager and is capable of receiving messages and Web content. Servers can push content to smart phones, including text messages and Wireless Web pages. In turn, the smart phones can ring or vibrate, attracting your attention so you can see the information pushed to the device.

The WAP Content Push Architecture

WAP's Push Access Protocol (PAP) extends WAP's concepts of the origin server and the gateway server, and providing pushed content to wireless clients. Figure 6-1 shows the deployment view.

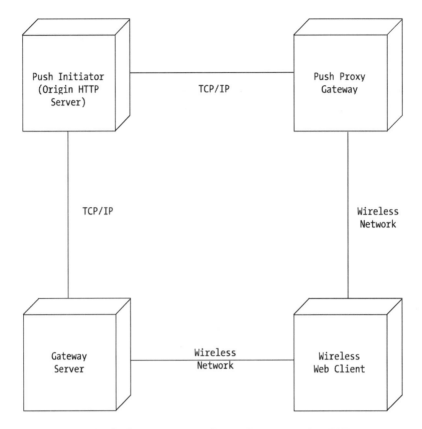

Figure 6-1. The deployment view of a service supporting PAP

The PAP framework adds a *Push Proxy Gateway* (PPG) to the wireless network. The PPG accepts requests from clients called *Push Initiators* (PIs). The PPG pushes messages to the wireless client on behalf of the PI, which then interprets the message and requests the content indicated in the message from the WAP gateway server. Figure 6-2 shows this process.

Figure 6-2 shows a hypothetical content push from the PI through the wireless client, and back to the application server as the wireless client requests content indicated by the PI's request. The process begins when the PI makes a PAP request of the PPG. The PPG can immediately forward the request to the wireless client over the air (OTA), but in practice, most PPGs queue the message for subsequent delivery and immediately respond to the PI. The return message contains a status result and assures the PI that the wireless service delivered the message.

Note, however, that while the wireless service makes its best effort to deliver the message, the wireless service can't actually assure the PI that the message will be read because users may choose not to look at the content the PI pushes. In the next step, the PPG makes an OTA request of the Wireless Web client, passing the

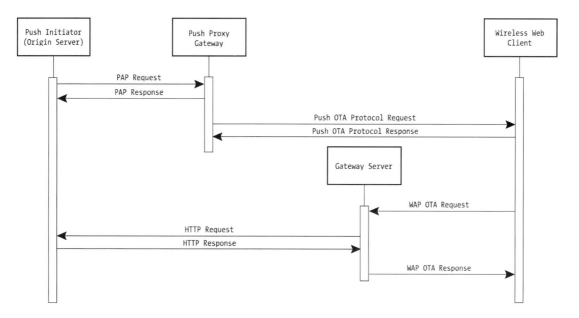

Figure 6-2. Sequence of events for a content push from a PI

PI's message. The Wireless Web client acknowledges the request, and makes a
WAP (actually a Wireless Session Protocol, see Chapter 2) request for the indicated
content. This request is intercepted by the WAP gateway, which translates the
request into a conventional HTTP request, where it proceeds to the origin server.
In turn, the origin server (in the figure, this is also the PI) produces the content
and an HTTP response, which the WAP gateway converts and sends to the client.

The PI may be a separate server responsible for only pushing content, or may
be your Wireless Web application server. Small services may be able to support
the cumulative load from the Web server, scripts, database, and scripts initiating
push requests, but most services should consider separating the responsibilities
of push initiation and content services, using separate hosts for each.

Can you guess what PAP looks like under the hood? Yep! It's a markup language;
in fact, it's an XML application, just as WML. PAP defines a series of tags that enable
you to delineate the destination smart phone's address, a URL that receives a
request when the smart phone actually receives the message, and the semantics
of the message itself. Additional tags, the *service indicator* and the *service load*
tags, enable you to specify a message the client displays or a page that the client
loads upon receipt of the message. To send these messages with markup to the
PPG, the PI uses HTTP and makes an HTTP POST request, posting the document
with the PAP request and, if necessary, the additional markup to perform a service
indicator or service load request.

A key part of PAP is how you specify which smart phone should receive the push content. The PAP address scheme enables you to identify the client using a number of mechanisms, such as the mobile subscriber number or address, using version 4 of the Internet Protocol. PAP also enables you to assign each push message a unique ID, so that you can cancel the push message before it's delivered if you need to.

While the PAP framework is elegant, in practice its deployment has some problems that limit its availability. There are two key problems: adoption and availability.

The PAP framework has been the slowest part of the WAP standard to reach the marketplace. Before WAP, a number of competing companies developed different push frameworks, which were later revised to support pushing WAP content to smart handsets. Wireless network providers, eager to provide functionality, rushed to implement the first-available push framework for the first smart phones they supported. Because these earlier systems are now working in the field, the PAP protocol has been slow to replace older push mechanisms. At the time of this writing, however, a number of networks have pledged to support PAP in the future.

Even as wireless carriers deploy PAP, it may not be available to all developers. As is discussed in more detail in the following section, pushed content is a sensitive subject for most consumers. A telephone handset is a very personal device; you expect content on smart phones to closely match your interests and needs. As with a pager, it is distracting and potentially damaging to receive undesired push content, as you may be responsible for paying for the costs associated with push delivery. Most network operators recognize this and are hesitant to provide open access to their PPG because unscrupulous or inadvertent use could flood subscribers with unsolicited push content. Because PAP does not provide mechanisms for filtering material from different sources, the network provider's only recourse is to limit access to their PPG to trusted content developers and partners. Understandably, given the limited resources of wireless carriers, most network providers can only offer this service for content providers willing to provide premium content or pay fees to access the PPG. Consequently, content push in many cases is restricted to large-scale content providers such as media companies, financial companies, and so on.

Because your application generates push requests in response to changes in your data, Web scripts generally don't create push requests. Instead, your application server will require additional code to watch your data for the conditions that require pushed content for your subscribers, initiating content push messages when conditions match your subscribers' selections. This is a very application-dependent problem; in some applications, you want to have the code responsible for accepting new or changed information trigger push requests, whereas in other cases you want to have a separate program periodically examine your application's data for relevant criteria, and generate push requests as appropriate. In either case, PHP probably isn't the best choice for your application. Although you can write stand-alone programs in PHP that run outside the Web server, (see "Using PHP Test and Debugging Aids" in Chapter 7), most of the time these applications are written in another high level language, such as C++, Java, or Perl.

Content Push User Interface Considerations

As alluded to in the previous section, content push is a touchy issue for consumers. While most consumers readily receive unsolicited print mail, and endure but resent unsolicited e-mail, consumers regard their wireless handset as a personal information source, giving their mobile phone number only to trusted colleagues and friends. In this environment, the user's implicit expectation is that *any* content appearing on a smart phone, from phone calls to Web pages to e-mail, appears only at their behest. Because most wireless providers charge additional fees for push delivery, typically several cents per push message, or a flat fee of a few dollars for a capped number of messages over the billing period, users also expect to receive only requested material. Worse still, smart phones have few mechanisms to enable you to separate your content from unsolicited content, so each pushed message means you must check the handset to see if the information delivered is meaningful to you or not.

In this environment, it's unreasonable to expect subscribers to accept—or appreciate—being bombarded with pushed content. With today's wireless network, the golden rule is simple: push no content unless asked to do so. This model, referred to as *opt-in* pushed delivery because the subscriber opts to have certain content delivered to the handset, gives the subscriber the greatest freedom in choosing appropriate content.

Most content providers pushing delivery offer a Web-based interface where subscribers can enter their mobile number and select the kinds of content they want pushed to their device. For example, the Sprint PCS enables subscribers to sign up for pushed content from trusted sources providing weather, news, and financial information.

If your site pushes information, it should be time-sensitive for subscribers. Mobile subscribers are busy people; your content interrupts them while they're on the go, so you should ensure that your information is useful to them. For example, I rely on pushed content for urgent e-mail notifications from my family and colleagues because these are often time-sensitive. I don't receive pushed content for regular e-mail because most of it can wait hours for a response.

As another example, MobileHelper doesn't use pushed content delivery. In a bona fide emergency, Coordinators contact Volunteers directly, even as they post open tasks to ensure the Volunteers own all tasks. Pushing open tasks would be a travesty because the open task list is constantly changing. Similarly, there's little point in pushing a message to Volunteers pointing out that the open task list has changed because emergencies are generally self-evident (few sleep through floods, hurricanes, or earthquakes!), and Volunteers know to check in with a Coordinator during these events. One possible use for content push for Volunteers would be an opt-in scheme as a push reminder prior to an event's beginning. However, this option is rarely used as most Volunteers use other tools (such as a paper calendar or PDA) to manage their schedules. Adding content push for task notification in this case becomes a nuisance as Volunteers become dependent on two scheduling systems: MobileHelper and their personal calendar.

You should apply this sort of reasoning when you examine your opportunities to push content. Pushed content must be intimately personalized, available on a simple-to-use opt-in/opt-out scheme, and inherently valuable to your subscribers. It is also equally important to maintain the same content guidelines for all the content you push.

As you saw in the previous section, pushed content traverses the same network as the content user's request. As a subscriber, you pay for both the content you request and the content pushed to you. Unlike Web-based push mechanisms, which can be used to stream large quantities of content to desktop computers, wireless push is only appropriate to deliver content tailored for wireless devices. As with your other wireless content, moderation is the word of the day.

First Steps

Let's begin by looking at a simple push request that instructs a client to load MobileHelper's main page. While pushing MobileHelper's main page isn't an appropriate use of push from a user's perspective, it gives us a target document with a well-known appearance for testing.

Setting Up the SDK

Few WAP SDKs support wireless push. The Nokia WAP Toolkit does, enabling you to create and test service load and service indicator requests from the Toolkit to see the results on the simulated Nokia phone.

To begin, check the **Push View** item of the **Show** item under the **Toolkit** menu. In turn, the Nokia WAP Toolkit shows the Push view, similar to what you see in Figure 6-3. Across the top half of the view, you can see a list of the push messages that the SDK has received. Along the bottom half of the window, you can see information about a particular push request.

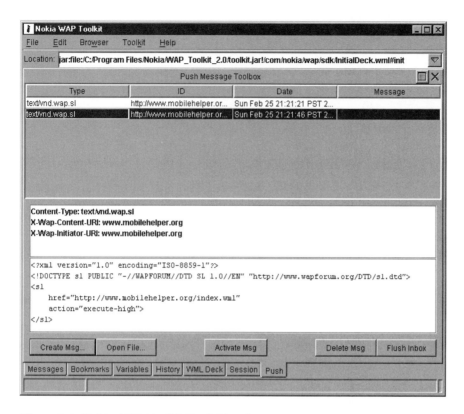

Figure 6-3. Nokia WAP Toolkit Push Simulator

You can use the **Create Msg…** button along the bottom to create a new push message, showing a dialog similar to what you see in Figure 6-4. In this box, you can enter the various attributes of the request (see the discussions in the following sections) and either add it to the push message list, or save the contents to load later. You can use saved push messages to test your content or as templates to create your own push messages if you're developing a server-side push solution.

From the Push view, you can open a previously saved push message (with the **Open File…** button), or activate a particular push message by selecting it and pressing the **Activate Msg** button. When you activate a message, the Toolkit follows the instructions in the push message and displays the result on the simulated phone. You can also delete a specific message using the **Delete Msg** button or remove all messages in the list with the **Flush Inbox** button.

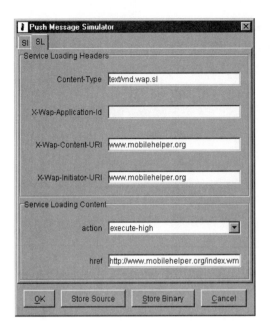

Figure 6-4. Nokia WAP Toolkit prompting for service load message attributes

A Simple Push Request

Your push request has two parts: the PAP request, telling the PPG you want to push content, and the service load request, which is the actual content pushed, telling the client to load a specific page. Listing 6-1 shows the PAP request.

```
01: <?xml version="1.0"?>
02: <!DOCTYPE pap PUBLIC "-//WAPFORUM//DTD PAP 1.0//EN"
03:    "http://www.wapforum.org/DTD/pap_1.0.dtd">
04:
05: <pap>
06:   <push-message push-id="260685-987379411@mobilehelper.org"
07:     ppg-notify-requested-to=
08:      "http://pi.mobilehelper.com/push-notify.php">
09:     <address
10:      address-value=
11:       "WAPPUSH=+011008885551234/TYPE=PLMN@ppg.provider.net"
12:      />
13:   </push-message>
14: </pap>
```

Listing 6-1. The PAP request

Listing 6-1 begins with the preamble associated with all XML documents, the `<?xml?>` tag identifying the document as an XML document on line 1. On line 2, the `<!DOCTYPE>` tag identifies this document as being a `pap` format document in accordance with the definition found at `http://www.wapforum.org/DTD/pap_1.0.dtd`. This line is important because the PPG may discard messages missing the proper identification, even if you correctly markup the rest of the document.

The push request itself is on lines 5–14, enclosed by a single `<pap>` tag. On line 6, the push message begins with the `<push-message>` tag that carries the message's unique ID, an optional result notification address, and the destination address. The unique ID stored in the `push-id` attribute is assigned by the PI, enabling it and PPG to uniquely refer to the push request. You may use any string you like for a `push-id` attribute, as long as it's unique. A good strategy is to use some concatenation of the current time in milliseconds from the epoch and a random number because that's virtually guaranteed to be unique. Lines 7 and 8 instruct the PPG to perform an HTTP POST request to the URL specified by the `ppg-notify-requested-to` attribute, `"http://pi.mobilehelper.com/push-notify.php"`, once the request is actually pushed to the handset. (Recall that the PPG probably only queues the request for later delivery upon your request.)

The `<address>` tag on lines 9–12 enables you to identify the destination for the push request using one of three basic schemes: network address, subscriber number, or subscriber identification. The address itself is labeled with the WAPPUSH identifier; following the address is a TYPE identifier that describes the type of address. In this case, the `address` tag is using the subscriber number, which includes the country code, mobile service identification assigned by that country's regulatory commission, and the mobile subscriber number itself. This address TYPE is PLMN, which happens to mean mobile subscriber number, and the network provider uses the trailing address to help process the request.

The PAP request is accompanied by a second document, either WML content or one of the service load or indicator requests. In general, you won't push WML content to the device directly; it's better to push a service load request because the user can opt to access the content or cancel the load, minimizing the impact on their time and billing. Listing 6-2 shows a typical service load request.

```
01: <?xml version="1.0"?>
02: <!DOCTYPE sl PUBLIC "-//WAPFORUM//DTD SL 1.0//EN"
03:   "http://www.wapforum.org/DTD/sl.dtd">
04: <sl
05:   href="http://www.mobilehelper.org/index.wml"
06:   action="execute-high"/>
```

Listing 6-2. The service load request message

The service load request message is yet another XML document, as you can see from the preamble on line 1. On lines 2 and 3, as with PAP and WML, the service load message identifies itself as an XML document of type sl, following the specification available at `http://www.wapforum.org/DTD/sl.dtd`.

The `<sl/>` tag *is* the service load message, and has two attributes: the `href` attribute and the `action` attribute. As you can guess, the `href` attribute contains the URL the client loads upon receipt of the `<sl/>` tag, and the `action` attribute enables you to select a priority for the message. Once the client receives the `<sl/>` tag, the client immediately loads the indicated URL.

> **CAUTION** *Don't confuse the* `<sl/>` *tag (or the* `<si/>` *tag you will see shortly) with the WML tags you learned in Chapter 2. The service tags are not WML tags, and not all smart phones understand them. Moreover, those smart phones that do understand these tags use them in the context of push requests, not in the context of your WML markup. Including these tags in a WML document is a mistake, causing the Wireless Web browser to show an error.*

The PAP and pushed document occupy a single request from the PI as part of a MIME document that specifies the two separate documents. Once the PPG receives this request (which the PI sends to the PPG using an HTTP POST request), the PPG responds with a status message such as the one in Listing 6-3.

```
01: <?xml version="1.0"?>
02: <!DOCTYPE pap PUBLIC "-//WAPFORUM//DTD PAP 1.0//EN"
03:   "http://www.wapforum.org/DTD/pap_1.0.dtd">
04:
05: <pap>
06:   <push-response push-id="260685-987379411@mobilehelper.org">
07:     <response-result code="1001"
08:      desc="Accepted for Processing/>
09: </pap>
```

Listing 6-3. The PAP response

The response message from the PPG is another XML document using the PAP markup tags, as lines 1–3 show. As it did with the request, the server wraps the response in a `<pap>` tag. This `<pap>` tag contains a single `<push-response/>` tag with the request's unique ID on line 6, and a `<response-result/>` tag on lines 7–8 that reports the result of the request.

The `<response-result/>` tag returns its response in two ways: as a computer-recognized numeric code similar to the HTTP status codes you saw in Chapter 1, and as a human-readable string. The `<response-result/>` tag returns the numeric code in its `code` attribute, and the human-readable string in the `<desc>` attribute. The result codes follow a specified numbering scheme; the value 1001 indicates the server successfully received, understood, and accepted the requested action.

Before you look at the different tags in the PAP, service load, and service indicator requests, let's look in more detail at the acceptable syntax for each of these requests.

Pushed Access Protocol Syntax

The rules for PAP and pushed content are the same as for WML. You intersperse your content with markup tags that identify the instructions for the PPG. You write these tags between angle brackets < and > (the greater-than and less-than symbols). Opening tags are written like `<this>`, and closing tags are written like `</this>`. You must write empty tags, such as the `<response-result/>` tag using a trailing solidus, such as this: `<response-result/>`. All tags are case-sensitive, so `<pap>` is *not* the same as `<PAP>`.

Because these messages are in XML, you need to be sure to include the `<?xml?>` and `<!DOCTYPE>` tags. The `<?xml?>` tag identifies the document as an XML document, and the `<!DOCTYPE>` tag identifies the kind of XML document, such as WML, PAP, or SL. Without these tags, the PPG may discard your message as incorrect, even if the remainder of the markup is correct!

PAP tags may have one or more attributes. An attribute is a name/value pair that provides additional information about a tag, such as the `code` attribute for the `<response-result/>`tag. The name follows the same rules as a tag name—begin with an alphabetic character or an underscore and follow with letters, numbers, hyphens, underscores, and periods. Attribute values are always strings, contained between double quotes.

You can use white space anywhere in the PAP and other pushed documents, as long as your white space does not break a tag or attribute name. Moreover, you can include comments in your PAP and pushed documents by delineating the comments using the symbols `<!--` and `-->`. In practice, comments aren't necessary because PAP documents are so verbose (even though short in length), they're often easy enough to read.

Going Further with the Pushed Access Protocol

PAP enables you to push content, as well as cancel a pending push message. Using the tags and attributes of PAP, you can also check the status of a pushed message, or enable your PI to track the status of messages as they are sent to subscribers.

Pushed Access Protocol Messages

PAP enables you to push messages, cancel a pending push, and obtain status on messages the PI queues for delivery to mobile clients. Each request is a single markup tag within the `<pap>` tag in your push request.

You examined the `<push-message>` tag in the last example. In addition to the `push-id` attribute, which you must include with each `<push-message>` tag, `<push-message>` has other attributes that enable you to control the push process. The `ppg-notify-requested-to` attribute enables you to specify a URL that the PPG will make an HTTP `POST` request to when the message is actually successfully delivered to the client. As you discover shortly, this request message contains another PAP document with a `<resultnotification-message>` tag that describes what happened to your push request. The `deliver-before-timestamp` and `deliver-after-timestamp` attributes enable you to supply a time before which (or after which, in the case of `deliver-after-timestamp`) the message should be delivered. The value of this attribute is a time in the form `YYYY-MM-DDThh:mm:ssZ`, where:

- `YYYY` is the four-digit year.

- `MM` is the two-digit numeric month number (from `01` to `12`).

- `DD` is the two-digit numeric day number (from `01` to `31`).

- `hh` is the two-digit hour number denoting hours past midnight (from `00` to `23`).

- `mm` is the two-digit number denoting minutes after the hour (from `00` to `59`).

- `ss` is the two-digit number denoting number of seconds after the minute (from `00` to `59`).

- `T` is the letter T.

- `Z` is the letter Z.

- `-` is a single hyphen.

- `:` is the colon symbol.

As with the HTTP protocol, all times are relative to Universal Coordinated Time.

The `<push-message>` tag takes one or more `<address>` tags indicating where the push message must go. Each address may be one of four types:

- PLMN, indicating that the address is a subscriber number with preceding country code and mobile operator code

- USER, indicating that the address is a subscriber-defined user-specific identification such as an e-mail address or registration number

- IPV4, indicating that the address is an IP address in accordance with Version 4 of the IP protocol

- IPV6, indicating that the address is an IP address in accordance with Version 6 of the IP protocol

Most of the addresses you use are either PLMN addresses, using a handset's subscriber number, or user-defined addresses based on a subscriber e-mail address. A few networks, notably CDPD, may support the IPV4 address scheme, also used by the Internet itself. In the future as wireless networks roll out higher-level protocols, you can expect to see growing support for the IPV6 scheme, which uses the IPV6-address notation developed for future versions of IP.

Addresses have two parts: the address itself and its type identifier, denoted as named values within the `<address>` tag's `address-value` attribute such as `WAPPUSH=address/TYPE=type@ppg`. The `type@ppg` code begins with the four-letter type abbreviation (one of the four types in the previous paragraph), and a network-specific identifier naming the PPG. Listing 6-4 shows a push message directed to three people, one each addressed using the PLMN, USER, and IPV4 types.

```
01: <?xml version="1.0"?>
02: <!DOCTYPE pap PUBLIC "-//WAPFORUM//DTD PAP 1.0//EN"
03:  "http://www.wapforum.org/DTD/pap_1.0.dtd">
04:
05: <pap>
06:   <push-message push-id="260685-987379411@mobilehelper.org"
07:    ppg-notify-requested-to=
08:     "http://pi.mobilehelper.com/push-notify.php">
09:     <address
10:       address-value=
11:        "WAPPUSH=+011008885551234/TYPE=PLMN@ppg.mobilehelper
    .net"
12:       />
13:     <address
14:       address-value=
15:        "WAPPUSH=ray_rischpater@mobilehelper.net/TYPE=USER@ppg
    .mobilehelper.net"
16:       />
```

```
17:      <address
18:        address-value=
19:         "WAPPUSH=205.179.20.1/TYPE=IPV4@ppg.mobilehelper.net"
20:        />
21:    </push-message>
22: </pap>
```

Listing 6-4. Various `<address/>` *tags*

The first address on lines 9–12 is a mobile phone number, `011008885551234`. The second address on lines 13–16 is a PPG-defined e-mail address, `ray_rischpater@mobilehelper.org`. This address must be known to the PPG and is defined by the network provider. The third address on lines 17–20 is the IP address of a specific device within the provider's network. Because this push message is addressed to multiple recipients, status information about this push message pertains to all three addresses. Thus, by using multiple `<address/>` tags you can send the same push message to multiple recipients.

Once a PPG accepts a message for delivery, you may want to cancel the message. The `<cancel-message>` tag, shown in Listing 6-5, cancels a message that's been queued for delivery *but has not yet arrived*. In other words, you can't cancel a message once the handset has received it.

```
01: <?xml version="1.0"?>
02: <!DOCTYPE pap PUBLIC "-//WAPFORUM//DTD PAP 1.0//EN"
03:   "http://www.wapforum.org/DTD/pap_1.0.dtd">
04:
05: <pap>
06:   <cancel-message push-id="260685-987379411@mobilehelper.org"
07:      <address
08:        address-value=
09:         "WAPPUSH=+011008885551234/TYPE=PLMN@ppg.mobilehelper.net"
10:        />
11:    </cancel-message>
12: </pap>
```

Listing 6-5. The `<cancel-message>` *tag*

Each `<cancel-message>` request must have the `push-id` attribute, giving the ID of the sent message that you want to cancel. You may include `<address/>` tags within the `<cancel-message>` tag, canceling the delivery of the message to the selected addresses only. If you omit the `<address/>` tag, message delivery is canceled to all clients.

Before canceling a message, you can test to see whether the PPG has successfully delivered a message. You can test by looking for `<resultnotification-message>` messages the PPG sends to the address you give with the `<push-message>` `ppg-notify-requested-to` attribute, but you can also use the `<statusquery-message>` message, providing the ID of the message in question. As with `<push-message>` and `<cancel-message>`, the `<statusquery-message>` message refers to *all* addresses unless you supply specific addresses using the `<address/>` tag. Listing 6-6, for example, requests the status of the message `260685-987379411@mobilehelper.org` being delivered to `ray_rischpater@mobilehelper.org`. Note, however, that between requesting the status for a message and attempting to cancel it, a lag time exists in which the message can be delivered, so even checking the status of the message and then canceling it doesn't ensure that the message won't be received.

```
01: <?xml version="1.0"?>
02: <!DOCTYPE pap PUBLIC "-//WAPFORUM//DTD PAP 1.0//EN"
03:   "http://www.wapforum.org/DTD/pap_1.0.dtd">
04:
05: <pap>
06:    <statusquery-message push-id="260685-987379411@mobilehelper.org">
07:       <address
08:         address-value=
09:           "WAPPUSH=ray_rischpater@mobilehelper.net/TYPE=USER@ppg
      .mobilehelper.net"
10:       />
11:    </statusquery-message>
12: </pap>
```

Listing 6-6. The `<statusquery-message>` *message*

For each of these requests you receive a response message telling you what happened to a particular request. The PPG sends one of the `<push-response/>`, `<cancel-response/>`, or `<statusquery-response/>` messages in response to a `<push-message>`, `<cancel-message>`, or `<statusquery-message>` message, respectively. Each of these responses has three attributes: `push-id`, `code`, and `desc`. The `push-id` attribute contains the ID of the message whose status is being reported, and a `<result>` tag that contains `code` and `desc` attributes contain a numeric and human-readable message describing the status of the delivery. Table 6-1 shows a list of defined status messages.

Table 6-1. PAP Status Codes

CODE	DESCRIPTION	LIKELY REASON
1000	OK	
1001	Accepted for processing	
2000	Bad request	PAP message is not correct.
2001	Forbidden	You do not have permission to make the request.
2002	Address Error	The address is not correctly formatted.
2003	Address	Not Found The address is wrong.
2004	push-id not found	You did not include a push-id attribute with your message.
2005	Capabilities mismatch	The client does not support the request in the message.
2006	Required capabilities not supported	The input is not in a form supported by the client.
2007	Duplicate push-id	The push-id in your message is already in use.
3000	Internal server error	The server could not process the request.
3001	Not implemented	The request is not supported by the server.
3002	Version not supported	The version of the request is not supported by the server.
3003	Not possible	The requested action is not possible because the message no longer exists.
3004	Capability matching not supported	The requested action is not supported by the server and client.
3005	Multiple addresses not supported	The server can only deliver messages to one client at a time.
3006	Transformation failure	The server could not transcode the message for the client.
3007	Specified delivery method not possible	The server could not deliver the message as requested.
3008	Capabilities not available	Client capabilities for the specified client are not available.

Table 6-1. PAP Status Codes (Continued)

CODE	DESCRIPTION	LIKELY REASON
3009	Required network not available	The desired network is not available.
3010	Required bearer not available	The bearer network is not available.
4000	Service failure	The service failed.
4001	Service busy	The service is too busy to handle the request.
5xxx	Mobile client aborted	The mobile client aborted reception of the message.

As you can see from Table 6-1, the status codes are divided into sections based on the thousands digit. Status codes in the range 1000–1999 indicate successful delivery of the message, whereas other messages report various failures. Broadly speaking, status codes in the range 2000–2999 are failures on the part of the PI, whereas status codes in the range 3000–3999 are failures on the part of the PPG. Failure codes between 4000 and 4999 are failures on the part of the service provider, and failure codes above 4999 indicate a problem with the mobile client to which you addressed the message.

In addition to the `code` and `desc` attributes of the various response messages, the `<statusquery-result/>` contains additional status information you can use when debugging push transactions. The `<statusquery-response>` message includes the `<statusquery-result>` tag, containing `<address/>` tags for the addresses of the message in question. The `<statusquery-result/>` message carries the attributes `event-time` and `message-state`, which specifies the last time the PPG did anything with the message, and what it did with the message. This state is a single word such as `"pending"`, `"rejected"`, `"canceled"`, `"expired"`, `"delivered"`, `"aborted"`, or `"timeout"`, with the obvious meaning attached to the word. Listing 6-7 shows a sample `<statusquery-response>` message for a successfully delivered push message.

```
01: <?xml version="1.0"?>
02: <!DOCTYPE pap PUBLIC "-//WAPFORUM//DTD PAP 1.0//EN"
03:   "http://www.wapforum.org/DTD/pap_1.0.dtd">
04:
05: <pap>
06:   <statusquery-response
07:   push-id="260685-987379411@mobilehelper.org">
08:     <statusquery-result code="1000" desc="OK"
09:      message-state="delivered">
```

```
10:        <address
11:          address-value=
12:           "WAPPUSH=ray_rischpater@mobilehelper.net/TYPE=USER@ppg
   .mobilehelper.net"
13:          />
14:      <statusquery-result/>
15:    </status-query>
16: </pap>
```

Listing 6-7. The <statusquery-response> *message*

PAP defines a message the PI may receive if the PI provides a URL in the
ppg-notify-requested-to attribute of the <push-message> tag. The PPG sends this
message to the PI using an HTTP POST request, sending a file with the MIME
type application/xml. The PI may use this message, which contains the
<resultnotification-message> tag to update its notion of the success or failure
of a message's delivery. The <resultnotification-message> tag has attributes
similar to the <statusquery-response> message. Listing 6-8 shows a sample
<resultnotification-message> tag.

```
01: <?xml version="1.0"?>
02: <!DOCTYPE pap PUBLIC "-//WAPFORUM//DTD PAP 1.0//EN"
03:   "http://www.wapforum.org/DTD/pap_1.0.dtd">
04:
05: <pap>
06:   <resultnotification-message
07:     push-id="260685-987379411@mobilehelper.org"
08:     code="1000" desc="OK"
09:     message-state="delivered"
10:     sender-address="205.179.20.1"
11:     sender-name="ppg.mobilehelper.org"
12:     received-time="2001-02-27T06:22Z"
13:     event-time="2001-02-27T06:43Z">
14:      <address
15:        address-value=
16:         "WAPPUSH=ray_rischpater@mobilehelper.net/TYPE=USER@ppg
   .mobilehelper.net"
17:        />
18:    </resultnotification-message>
19: </pap>
```

Listing 6-8. The <resultnotification-message> *tag*

The names of the `<resultnotification-message>` tag's attributes allude to their meanings. The `push-id`, `code`, `desc`, and `message-state` tags all serve the same purpose as they do for the `<statusquery-response>` tag, providing the message's unique identification and status. The `sender-address` and `sender-name` attributes enable you to match the `<resultnotification-message>` request to a particular PPG within your network, handy if you're using multiple PI's to distribute load or push different kinds of messages. The `received-time` and `event-time` attributes, on the other hand, indicate the time at which the PPG received the message and at which the PPG last manipulated the message. As with the times for the `<push-message>` tag, the server expresses these times tersely using the `yyyy-mm-ddThh:mmZ` notation.

When your PI receives a `POST` containing a `<resultnotification-message>` tag, it must respond with a `<resultnotification-response>` message. This assures the PPG that the notification was successfully handled, and closes the loop between PI and PPG. The `<resultnotification-response>` message has three attributes: `push-id`, `code`, and `desc`, which the PI fills out using the status codes in Table 6-1. Listing 6-9 shows the PI's response to the `<resultnotification-message>` in Listing 6-8, acknowledging the message with a successful status code.

```
01: <?xml version="1.0"?>
02: <!DOCTYPE pap PUBLIC "-//WAPFORUM//DTD PAP 1.0//EN"
03:   "http://www.wapforum.org/DTD/pap_1.0.dtd">
04:
05: <pap>
06:   <resultnotification-response
07:     push-id="260685-987379411@mobilehelper.org"
08:     code="1000" desc="OK">
09:     <address
10:       address-value=
11:         "WAPPUSH=ray_rischpater@mobilehelper.net/TYPE=USER@ppg
    .mobilehelper.net"
12:       />
13:   </resultnotification-response>
14: </pap>
```

Listing 6-9. The `<resultnotification-response>` *message the PI sends upon receipt of the* `<resultnotification-message>` *message in Listing 6-8.*

Either your application's Web server or your push server can handle the `<resultnotification-message>` and `<resultnotification-response>` messages In either case, handling these messages is generally the responsibility of push framework, and it's unlikely you will choose to code this in PHP. Often, it makes the most sense to build this as a separate subsystem within the rest of your push application using a language such as Java, C++, or Perl.

Service Indicator Messages

Service indicator messages notify subscribers that a particular service or URL is available, and gives them an opportunity to load indicated content. It's similar to a service load message, in that it primes the smart phone to load a particular URL, but does not actually load the URL unless the user chooses to do so.

As with the service load message that you saw in Listing 6-2, the service indicator message is an XML document. Listing 6-10 shows a simple service indicator message; Figure 6-5 shows the result in the Nokia Toolkit.

```
01: <?xml version="1.0"?>
02: <!DOCTYPE si PUBLIC "-//WAPFORUM//DTD SI 1.0//EN"
03:  "http://www.wapforum.org/DTD/si.dtd">
04: <si>
05:   <indication
06:    href="http://www.mobilehelper.org"
07:    si-id="message@pi.mobilehelper.org"
08:    created="2001-02-27T06:22Z"
09:    si-expires="2001-02-27T06:22Z"
10:    action="signal-medium">
11:     Load MobileHelper?
12:   </indication>
13: </si>
```

Listing 6-10. A service indicator message

Figure 6-5. Nokia WAP Toolkit showing push message

As the first three lines of Listing 6-10 indicate, all service indicator messages conform to the WAP Forum SI format, described at http://www.wapforum.org/DTD/si.dtd. The service indication message itself consists of an <indication> tag, containing the prompt the user sees when the client receives the indication. Most clients have a mailbox metaphor that enables you to see various indications as they arrive, selecting which ones you want to view and which ones you want to delete.

The `<indication>` tag has several optional attributes, all of which are shown in Listing 6-10. The `href` attribute tells the client the URL to load when you accept the service indication. If you don't include an `href` attribute, the client displays the indication with no prompt to load a page.

The `si-id` attribute is a unique identifier for the service indication. If you don't provide one, the client uses the `href` attribute as the unique identifier. Clients use this ID when determining which service indications are new messages and which are copies of messages already received. If a client receives an indication with the same ID as one already in memory, the older one is silently discarded.

You can use the `created` and `si-expires` attributes to assign creation and expiration dates to your content, which the client may use when displaying the prompt. Some smart phones show the date and time the message was created, and can delete messages that live past the time in the `si-expires` attribute. As with PAP, the times must be in UTC in `yyyy-mm-ddThh:mmZ` format.

The `action` attribute tells the client what action to take to obtain your attention when receiving the indication. Five values of `action` are possible, with each value having an increasingly intrusive impact to the user interface:

- `"signal-none"` indicates that no action should be taken.

- `"delete"` indicates that pending indications with the same ID should be deleted.

- `"signal-low"` indicates that the message should be silently saved for your review.

- `"signal-medium"` indicates that the client should display an alert regarding the content's arrival as soon as it can without interrupting you.

- `"signal-high"` indicates that the client will immediately display the indication.

Clients can sort incoming service indications by their `action`, so that higher-priority indications always receive greater attention than lower priority indications.

Some clients enable you to provide additional information in the service indication, corresponding to the body of an e-mail message. You wrap this information in an `<info>` tag within the indication, consisting of one or more `<item>` tags. Each `<item>` has a client-specific `class` attribute that instructs the client how to display the `<item>` tag's contents. For example, the Nokia WAP browser supports the `"MoreInfo"` class of information, corresponding to a paragraph describing the service indication. Listing 6-11 shows an example.

```
01: <?xml version="1.0"?>
02: <!DOCTYPE si PUBLIC "-//WAPFORUM//DTD SL 1.0//EN"
03:  "http://www.wapforum.org/DTD/si.dtd">SI
04: <si>
05:   <indication
06:    href="http://www.mobilehelper.org"
07:    si-id="message@pi.mobilehelper.org"
08:    created="2001-02-27T06:22Z"
09:    si-expires="2001-02-27T06:22Z"
10:    action="signal-medium">
11:     Load MobileHelper?
12:   </indication>
13:   <info>
14:     <item class="MoreInfo">
15:       You haven't checked your task list this week.
16:     </item>
17:   </info>
18: </si>
```

Listing 6-11. The <info> *tag in a service indication*

Because the <info> tag's interpretation strongly depends on the client, it's seldom suitable for general use.

Service Load Messages

With each PAP message, the PI sends a second document containing the actual content the PI is pushing to the client. In its simplest form, this message may be a text document or WML deck. Far more often, however, you send a service load message, instructing the client to load a specified URL on your application server.

Using a service load message instead of sending a WML deck has two key advantages. First, the service load message is smaller, ensuring faster delivery to the recipient, often incurring lower cost. Second, it frees your push application from needing to deal with the vagaries of content production. Instead, producing displayable content remains the sole responsibility of your Web scripts; the push application need only generate and send a URL to the target content.

> **NOTE** *If you want your subscriber to have a choice as to whether or not to view the pushed content, you should use a service indication message, which prompts the user before loading the pushed content.*

The service load message is simple; in fact, you've already seen it in its entirety in Listing 6-2. Listing 6-12 shows a copy of Listing 6-2 for your perusal.

```
01: <?xml version="1.0"?>
02: <!DOCTYPE sl PUBLIC "-//WAPFORUM//DTD SL 1.0//EN"
03:    "http://www.wapforum.org/DTD/sl.dtd">
04: <sl
05:    href="http://www.mobilehelper.org/index.wml"
06:    action="execute-high"/>
```

Listing 6-12. The service load message

The service load message consists of an `<sl/>` tag with two attributes. The `<sl/>` tag's href attribute points to the fully qualified URL for the document the client should load, and the action attribute indicates what action the client takes when loading the content. The action attribute may be one of `"execute-high"`, `"execute-low"`, or `"cache"`, denoting the relative priority of the message. The client handles each of these differently.

When the action attribute is equal to `"execute-high"`, the client loads content immediately and may disturb the user interface to alert the user. This disturbance may be a ring, beep, vibration, or dialog box. On the other hand, if action is equal to `"execute-low"`, the client loads content immediately, but does not disturb the user interface. Finally, if action is equal to `"cache"`, the client attempts to cache the content at the URL, but does not display the content. If the device has no cache or there is no room for the content, the client discards the message.

You should avoid using the `"cache"` action for pushed content *unless* the receiving client has a flat-rate billing service to the network because the client bears the cost of pushed content delivery. Pushing content to update client caches in anticipation of user requests can quickly congest wireless networks and bring user costs to an unacceptable level.

On the CD-ROM

This chapter sports no additions to MobileHelper, so you will only find the numbered listings in the ch06 directory of the CD-ROM.

Because of the highly operator-specific nature of server-pushed messages, it is suggested that you check with the wireless network provider for your handsets before experimenting with server push. If they support server push, they can provide you with additional documentation for using their network to access their devices, often including a software development kit and sample code.

Food for Thought

- Determine whether your wireless provider enables independent developers to access their content push framework. Does your wireless provider support the WAP standard, or do they use an alternate framework?

- MobileHelper makes use of service push in two ways: pushing reminders to users just before a task starts, and enabling messages to be entered by one volunteer and be sent to another (such as a simple wireless chat or e-mail). Sketch a design for either of these features, being sure to include support for opt-in/opt-out. How does your design affect the various database tables discussed in the last chapter?

- When might pushing content directly from a PHP script be appropriate?

- Would a wireless chat application best use the service indicator, service load messages, or neither? Why? How can such an application work?

#### CHAPTER 7

Making It Work: Testing and Debugging

AS YOU WRITE SCRIPTS, some things inevitably go wrong. The vast majority of problems occur within the scripts you write, rather than within other parts of your system, such as the Web server, script interpreter, or database.

You can avoid many of these problems with a little forethought and discipline. In this chapter, I show you some of the tricks of the trade to help you write programs correctly. I also show you some specific techniques to help you test and debug scripts written using PHP and WMLScript.

Doing It Right

Before I show you what you can do when things go wrong, let's spend some time talking about how you can make sure that things go right. Programming is a human endeavor, fraught with opportunity for mistakes.

Your programs fail when you make mistakes. Defects—or bugs, as many people call them—don't creep in; they're there because you made a decision to do something a particular way, and that way was wrong. Admitting that your work contains errors is the first step toward making fewer mistakes.

"Why worry?" you may ask. After all, everyone makes mistakes, and that's how people learn. But the cost of fixing a mistake in software grows quickly as long as the defect remains undetected. A mistake that takes you a minute to avoid today may take you an hour to find tomorrow, and a full day next week, and it can cause untold problems once your application is in the hands of customers.

Aside from cost, there's a second reason to be careful and do it right the first time: professional pride. You don't have to look hard to find stories of software problems leading to personal or business problems. It's only a matter of time before the public realizes that software failures are our failures, and when this happens, our jobs become much harder.

You can form a number of good work habits that help you avoid making mistakes. Many of these are so obvious you may wonder why they're overlooked; others are more subtle. The underlying principles behind all good work habits are *simplicity* and *consistency*. A simple program is easier to understand and debug. It's easier to write, too, because you have to think about fewer things as you write your program. By doing things consistently you build good working habits and eliminate opportunities for error.

One of the best habits you can form is to keep a notebook. In this notebook you should record not just what you do and how you're doing it, but what you learn, and most importantly, what kind of mistakes you make. By periodically reviewing your notebook, you see where you make mistakes and how you can avoid those mistakes in the future. It doesn't matter if the notebook is paper or electronic: what's important is that you record what works for you and what doesn't, and that you improve as you work.

The Right Way to Write Code

As you write a program, you're faced with choices concerning how the program should work. You make fundamental decisions throughout the inception and elaboration phases, while during construction you actually put together the logic behind the program. The actual process of writing a program, however, has its own set of decisions you need to make. You need to address questions such as how to organize your program, how to format lines of code, and how to report errors. Regardless of the application you write, you can answer many of these questions by following the same basic principles, thus minimizing the mistakes you might make.

For example, consider how you format your code. Obviously, the code should be organized so that you and others can read it. There are a number of conventions that most people accept as part of well-formatted code, including:

- **Ample white space.** Use white space generously between operations and statements. White space gives the reader space to consider the meaning of a statement, and gives you the opportunity to highlight parts of your code.

- **Consistent naming.** Clearly and consistently name your variables and functions. Readers should be able to tell the purpose of a variable or function just by looking at the name, rather than reading the code.

- **Ample line breaks.** Use blank lines between statements to indicate a change in purpose or logic. There's seldom a good reason to have more than one statement on a line.

- **Consistent indenting.** Indent structural blocks of your program to help readers keep their place.

- **Short functions.** Keep functions short. Any function longer than a page is too long.

- **Clear comments.** Use comments to describe the purpose of parts of your code, as well as what the code actually does. Write and change comments first and code second. This way, you don't forget to change a comment when you change code.

Good comments in your code improve legibility. Well-commented code tells the reader what you intend to do in your program, and how the code itself does what you intend, rather than just reiterating the meaning of a statement or function. In addition, you use large blocks of comments to call attention to key parts of your scripts such as function declarations. As I discussed in the Introduction, I believe that comments play such an important role that they deserve to start at the first column of code so your eye is drawn to comments before code.

I find it helpful to have a style file for each project that contains template comments for things such as function banners and function declarations. For example, as I wrote MobileHelper, I created each of the functions by copying a template out of my style file, and then customizing it for the function I was writing. At the bottom of the style file are notes to myself with details such as the number of spaces to indent blocks, where to use white space, and so on. If you use a powerful text editor like emacs, you can automate many of these details with keyboard macros, too.

When writing your code, you should be sure to test any assumptions you make, and call out areas where they may fail. When you define a function, the function should test its arguments to be sure that they're correct and report an error if they aren't. Similarly, you should check the results from functions—both your own and those provided by the libraries you use—and see if an error occurred.

As you do this, you need to come up with a strategy for handling errors. How you handle errors will differ from application to application. It might be okay for a prototype to fail with a cryptic error message, but an application you're preparing for production should behave significantly better. You need to decide how your application transitions from normal operation to error reporting and back to normal operation again. In most Web applications you can report an error to the user and urge her to try back later, logging the event for a system administrator to investigate. Of course, reported problems should be rare, or your users won't bother coming back to your site.

In some cases, you can use other techniques to avoid revealing potential errors to your users. Retrying a connection before failure, for example, or maintaining running backup servers can help mitigate the risk from software failures.

You should review your code before testing it, preferably with a colleague or partner. Code reviews can be informal; simply skimming a program listing often points out possible errors. To get the most out of a code review, though, you should ask yourself questions as you read the code, including:

- Is the code legible? Do you immediately understand what it does and what side effects it might have?

- How can the code fail? What will the program do if it does?

- What data does this statement manipulate? What are the results?

- As you read the code, follow the logic as if you were the computer, and see what happens. Does the code do what you expect?

- Does this statement use data stored by another program (or part of the program)? Are there side effects from this relationship?

Reading your own code helps you find mistakes, just as reading something you've written helps you pick out spelling and grammatical errors. Having the opportunity to read someone else's code is even better because you can learn from them.

Once you write and read your code, it's time to test it. Testing is a three-step process. First, you eliminate any obvious mistakes in your code that keep the computer from understanding it. This is often called *building* because in applications using compiled languages the computer builds the application from the source code you write. Next, you actually run the code to see how it behaves using *unit tests* that enable you to test your code in isolation to make sure it behaves the way you expect. Then, you integrate the new code with your existing work and perform *integration tests* that enable you to verify how the new system—the union of your existing code and the new code—performs.

The Right Way to Test Code

As you build your code, you should stop frequently and test what you write. As you do, you will find both problems in the syntax of your code, which the PHP interpreter will immediately call to your attention, and problems in the implementation as you run your code.

When trying to run code you've just written, you will see the occasional error message from the interpreter. For example, in working on a PHP script for this book, I got the error message shown in Figure 7-1 the first time I tried to load the page with a Web browser.

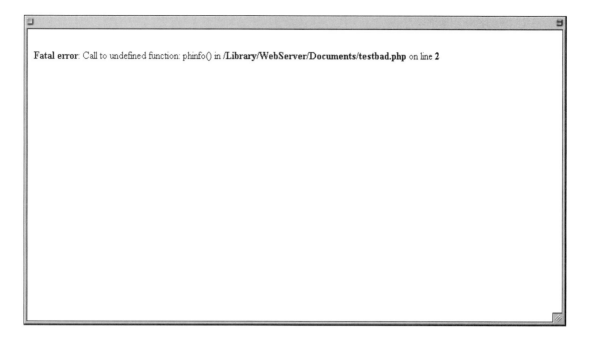

Fatal error: Call to undefined function: phinfo() in **/Library/WebServer/Documents/testbad.php** on line **2**

Figure 7-1. A PHP error message

The meaning of this error message is obvious: I misspelled the name of the function phpinfo. Sometimes, however, you might not understand an error message, or the message is a warning and your code still runs.

Do not ignore these error messages! Just because your script executes doesn't mean that there's no problem. Warnings like these often point to things that break in the future, such as a change to a function call parameter or the possibility of a run-time error.

> **CAUTION** *If you ignore build-time messages, it's an invitation for disaster.*

You unit test your functions separately, ensuring that they work before putting them together. Unit testing often requires a *scaffold*, code that calls your function and reports the results. A software scaffold is similar to a real scaffold: material erected for support around something you're building. Most scaffolds are crude, often a simple set of logging functions that you include in a stand-alone script that calls your function with some values and checks the results. As you test your function through your scaffold, you can see how your function operates.

Unit testing should test a function's boundaries. Write unit tests that call your function under a host of conditions, both expected and abnormal. For example, if you're writing a function that finds a record in a database, you should include a unit test that results in no records being found.

Once you're sure your function works, you can test it within your application. This testing is called *integration testing* because you're integrating new functionality within your application. When you test your integrated application, you exercise your application, and your scaffold becomes largely secondary. As long as your application works correctly, you won't rely on your scaffold. When things fail, however, you still use your scaffold to quickly pinpoint the problem.

To find a problem in your code you use the scientific method, following these steps:

1. Gather information about the problem.

2. Form a hypothesis that accounts for the information.

3. Design an experiment to prove the hypothesis.

4. Use the experiment to prove or disprove the hypothesis.

5. Repeat as needed.

In the first step, you look at all the information about the failure. The value of variables, the flow of execution through each statement, the code itself, and the status of the server and network can all provide clues as to the cause of the failure. When you can, focus on making the problem reproducible so that you can collect all the information that might be available.

With the information at hand, you can often make an educated guess as to what has happened. Your hypothesis may point to your code or external factors, although you should take care: odds are quite high that the problem is in your code, no matter how skilled you are. It's far less common to find problems with someone else's application or network than it is to find mistakes in your own work. Moreover, it's often easier to verify your own work first, so even if you suspect an external cause, be sure your work is in good standing before you search elsewhere.

Once you have your hypothesis, you devise an experiment to test your hypothesis. Often the easiest experiment is changing the code. Usually this change is a prospective fix, although sometimes it's just a change that you make to help collect more information. Other times, you may find it easier to change another aspect of your application's environment, such as consolidating the Web server and database server on a machine, or switching from using a wireless client to a WAP SDK. This is often helpful when the problem is complex or hard to reproduce because you can eliminate variables that could contribute to the problem.

Performing your experiment enables you to prove or disprove your hypothesis. Disproving your hypothesis is as good as proving it: it provides more data as you continue to collect more information about the problem.

Debugging can be a tedious process, but by sticking to an established methodology, you avoid getting stuck and being unable to make progress finding a fix. Without a clear methodology, you might be tempted to just make a change to see if it fixes the problem, or fixate on a particular theory. You can waste far more time than by simply rolling up your sleeves, digging in, and performing a little detective work.

First Steps Debugging

The basic principles of debugging—collect information, form a hypothesis, test the hypothesis—are the same regardless of the language and platform you use. Let's begin by looking at a mistake in the DBGetOpenTasks function, defined in db.php, and build a test framework that lets you collect additional information about the mistake.

Finding the Bug

Listing 7-1 shows an early version of DBGetOpenTasks in db.php. This version of DBGetOpenTasks has a minor bug.

```
01: <?php
02: // exerpt from db.php
03:
04: /*****************************************************
05:  * FUNCTION: DBGetOpenTasks( )
06:  *
07:  * DESCRIPTION: Returns an array of open assignments.
08:  *
09:  * RETURNED: array of event hashes or 0
10:  *****************************************************/
11: function DBGetOpenTasks()
12: {
13:
14:   LogMsg( "db.php: in DBGetOpenTasks", SCAFFOLD_LOG_DEBUG );
15:
16: // Do the query, return the record or null
17:
```

```
18:    $dbqr = mysql_query(
19:      "SELECT * FROM event " .
20:      "WHERE state=" . DBTASKOPEN . " " .
21:      "ORDER BY start ASC"
22:    );
23:
24: // Validate
25:
26:    if ( !$dbqr )
          LogMsg( "db.php: mysql_query failed!", SCAFFOLD_LOG_ERR );
27:
28:    if ( !$dbqr )
29:      return 0;
30:
31: // We've got something... create a result array and return
32:
33:    LogMsg( "db.php: " . mysql_num_rows( $dbqr ) .
          " rows.", SCAFFOLD_LOG_DEBUG );
34:
35:    $result = array();
36:
37:    while( $row = mysql_fetch_array( $dbqr ) );
38:    {
39:      array_push( $result, $row );
40:    }
41:
42:    return $result;
43: }
44: ?>
```

Listing 7-1. A broken DBGetOpenTasks

The flow of DBGetOpenTasks is straightforward: issue a database query, and iterate over the resulting rows to create an array of table rows. LogMsg, which the script calls on lines 14, 26, and 33, is a function in my scaffold I use to record debugging messages as the function runs.

To find the bug in Listing 7-1, I use one of the unit tests I wrote when I first wrote DBGetOpenTasks. Written in PHP, the test is crude, requiring you to use both the test script with a browser and run a separate MySQL monitor to execute a query. You can compare the results from the test script with the query you execute to determine whether DBGetOpenTasks operates correctly. The test script itself calls DBGetOpenTasks and shows the result in HTML. By using HTML, I can interactively test my PHP scripts on a single machine using a text editor, the host's Web server with PHP, and a Web browser without running a WAP SDK. Listing 7-2 shows the test script.

```
01: <?php
02: /*********************************************************
03:  * testdb_dbgetopentasks.php
04:  *
05:  * Tests DBGetOpenTasks in db.php by calling & showing
06:  * results using a foreach(). Tester should compare
07:  * resulting HTML page with a MySQL monitor statment
08:  *
09:  *    SELECT * FROM event WHERE state=0
10:  *
11:  *********************************************************/
12:
13: include "log.php";
14: include "db.php";
15:
16: LogSetLevel( LOGLEVEL_ALL );
17: LogSetWhere( SCAFFOLD_LOG_FILE );
18:
19: // Describe what we're doing and what we expect.
20:
21: echo( "<h1>DBGetOpenTasks Test</h1>\n" );
22: echo( "<p>Compare this page with the result of a<br>\n" );
23: echo( "<tt>" );
24: echo( "SELECT id,name FROM event WHERE state=0" );
25: echo( "</tt><br>\n" );
26: echo( "at a MySQL monitor near you. The table  " );
27: echo( "generated by that request and the table on " );
28: echo( "this page should match.</p>" );
29:
30: // Test the function
31:
32: $taskList = DBGetOpenTasks();
33:
34: // Say what we got
35:
36: if ( $taskList && $taskList[ 0 ] )
37: {
38:   echo( "<p>Query returned " );
39:   echo( count( $taskList ) );
40:   echo( " rows.</p>\n" );
41: }
```

```
42: else
43: {
44:   echo( "<p>Query returned 0 rows.</p>\n" );
45: }
46:
47: // Produce a result table
48:
49: echo( "<table>\n" );
50:
51: for ( $i = 0; $i < count( $taskList); $i++ )
52: {
53:   $item = $taskList[ $i ];
54:
55:   echo( "  <tr>\n" );
56:   echo( "    <td>" );
57:   echo( $item[ "id" ] );
58:   echo( "</td><td>" );
59:   echo( $item[ "name" ] );
60:   echo( "</td>\n" );
61:
62:   echo( "  </tr>\n" );
63: }
64:
65: echo( "</table>\n" );
66: ?>
```

Listing 7-2. The unit test harness for DBGetOpenTasks

After including the scaffold on line 13, I include the db.php file that defines functions such as DBGetOpenTasks. Lines 16 and 17 initialize the logging scaffold to report all log messages to an external file; each time I access the script, any calls to LogMsg appends messages to the log file.

The remainder of the file generates the HTML that describes the test. On lines 21–28, the script outputs HTML that describes what the test does and what output you should expect. After describing the expected output, I call DBGetOpenTasks and store the results in $taskList on line 32. The script shows the number of rows in $taskList on lines 36–45, and builds a table with the results from DBGetOpenTasks on lines 49–63.

This version of DBGetOpenTasks is supposed to return an array of tasks that are marked as open in the database. As you can see by comparing Listing 7-3 with Figure 7-2, something's wrong. The SELECT FROM query in Listing 7-3 returns three open tasks, yet the test case result in Figure 7-2 says that DBGetOpenTasks returns an empty array.

```
01: [localhost:~] dove% mysql -u dove -p
02: Enter password:
03: Welcome to the MySQL monitor.  Commands end with ; or \g.
04: Your MySQL connection id is 7 to server version: 3.23.28-gamma
05:
06: Type 'help;' or '\h' for help. Type '\c' to clear the buffer
07:
08: mysql> USE users;
09: Database changed
10:
11: mysql> SELECT id,name FROM event WHERE state=0;
12: +----+-------------+
13: | id | name        |
14: +----+-------------+
15: |  1 | First Night |
16: |  2 | Communications |
17: |  3 | Communications |
18: +----+-------------+
19: 3 rows in set (0.01 sec)
20:
21: mysql> Bye
```

Listing 7-3. The SELECT FROM *query results*

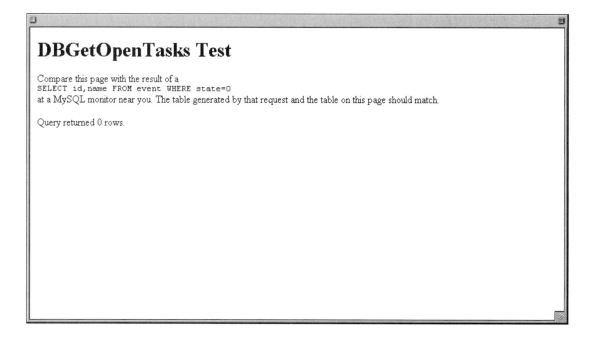

Figure 7-2. Test case result

It's time to put all these facts together and come up with a theory as to why DBGetOpenTasks isn't working correctly. This might be for one of two reasons: either it couldn't access the database (lines 28–29 of Listing 7-1), or the resulting table from the database query itself is empty (lines 35–43 of Listing 7-1).

A look at the scaffold log in Listing 7-4 tells you that there were no problems accessing the database. (If there were, you'd see a message reading **db.php: mysql_query failed** in the log.) Perhaps I'm creating the result array incorrectly? Let's look at lines 35–42 of Listing 7-1 more closely.

```
01: 980034552.84187 [20/Jan/2001:15:49:12] db.php: in
    DBGetOpenTasks
02: 980034552.84665 [20/Jan/2001:15:49:12] db.php: 3 rows.
```

Listing 7-4. Excerpt from the scaffold log

Aha! On line 37, the while statement ends with a semicolon. That's not right—the while statement alone executes for every row in the result table, until mysql_fetch_array returns zero. Once it does, execution continues on line 38, and the script pushes the zero in $row on to the end of the array $result on line 39. I need to remove the semicolon, so the block on lines 38–40 gets executed each pass through the while loop. Removing the semicolon does, in fact, fix the problem, as you see in Figure 7-3.

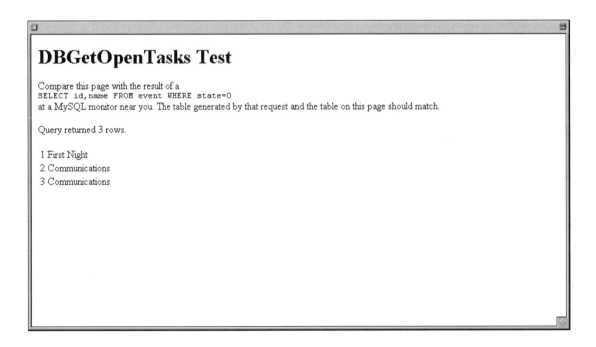

Figure 7-3. Test case result after the fix

Using PHP Test and Debugging Aids

One of the handiest ways to test PHP scripts is to run them standalone, outside the Web server. You need a version of PHP built to support the Common Gateway Interface (see the sidebar). This version of PHP is an application named **php.exe** under Microsoft Windows, or **php** under UNIX.

PHP CGI Support

The Common Gateway Interface is a standard interface between a Web server and other programs that enables them to share data. PHP supports CGI through an application called **php.** This application may or may not be on your system, depending on whether you built PHP from scratch. Some binary releases—notably the Windows version—include a CGI binary by default, while others do not.

If you don't have the **php** application, you can build one. If you don't have the sources, get them from www.php.net or from the CD-ROM. Unpack the source archive using **rpm** or **tar**, and follow the instructions to build the CGI version. Don't forget to give PHP's **configure** script a list of the options you want, such as –with-my-sql to include MySQL support.

You use **php** from the command line as you do any other application. Simply type **php** followed by the name of the file it should execute, and the computer displays the results. Listing 7-5 shows **php** running the DBGetOpenTasks test script from Listing 7-2.

```
01: [localhost:~] dove% php testdb_dbgetopentasks.php
02: X-Powered-By: PHP/4.0.1pl2
03: Content-type: text/html
04:
05:
06:
07:
08:
09: <h1>DBGetOpenTasks Test</h1>
10: <p>Compare this page with the result of a<br>
11: <tt>SELECT id,name FROM event WHERE state=0</tt><br>
12: at a MySQL monitor near you. The table  generated
13: by that request and the table on this page should
14: match.</p>
15:
```

```
16: <p>Query returned 3 rows.</p>
17:
18: <table>
19:   <tr>
20:     <td>1</td><td>First Night</td>
21:   </tr>
22:   <tr>
23:     <td>2</td><td>Communications</td>
24:   </tr>
25:   <tr>
26:     <td>3</td><td>Communications</td>
27:   </tr>
28: </table>
29:
30: [localhost:~] dove%
```

*Listing 7-5. Running **php** from the command line*

As you can see from Listing 7-5, **php** returns exactly the content that the Web server would send to the client. The top four lines show the HTTP headers generated by PHP, while the remainder of the body is the content generated by the script itself. The **php** application is suited to when you first write a file because you can quickly run **php** from a command line and return to your text editor to fix any syntax errors you made. Some editors, such as emacs, enable you to have a command line open within the editor, letting you work entirely within emacs as you write and debug your PHP scripts. Eventually, however, you'll want to start using your PHP scripts with the Web server and clients, rather than reading through reams of WML or HTML.

Another feature PHP offers is *syntax coloring*, which enables you to see different parts of your PHP script in different colors. Syntax coloring helps you distinguish between comments, statements, and variables. This comes in handy when you have a lot of scripts to read, such as during a review with your peers. By including the MIME type application/x-httpd-php-source and matching it to a file suffix such as .phps, you can use your Web browser to see your script with different keywords in different colors, as Figure 7-4 shows. (Of course, Figure 7-4 shows the colors as various shades of gray.)

> **CAUTION** *Don't map the MIME type application/x-httpd-php-source to the same extension that you want to use for PHP scripts. If you do so, your Web server will either fail to syntax color your source code when you load a script or won't execute a script because one MIME type for the script suffix will overwrite the other.*

> **NOTE** *Syntax coloring isn't fully supported under Microsoft Windows. You can use either a PHP script that uses the function* show_source() *with the name of the script you'd like to see in color, or you can use the* **php.exe** *command with the* −s *option.*

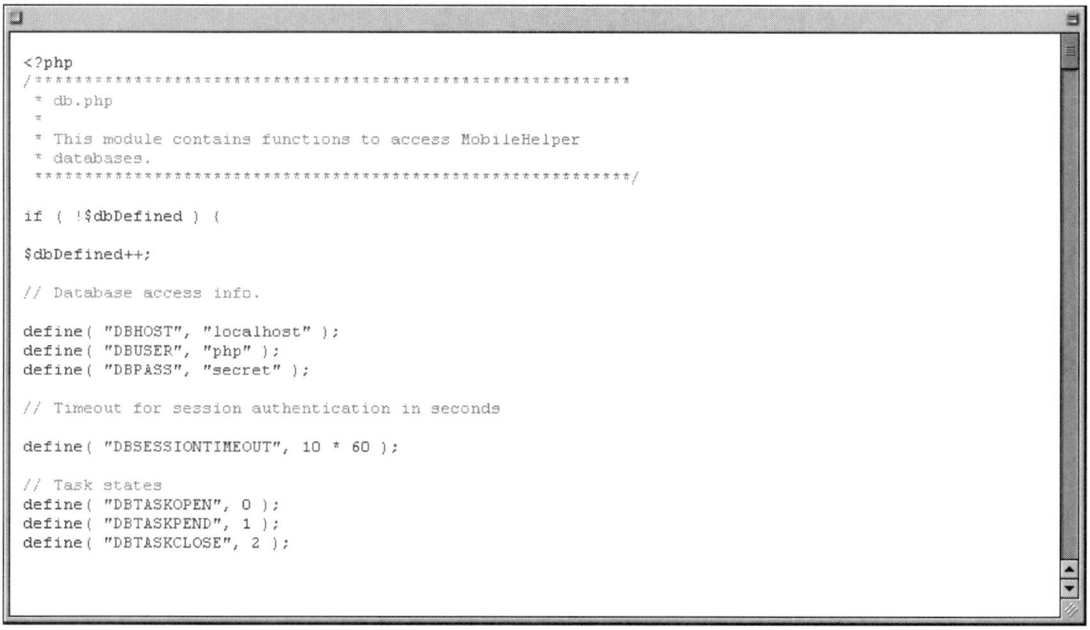

```php
<?php
/*****************************************************************
 * db.php
 *
 * This module contains functions to access MobileHelper
 * databases.
 *****************************************************************/

if ( !$dbDefined ) {

$dbDefined++;

// Database access info.

define( "DBHOST", "localhost" );
define( "DBUSER", "php" );
define( "DBPASS", "secret" );

// Timeout for session authentication in seconds

define( "DBSESSIONTIMEOUT", 10 * 60 );

// Task states
define( "DBTASKOPEN", 0 );
define( "DBTASKPEND", 1 );
define( "DBTASKCLOSE", 2 );
```

Figure 7-4. PHP syntax coloring

Early versions of PHP—PHP3, to be exact—supported a simple debugger that logged error and status messages to a server listening on a TCP socket. Messages from the debugger include not just errors and warnings, but the file and line on which they occur. Sadly, this functionality is missing from the version of PHP available as this went to press, but you should check the PHP documentation at www.php.net to see if it or a similar feature is now available. The messages from the PHP debugger are a valuable addition to a good scaffold.

Using WMLScript Test and Debugging Aids

The level of test and debugging aids varies widely between different WAP SDKs. Some SDKs, such as the Phone.com UP.SDK, provides little more than a phone emulator with WML support. Other SDKs, such as the Yospace SPEDE, have a number of unique features that make debugging WMLScript easier.

When debugging WMLScript, the most common strategy is to embed calls to `Dialogs.alert` in your code. The `Dialogs.alert` function stops the execution of a script and displays the string you give it until you press a key. You can use the `Dialogs.alert` function to display a WMLScript variable or the equivalent of a "You are here" message in your code. The code snippet in Listing 7-6 does this when the WML variable debug is set to the string "true".

```
01: // Inside a WMLScript function...
02:
03:   var debug=WMLBrowser.getvar("debug") == "true";
04:
05:   var x;
06:
07: // Your code here does things with x.
08:
09: // When you want to check the value of x:
10:
11:   if ( debug ) Dialogs.alert( "x=" + x );
12:
13: // Your code continues here...
```

Listing 7-6. Checking a WMLScript variable using `Dialogs.alert`

On line 3, the WMLScript variable var is set to true if the WML variable is set to the string "true", enabling you to turn on and off debugging messages from within your WML deck. After line 3, when you want to see something—say, the value of x–you can do so by testing debug and calling `Dialogs.alert`, as on line 11. When your scripts go into production, you can either make sure that you never set the variable var in any of your decks, or go back and remove the lines testing debug and calling `Dialogs.alert`.

Similarly, you can store values in a WMLScript variable and return them to a WML variable as your script exits. In your WML, you can provide a navigation element like a soft key assignment to a card that lets you view the WML variable. Once you finish testing, you can remove the navigation element, hiding the debug data, or remove both the WMLScript and the navigation element and card. This is a better method if you don't want to deal with alerts within your script, such as during a loop's execution.

The Nokia WAP Toolkit includes a variable viewer that enables you to see and edit the value of all WML variables (see Figure 7-5). By clicking a value in the window, you can change it without altering the WML deck, which gives you the capability to adjust variables while testing a deck. It also has a message viewer (see Figure 7-6) that enables you to read the SDK's internal debugging messages. Neither the variable or message views is terribly useful when debugging WML-Script, however, except right at the layer between WML and WMLScript where the client exchanges values between the two contexts.

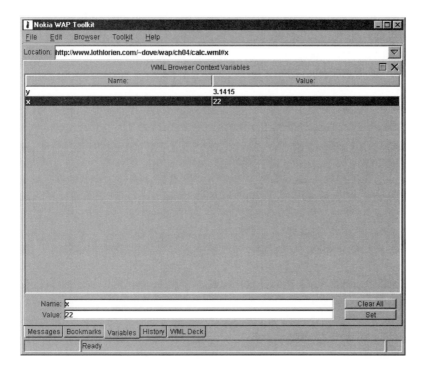

Figure 7-5. Nokia WAP Toolkit variable viewer

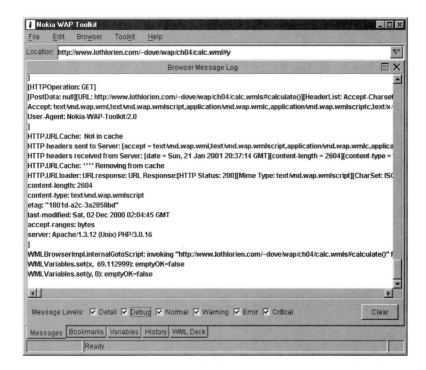

Figure 7-6. Nokia WAP Toolkit message viewer

In contrast, the latest versions of the Yospace SPEDE are downright luxurious in the features they offer to help you debug. Using WMLScript and the Yospace SPEDE libraries, you can interactively edit and run WMLScript code and control the browser's behavior through Yospace's SPEScript. Figure 7-7 shows the SPEScript tool in action.

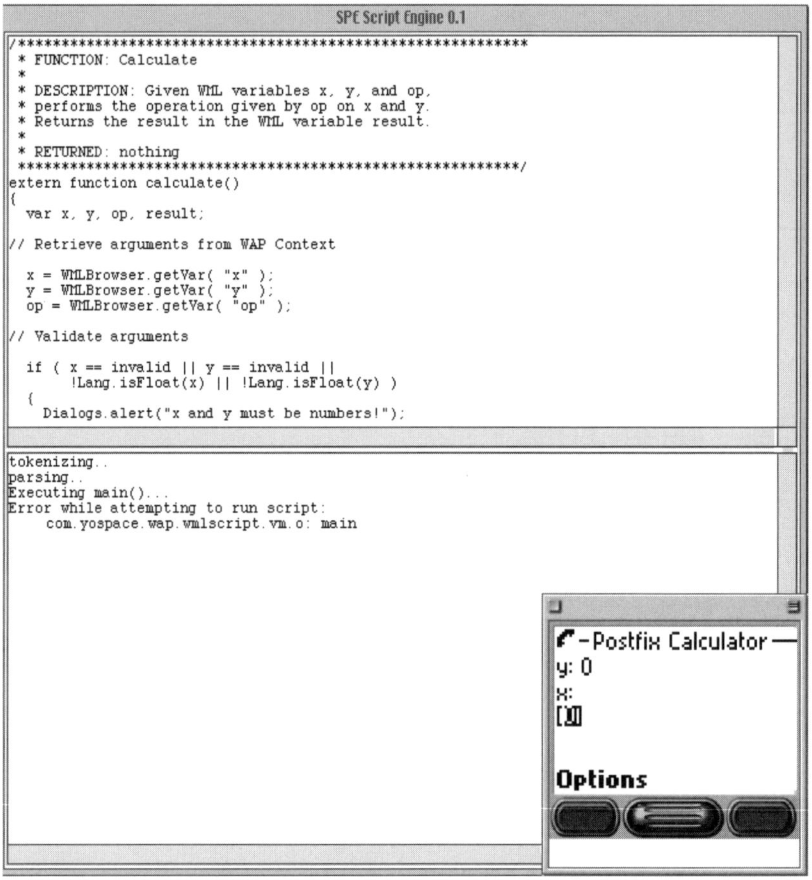

Figure 7-7. Yospace SPEDE SPEScript environment

One of the best ways to use SPEScript is to quickly check the syntax of your WMLScript. You can write your scripts using SPEScript, and use it to check your script's syntax as you go. When you do so, the SPEScript environment compiles and executes your script, reporting any errors that it encounters.

SPEScript points out syntax errors, but if you include an `extern main` function in your WML, it actually executes the `main` function as well. Your `main` function can call the other functions in your WMLScript, enabling you to write test cases for each WMLScript function directly within the SPEScript environment.

In addition, your `main` function can use the WMLScript libraries provided by the SPEScript. These libraries enable you to load and save data to and from files on your development system, navigate the browser to different pages, and capture the contents of the browser's screen to a bitmap (useful when you want to compare the contents of different screens). Together, you can use WMLScript to automate testing of both WML and WMLScript content, making it easier to test large wireless applications.

> **NOTE** *At this writing, the SPEScript environment is in its infancy. You should check the Yospace Web site at* `http://www.yospace.com` *for the latest information about SPEScript.*

Debugging MobileHelper

By far the most useful tool when testing and debugging PHP scripts is a good scaffold that enables you to see what your code is doing. In the section "The Bug," you saw how I use my scaffold, defined in log.php.

The scaffold defines three public functions: `LogMsg`, `LogSetLevel`, and `LogSetWhere`. The `LogMsg` function logs a message at a given priority. To see messages `LogMsg` records, you must first tell the scaffold where the messages should go and what priority messages it should display. `LogSetLevel` selects to what priority messages the scaffold displays, while `LogSetWhere` tells the scaffold where it should send messages. Listing 7-7 shows the code for the PHP scaffold.

```
01: <?php
02: /****************************************************
03:  * log.php
04:  *
05:  * This module contains log functions used when unit
06:  * testing and debugging.
07:  ****************************************************/
08:
09: // Some standard log levels
10: define( "SCAFFOLD_LOG_EMERG", 0 );
11: define( "SCAFFOLD_LOG_ALERT", 1 );
12: define( "SCAFFOLD_LOG_CRIT", 2 );
13: define( "SCAFFOLD_LOG_ERR", 3 );
14: define( "SCAFFOLD_LOG_WARNING", 4 );
15: define( "SCAFFOLD_LOG_NOTICE", 5 );
16: define( "SCAFFOLD_LOG_INFO", 6 );
```

```
17: define( "SCAFFOLD_LOG_DEBUG", 7 );
18: define( "LOGLEVEL_ALL", SCAFFOLD_LOG_DEBUG );
19:
20: // Default is no logging.
21:
22: $logLevel = SCAFFOLD_LOG_EMERG-1;
23:
24: // Where do we log?
25:
26: define( "SCAFFOLD_LOG_NONE", 0 );
27: define( "SCAFFOLD_LOG_CLIENT", 0x01 );
28: define( "SCAFFOLD_LOG_FILE", 0x02 );
29: define( "SCAFFOLD_LOG_ALL",
30:   SCAFFOLD_LOG_CLIENT | SCAFFOLD_LOG_FILE );
31: $logWhere = SCAFFOLD_LOG_NONE;
32:
33: // Log file location
34: // On Windows, change to something like
35: // define( "SCAFFOLD_LOG_FILE", "C:\\TMP\\MYPHPLOG.txt" );
36:
37: define( "SCAFFOLD_LOG_FILENAME", "/tmp/myphplog" );
38:
39: /*****************************************************
40:  * FUNCTION: LogSetLevel
41:  *
42:  * DESCRIPTION: Sets the log level. Messages with a level
43:  * greater than the level set are logged.
44:  *
45:  * RETURNED: previous log level
46:  *****************************************************/
47: function LogSetLevel(
48:   $level  // (in) new log level
49: )
50: {
51:   global $logLevel;
52:
53:   $result = $logLevel;
54:
55:   $logLevel = $level;
56:
57:   return $result;
58: }
59:
```

```
60: /*****************************************************
61:  * FUNCTION: LogSetWhere
62:  *
63:  * DESCRIPTION: Sets where to send log messages
64:  *
65:  * RETURNED: previous destinations
66:  *****************************************************/
67: function LogSetWhere(
68:   $where  // (in) flags indicating where to log
69: )
70: {
71:   global $logWhere;
72:
73:   $result = $logWhere;
74:
75:   $logWhere = $where;
76:
77:   return $result;
78: }
79:
80: /*****************************************************
81:  * FUNCTION: LogMsg
82:  *
83:  * DESCRIPTION: Logs the message if its level is less
84:  * than or equal to the log level.
85:  *
86:  * RETURNED: nonzero if log message recorded.
87:  *****************************************************/
88: function LogMsg(
89:   $msg,  // (in) message to log
90:   $level // (in) msg log level
91: )
92: {
93:   global $logLevel;
94:   global $logWhere;
95:
96:   $result = 0;
97:
98: // Log if logging is on and the level of the message is
99: // below (higher priority) or equal to our message
100:
101:   if ( $level <=  $logLevel )
102:   {
103:
```

```
104:     $logMsg = _LogFormatMsg( $msg );
105:
106: // Log results to file if appropriate
107:
108:     if ( ( $logWhere & SCAFFOLD_LOG_FILE ) > 0 )
109:     {
110:       $result |= _LogToFile( $logMsg );
111:     }
112:
113: // Log results to client if appropriate
114:     if ( ( $logWhere & SCAFFOLD_LOG_CLIENT ) > 0 )
115:     {
116:       $result |= _LogToClient( $logMsg );
117:     }
118:   }
119:
120:   return $result;
121: }
122:
123: /*******************************************************
124:  * FUNCTION: _LogFormatMsg
125:  *
126:  * DESCRIPTION: Formats a message for the log
127:  *
128:  * RETURNED: Formatted message
129:  *******************************************************/
130: function _LogFormatMsg(
131:   $msg   // (in) message to log
132: )
133: {
134:
135: // Create the timestamp including microseconds
136:
137:   $now = microtime();
138:   sscanf( "$now", "%f %d", &$msec, &$sec );
139:   $now = $sec + $msec;
140:
141: // Create the log message
142:
143:   return "$now " .
144:   date( "[d/M/Y:H:i:s] " ) .
145:   "$msg\n";
146:
147: }
148:
```

```
149: /********************************************************
150: * FUNCTION: _LogToFile
151: *
152: * DESCRIPTION: Logs message to file
153: *
154: * RETURNED: nonzero on success
155: ********************************************************/
156: function _LogToFile(
157:    $msg   // (in) message to log
158: )
159: {
160:    $result = 0;
161:
162: // Open the log file
163:
164:    $fp = fopen( SCAFFOLD_LOG_FILENAME, "a" );
165:    if ( $fp )
166:    {
167:
168: // Lock the log file so no one else writes
169:
170:       if ( flock( $fp, LOCK_EX ) )
171:       {
172:
173: // Write the log message
174:
175:          fputs( $fp, $msg );
176:
177: // Unlock the log file
178:          flock( $fp, LOCK_UN );
179:       }
180:
181: // Close the log file
182:
183:       fclose( $fp );
184:       $result |= SCAFFOLD_LOG_FILE;
185:    }
186:
187:    return $result;
188: }
189:
```

```
190: /*********************************************************
191:  * FUNCTION: _LogToClient
192:  *
193:  * DESCRIPTION: Logs message to client
194:  *
195:  * RETURNED: nonzero on success
196:  *********************************************************/
197: function _LogToClient(
198:    $msg  // (in) message to log
199: )
200: {
201:
202:    echo( "$msg<br/>\n" );
203:
204:    return SCAFFOLD_LOG_CLIENT;
205: }
206: ?>
```

Listing 7-7. The log.php file

Lines 9–22 of Listing 7-7 define the message priorities. LogMsg logs all messages above the priority threshold that you set with LogSetLevel, letting you choose just how verbose your log will be. As you start testing, you want a low threshold, so you can see in detail what your script does. As you continue to test and fix any defects, you gradually increase the threshold, until in a production environment, you will only log urgent messages with a high priority.

Lines 24–31 use a flag to determine where log messages should go. A *flag* is a value that can be on or off, similar to a Boolean value. Unlike Booleans, however, flags usually control functionality, and there can be more than one flag, making flags similar to the MySQL SET type discussed in Chapter 5. While PHP doesn't have any built-in support for flags, you can use the bits in an integer to reflect the value of specific flags, as I do on lines 27–28, by defining each flag value as a unique power of two. You can then use the binary operands |, &, and ~ to set and clear flag values, and the binary operand & to test flag values. I define two unique flags, SCAFFOLD_LOG_FILE and SCAFFOLD_LOG_CLIENT, which the script stores in the $logWhere variable. If you assert the SCAFFOLD_LOG_FILE flag in $logWhere using LogSetWhere, LogMsg logs to a log file; similarly, if you assert SCAFFOLD_LOG_CLIENT, log messages are displayed on the client. By using a flags and the binary OR operator |, you can assert both by writing SCAFFOLD_LOG_FILE | SCAFFOLD_LOG_CLIENT. Similarly, you can test if a flag is set by using the binary AND operator &, ANDing $logWhere with the flag of interest.

Line 37 sets the location of the log file used by log.php. The log file name is arbitrary, although of course it must meet the requirements of the operating system. On UNIX, you need to choose a path and file the Apache Web server can write to, such as /tmp. Under Microsoft Windows, the path string should include your drive specification as well as the directory. (Remember to escape the solidus \ symbols in a Windows path or define the path in single quotes.)

The LogSetLevel function on lines 39–58 is a mutator that lets you set the priority threshold. Obviously, you don't want scripts changing $logLevel directly because, in the future, if you change log.php, scripts relying on the existence of $logLevel may break. Instead, to set the priority threshold, scripts call LogLevel, which sets $logLevel to the desired value and returns the previous priority threshold. By returning the current threshold, you can use multiple calls of LogSetLevel around problematic code to lower the threshold for increased detail and raise it again when you're through, giving greater detail in the parts of your application that need it. Simply save the value LogSetLevel returns before the troubled code, and call LogSetLevel again with the saved value after the code.

The LogSetWhere function on lines 60–78 is a mutator function that is responsible for setting the $logWhere variable. Using a mutator is especially important with flags because it enables you to change how db.php stores flags without impacting the scripts that use its functions.

The LogMsg function on lines 80–121 logs messages above the priority threshold. At line 101, I check the incoming log level to see if it's a higher priority than $logLevel. Line 101 must use a less than or equal comparison because higher priorities are denoted with *lower* numbers. (Look back at their definition on lines 9–22.)

Line 104 creates the log message using the private function _LogFormatMsg. This function, defined later in db.php, uses the message you give to LogMsg and the current time to create a log message with a timestamp so you can investigate how long parts of your script take to execute.

Lines 108–117 write the resulting message to the log file and the client, depending on the flags set in $logWhere using the private _LogToFile and _LogToClient functions. The script uses the binary AND operator (&) to test the value of each flag bit in $logWhere. The parentheses in the if statements on lines 108 and 114 are necessary because the & operator's precedence is lower than >. If I hadn't included the parentheses in each statement, PHP would have compared SCAFFOLD_LOG_FILE (or SCAFFOLD_LOG_CLIENT, on line 114) with 0, obtained 1, and then binary-ANDed that value with the value of $logWhere.

> **NOTE** *The order and precedence of operations—especially when using the binary arithmetic operators |, &, and ~—can trip you up, causing subtle and hard-to-find bugs in your code. If you're hazy about the precedence of operators, review the section "Operations" in Chapter 3, especially Table 3-2.*

The log.php function defines three private functions, which other scripts should not call. As I do elsewhere in the book, I denote private functions with a leading underscore (_) because PHP doesn't provide a mechanism to hide private functions.

The _LogFormatMsg function defined on lines 123–137 formats its argument with a preceding timestamp. The function presents the timestamp in two formats: fractional seconds after the epoch and a human-readable time and date with hours, minutes, and seconds. The PHP function microtime on line 137 returns a string containing two integers, one containing the number of seconds since the epoch, and the other a fraction indicating the number of microseconds since the last second. On line 138, the sscanf function breaks the string microtime returned into two pieces, storing one piece in $msec and the other in $sec. You can use sscanf for simple parsing like this, although for more sophisticated applications strtok (see "Task Management" in Chapter 5) is easier.

The _LogToFile function on lines 149–188 writes the log message to the log file using PHP's file functions. Writing to the log file is a little tricky because you need to lock the log file to be sure no more than one script attempts to update the log file at once. Multiple accesses to the file can happen when more than one client accesses a script, calling LogMsg at the same time.

On line 164, _LogToFile opens the log file using the fopen function. PHP's fopen is similar to the C fopen function, taking the name of the file to open as its first arguments and how to access the file—the *mode*—as the second argument. The script uses the "a" mode to append new log entries to the end of the file. Table 7-1 shows different modes that you can give to fopen to open a file to read and write data.

Table 7-1. File Modes fopen *Supports*

MODE	PURPOSE
r	Open the file for reading, starting at the beginning of the file.
r+	Open the file for reading and writing, starting at the beginning of the file.
w	Open the file for writing, starting at the beginning of the file, and truncate to zero length. Attempt to create the file if it does not exist.
w+	Open the file for reading and writing starting at the beginning of the file, and truncate to zero length. Attempt to create the file if it does not exist.
a	Open the file for writing, starting at the end of the file. Attempt to create the file if it does not exist.
a+	Open the file for reading and writing, starting at the end of the file. Attempt to create the file if it does not exist.

On line 170, the script locks the file using flock. Like a locked record in a database, other programs can't access a locked file until it's unlocked. PHP provides *advisory locking*, meaning that all parts of your code must use `flock` the same way to ensure that the file is locked and unlocked at the appropriate times. Line 170 requests an exclusive lock using `LOCK_EX`, telling the operating system that no other file may read from or write to the log file while its locked. (You can also request a shared lock, letting others read the file, using `LOCK_SH`.) PHP waits until the first script unlocks the file before continuing.

On line 175, the script writes the log message using `fputs`. The `fputs` function writes a string to the specified file; PHP defines the corresponding `fgets` function to read a line from a file if you need it.

On line 178, the script unlocks the file using `flock` with the `LOCK_UN` constant. It's imperative that you unlock the file; if you don't, other scripts won't be able to use the file after you, and they'll simply hang, waiting forever for the original script to release the lock.

> **CAUTION** *In heavily used applications, shared resources such as locked files quickly become bottlenecks because only one user can access the resource at a time. You should always be sure that your scripts keep resources (files, database records, or anything of that nature) locked for as little time as possible, or even avoid locking altogether if you can.*

Once the script unlocks the file, it closes the file on line 183 and returns a flag indicating that it's written to the log file.

The `_LogToClient` function on lines 190–205 is similar, but much simpler, using the PHP `echo` function to send the message to the client. Ending the string on line 202 with a `<br/>` tag is a sneaky trick: it gives me a line break anywhere in HTML or WML within the context of a paragraph. Of course, if you call `MsgLog` while logging to a WML client when you haven't yet defined a card and paragraph, you generate invalid WML, but you can still use your WML SDK's view source function to see the log message in the WML source itself.

Throughout my development of MobileHelper, I left calls to `MsgLog` scattered throughout my code to log errors, status, and other information. As I tested the code, I could always go back and look at my log file when errors occurred. As I neared completion in each chapter, I raised the message threshold so the log file only flagged outright errors instead of all my state information.

Sometimes you don't want to leave the calls to the scaffold code in place in a finished product. For example, I chose not to include the calls to the scaffold code in the listings in Chapters 5 and 6 or on the CD-ROM because it would distract you as you learn about PHP and wireless development. Similarly, you might find that, in some high-performance applications, including calls to the scaffold slows your scripts more than you can afford. Manually stripping scaffold calls is a dangerous proposition: you might miss one, or you might delete other code by mistake. While some languages, such as C and C++, provide a preprocessor that enables you to include code only on certain conditions, PHP doesn't have a similar feature.

Instead, if you identify all lines in your code that use your scaffold with a unique comment such as `// DEBUG` at the end of the line, you can use a tool such as grep or Perl to remove the lines calling your scaffold from your script.

On the CD-ROM

You can find all of the listings in this chapter on the CD-ROM in the folder ch07, including the scaffolds for both PHP and WMLScript. You can also find a copy of my style guide in the file style.txt in Chapter 7's directory.

You won't find a version of MobileHelper for this chapter, however. To make things easy for you to follow throughout the book, I removed the calls to the log.php scaffold before making the CD-ROM. However, you can see how the log.php functions are used from the example in this chapter, and use the script in your own work.

Food for Thought

- What types of information do you keep in your notebook? How often do you go back and review what you've learned? How helpful is this for you? How might you improve how you use it?

- The unit test harness for DBGetOpenTasks, shown in Listing 7-2, requires that you run both this PHP script and a separate query against the database using **mysql**. Can you think of a way to skip the manual step of running a separate query and checking the result by hand? What are the benefits and costs of the manual method versus a method that doesn't require any manual intervention?

- PHP provides an interface to your computer's system logger using the function `syslog`, which takes a message and a priority. How would you extend log.php to offer logging to the system logger as well as to the client and log file? What advantages would logging to the system logger bring to a production application?

CHAPTER 8
Graphics

THE CONSTRAINTS OF WIRELESS TERMINALS make graphics particularly challenging. Limited memory, slow processors, low-bandwidth networks, and, above all, small screens call for new strategies to make Wireless Web images successful.

In this chapter, you learn the important strategies for making Wireless Web images successful, beginning with examining why most graphics aren't appropriate for the Wireless Web. You'll also be introduced to new uses for graphics that are better suited to today's wireless devices and you'll be shown WAP's support for images and PHP's support for creating images with your scripts. Because Mobile-Helper has little use for the WAP-supported images, you will see examples from other applications throughout this chapter instead.

Images on the Wireless Web

While you're already familiar with the constraints of the Wireless Web, chief among these are two factors that limit your use of graphics: the physical size of the wireless handset and the user's attention span. These limitations are human rather than electronic constraints, and thus, they're unlikely to change any time soon.

The size of a wireless handset dictates the size of its screen. The majority of people won't carry a device much larger than a cellular phone, which significantly limits the screen size available for graphics. Because the human eye can't distinguish shapes smaller than a fraction of an inch, increasing display resolution doesn't change the overall complexity of a viewable image. Moreover, when you use a mobile terminal you're likely to be doing other things, such as talking or walking. Your attention can't be diverted to discern subtle differences. Even in special cases such as playing a game, you're not wholly focused on your wireless terminal because the small screen enables you to remain aware of your surroundings.

Consequently, graphics perform a very different role in wireless applications. Most traditional uses of images for advertising and corporate identification simply don't work on the Wireless Web. As with each word on a Wireless Web page, you must choose every image carefully to make the most of the limited space and your viewer's attention. Your images can replace selected words on your site, making your pages faster and more accessible for your users.

Wireless Image Fundamentals

WAP's support for graphics is Spartan but appropriate for the delivery platform. WML includes an <img/> tag that enables you to insert images in your content. The tag specifies the URL of an image, along with a mandatory text tag that a browser displays instead of the image if it cannot display the image. The WML standards do not specify whether clients must be able to scroll images or flow text, giving clients the freedom to present the image in whatever way is most appropriate for the client application and hardware. In turn, most clients display the specified images with the <img/> tag centered on the display on their own line. Images larger than the screen may be cropped, or, more often, cropped horizontally but scrollable vertically.

Unlike HTML, image maps are not supported. You can't use images for navigation, although you can use an image inside an anchor to simulate a button. However, this is considered to be in poor form because not all clients can display images.

WAP also defines the Wireless Bitmap format (WBMP), optimized for small clients. Unlike other image formats, it is a monochrome format for small images that don't use compression, making it especially suited to small devices with limited memory and processors that may be unable to decompress or display more complex formats. The WBMP image format is based on an uncompressed single-color Windows BMP files format, but with some minor differences, including that it has the MIME type image/vnd.wap.wbmp.

Your images should be stored in the WBMP format, rather than the GIF, PNG, or JPEG formats used on the Web. Most commercial drawing programs now support the WBMP format, making it dangerously easy to create content for wireless handsets. To see why it's dangerous, let's look at two hypothetical applications, which are both becoming increasingly popular for handheld computers with use on the Wireless Web.

A number of companies offer online Web photo albums enabling you to take pictures (digital or film) and post them to a Web site. With the widespread adoption of handheld computers, some of these firms have expanded into the handheld market, providing handheld photo viewing software that draws content from their Web site. On a device such as a Palm-powered organizer, these applications can be strikingly attractive, enabling people to carry photos as they would in a wallet or purse. It begs the question: why not a WAP version of the same service?

Figures 8-1, 8-2, and 8-3 demonstrate clearly why not. Figure 8-1 shows a typical family snapshot reduced to grayscale and cropped to fit an average Web page. To be stored in the WBMP format and displayed on a screen phone, the image must be processed further by significantly reducing its dimensions and converting it to a monochrome image.

In the first step of this process, the image must be resized and its contrast enhanced, creating an image that fits on a screen phone. Because this is a hypothetical example, I choose a spacious image size of 40 by 48 pixels, rather than the scant 24 pixels of display height for WAP content afforded by many of today's screen phones. This is a manual process, although a glance at any book on image processing, such as Al Bovik's *Handbook of Image and Video Processing*, points you to algorithms you can use in programs to automate the process your production server could use before reducing an image to monochrome.

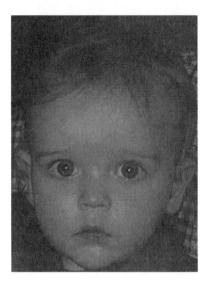

Figure 8-1. A family snapshot

Figures 8-2 and 8-3 show the results. Even with a great deal of fiddling around to find the best results—which would be devilishly hard to automate—Figure 8-2 is barely recognizable. In this figure, the image is halftone, using speckled pixels to emulate shades of gray. In Figure 8-3, on the other hand, the image is a threshold; all the pixels darker than half black are turned to black. These transformations were taken from several trials performed using Adobe Photoshop; many others looked much worse than what appears here.

Over time as handset displays improve and protocols take advantage of the improvements, you can expect modest improvements in the display of photographs such as these. At some point, this kind of image display might satisfy a niche demand—for those willing to accept postage-stamp-sized pictures, anyway.

Figure 8-2. Snapshot reduced to WBMP using a halftone

Figure 8-3. Snapshot reduced to a WBMP using a threshold

Consider instead a second application, the hypothetical navigation site CaféNavigator. Unlike photographs, maps—and many other kinds of diagrams—are a little better suited to low-fidelity displays because they generally use only a few colors and line weights. Our hypothetical site CaféNavigator caters to coffee aficionados, providing site-visitors with reviews, turn-by-turn directions to coffee shops, and other content.

Figure 8-4 displays a page from CaféNavigator showing you how to get from one favorite coffee shop to the other in town. For the delight of writers, the shops are located only a few blocks from each other, so you can work and drink your fill at one, walk off the buzz, and arrive at the other just in time to begin again. Because most maps contain a great deal of extraneous detail that wouldn't fit on a WBMP, this map was drawn by hand, simulating a mapping engine optimized for small-scale devices.

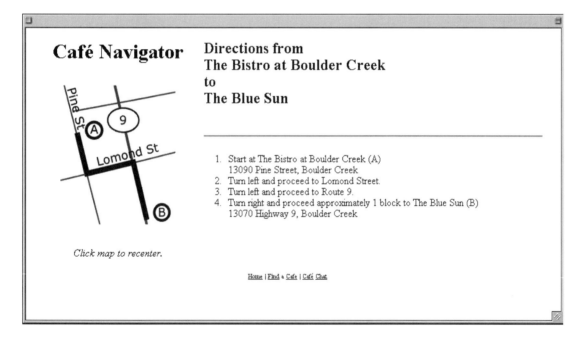

Figure 8-4. CaféNavigator Web page showing a map

While more legible than a rendered photograph, the WBMP in Figure 8-5 still doesn't add much to the page. In shrinking to fit on a screen phone, the map loses much of the additional context such as cross street names, relative distances, and landmarks that it originally contained. It's at least obvious that it's a map, but you can gain the same insight by reading the text directions that follow. Moreover, the map occupies valuable space, forcing you to scroll in order to see the text directions.

Figure 8-5. CaféNavigator Wireless Web page showing a map

Figure 8-6 shows a much better use for graphics in CaféNavigator. In the figure, which shows the first two cards of a deck with the same directions, icons replace the map, giving you clear and immediate directions as to how to proceed.

Figure 8-6. CaféNavigator Wireless Web page with icons

Unlike pictures or diagrams, icons are more appropriate for the Wireless Web. Not only are they simpler, being both small and monochrome, but they carry clear meaning with viewers. You can use icons on many kinds of sites to represent common concepts such as weather, direction (both spatial direction and numerical directions, such as an up arrow by a company's stock quote), and so forth. Just as WAP provides binary compression for your text content, a good icon provides *conceptual* compression, speeding your message's delivery from the handset to the brain.

Of course, to be effective your icons must be clear and easily recognizable. Take pains to localize your icons for different countries. For example, consider Figure 8-7. Americans tend to recognize the left-hand icon as a stop sign more quickly than the right, while the rest of the world is more likely to recognize the right-hand symbol.

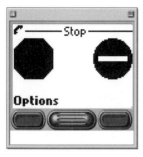

Figure 8-7. CaféNavigator Wireless Web page with icons

When deciding to add icons to your wireless application, carefully consider whether they add value for your viewers. Adding icons does not make a site easier to read or use, and in fact, icons can slow access to your site because clients need to download images as well as text.

You should limit the number of icons you use throughout your deck, typically keeping to less than seven distinct icons. Doing so keeps viewers from being bewildered by the number of different things they see. The human mind is capable of juggling between five and seven items in its short-term memory, including icons and text, so it's more effective to adhere to that number than present a larger number of icons. Equally important, your icons consume valuable space in the device's cache (or take time to download), and you don't want devices caching your icons and repeatedly hitting your server for the same content.

It's not only important to limit the number of different icons you use, but it's also important to limit how often you use them. Again, *sparingly* should be your modus operandi. Pictograms aren't used in today's writing because alphabets are easier to read. The same is true with icons; filling a card with icons makes it more difficult to read.

Finally, icons seem to have an optimal size, making them easily distinguishable from pictures, so the mind doesn't confuse their apparent meanings. In general, icons on a wireless handset should be between 8 by 8 and 16 by 16 pixels. This size amounts to about a quarter inch on the best screens today, or about two lines of text.

PHP Image Fundamentals

Although PHP was conceived to create dynamic HTML content, its originators quickly added to it the capability to create images dynamically as well.

PHP uses the gd library provided by Thomas Boutell at `http://www.boutell.com/` to add scripting functions to draw pictures. While not part of the base PHP package, this library is freely available on the Internet, so that any PHP user can add support for dynamic graphics generation.

With gd and PHP, you can draw images consisting of text, lines, boxes, and arcs. It's suitable for many simple kinds of images, including basic graphs, charts, and simple icons. You can format the resulting images in PNG, JPEG, or WBMP, saving them to either the local file system or returning them for a client to display.

As with most simple graphics packages, the gd library starts with the notion of a *canvas*, the empty space in which you draw. You place a point on the canvas, called a *pixel* (short for *pixel element*) by specifying its position and color. To denote a position, you use a coordinate in Cartesian coordinates, just as you did in high school mathematics. The x-axis stretches horizontally and the y-axis stretches vertically. By convention, coordinates are written as ordered pairs in parentheses, with the *x* coordinate first and *y* coordinate second. Also by convention, coordinates are numbered starting with (0, 0) at the upper left, and increasing as you move down and across. Figure 8-8 shows a small canvas containing a few points.

Unlike the imaginary points (which have no width or breadth) in mathematics, pixels occupy space. The pixels in gd have a unit width and height, so you can shade parts of the canvas by specifying pixels and their color. In Figure 8-8, the pixels at (2, 2), (6, 2), (4,4), (2, 6), (6, 6), (3, 7), (4, 7), and (5, 7) are black.

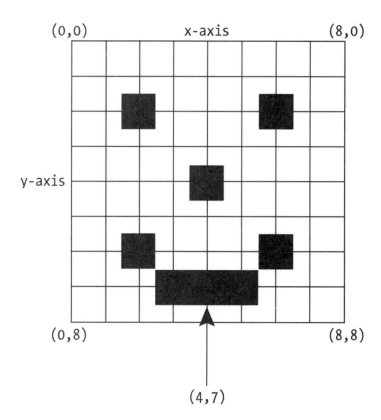

Figure 8-8. A gd canvas with a simple image

The gd package supports drawing in color as well as black-and-white. Each color is a unique mix of the three primary colors: red, green, and blue. To create purple, for example, you mix red and blue, whereas you create yellow by mixing red and green. For WBMP images, of course, you're only interested in black (a combination of red, green, and blue), and white (no color at all). Each of gd's color values are specified as a number from 0 to 255, indicating the amount of a color needed for the mix. Purple, for example, is (255,0,255), whereas black is (255, 255, 255).

Drawing an image with gd in PHP requires four steps using the PHP image functions:

1. Create the image's canvas.

2. Create any colors your picture contains.

3. Draw your picture using one or more of the PHP image drawing functions.

4. Send the image to the client or a file in the format you want.

PHP's image drawing functions enable you to set individual pixels, draw lines, rectangles, and arcs, and draw text, in addition to copying parts of one image to another. The functions themselves are primitive: there's no text wrapping, for example, when you draw text. Because these functions are crude, it's a good idea to spend some time laying out your image before you create the code. You can sketch your image on graph paper and determine the approximate coordinates for the various shapes in your image, and then write the code that draws each shape.

In HTML, developers use PHP's image support for a variety of purposes, notably real-time charts and graphs. Scripts reporting server usage statistics, for example, can create graphs using PHP.

However, these applications are less likely to be used with WAP because most screens are too small to present graphs or charts clearly. A good use for PHP's dynamic image support is to dynamically draw icons tailored to the wireless handset's screen size. Handset screens come in a number of sizes, ranging from too small to barely adequate for graphics. In some cases, the handset returns HTTP headers to the server during a request indicating the screen size, so your PHP scripts can use the information in these headers to determine how large an icon should be.

> **CAUTION**   *Using PHP's graphics support consumes additional resources on your Web server. Sites generating large images or numerous different small images for many clients at once may need more RAM and faster processors to adequately handle the load generated by the scripts. If you're designing a site that needs optimum efficiency, be sure to carefully consider your use of dynamic graphics.*

First Steps with Graphics

Using graphics with WAP and PHP is easy—too easy, by some accounts. When you first start out, you may be tempted to include graphics gratuitously, which detract from your Wireless Web site. As you read the following sections, carefully consider how you can use this information to make your site easier to view and easier to navigate.

Setting Up the Server

Setting up your Web server to port graphics with WAP takes two steps, although you can skip either one or the other depending on whether you want to serve only static WBMP images or use PHP to create dynamic images.

In order to make WBMP images available to clients, you must configure your server to send the correct MIME type for the WBMP image files. If you're running a current version of Apache—almost anything after 1.3.14 or so—you won't even need to do this; it comes preconfigured for you. To see if you need to set the MIME type for your server, check the MIME type configuration file (usually mime.types in your server's configuration file directory) and look for the line that reads `image/vnd.wap.wbmp wbmp`. If you see one, you're set—if not, just add it to the file and restart your Web server. With this line in place, your Web server sends the MIME type image/vnd.wap.wbmp to clients whenever they request a file ending in .wbmp.

For dynamic image support, you may have a little more work to do. You must determine if your installation of PHP supports the gd library using the PHP function `phpinfo`, described in Chapter 5. If your server supports dynamic images, the page returned by `phpinfo` will include text as is shown in Figure 8-9. Often, this occurs if you're using a system installed with Red Hat Linux or another Linux distribution that includes both gd and PHP. If not, you need to get the sources for gd and PHP and recompile PHP (see the sidebar in this section).

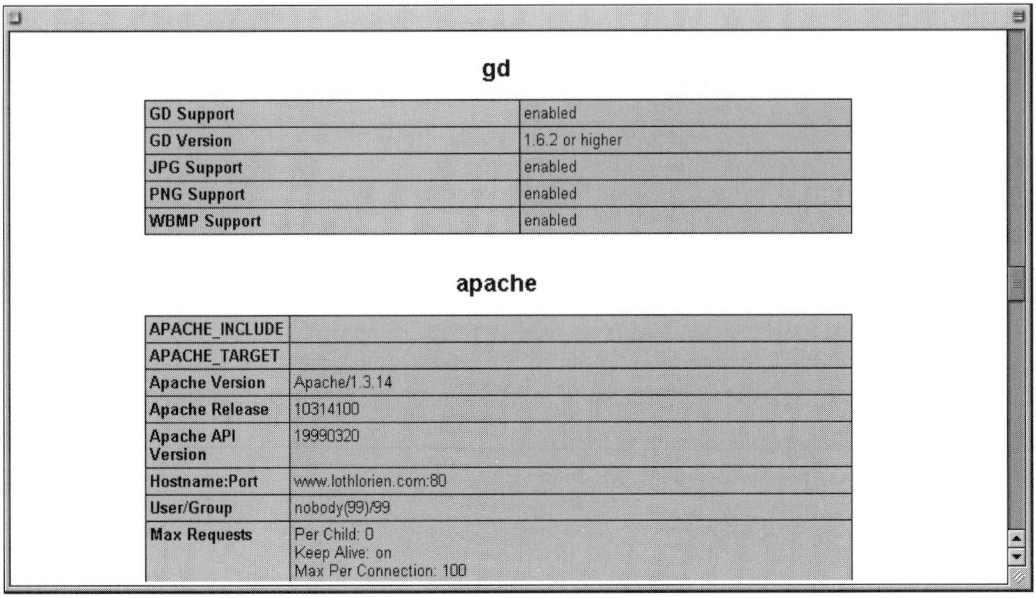

gd	
GD Support	enabled
GD Version	1.6.2 or higher
JPG Support	enabled
PNG Support	enabled
WBMP Support	enabled

apache	
APACHE_INCLUDE	
APACHE_TARGET	
Apache Version	Apache/1.3.14
Apache Release	10314100
Apache API Version	19990320
Hostname:Port	www.lothlorien.com:80
User/Group	nobody(99)/99
Max Requests	Per Child: 0 Keep Alive: on Max Per Connection: 100

Figure 8-9. Results from phpinfo *when dynamic image support is available*

Installing gd for PHP

Getting gd and PHP to work isn't difficult, but it can be very time consuming. The gd package itself depends on three other packages. To get gd running for PHP, you'll need to spend time tracking down these three packages.

If you're using Microsoft Windows, the prebuilt binary includes support for gd, including the underlying packages required by gd itself.

UNIX users aren't so fortunate. If you're on a UNIX host that offers the Red Hat package manager rpm, you want to ensure that you have zlib, libjpeg, and libpng packages, in addition to the gd package. You can use the rpm -q command to see if they're installed, such as the following:

```
# rpm -q libpng
libpng-1.0.3-4
# rpm -q libjpeg
package jpeg is not installed
# rpm -q zlib
zlib-1.1.3-5
# rpm -q gd
package gd not installed
```

Here, the system already has libpng and zlib, but not the libjpeg package or the gd package.

You can get the packages you're missing from well-known sites such as www.redhat.com or www.rpmfind.com, and install them with rpm using the rpm -i command.

If you don't have rpm, you need to build each of these from their source code. You can get each of these packages as compressed tar files from the following sources:

- zlib is at http://www.freesoftware.com/pub/infozip/index.html.

- libjpeg is at ftp://ftp.uu.net/graphics/jpeg/.

- libpng is at http://www.libpng.org/pub/png/.

- gd is at http://www.boutell.com/gd/.

Download and install each of these packages, following the instructions that come with them.

Once you've installed these packages, you can rebuild and reinstall PHP. PHP *should* find these packages automatically, but it doesn't hurt to include –with-gd and –with-jpeg-dir options to the **configure** script. Of course, don't forget any other options you may want, such as support for MySQL.

Including an Image

You use the WML `<img/>` tag to include an image within a card. Listing 8-1 shows the WML that creates the sample shown in Figure 8-2 of this chapter.

```
01: <?xml version="1.0"?>
02: <!DOCTYPE wml PUBLIC "-//WAPFORUM//DTD WML 1.1//EN"
03:  "http://www.wapforum.org/DTD/wml_1.1.xml">
04: <wml>
05:   <card title="Jarod">
06:     <p align="center">
07:       <img alt="Jarod" src="jarod.wbmp"/>
08:     </p>
09:   </card>
10: </wml>
```

Listing 8-1. The WML `<img/>` tag

The `<img/>` tag shown in Listing 8-1 shows the two attributes the `<img/>` tag requires: `alt` and `src`. As with the HTML `<img>` tag, the `<img/>` tag uses these to specify an image's name and URL, respectively. Because not all WAP clients can display images, the WML specification requires you to include a descriptive title in the `alt` tag. Browsers unable to display your image, display the `alt` tag instead.

> **CAUTION** *You should give a descriptive to the* `alt` *content that succinctly describes the image, such as "cloud," "sun," "rain," "left," "right," or "stop," instead of the HTML standby "image." Viewers without the ability to see images resent seeing the text* **[image]** *gratuitously scattered over a deck that uses graphics, even if they know that their handset won't display the content. Better yet, avoid the use of images altogether, or detect the client type (discussed later in this chapter) and only present images to those clients that can display them.*

The `<img/>` tag has a third attribute, the `localsrc` tag, that you can use to specify an on-device image. Some handsets, notably those running the Phone.com browser have a number of standard images in the device's read-only memory (ROM). You use `localsrc` images just as you would use conventional images, giving a `src` and an `alt` tag. If the handset has the image you name with the `localsrc` attribute in ROM, it displays that image. Otherwise, if it has image support at all, it fetches the image you name with the `src` attribute, or if it cannot display graphics, it displays the `alt` attribute's message. Listing 8-2 shows a simple example.

```
01: <?xml version="1.0"?>
02: <!DOCTYPE wml PUBLIC "-//WAPFORUM//DTD WML 1.1//EN"
03:   "http://www.wapforum.org/DTD/wml_1.1.xml">
04: <wml>
05:   <card title="Clock">
06:     <p align="center">
07:       <img alt="Clock" src="clock.wbmp"
08:        localsrc="clock"/><br/>
09:       <big>9:23:21 AM</big>
10:     </p>
11:   </card>
12: </wml>
```

Listing 8-2. The `<img/>` `localsrc` *attribute*

Figure 8-10 shows the results using the Yospace SPEDE, which does not define a `"clock"` image for the `<img/>` `localsrc` attribute. In Figure 8-10, the WBMP image clock.wbmp is loaded from the server instead. In Figure 8-11, however, you can see the "clock" image provided by the Phone.com UP.SDK.

Figure 8-10. Yospace SPEDE without localsrc *image for* "clock"

Figure 8-11. Phone.com UP.SDK with localsrc *image for* "clock"

When you use localsrc images you improve your application's performance because the browser does not need to use the network to fetch images it already has in ROM. Of course, you have no guarantee that the images are there, so the performance gain isn't guaranteed.

> **NOTE** *While the WML standard dictates that all clients must understand the* localsrc *tag, it does not dictate what images a client must cache. Thus, you should plan on using* localsrc *images only when you have some knowledge of your client's capabilities, or be sure to select appropriate-looking images for the image's* src *attribute. The* localsrc *attribute is especially suited for vertical applications where your viewers use only a predetermined manufacturer's wireless handset because you can match the handset's support for* localsrc *with your content.*

Drawing an Image with PHP

For our first dynamic image, let's draw a happy face such as the image in Figure 8-12. Because you could easily do this using a paint program and a static WBMP image, let's make things interesting: the script should change the shape of the mouth in the image depending on how happy the face should look.

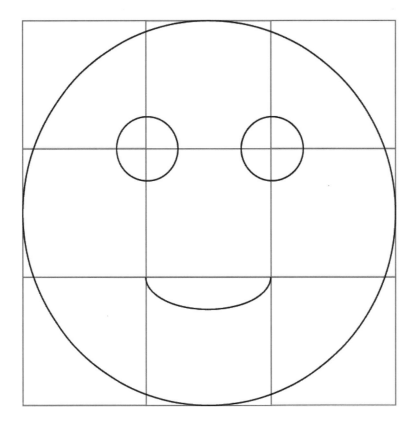

Figure 8-12. Sketch of our first dynamic image

The face itself has two parts: the eyes and the mouth. All of these shapes are arcs; the eyes are circles, and the mouth is a half-ellipse. To find out where to place each shape, divide the face up into nine equal squares (shown in gray in Figure 8-12). Place the eyes at the corners of the first and third regions, and the corners of the mouth are on the corners of the seventh and ninth squares.

Listing 8-3 shows a script that draws a similar face, returning a WBMP image to the client such as the one in Figure 8-13.

Figure 8-13. Happy face drawn by smile.php

```
01: <?php
02: /*****************************************************
03:  * smile.php
04:  *
05:  * This module draws a face in a wbmp.
06:  * $happy - the amount happiness between 0 (unhappy) and
07:  * 100 (happy) to show.
08:  * $width – image width (pixels)
09:  * $height – image height (pixels)
10:  *
11:  *****************************************************/
12:
13: // Initialize unset variables
14:
15: if ( !isset( $happy) )
16: {
17:   $happy = 90;
18: }
19:
20: // Validate input value if needed
21:
22: $happy = $happy < 0 ? 0 : $happy;
23: $happy = $happy > 100 ? 100 : $happy;
24:
25: if ( !isset( $width ) )
26: {
27:   $width = 32;
28: }
29:
```

```
30: if ( !isset( $height ) )
31: {
32:   $height = 32;
33: }
34:
35: // Create the image to hold the face
36:
37: $image = ImageCreate( $width, $height );
38:
39: // Allocate colors
40: // WARNING: WBMP appears to swap black and white.
41:
42: $colorWhite = ImageColorAllocate( $image,
43:   0, 0, 0 );          // R, G, B
44: $colorBlack = ImageColorAllocate( $image,
45:   255, 255, 255 );    // R, G, B
46:
47: // Draw face
48:
49: ImageArc( $image,       // canvas
50:   $width / 2, $height / 2,  // center coordinate
51:   $width, $height,      // width & height
52:   0, 360,               // start, stop degrees
53:   $colorBlack );        // color
54:
55: // Draw eyes
56:
57: $pupilX = $width / 3;
58: $pupilY = $height / 3;
59: $pupilW = $width / 6;
60: $pupilH = $height / 6;
61:
62:
63: // Left eye first.
64:
65:   ImageArc( $image,     // canvas
66:     $pupilX, $pupilY,   // center
67:     $pupilW, $pupilH,   // width & height
68:     0, 360,             // start, stop degrees
69:     $colorBlack );      // color
70:
71: // The right eye next
72:
```

```
73:    ImageArc( $image,    // canvas
74:      2 * $pupilX, $pupilY,   // center
75:      $pupilW, $pupilH, // width & height
76:      0, 360,            // start, stop degrees
77:      $colorBlack );    // color
78:
79: // Draw smile
80:
81: $smileX = $width / 2;
82: $smileY = 2 * $height / 3;
83: $smileW = $width / 3;
84: $smileH = $height / 3 * abs( 50 - $happy ) / 50;
85:
86: // Draw upper half of oval if unhappy, lower if happy.
87:
88: $start = $happy < 50 ? 180 : 0;
89: $stop = $happy < 50 ? 360 : 180;
90:
91: ImageArc( $image,     // canvas
92:    $smileX, $smileY,    // center coordinate
93:    $smileW, $smileH,    // width & height
94:    $start, $stop,       // start, stop degrees
95:    $colorBlack );    // color
96:
97: // Output the image
98:
99: header( "Content-type: image/vnd.wap.wbmp" );
100:
101: ImageWBMP( $image );
102: ?>
```

Listing 8-3. The smile.php script to draw a happy face

The script in Listing 8-3 begins by initializing the default variables $happy, $width, and $height. By making these variables tested and set at the beginning of the script, you can use this script to draw faces of various sizes and dispositions simply by adding values for the PHP variables to the URL. For example, to see a very large, unhappy face, the WML invoking smile.php could be smile.php?happy=10;width=60;width=60. Because PHP extracts HTTP GET variables from the request URL, the script begins with the variables $happy, $width, and $height set to the values specified by the URL.

Lines 15–24 accomplish this for the variable $happy. The script uses isset function to see if $happy was previously set by the incoming URL. If $happy is not set by the incoming URL, it defaults to the value 90 on line 17. Lines 22 and 23 check the value of $happy to be sure it's greater than zero and less than one hundred.

Lines 25–28 specify a default value for the image's width, and lines 30–33 specify a default value for the image's height. As with the value of $happy, these values, stored in $height and $width, may be overridden by the request URL.

Line 37 creates the canvas that contains the resulting image. The PHP function ImageCreate takes a height and width and returns an opaque structure, containing an image with the specified size.

Although WBMP images support only two colors—black and white—we still need to define those colors. On lines 42–44, we use the PHP function ImageColorAllocate to create two colors. Lines 42–43 create the color white, using the value 0 for each of red, green, and blue. Paradoxically, the PHP support for WBMP appears to reverse white and black, resulting in the color white. Similarly, specifying full values for red, green, and blue on lines 44–45 result in the color black.

Our face begins to take shape on lines 49–53, where we use the PHP function ImageArc to draw the face on the canvas $image. ImageArc takes the arc's center point, along with its width and height—for a circle, this is its diameter, whereas for an ellipse, this is the length of its major and semimajor axes. It also takes the start and stop positions for drawing, so you can draw arcs smaller than a full circle or ellipse. ImageArc, like the other drawing functions, also takes the color to use when drawing. We specify a full 360 degrees, so ImageArc draws an entire circle.

The eyes are smaller circles, spaced at one-third intervals across and down the face (see Figure 8-12), and each eye is one-sixth the size of the face. On lines 57–58, the script calculates the center points for the eyes, and on lines 59–60, it calculates the width and height of each eye. These numbers are somewhat arbitrary; chosen after pushing circles of various sizes around on a sheet of graph paper to see what looks reasonable.

On lines 63–77, the script draws the two eyes using two calls to ImageArc. As with the face, these are full circles.

Drawing the mouth is a little trickier. If the face is unhappy, the middle of the mouth bends upwards, into a frown. Otherwise, if the face is happy, it bends downward, into a smile. Do this by drawing an arc, corresponding to either the top or bottom half of an ellipse using ImageArc. ImageArc takes two arguments that determine what segment of an arc to draw in degrees. A position of zero degrees corresponds to a point at the three o'clock position. Degrees are numbered counterclockwise. Thus, the arc corresponding to the bottom half of an ellipse begins at zero degrees and ends at 180 degrees, whereas the top half of the ellipse begins at 180 degrees and ends at 360 degrees.

In addition to deciding which arc segment to draw, the script must determine the height of the arc segment. The happier (or unhappier) the face appears, the more distorted the mouth. For instance, if $happy is equal to fifty, the mouth appears as a straight line, and as $happy approaches zero or one hundred, the mouth reaches maximum deflection up or down, respectively. To achieve this effect by changing the arc, scale the arc's height by the difference between $happy and 50. Thus, when $happy is near an extreme, the difference between $happy and 50 is large, and the arc height approaches its maximum. When $happy is near 50, on the other hand, the difference is small, and the arc's height is near zero.

Lines 81–84 compute the location of the arc's center. The smile is centered horizontally ($smileX is half of the image's width) and spaced two-thirds of the way down the face ($smileY is two-thirds the image's height). The smile always spans one-third the face, whereas its height depends on the value of $happy. Line 84 scales the height of the arc using the technique just discussed.

Lines 88–89 determine what segment of the arc the script draws by testing $happy and conditionally setting the $start and $stop variables. Then, on lines 91–95, the script draws the arc on the canvas.

Finally, the script needs to return the image to the browser. To do this, it must first send the appropriate MIME type for the image, followed by the image data itself. The call to the header function on line 99 sends the WBMP MIME type to the client, whereas the ImageWBMP function on line 101 converts the image canvas to a WBMP and sends the resulting data to the client. (PHP also has the functions ImagePNG and ImageJPEG to create PNG and JPEG images, respectively.)

Unlike a Web browser, most WML browsers won't directly load an image URL. Instead, to display an image you must reference it from a WML deck. To see the output from Listing 8-3, we need a simple WML deck that shows an image. Listing 8-4 shows the WML used to create Figure 8-13.

```
01: <?xml version="1.0"?>
02: <!DOCTYPE wml PUBLIC "-//WAPFORUM//DTD WML 1.1//EN"
03:   "http://www.wapforum.org/DTD/wml_1.1.xml">
04: <wml>
05:   <card title="Smile">
06:     <p align="center">
07:       <img src="smile.php" alt="smile!"/>
08:     </p>
09:   </card>
10: </wml>
```

Listing 8-4. WML deck using smile.php

Line 7 of the listing invokes the smile.php script on the server, which returns the WBMP image on lines 99–101 of Listing 8-3. Note that you could send different values for $happy, $width, and $height; consider Listing 8-5 which produces the image in Figure 8-14.

```
01: <?xml version="1.0"?>
02: <!DOCTYPE wml PUBLIC "-//WAPFORUM//DTD WML 1.1//EN"
03:   "http://www.wapforum.org/DTD/wml_1.1.xml">
04: <wml>
05:   <card title="Smile">
06:     <p align="center">
07:       <img src="smile.php?happy=50;width=16;height=16;"
08:         alt="smile!"/>
09:     </p>
10:   </card>
11: </wml>
```

Listing 8-5. WML deck using smile.php with different values

Figure 8-14. Unhappy face drawn by smile.php from Listing 8-5

Going Further with Graphics

Now that you've seen how to include graphics in your WML content and how you can draw simple pictures using PHP, let's take an in-depth look at the PHP functions for graphics. This chapter closes with a detailed discussion of how you can use the PHP graphics functions to scale your icons so they best fit a wireless handset's display.

PHP Graphics Functions

PHP's graphics functions share a common interface. All are named with the leading word Image, and most have similar arguments, making them easy to use. We saw a handful of them in Listing 8-3, but there are others you should know about as well.

When you create a new image canvas, you can use the ImageCreate function, or you can use one of the ImageCreateFrom functions (ImageCreateFromJPEG,

`ImageCreateFromPNG`, `ImageCreateFromWBMP`) to initialize your canvas with the contents of an image from a file or a particular URL. You can give these functions the name of a file or the URL for an image, and they return a canvas containing the image. The `ImageCreateFrom` functions are good when you need to embellish an image with dynamic content because you can draw a template of the image using a drawing program. Then, you can simply draw the dynamic content over the image.

CAUTION   *The* `ImageCreateFrom` *functions enable you to load graphics from other Web sites by specifying an image's URL, but be sure you have the rights to change and reuse the images. If you don't, you may be violating copyright laws.*

When using an image as a drawing template, you need to determine the size of the image. The `ImageSX` and `ImageSY` functions return the width and height of an image, respectively. In addition, you can use images you load using the `ImageCreateFrom` functions when copying images with `ImageCopy` and `ImageCopyResized`; these copy part or all of one image into another image. Using `ImageCopyResized` you can even resize an image during copying if you need to, although the results aren't pretty with monochrome images.

After creating your canvas, you can specify what colors your picture uses with the `ImageColorAllocate` function. This function takes a color's red, green, and blue values and returns an integer that uniquely denotes this color. The function also stores information about the color in an image, so you should always create new colors for each image you draw.

You can draw both empty and filled shapes on your canvas. The `ImageArc`, `ImagePolygon`, and `ImageRectangle` functions enable you to draw empty shapes, showing just the outline of the shape you specify. The `ImagePolygon` function takes an array of coordinates specifying polygon's vertices and the desired color, while `ImageRectangle` draws a rectangle with the given two points and color. Similarly, the `ImageFilledPolygon` and `ImageFilledRectangle` functions draw filled shapes. There's no `ImageFilledArc` function, however. To draw a filled arc, you need to first draw an empty arc with `ImageArc` and fill it using `ImageFill`.

You can fill arbitrary regions—called a *flood fill* because the color floods to fill an entire shape—using the `ImageFill` and `ImageFillToBorder` functions. Both functions take an argument specifying the point at which the fill operation should start, along with the color that PHP uses to fill the region. `ImageFill` fills the region until it encounters pixels of the same color as the fill, and `ImageFillToBorder` fills the region until it encounters pixels the same color as a color you specify. Thus, `ImageFill` is the same as `ImageFillToColor` called with equal fill colors and the border colors.

You can draw solid and dashed lines using the `ImageLine` and `ImageDashedLine` functions. These functions take both the image and the line's start and end coordinates and color, drawing a line that connects the two points.

PHP has a number of text-drawing functions that enable you to draw individual characters on an image. These functions use either a font built into GD, or True-Type fonts you load with gd's TrueType support. You won't want to use TrueType fonts in your image because most result in images that are too large for wireless handsets to display. Instead, use one of the internal fonts, identified by a number from 1 to 5. Larger fonts have progressively higher numbers, so font 2 is larger than font 1, and font 5 is the largest of all.

To determine the size of a string in a particular font, call the `ImageFontWidth` and `ImageFontHeight` functions. These return the pixel width of a character in the indicated font; you can find out how large a string is by multiplying the pixel width of the font character by the number of the characters in the string. You can call these functions once for each font your image uses. The resulting values help determine how large each bit of text is and where you should place it on an image.

To actually draw text, you use the `ImageChar` and `ImageString` functions. These take a character or string respectively, along with the desired position for the text, color, and text font. `ImageChar` and `ImageString` draw the text horizontally from left to right. If you need to draw vertical text, you can do so using the `ImageCharUp` and `ImageStringUp` functions.

Sometimes you may want to access an individual pixel in an image. The `ImageColorAt` function returns the color at a specified point in an image, and the `ImageSetPixel` sets a specific pixel to the desired value.

Once you finish drawing on the canvas, use one of the functions `ImagePNG`, `ImageJPEG`, and `ImageWBMP` to save the image in your desired format. Called with only an image, these functions send the bits of the image in the desired format to the client. If you provide a filename, PHP writes the image in the desired format to the file you specify, enabling you to cache dynamically created images for later use by multiple clients.

Finally, you can destroy the image using `ImageDestroy`. This is a good idea if your script creates a lot of images, or if it continues running for some time after it creates and saves the image.

PHP's graphics support also includes functions for color matching, True Type font rendering (through the external FreeType package). These functions aren't terribly useful for WBMP generation because WBMP images wouldn't use these features. If you're interested in using PHP and gd to generate PNG or JPEG images as well, be sure to see the documentation that accompanies PHP.

Using PHP to Scale Graphics

The best use for PHP's dynamic image support with WBMP images is to dynamically scale images to fit a client's screen. You won't do this with `ImageCopyResized` because while you can resize source images with that function, the results aren't pretty in a monochrome image. `ImageCopyResized` attempts to stretch or shrink the image as it is copied, resulting in jagged shapes in monochrome images that look awful or incomprehensible.

Instead, you can draw an entirely new icon depending on the screen size. To do this, of course, you must write the code that draws your image, rather than simply using a WBMP you draw from a paint program. Fortunately, most icons are aggregates of simple shapes such as squares, circles, and lines, making this easy to do.

Consider a WAP application to show an analog clock with the current time, such as the one in Figure 8-15. Clearly, it's easiest to generate the clock image dynamically because there are 720 images for a given screen size (one for each minute in half of the day). To create an easy-to-read clock, its face should be as large as the device's screen, but no larger because you would need to scroll the display to see the entire clock face.

Figure 8-15. WAP analog clock application

Determining client screen size

Before you can scale a drawing to fit the client display, you need to know how big the display is. Determining the client's screen size takes a bit of detective work, however. Some browsers, notably the Phone.com browser, report nicely on the device's screen size using an HTTP header. Others, such as the current version of the Nokia browser on the Nokia 7110 screen phone, do not. Thus, finding the display size of a particular client involves a series of tests, including initially checking for a header that describes the screen size. If no header is available, you must make a reasonable guess from the browser identification. It's educated guesswork, so applications using this technique should check the results and substitute adequate defaults, if necessary. Listing 8-6 shows a function extending wml.php that does this.

```
01: <?
02: // Extracted from wml.php
03:
04: /*****************************************************
05:  * FUNCTION: WMLClientScreenSize
06:  *
07:  * DESCRIPTION: WMLClientHasWMLScript checks the
08:  * HTTP headers to try to find the screen size.
09:  *
10:  * RETURNED: hash containing three slots
11:  *  "width"   => screen width
12:  *  "height"  => screen height
13:  *  "success" => either 0 (nothing found) or how
14:  *    size determined
15:  *****************************************************/
16: function WMLClientScreenSize()
17: {
18:
19: // List of the browsers we know
20:
21:   $uaScreens = array(
22:     "Nokia 7110" => "96,45",
23:     "Nokia 6210" => "96,40",
24:     "Nokia 6250" => "96,40",
25:     /* Add more browsers here if you like... */
26:   );
27:
28: // Assume the worst.
29:
30:   $result = array(
31:     "success" => 0,
32:     "width" => 0,
33:     "height" => 0 );
34:
35: // Extract HTTP headers
36:
37:   $headers = getallheaders();
38:
39:
40: // Look for the Phone.com info first.
41:
42:   $pixels = $headers[ "x-up-devcap-screenpixels" ];
43:
44:
```

```
45:   if ( $pixels )
46:   {
47:
48: // Aha! We got something.
49:
50:     $result[ "success" ] = "x-up-devcap-screenpixels";
51:   }
52:   else
53:   {
54:
55: // Hrm. Maybe we can guess from the user agent.
56:
57:     $ua = $headers[ "User-Agent" ];
58:
59:     for ( reset( $uaScreens );
60:       $index = key( $uaScreens );
61:       next($uaScreens) )
62:     {
63:       if ( stristr( $ua, $index ) )
64:       {
65:         $pixels = $uaScreens[ $index ];
66:         $result[ "success" ] = "user-agent";
67:         break;
68:       }
69:     }
70:   }
71:
72: // $pixels is now a string of the form "x,y" or is empty.
73:
74:   if ( $pixels )
75:   {
76:
77: // Extract x, y values
78:     sscanf( $pixels, "%d,%d",
79:       &$result[ "width" ],
80:       &$result[ "height" ] );
81:   }
82:
83:   return $result;
84: }
85: ?>
```

Listing 8-6. WMLClientScreenSize *in wml.php*

> **NOTE** *Because this function uses the PHP Apache function* getallheaders, *it only works when you use PHP with Apache.*

The WMLClientScreenSize function is essentially a series of conditional expressions, starting with checking HTTP headers and looking at the HTTP User-Agent header specifically.

It begins on lines 21–26 by storing a very short list of known WML browsers that don't provide screen size information using a specific HTTP header in the array $uaScreens. These values are taken from the Nokia developer documentation; you could easily add information about other browsers here. At the time of this writing, the Phone.com and Nokia browsers constitute about 80 percent of the North American user base, so together this function captures information about the majority of clients.

These screen sizes indicate the client's usable screen size, that is the total screen size less any space used by soft key labels, annunciators, and so on.

Lines 30–33 initialize the result array, which has three slots. The result array contains information so that the caller can judge whether the function succeeded or failed, as well as the actual screen dimensions. The slot "success" contains a string on success indicating how the screen size was determined, and the reported screen size is returned in the width and height slots.

WMLClientScreenSize first gets the HTTP headers using getallheaders on line 37 to look for the x-up-devcap-screenpixels header Phone.com clients send. If it exists, the script puts its value in pixels on line 42, and notes success on line 50.

Otherwise the script gets the User-Agent header value on line 57 and uses it to search the array $uaScreens for information about the client. The key of each slot in $uaScreens is the name of a browser, but clients can send additional information to the server within the User-Agent header, so you can't just use the User-Agent header to index $uaScreens. Instead, the script tests each key of $uaScreens on lines 59–70 to see if the key's value is part of the User-Agent header value.

For example, the Yospace SPEDE sends the string "Nokia 7110 v0.13 (compatible; YOSPACE SmartPhone Emulator 1.2)". The if statement on line 63 matches this user agent with the key "Nokia 7110", setting $pixels to "96,45".

The last thing WMLClientScreenSize does is extract the width and height data from the string in $pixels. Within the string a comma separates the numbers, so a simple sscanf suffices to extract the width and height on lines 79–80.

WMLClientScreenSize doesn't check if the client supports graphics. While you could test the HTTP Accept header and look for the MIME type image/vnd.wap.wbmp, some clients send this MIME type in the Accept header *only* when they request an image, falsely indicating that the client cannot accept images, when in fact, it can.

Drawing the clock

Once you know the screen size, you can draw the clock. Drawing the clock face is easy; it's just a circle, so the script can call `ImageArc`, centering the circle in the image. Drawing the hands and dial markings is a little more challenging, however.

To draw the clock hands or the dial markings, you need to know the pixel coordinates for various points along the clock face's circle. Looking back to high school geometry, the equation for a point *(x, y)* that is *t* degrees around a circle centered at the point *(c_x, c_y)* with radius *r* is:

$$x = r \cos t + c_x$$
$$y = r \sin t + c_y$$

Fortunately, PHP has trigonometric functions, so it's easy to use this equation in our script. However, PHP's trigonometric functions take angular measurements in radians (there are 2π radians in a circle, which is 360 degrees), so you need to ensure that the script converts measurements from degrees to radians before calling PHP's `sin` and `cos` functions. You can do this using the `DegToRad` function in Listing 8-7.

```
01: <?php
02: // Extracted from clock.php
03:
04: /********************************************************
05:  * FUNCTION: DegToRad
06:  *
07:  * DESCRIPTION: Converts from degrees to radians
08:  *
09:  * RETURNED: number of radians
10:  ********************************************************/
11: function DegToRad(
12:    $deg  // (in) degrees
13: )
14: {
15:    $pi = 3.1415926536;
16:
17:    return ( $deg / 360 ) * ( 2 * $pi );
18: }
19:
20: ?>
```

Listing 8-7. The `DegToRad` *function in clock.php*

The DegToRad function is a straightforward arithmetic computation, as is the PointOnCircle function that implements the equation of a circle shown previously. PointOnCircle, shown in Listing 8-8, returns an array where the first value is the *x* coordinate and the second value is the *y* coordinate of the point on the circle.

```
01: <?php
02: // Extracted from clock.php
03:
04: /********************************************************
05:  * FUNCTION: PointOnCircle
06:  *
07:  * DESCRIPTION: Given degrees on circle with center and
08:  * radius, returns x and y coordinates of point at
09:  * degrees.
10:  *
11:  * RETURNED: x, y in $x, $y
12:  ********************************************************/
13: function PointOnCircle(
14:     $deg,    // (in) degrees around circle
15:     $centerX,   // (in) center of circle
16:     $centerY, // (in) center of circle
17:     $radius    // (in) radius of circle
18: )
19: {
20:
21: // equation for unit circle is ( cos(theta), sin(theta) )
22:
23:     $x = $radius * cos( DegToRad( $deg ) ) + $centerX;
24:     $y = $radius * sin( DegToRad( $deg ) ) + $centerY;
25:
26:     return ( array( $x, $y ) );
27:
28: }
29:
30: ?>
```

Listing 8-8. The PointOnCircle *function in clock.php*

There's one more catch before you can draw the clock hands and face markings, however. By definition, zero degrees on a mathematical circle is at the three o'clock position on a clock dial. It is more natural for us to think of zero degrees at the twelve o'clock position on a clock dial, so we can use the hours and minutes in the time to determine how far the hands should sweep. To keep things clear, use the ClockDegToMathDeg function in Listing 8-9 to do the conversion.

> **CAUTION** *It's easy to confuse mathematical degree measurements, which begin at the three o'clock position and sweep clockwise, with the PHP* ArcImage *function's measurement of degrees, which starts at the three o'clock position and sweeps counterclockwise.*

```php
01: <?php
02: // Extracted from clock.php
03:
04: /*******************************************************
05:  * FUNCTION: ClockDegToMathDeg
06:  *
07:  * DESCRIPTION: Given degrees from 12 o'clock, returns
08:  *   degree position on unit circle.
09:  *
10:  * RETURNED: number of degrees
11:  *******************************************************/
12: function ClockDegToMathDeg(
13:    $deg  // (in) degrees
14: )
15: {
16:
17: // Move back a quarter circle.
18:
19:    return $deg - 90;
20: }
21:
22: ?>
```

Listing 8-9. The ClockDegToMathDeg *function in clock.php*

Whew! It's time to do some drawing. The clock face is centered in the image. Once you know its display size, you can calculate its center and radius. You also need to know how many degrees around the circle to draw each hour's tick mark, and how many degrees one hour and minute sweep on the clock face. The twelve hours on a clock face are one circle equaling 360 degrees. Dividing 360 by twelve yields 30 degrees per hour; similarly, there are 6 degrees per minute. The clock hands are lines from the center of the clock face out a fraction of the face's radius to the point in degrees representing the time, whereas the clock face hour mark-ings are lines *inwards* from the clock face's circle towards the center of the circle.

Drawing the hands and tick marks

Listing 8-10 shows the remainder of clock.php, which creates a canvas as large as the client's displayable area, drawing a clock face with hour markings, and the hour and minute hand.

```php
01: <?php
02: /****************************************************
03:  * clock.php
04:  *
05:  * This module draws a face in a wbmp.
06:  * $happy - the amount happiness between 0 (unhappy) and
07:  * 100 (happy) to show.
08:  * $width - image width (pixels)
09:  * $height - image height (pixels)
10:  *
11:  ****************************************************/
12:
13: // Functions in clock.php shown previously...
14:
15:
16: include "wml.php";
17:
18: // Setup: get the client screen size
19:
20: $clientInfo = WMLClientScreenSize();
21:
22: if ( $clientInfo[ "success" ] )
23: {
24:
25: // Make it square
26:
27:   $height = $clientInfo[ "height" ];
28:   $width = $height;
29: }
30:
31:
```

```
32: if ( !isset( $width ) )
33: {
34:   $width = 32;
35: }
36:
37: if ( !isset( $height ) )
38: {
39:   $height = 32;
40: }
41:
42: // Position of clock face
43:
44: $radius = $height / 2;
45: $originX = $radius;
46: $originY = $radius;
47:
48:
49: // Time
50:
51: sscanf( date( "h,i" ), "%d,%d", &$hour, &$min );
52:
53:
54: // Create the image to hold the clock face
55:
56: $image = imagecreate( $width, $height );
57:
58: // Allocate colors
59: // WARNING: WBMP appears to swap black and white.
60:
61: $colorWhite = imagecolorallocate( $image,
62:   0, 0, 0 );
63: $colorBlack = imagecolorallocate( $image,
64:   255, 255, 255 );
65:
66: // Draw face
67:
68: imagearc( $image,        // canvas
69:   $width / 2, $height / 2,  // center coordinate
70:   $width, $height,     // width & height
71:   0, 360,        // start, stop degrees
72:   $colorBlack );       // color
73:
74:
```

```
75: // Draw each hour tick mark
76:
77: for ( $i = 0; $i < 12; $i++ )
78: {
79:
80:   // Ticks are 30 degrees apart.
81:
82:   $tickDeg = ClockDegToMathDeg( $i * 30 );
83:   $p1 = PointOnCircle( $tickDeg,
84:     $originX, $originY, 4 * $radius / 5 );
85:   $p2 = PointOnCircle( $tickDeg,
86:     $originX, $originY, $radius );
87:
88:   ImageLine( $image, $p1[0], $p1[1],
89:     $p2[0], $p2[1], $colorBlack );
90: }
91:
92: // Hour hand— each hour occupies 30 degrees.
93:
94: $hourDeg = ClockDegToMathDeg( $hour * 30 );
95: $point = PointOnCircle( $hourDeg,
96:     $originX, $originY, $radius / 3 );
97:
98: ImageLine( $image, $originX, $originY,
99:   $point[0], $point[1], $colorBlack );
100:
101: // Minute hand— each minute occupies six degrees.
102:
103: $minDeg = ClockDegToMathDeg( $min * 6 );
104: $point = PointOnCircle( $minDeg,
105:   $originX, $originY, 2 * $radius / 3 );
106:
107: ImageLine( $image, $originX, $originY,
108:   $point[0], $point[1], $colorBlack );
109:
110: // Output the image
111:
112: header( "Content-type: image/vnd.wap.wbmp" );
113:
114: ImageWBMP( $image );
115:
116: ?>
```

Listing 8-10. The clock.php script

The script begins by defining the functions you just saw and then including the wml.php script on line 16. It then uses the new `WMLClientScreenSize` function to get the client's screen size if it can. On lines 22–29, the script sets `$width` equal to `$height` to create a square canvas if `WMLClientScreenSize` succeeded; if it didn't, `$width` and `$height` will be set to 32 on the subsequent lines 32–40.

Lines 42–46 calculates how big the clock face is and where to center the face. The radius of the face is half the height of the image (line 44), and the circle is centered in the image (lines 45 and 46).

On lines 49–51 the script gets the current time and breaks it into hour and minute variables `$hour` and `$min` using `sscanf` and `date`. When you call `date` with only a format string, it returns the current date; you can also call `date` with a time from `time` (or `gmtime`, see "Food for Thought" later in this chapter) to obtain a formatted time string of a particular time.

Lines 54–65 perform the necessary bookkeeping for the script to draw the image. Line 56 creates the image canvas and lines 61–64 create black and white colors so the script can draw.

Lines 68–72 draw the outside circle for the clock face.

Lines 77–90 draw each tick mark on the clock face. Each tick mark is a line from a circle four-fifths of the diameter of the clock face to the clock face itself. For each hour tick mark, the script first calculates the degree position around the circle for the mark on line 82, storing the result in `$tickDeg`. The script then uses `PointOnCircle` to find the beginning and ending of the tick marks to draw. On lines 83–86, the script uses `$tickDeg` along with the clock face's center and radius to calculate the start and end points for the line representing the tick mark. The script draws the line on line 88 with `ImageLine`.

To draw the hour and minute hand, lines 92–109 operate similarly. First, on line 94, the script determines how far around the circle to place the hour hand. The script then finds the coordinates of that point on a circle one-third the radius of the clock face on lines 95–96, and draws the hour hand on lines 98–99 with `ImageLine`. The process is the same for the minute hand, although the script uses a line two-thirds the size of the clock face for the minute hand.

Finally, the script outputs the MIME header for the WBMP image itself on lines 112–114.

Although line 112 generates a WBMP in the listing, when writing this function, I used the MIME type `"image/jpeg"` on line 112 and called `ImageJPEG` instead of `ImageWBMP` on line 114. That way, the script could be quickly run from my desktop computer's Web browser to inspect the results. Once it was working correctly, I replaced the MIME type and `ImageJPEG` function call with the MIME type and function for WBMP images.

No man is an island; neither are WBMP images. To view the WBMP image, we need the deck in Listing 8-11. As with the deck in Listing 8-4, this deck shows a single card with an `<img/>` tag that invokes our PHP script.

```
01: <?xml version="1.0"?>
02: <!DOCTYPE wml PUBLIC "-//WAPFORUM//DTD WML 1.1//EN"
03:  "http://www.wapforum.org/DTD/wml_1.1.xml">
04: <wml>
05:   <card>
06:     <p align="center">
07:       <img src="clock.php" alt="smile!"/>
08:     </p>
09:   </card>
10: <wml>
```

Listing 8-11. Deck displaying the clock image generated by clock.php

On the CD-ROM

Although this chapter doesn't make any changes to MobileHelper, the ch08 directory includes all of the listings from this chapter, along with each example in a folder.

In addition to the Clock, CafeNavigator, PhotoAlbum, Smile, and Stop examples, the CD-ROM includes a version of wml.php with the WMLClientScreenSize function.

Food for Thought

- Would icons add clarity to your Wireless Web site? Why or why not?

- How could the clock.php function add value to MobileHelper? Would it be better for users to see task times as text or images?

- Write a WML deck that enables you to change the various parameters—$happy, $width, and $height—passed to smile.php using <select>/<event> or <input> tags. What happens if you call smile.php with rectangular shapes where the image's width and height are unequal?

- WMLClientScreenSize uses an in-code array to store screen size data for clients. This isn't the best solution, because as you learn about new clients, you need to make changes to wml.php. How would you read this information from a static file? (Hint: See the discussion of PHP file I/O functions in the last chapter, or consult the section on PHP file I/O in the PHP manual.) Better yet, from a functional standpoint, how would you store this information in a database?

- How would you modify clock.php to draw a line of text below the clock face with the current time? Which is easier, including the text in the image or in the deck? Why?

- The clock.php script has one problem that makes it unusable for many: it shows the local time on the server, not the user's current time. PHP offers the gmtime function, which returns the current time in GMT. How would you modify clock.php and clock.wml to enable the user to set and store their timezone and show the time at the user's location rather than the server's location?

#### CHAPTER 9

Client Independence

WHEN BUILDING MORE COMPLEX Wireless Web sites, you're faced with the challenge of supporting different kinds of clients. Many different Wireless Web browsers—*user agents*—access your Wireless Web content. To make your site compelling for your customers, you want to tune your presentation for each user agent. Moreover, many Wireless Web sites need to offer their content to non-WAP clients, such as PDAs running Web browsers over wireless modems. Fortunately, you can use scripts to minimize the work you must do to bring your content to different user agents.

In this chapter, I look at two of the most common techniques using PHP, *per-agent content* and *XML style sheets*. Neither is specific to PHP, so as you read about these you can apply what you learn to other active server platforms, including Java servlets and Microsoft ASP. I begin with an overview of the two approaches so that you determine which is appropriate for your site. Then I look in detail at each, and show you how to use XML style sheets so that both WAP and HTML browsers can access MobileHelper.

Fundamentals of Client Independence

The crux of the client independence problem is simple: different user agents support different features. For example, although WAP is a standard, handsets running the Nokia browser and handsets running the Phone.com browser support different font options and a different interface for customized user interfaces. As a developer, you want your content to look good, regardless of the platform; to look its best, your material should take advantage of as many platform features as are available. At the same time, you want to minimize the effort you expend to support different platforms. This problem is exacerbated if you're adding wireless support to an existing Web site, or you want to offer your material to users on both the Wireless Web and the Web. Suddenly, you need to support both WAP and HTML.

You have three options. First, you may be able to create content that is available to all platforms. This is an option for many WAP developers producing smart phone content because most smart phones support the same WAP features, differing only in small things such as soft key presentation. It's not an option if you need to support drastically different devices (PDAs and smart phones running WML browsers, for example) or different markup languages, such as WML and HTML.

A second approach is to divide the kinds of hardware that will access your site into similarly featured classes and create unique content for each class of device. This method, which I call *per-agent content*, enables you to tune your content to different sets of devices, making as few tradeoffs as possible. This method works well if you can afford to manage different versions of your content, especially if the number of device classes is small and you have a limited amount of content with which to work.

A third approach combines the best of both worlds. You can abstract your content from its presentation using the eXtensible Markup Language, and let your scripts merge your content with the appropriate formatting, using style sheets on the server as a client requests a document. This method, which I call *content abstraction,* is more complicated because you need to spend extra effort up front defining your content's XML representation and how it will be formatted on each client. On the other hand, once your site has transitioned, content developers need not worry about the details of presentation, unless they need to add support for wholly new devices or markup languages.

Let's look more closely at per-agent content and content abstraction to see how each applies to your content.

Per-Agent Content

Per-agent content is the simplest way to handle divergent user agents such as WAP and HTML browsers. In many cases, it's as simple as posting two different sets of content to two different URLs, such as `http://wap.yourservice.com` and `http://www.yourservice.com`. This is a good way to tackle the problem when you have static content or your content changes only infrequently.

In other cases, you may want more granularity. For example, one site I maintain needs to provide support for three different kinds of browsers: desktop Web browsers, PDA browsers that synchronize with the Web, and WAP browsers. Each of these has its own unique requirements. For example, desktop Web browsers have large screens and high-speed Web connections that make the traditional site-of-many pages approach appropriate. Synchronized browsers on PDAs, however, must download a snapshot of all the content the user wants, and store it on a small device in very little memory. Consequently, they need access to pared-down content that makes little use of tables, graphics, or other fancy Web features. Moreover, the WAP version must be slimmer still and marked up using WML. In this case, offering different URLs for each site isn't just tacky; it's downright confusing.

Instead, the scripts that serve the site look at the HTTP headers to determine which version of content to return to each client. As a client requests the base

URL, the server examines the incoming HTTP headers and produces content appropriate for a desktop computer, handheld computer, or WAP terminal.

The two headers best suited to determining the kind of client to serve are the HTTP `Accept` and `User-Agent` headers. With the `Accept` header, you can check to see if the client accepts HTML or WAP, while with the `User-Agent` header you can often tell whether the client is a high-bandwidth client such as a desktop computer or a low-bandwidth computer such as a PDA running AvantGo. If you need to support localized content in different languages, you want to use the HTTP `Accept-Language` header as well.

The simplest way to use scripts to support per-agent content is to use them to detect the client's attributes and select a static Web site based on the characteristics the script detects. For example, your server can have static content in HTML and WML in separate directories, and the scripts can load content from the appropriate directory. This works well for small sites with static content or only the occasional dynamic page, but of course you have to keep all the different versions of the content current.

Other times you can organize your content so your scripts insert markup tags within your content before passing it to the client. Much as MobileHelper's scripts insert WML tags after fetching tasks from the database, this trick works well for simple dynamic sites.

The problem with this approach becomes apparent as your site grows. To add a new kind of client, you must update the script's criteria for matching clients with HTTP headers, and add new code to format your content for the new device. This quickly becomes impractical in many situations because modifying the scripts requires programming skills most content developers simply don't have. While you can mitigate these problems using tools that automate some of the process, as you invest more time in developing tools, you approach exactly the solution that XML provides. Consequently, if your site changes often enough that per-agent content isn't practical, it's probably easiest to move to abstracting your content with XML.

Content Abstraction

Rather than keeping multiple copies of your content in different formats, one solution is to keep one copy of your content in a format that scripts for all clients can access in their native formats.

You can do this using custom software and your own markup language, but it's much easier to use the industry-standard XML for this because tools abound to help you. Although using XML can be complicated, it is easier to learn to use standard technologies instead of developing your own custom solution, which won't be as flexible in the long run. Figure 9-1 shows a deployment diagram demonstrating how this works.

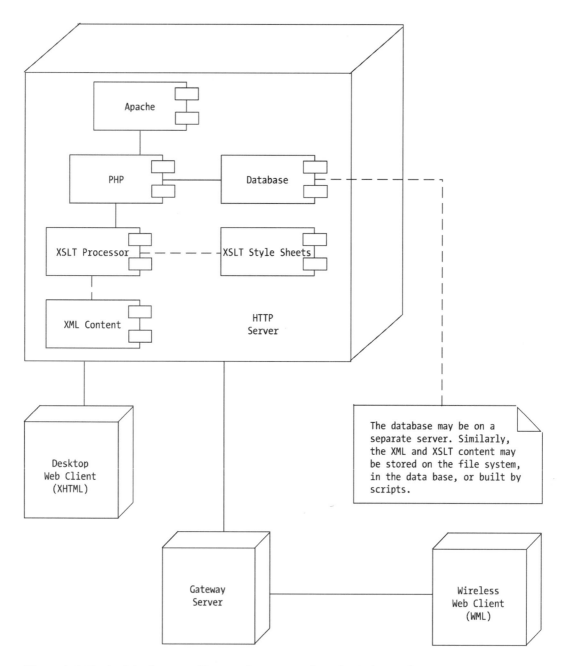

Figure 9-1. Typical deployment diagram for an XML-based Wireless Web service

This diagram has a number of new components you haven't encountered before. In addition to the Apache Web server, PHP interpreter, and database that are at the heart of an active Web site, there are also the *XSL processor, XML content,* and *XSL style sheets.* Together, these enable you to write your content in an abstract markup language based on XML and free of device constraints, specify how your markup language should be formatted on different clients using XSL style sheets, and merge real-time content in response to client requests using the XSL processor.

To develop a site that uses content abstraction, you proceed through your inception and elaboration phases a little differently. As you begin your design, you need to answer additional questions, including:

- What kinds of clients will access your site?

- What markup language does each class of client use to the greatest advantage?

- What scripting language does your server use?

- What content-specific markup tags do you need to describe your content?

- Is there an XML language you can use to describe your data?

For most sites, the last two questions are most important. With XML, you define your own markup language specific to your application. As I show you in Chapter 1, XML describes a common syntax for a family of markup languages. In some cases, you can find a markup language based on XML that describes your content; this is especially true for commonly accessed content such as news stories or financial market information.

You create tags for each separate datum in your content. For example, MobileHelper has tags to describe task titles, descriptions, and task links to tasks, as well as location titles and location information. The markup language you create is similar to the schema you use to describe your data, although some key differences exist.

First, while a schema must describe the bits-and-bytes representation of your data in a database, your XML markup language need only provide tags that describe the nature of your content. In other words, XML describes the meaning of each piece of your content, rather than its representation.

Second, your XML language doesn't need to worry about the independence between different kinds of records. When creating a schema you use indirection to ensure that you store each piece of information only once, but XML doesn't suffer from this restriction.

Nonetheless, your schema has valuable hints. In general, any column whose data is displayed to the user is a candidate for inclusion as a tag. Similarly, those columns that your scripts only use to maintain your data—such as id columns or columns that refer to ids in other tables—probably don't need to have an XML tag.

Once you identify the tags that describe your data in XML, you need to decide how each client should format the contents of each XML tag. Different browsers use different styles; for example, MobileHelper's HTML clients use the HTML header `<h1>` tag to display a task's title, while WML clients might use a more prosaic centered paragraph through `<p align="centered">`.

You code this format information using the XML style sheet language XSL, itself an XML markup language. In XSL you describe the relationship between your content's markup tags and the destination markup language (such as WML or HTML) tags. You write one XSL document describing this relationship for each class of device your site supports. Using XML and XSL, you can convert XML documents from one XML application, such as WML, to another, such as XHTML, the XML-compliant version of HTML. Because most modern browsers support XHTML, the XML/XSL combination enables you to separate your document's markup from its presentation.

> **NOTE** *XHTML is similar enough to HTML that you will understand it as soon as you see it. The key difference between HTML and XHTML is the distinction between tags with content, such as `<p>`, and empty tags, such as `<br/>`. In HTML, you can get away with writing `<br>`, and the browser understands that there is no trailing `</br>`. In XHTML, you must write `<br/>` because the `<br/>` tag is an empty tag with no content and ending `</br>`. XHTML is based on HTML 4.01.*

Before you can see your content, some application—either a user-agent, server-side script, or external program—must merge your content in XML with the XSL page for the user-agent you use. Some desktop browsers such as Microsoft Internet Explorer can work directly with XML and XSL pages, although of course Wireless Web clients cannot because XML and XSL are too expensive for today's wireless handsets and networks. Instead, it's more common for servers to do the necessary transformation on behalf of user agents as they access each document.

If all of this appears to be a lot of work, that's because it is! XML-based solutions are commonplace for large-scale servers such as those used by major Web site portals and large-scale intranet sites, but they're seldom a choice for small sites. It's only been within the last eighteen months (as I write this) that developers have assembled the components you need to create full-scale content abstraction solutions, even though all of the pieces have been around for some time. Over the coming year, expect to see a number of applications and tools to make it all easier.

When choosing whether per-agent content or XML-based content abstraction is right for your site, consider the tradeoffs inherent in each. Setting up a site that serves content on a per-agent basis is relatively simple, but maintaining the site can quickly become a nightmare. On the other hand, a robust content abstraction strategy requires that you understand not just WML, HTML, and a server-side scripting language, but XSL, the essence of creating a markup language with XML, and the additional support your server-side scripting language provides for merging XML with style sheets. Together, all of this information makes getting your site up and running much more difficult. Once it's operational, however, you can quickly and easily support new clients just by adding additional style sheets.

Getting Started with Per-Agent Content

The most difficult part of setting up a site to support per-agent content is defining what classes of clients your server supports. Once you determine what classes of clients your site will support, it's fairly easy to rework your scripts so that the appropriate content is sent to each kind of client.

Setting Up The Server

If you plan to use only the HTTP `Accept` and `User-Agent` strings to identify the user agent, the only work you need to do on the server is decide how to organize scripts for each class of user agent your site supports.

As a general rule of thumb, I like to create a separate script directory for each class of client. In the following example, in which I adapt MobileHelper to support both HTML and WML clients, I divide the scripts into two directories: html and wml. If I need to, I can add additional directories, such as html-small for small devices like PDAs or smart phones that display HTML.

A related strategy if you store your content in a database is to use separate tables to store the content for each markup language. This works well if your organization has application-specific tools that let you maintain content independent of a markup language, although if you're doing that on your own, you might as well just use XML and XSL and get all the benefits of a standard solution.

HTTP `Accept` Header Example

Let's look at a simple script that uses the HTTP `Accept` header to decide whether to send HTML or WML to the client. Listing 9-1 shows login.php, which selects either the login.html or login.wml page when you access the script.

```
01: <?php
02: /*******************************************************
03:  * login.php
04:  *
05:  * This module examines the HTTP Accept header and sends
06:  * either an HTML or a WML file depending on the browser's
07:  * preference.
08:  *******************************************************/
09: if ( strstr( $HTTP_ACCEPT, "wml" ) )
10: {
11:   header( "Content-type: text/vnd.wap.wml" );
12:   readfile( "login.wml" );
13: }
14: elseif (strstr( $HTTP_ACCEPT, "*/*" ) ||
15:        strstr( $HTTP_ACCEPT, "html" ) )
16: {
17:   header( "Content-type: text/html" );
18:   readfile( "login.html" );
19: }
20: ?>
```

Listing 9-1. The login.php script using the HTTP Accept *header*

The conditional statements on lines 9, 10, and 15 are trivial. On lines 9 and 15, I use the PHP string search function strstr to look for "html" and "wml", respectively. On line 15, the script checks for the Accept value of */*, signifying any MIME type. Desktop browsers such as Microsoft Internet Explorer use this value to indicate support for MIME types supported by their plug-ins, rather than sending a long list of supported types.

The script uses the HTTP header function on lines 12 and 17 to send the appropriate MIME type to the client because, although it may ask for a particular MIME type, it makes no assumptions about the resulting MIME type. On lines 13 and 18, the script uses the PHP function readfile, which opens the file given and sends its contents to the client.

NOTE *Some browsers, notably the Phone.com UP.SDK, include text/html as a valid MIME type in the HTTP* Accept *header even though they fail to display HTML. Consequently, code such as Listing 9-1 must either preferentially send WML to those clients that prefer it, or examine the* User-Agent *string in addition to the* Accept *string to work around this problem.*

Getting Started with Content Abstraction

Using content abstraction with your site is more complex than using per-agent content. You need to add support for XML and XSL to PHP and structure your content using XML instead of WML. Then, you need to write the XSL files for each class of device that accesses your site, and write the PHP scripts that will merge your style sheets and XML content.

Setting Up the Server with XML and XSL

PHP supports XML and XSL via two external modules: the XML module and the XSL module. These modules add functions to PHP that enable you to interpret XML documents and XSL documents. In turn, these modules require additional components: the expat library written by James Clark, and the Sablotron library, written by Ginger Alliance. Like PHP, these are freely available, but not part of the source distribution (see the sidebar). The Sablotron and expat libraries may not be included with all binary builds of PHP; you can test for their existence using the phpinfo function as I describe in Chapter 5. Look for the *sablot* and *xml* modules.

Installing expat and Sablotron for PHP

The expat library—and its incorporation in PHP—has been around virtually forever, at least in terms of Web time. PHP includes a lightweight version of the expat library by default, although to use Sablotron you'll need the latest version of the full expat library. As I write this, Sablotron support in PHP is well-established, but the underlying Sablotron library is undergoing regular change. Consequently, you should visit www.php.net to update PHP before trying to use the Sablotron module.

The version of PHP precompiled for Microsoft Windows includes Sablotron as this goes to press (on Microsoft Windows, be sure the folder containing PHP's DLL files is named in your %SYSTTEMPATH% so PHP can load the DLLs when it needs them), but most of the other platforms require you to rebuild PHP with full expat and Sablotron support. To do this, you must get expat from http://www.jclark.com/xml/expat.html and Sablotron from http://www.gingerall.com.

By now, you know the drill: download the sources, follow the installation instructions for both expat and Sablotron, and rebuild PHP using the **configure** options for expat and sablotron (--with-xml and --with-sablot) in addition to any other options such as --with-mysql that you want to use. After reconfiguring, be sure to rebuild with the **make** and **make install** commands as well.

Together, the XML and XSL modules add a number of new functions to PHP that enable you to parse XML documents, parse XSL documents, and apply XSL documents to XML documents. In normal use, you use only a few XSL functions that initialize an XSL parser and merge your XML with an XSL document.

Abstracting Content

MobileHelper uses XML tags to mark up tasks, locations, task lists, and so on. I define the XML tag <message> to contain a plain text message, such as an error or illegal login message. Let's look at how MobileHelper converts an XML <message> tag to either WML or HTML.

Generating the XML

As you saw in Chapter 5, the logininvalid.php script tells you when you mis-enter your MIN and PIN. Listing 9-2 shows the logininvalid.php script using XML and XSL.

```
01: <?php
02: if ( !$dbLink ) include "db.php";
03: // Filter our output through the client stylesheet.
04:
05: $xsltref = xslt_create();
06: $xslt = join( '', file( DBStyleSheetForClient() ) );
07:
08: // Invalid MIN or PIN.
09:
10: $content = '<?xml version="1.0" standalone="yes"?>' .
11:    "\n<mobilehelper key=\"$key\" " .
12:    "action=\"login.php\" alabel=\"Log In\">\n";
13:
14: $content .= "<message>" .
15:    "Either the MIN or PIN you entered was invalid. " .
16:    "Please try again, or contact your Coordinator " .
17:    "for a new PIN.</message>\n";
18:
19: $content .= "</mobilehelper>\n";
20:
21: // Send results
22:
23: header( "Content-type: " . DBMimeTypeForClient() );
24: header( "Cache-control: 300" );
25:
```

```
26: xslt_process( $xslt, $content, $result );
27:
28: print( $result );
29:
30: // Clean up XSLT Processor
31:
32: xslt_free($xsltref);
33:
34: ?>
```

Listing 9-2. The logininvalid.php script

Most of this should be familiar to you so let's focus on the XML support. The script builds a simple XML document in `$content`; by line 20, `$content` contains the XML shown in Listing 9-3.

> **NOTE** *Because XML doesn't preserve white space, the actual results from the XML and XSL processing can be rather ugly to read. In Listing 9-3 and subsequent listings in which I show the XML output from the XSL processor, I've added white space to make the XML more readable.*

```
01: <?xml version="1.0" standalone="yes"?>
02:
03: <mobilehelper key="nutmeg" action="login.php" alabel="Log In">
04:   <message>
05:     Either the MIN or PIN you entered was invalid.
06:     Please try again, or contact your Coordinator
07:     for a new PIN.
08:   </message>
09: </mobilehelper>
```

Listing 9-3. XML contained in `$content` *in Listing 9-2*

This looks strikingly like a WML document because WML itself is an XML-based markup language. On the first line, the document declares that it's an XML document using XML 1.0, and that it does not rely on other documents for processing directives. Because it's *my* XML application, however, I define my own tags: `<mobilehelper>` and `<message>`.

I use the `<mobilehelper>` tag to denote MobileHelper documents. I show you the various attributes I define for this tag later in this chapter; for now, you can see that the tag has three attributes: a `key` attribute defining the session key, an `action` attribute defining a destination URL (login.php) and an `alabel` attribute that labels any link to this URL. The `<message>` tag bears the document's message: a simple error message telling you that you mis-entered your MIN and PIN.

Converting from XML to WML or XHTML

Of course, browsers don't understand the `<mobilehelper>` and `<message>` tags. Some browsers—notably Netscape 6.0 and Microsoft Internet Explorer 5.0—do a tolerably good job of displaying XML documents like this, using syntax coloring to show the various tags and their contents. However, that's not what I want; I want to use PHP and an XSL document to translate these application-specific tags into conventional formatting tags in either HTML or WML.

Returning to Listing 9-2, line 5 uses the PHP function `xlst_create`, defined by the XSL module, to load the XSL interpreter.

On line 6, the script first selects a style sheet using my `DBStyleSheetForClient` function, defined in db.php. This function, which I discuss in detail in the section "The MobileHelper Scripts" later in this chapter, uses logic similar to Listing 9-1 to decide whether the script should use the wml.xsl or html.xsl style sheet to convert my XML into WML or HTML, respectively. Line 6 then uses the `file` function to load the contents of the selected style sheet into an array, one entry in the array per line of the file. The `file` function is handy when you need to quickly load the contents of an entire file into an array. This array is then merged into a single string using `join`, which iterates over each item in the array, concatenating the array element with the given string to create one big string. Thus, after line 6 executes, the variable `$xslt` contains either the contents of wml.xsl or html.xsl.

On line 23, the script reports the resulting MIME type—either text/html or text/vnd.wap.wml—to the client. `DBMimeTypeForClient`, like `DBStyleSheetForClient`, simply uses the HTTP `Accept` header to determine the appropriate MIME type. (Of course, the logic in these functions ensures that the MIME type `DBMimeTypeForClient` matches the style sheet indicated by `DBStyleSheetForContent`.) Line 24 simply provides a `Cache-control` HTTP header, indicating that this file should remain in the browser's cache for five minutes.

The XML translation occurs with the magic invocation on line 26. The PHP XSL module function `xslt_process` takes an XSL document and an XML document, and converts the XML document using the XSL instructions to return a new XML document. The resulting XML document—either WML or XHTML—is sent to the client on line 28, and on line 32,the XSL processor is freed.

The XSL style for the <message> tag

Listing 9-4 shows a fragment of html.xsl that Listing 9-2 uses to generate the XHTML document shown in Listing 9-5. XSL is a *transformational* markup language: its tags specify transformations that the XSL processor should make when moving the XML document from one XML dialect to another.

```
01: <?xml version="1.0"?>
02:
03: <xsl:stylesheet
04:  xmlns:xsl="http://www.w3.org/1999/XSL/Transform"
05:  version="1.0">
06:
07: <!-- Match the document itself -->
08: <xsl:template match="/">
09:   <html>
10:     <head>
11:       <title>
12:         MobileHelper
13:       </title>
14:     </head>
15:     <xsl:apply-templates/>
16:   </html>
17: </xsl:template>
18:
19: <!-- Match the mobilehelper tag -->
20: <xsl:template match="mobilehelper">
21:   <body>
22:     <h1>
23:       MobileHelper
24:     </h1>
25:     <xsl:apply-templates/>
26:     <xsl:if test="@action|@prev">
27:       <p align="center">
28:         <hr/>
29:         <xsl:if test="@action">
30:           <a href="{@action}?key={@key}">
31:             |<xsl:value-of select="@alabel"/>|
32:           </a>
```

```
33:        </xsl:if>
34:        <xsl:if test="@prev">
35:          <a href="{@prev}?key={@key}">
36:            |<xsl:value-of select="@plabel"/>|
37:          </a>
38:        </xsl:if>
39:      </p>
40:    </xsl:if>
41:  </body>
42: </xsl:template>
43:
44: <!-- Match the message tag -->
45: <xsl:template match="message">
46:   <p>
47:     <xsl:value-of select="."/>
48:   </p>
49: </xsl:template>
50: </xsl:stylesheet>
```

Listing 9-4. A fragment of html.xsl.

Listing 9-4 begins with the usual XML preamble. The first line states the version of XML the file uses, while the second line states that this file is an XSL style sheet in accordance to the version 1.0 definition found at `http:// www.w3.org/1999/XSL/Transform`.

> **CAUTION** *XML standards, including those for XSL, require parsers to expect well-formed XML documents that include things like the `<?xml?>` and `<xsl:stylesheet/>` tags. Consequently, XSL interpreters such as the Sablotron interpreter PHP uses are notoriously picky and won't interpret your XSL files unless you include these tags. Forgetting these tags can be a common source of frustration for you as you start out.*

With XSL, you define *templates* that the interpreter applies as it finds matching patterns, such as tags and attributes. Listing 9-4 defines three templates: the document itself (matched by the special pattern "/"), the `<mobilehelper>` tag, and the `<message>` tag. You define each template using the `<xsl:template>` tag, which contains XML markup the interpreter inserts in lieu of the matching tag.

The first template, on lines 8–17, matches the entire document. As the XSL processor parses the XML document, it automatically applies the template matching the "/" (pronounced "root"). Thus, the processor replaces the input document with the `<html>…</html>` tags on lines 9–16.

XSL defines additional tags, such as the `<xsl:value-of/>` and `<xsl:apply-templates/>` tags that enable you to access pieces of the source document when creating the final document. For example, the `<xsl:apply-templates/>` tag on line 15 instructs the processor to look for tags matching the other templates in the input after outputting the closing `</head>` tag.

Thus, the processor creates the XHTML in Listing 9-5 from the XML in Listing 9-3 using the following steps:

1. The processor matches the root of the document, and outputs an XML preamble and the beginning `<html>` tag as well as the `<head>` tag on lines 9–15 of Listing 9-4.

2. The processor scans the input file looking for tags that match either of the other two templates in Listing 9-4.

3. The processor matches the `<mobilehelper>` tag in the input XML.

4. The processor outputs the beginning of `<body>` tag and the `<h1>` tag on lines 21–24 of Listing 9-4 before continuing to look for `<mobilehelper>` or `<message>` tags.

5. The processor matches the `<message>` tag in the input XML.

6. The processor outputs an opening `<p>` tag according to line 46 of the style sheet, followed by the contents of the `<message>` tag and then the closing `</p>` tag.

7. The processor finds no more tags in the input XML.

8. The processor evaluates the `<xsl:if>` tags on lines 26–38, which test for `<mobilehelper>` attributes named `<action>` and `<prev>`. On line 26, the `<xsl:if>` test matches the action attribute in the input, and the processor outputs the `<p align="center">` and `<hr/>` tags before matching the next `<xsl:if>` tag on line 29.

9. The processor successfully matches the `<xsl:if>` tag on line 29 with the action attribute of the `<mobilehelper>` tag in the input, and outputs the XHTML `<a>` anchor tag and the value of the `<mobilehelper>` alabel tag on line 31.

10. The processor fails the `<xsl:if>` test looking for a `<mobilehelper>` prev attribute on line 34, and continues by outputting the closing paragraph and closing body tags on lines 39 and 41.

11. The processor returns to the root template, and outputs the closing `</html>` tag.

12. The processor exits.

Listing 9-5 shows the XHTML output from the XSL processor, while Figure 9-2 shows the XHTML in Microsoft Internet Explorer and the WML (not listed here) in the Yospace SPEDE.

```
01: <html>
02:   <head>
03:     <meta http-equiv="Content-Type"
04:       content="text/html;
05:       charset=UTF-8">
06:     <title>
07:     </title>
08:   </head>
09:   <body>
10:     <h1>
11:       MobileHelper
12:     </h1>
13:     <p>
14:       Either the MIN or PIN you entered was invalid.
15:       Please try again, or contact your Coordinator
16:       for a new PIN.
17:     </p>
18:     <p align="center">
19:       <hr/>
20:       <a href="login.php?key=">
21:         |Log In|
22:       </a>
23:     </p>
24:   </body>
25: </html>
```

Listing 9-5. The XHTML rendition of Listing 9-3

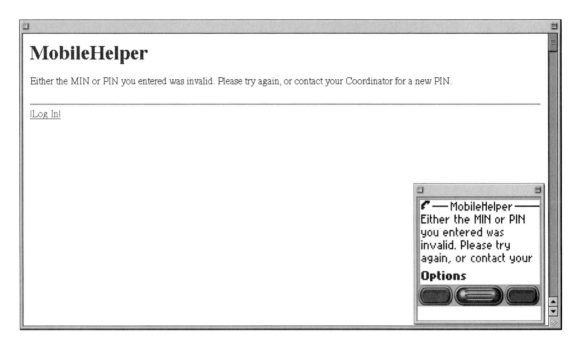

Figure 9-2. The XHTML of Listing 9-5, along with a browser showing comparable WML

Going Further with Content Abstraction

Although XML, XSL, and the PHP functions that support XML and PHP aren't complicated, piecing them altogether can be. It's a lot like painting: each of the individual colors and brushes are pretty easy to understand, but making the canvas look like something other than a muddy field takes a bit of forethought and a lot of practice.

XML Syntax

So far, I've largely neglected XML syntax. Because other markup languages—such as WML—are based on XML, it's easiest for you to learn XML by example. XML is an extendible language—you define the tags and their meanings, rather than using tags with set meanings like paragraph, task, and so on. By now, these rules are familiar to you because you have spent so much time working with WML.

As with other markup languages, XML uses tags interspersed with your content to denote meaning. You write XML tags as text between angle brackets < and > (the greater-than and less-than symbols). Opening tags are written like <this>, while closing tags are written like </this>. Tags without content—so-called *empty tags*—are written using a trailing solidus, like this: <br/>. Tag names must begin with a letter or an underscore _, and may contain letters, digits, underscores, hyphens, and periods. XML tags are case-sensitive, so `<p>` is *not* the same as `<P>`.

XML has a few special tags, too, which you've already seen. The `<?xml?>` tag identifies an XML document, while the `<!DOCTYPE>` tag identifies the kind of XML document, such as WML or XHTML. A number of XML applications, such as the Document Type Definition, which you can use to specify a formal syntax for your XML tags, uses other tags delimited by `<!` and `>`. (You can share a DTD with other developers, who can use the DTD to ensure that the XML they write matches your specification.)

XML tags belong to one or more *name spaces*. A *name space* is simply a well-defined prefix that enables developers to create a unique set of tag names without using tags that another XML application is using. For example, XSL uses tags within the `xsl` name space. To refer to a tag in a specific name space, you prefix the name of the tag with the name of the name space and a colon, like this: `<xsl:stylesheet>`.

Any tag may have one or more attributes. An attribute is a name/value pair that provides additional information about a tag. The name follows the same rules as a tag name: begin with an alphabetic character or an underscore, and follow with letters, numbers, hyphens, underscores, and periods. Attribute values are always strings contained between double quotes.

XML defines four entities to represent special characters that XML reserves for its own use. Table 9-1 shows these entities.

Table 9-1. XML Entities

ENTITY	CHARACTER	NOTE
&amp;	&	Ampersand
&lt;	<	Less than symbol
&gt;	>	Greater than symbol
&quot;	"	Quote

You can include comments in your XML, too, by enclosing the comments within the `<!--` and `-->` characters, as I did on lines 7, 19, and 44 of Listing 9-4. You can't put comments before the `<?xml?>` declaration, however, or within a tag itself. You can also use white space wherever you like, except between characters of a tag or attribute.

XML provides the notion of the *well-formed* XML document, which XML parsers must be able to interpret. Well-formed XML documents have the following properties:

- The `<?xml?>` declaration must be the first thing in the document.

- The document should contain exactly one tag that encloses all other tags.

- Tags may be nested but may not overlap other tags.

- Tags that contain content must have matching start and end tags.

- Tags that do not contain content must end in `/>`.

- Attribute values must be quoted using `""`.

By following these rules, any XML document can be represented as a *tree*. A tree is a data structure that has connected nodes, beginning with a single node called the "root." In turn, the root connects to one or more nodes, called *children*, which themselves may have children. For example, Figure 9-3 shows the XML document in Listing 9-6 as a tree.

```
01: <?xml version="1.0" standalone="yes"?>
02:
03: <mobilehelper session="Nutmeg">
04:
05:    <tasklist name="Open Tasks">
06:
07:    <task id="1">
08:       <name>First Night</name>
09:       <sstart>
10:          <date>01-01-2001</date>
11:          <time>12:00</time>
12:       </sstart>
13:       <sstop>
14:          <date>01-01-2001</date>
15:          <time>14:00</time>
16:       </sstop>
17:    </task>
18:
19:    </tasklist>
20: </mobilehelper>
```

Listing 9-6. An XML document

Listing 9-6 shows more XML tags used by MobileHelper to represent a list of tasks, such as the lists of open or assigned tasks displayed by the Web application.

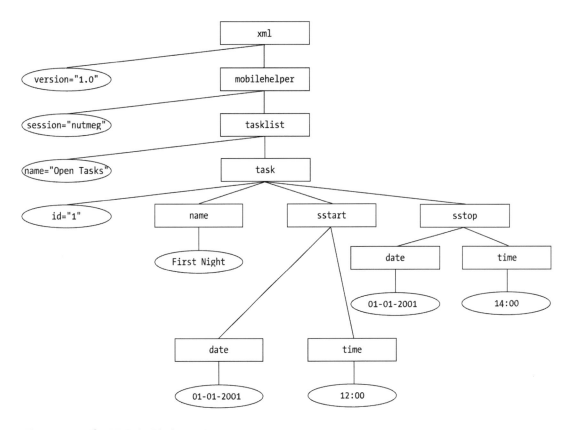

Figure 9-3. The XML in Listing 9-6 as a tree

IIn the figure, the `<task>` tags are children of the `<mobilehelper>` tag, while the `<location>` tags are children of `<task>` tags. Note that tag attributes are nodes as well, as are XML comments.

Many aspects of XML—including XSL—use this notion of a document as a tree. XSL, for example, lets you refer to tags and attributes within the structure of the tree, giving you very fine granularity when selecting tags and attributes for transformations.

You should be aware of two parts of XML that help you exchange your XML applications with other developers. XML provides the Document Type Definition (DTD), which you can use to describe the precise syntax of your tags, including details such as which attributes work with which tags, and which tags may contain other tags. Organizations such as the WAP Forum use a DTD to formalize their markup language (in the case of WAP, it's the WML DTD, found at http://www.wapforum.org/DTD/wml_1.1.xml). A newer mechanism, XML schemas, enables you to do the same thing using a more flexible language. Both of these actually use the XML syntax so you need only learn the tags for these XML applications to begin formalizing your own XML applications.

XSL Syntax

XSL enables you to define *templates* that specify how the XSL processor maps XML tags from one XML application to another. As you already know, XSL is an XML application itself: the tags and syntax follow the same rules as XML. All XSL tags are in the `xsl` name space, so XSL tags won't conflict with your XML tags.

XSL documents begin with the `<?xml?>` preamble, followed by the `<xsl:stylesheet>` tag. This tag contains the XSL style sheet and defines the `xsl` name space. The optional `version` attribute for the `<xsl:stylesheet>` tag—which you should be in the habit of including—states the version of XSL your document uses.

Within the `<xsl:stylesheet>` tag, your XSL document contains one or more `<xsl:template>` tags, each of which defines a pattern the XSL processor matches in the sourcpe document. The XSL processor begins by matching the template that identifies the root of the source document, and continues matching when it encounters additional `xsl` tags such as `<xsl:apply-templates/>`. The templates you write use the tag's `match` attribute to identify the XML you want to match. This `match` attribute takes advantage of XSL's pattern matching to let you test the incoming XML for tags, tag hierarchies, or tags possessing specific attributes. Within the `match` attribute, you use the XML document's tree representation to refer to specific tags, also called *nodes*, on the document tree. Like documents on your hard drive, you begin by denoting the tree's root, with a single solidus (/), and then the names of each tag, delimited by solidus (/) characters.

You can specify absolute positions on the tree, such as / (the root), or relative positions on the tree by omitting the leading / designation. Looking back at Figure 9-3, `/mobilehelper` refers to the top node of Listing 9-6, contained within the `<mobilehelper>` tag. You can refer to each of the `task` tags in a number of ways: `/mobilehelper/tasklist/task`, `mobilehelper/tasklist/task`, `tasklist/task`, or simply `task`. If you want to express ancestor-child relationships in the tree in a more general way, you can use two / characters in succession. For example, a `match` attribute `/mobilehelper//task` specifies nodes of `task` tags that have the `mobilehelper` tag as an ancestor anywhere, matching the `<task>` tags in Listing 9-6 as well. You can also specify nodes with wildcards; `/mobilehelper/*/task` matches `<task>` tags contained within any tag that is an immediate child of the `<mobilehelper>` tag.

Two less commonly used symbols you use when specifying nodes are .. and |. The .. lets you refer to the immediate parent of a node; for example, `../task` matches task nodes that are siblings (children of the current node's parent) of the current node, while .. simply matches the current node's parent. The | symbol, on the other hand, enables you to express multiple tags. For example, `timeinput|dateinput` matches either the `<timeinput>` or the `<dateinput>` tags.

In addition to writing paths, you can specify tests that enable you to test for paths containing attributes, paths without attributes, or either-or combinations of tags. XSL defines a number of functions you can use within path expressions, such as `not`. Test expressions are written within square brackets [ ], like the templates shown in Listing 9-7.

```
01: <?xml version="1.0"?>
02:
03: <xsl:stylesheet
04:  xmlns:xsl="http://www.w3.org/1999/XSL/Transform"
05:  version="1.0">
06:
07: <!-- excerpt from html.xsl -->
08:
09: <xsl:template match="tasklist[task]">
10:   <h2>
11:     <xsl:value-of select="@name"/>
12:   </h2>
13:   <p>
14:   <table>
15:     <xsl:for-each select="task">
16:       <tr>
17:         <td>
18:           <p>
19:           <xsl:value-of select="sstart/date"/>
20:           <xsl:text> </xsl:text>
21:           <xsl:value-of select="sstart/time"/>
22:           </p>
23:         </td><td>
24:           <p>
25:           <a href="{../@action}?id={@id}&#38;
    key={../../@key}">
26:             <xsl:value-of select="name"/>
27:           </a>
28:           </p>
29:         </td>
30:       </tr>
31:     </xsl:for-each>
32:   </table>
33:   </p>
34: </xsl:template>
35:
36: <xsl:template match="tasklist[not(task)]">
37:   <p>
38:     <xsl:value-of select="."/>
39:   </p>
40: </xsl:template>
41:
42: </xsl:stylesheet>
```

Listing 9-7. XSL templates with tests

The two templates in Listing 9-7 match lists of tasks to create an HTML table or a single paragraph if a task list is empty. In MobileHelper's XML, you write a list of tasks using `<task>` tags contained within a `<tasklist>` tag, all enclosed by the `<mobilehelper>` tag, as I did back in Listing 9-6. The first template, on lines 9–34, matches `<tasklist>` tags with one or more `<task>` tags. (Note that this template matches the `<tasklist>` tag, not the `<task>` tags within the `<tasklist>` tag; you'd match these `<task>` tags using either task or tasklist/task. The difference is subtle!). The second template, on lines 36–40, uses XSL's not function to test for `<tasklist>` tags that have no `<task>` childrenXSL.(More about the other tags in these templates in the next few pages.)

In addition to the not function, which matches any tag but its argument, XSL also has the four functions first-of-type, last-of-type, first-of-any, and last-of-any. You use the first two to match either the first or last use of a specific tag, while the other two match the first tag of any type and last tag of any type. Thus, the expression tasklist[first-of-type(task)] matches the first `<task>` tag within the `<tasklist>` tag, while the expression tasklist[first-of-any()] matches the first tag of any type within the `<tasklist>` tag. These functions enable you to create templates for elements that require initial or closing tags, such as tables or forms. There is also the comment function, which matches XML comment nodes in your document's tree.

> **NOTE** *It's bad practice to rely on comments in your XML for formatting information or other transformations. Comments are meant for people, not computers, to read. Use the* comment *function with care in specific circumstances only, such as creating human-readable documentation from an XML document that stylizes comments.*

To match an attribute, you need only precede the attribute with an @ symbol in a test. For example, task[@id] matches `<task>` tags with id attributes. As you saw in the section "Abstracting Content" previously in this chapter, the @ attribute enables you to match an attribute elsewhere, too, such as when extracting the value of an attribute to include in the output document.

Within the `<xsl:template>` tag you place the content that the style sheet processor copies from your template to the output document, as well as XSL markup directing the processor to copy pieces of your input document to your output document. All of the markup within the `<xsl:template>` (except, of course, for tags in the xsl name space, which are interpreted by the XSL processor), along with the markup's contents, are copied from the template to the output document.

Also within the `<xsl:template>` tag, you use the `<xsl:value-of/>` tag to copy the value of the tag or attribute you name in its select argument. As with the `<xsl:template>` tag, the select attribute may contain the name of a tag, or the name of an attribute, by preceding the attribute name with an @ symbol, or tests using XSL functions. You've already seen several examples of this; for example, the tag on line 26 in Listing 9-7 copies the contents of any `<name>` tags from the input to the output.

Sometimes you want to refer to the contents of a tag or an attribute in your input document from inside a tag of your template. You do this by writing the XML tag in the ordinary way, and including the attribute you want to include in curly braces {}. For example, the `tasklist[task]` template in Listing 9-7 on lines 9–34 must create a hyperlink between the task item and the server-side script that displays the task. It does this on line 25, where it constructs the `href` attribute of an `<a>` tag using attributes of the `<mobilehelper>`, `<tasklist>`, and `<task>` tags. Each `<task>` tag has an `id` attribute, which is the same as the `id` field in MobileHelper's database. To include the `id` attribute, I use {@id}, which fetches the `id` attribute of the current tag (a `<task>` tag, in this case). To obtain the name of the script in the target URL, the XSL processor converts the {../@action} expression at the beginning of the `href` attribute to the value of the `action` attribute belonging to the `<task>` tag's parent, `<tasklist>`. Similarly, the processor fetches the MobileHelper session key, given in the XML as the `key` attribute of the `<mobilehelper>` tag, using the expression {../../@key}.

As your template specifies the output document, it often needs to refer to other tags. For example, when creating a task list, a style sheet formatting MobileHelper's `<tasklist>` tag must show the contents of its `<task>` tags. You can do this in two ways: by applying other patterns in your style sheet using `<xsl:apply-templates/>`, or by iterating over tags within the current tag using `<xsl:for-each>`.

Most of the time you use `<xsl:apply-templates/>`, such as when you want to continue processing from your document's base tag. For example, MobileHelper's style sheet uses the `<xsl:apply-templates/>` tag within the template matching the `<mobilehelper>` tag to continue processing all tags within the `<mobilehelper>` tag (refer to Listing 9-4). You can also direct the XSL processor to apply templates for only certain tags, using the `<xsl:apply-templates/>` select attribute.

Occasionally, you won't want to use a tag's template, but instead want to format a tag differently. I have exactly this problem with `<task>` tags within a `<tasklist>`: `<task>` tags show all the information about a task, including its owner and location, but within a task list, the `<task>` tag shows only the task's time and title. Rather than creating two different tags, such as `<task>` for an entire task and `<tasklistitem>` for items within a task list, I use the `<xsl:for-each>` tag within the template for `<tasklist>` to select and format each `<task>` tag on lines 9–34 of Listing 9-7. On line 15, the `<xsl:for-each>` tag instructs the processor to iterate over all `<task>` tags, including the contents of the `<xsl:for-each>` tag between lines 15 and 31. Thus, for each `<task>` tag, the processor begins by writing opening table row (line 16), table cell (line 17), and paragraph (line 18) tags. Then it writes out the contents of the `<date>` tag within the `<sstart>` tag, followed by a single space within the `<xsl:text>` tag, and the contents of the `<time>` tag within the `<sstart>`

tag. Then the processor closes the paragraph and table cell (lines 22–23), and begins a new table cell and paragraph (lines 23–24) for the task's title. As I mentioned, the processor builds a unique URL for the title using the ‹tasklist› action attribute and ‹task› id attribute on line 25, including the name of the task on line 26 to identify the hyperlink. The style sheet then closes the hyperlink, paragraph, table cell, and table row.

In the section "Abstracting Content" earlier in this chapter, you encountered the ‹xsl:if› tag, which lets you conditionally include content if its test attribute is true. XSL also has the ‹xsl:choose› tag, which lets you specify a number of conditions, each with a ‹xsl:when› tag bearing a test attribute. The ‹xsl:choose› ‹xsl:when› tag pair is similar in concept to a chain of if-else-if statements; each ‹xsl:when› clause corresponds to a single if statement.

You can't directly include certain kinds of output in your template for your output document, such as the ‹!DOCTYPE› tag, comments, or literal white space. XSL provides the ‹xsl:output› tag to create a ‹!DOCTYPE› tag. As you can see from Listing 9-8, the tag enables you to state both the document's system using the doctype-system attribute and the public DTD of the document using the doctype-public attribute. Listing 9-8 creates the ‹!DOCTYPE› tag shown in Listing 9-9.

```
01: <xsl:output
02:   doctype-system="http://www.wapforum.org/DTD/wml_1.1.xml"
03:   doctype-public="-//WAPFORUM//DTD WML 1.1//EN"/>
```

Listing 9-8. The ‹xsl:output› *tag*

```
01: <!DOCTYPE wml PUBLIC "-//WAPFORUM//DTD WML 1.1//EN"
02:   "http://www.wapforum.org/DTD/wml_1.1.xml">
```

Listing 9-9. The results of the ‹xsl:output› *tag in Listing 9-8*

You use the ‹xsl:comment› to insert comments in your XML output document from your XSL. The contents of the ‹xsl:comment› tag are embedded in an XML comment, enabling you to add clarification to obtuse markup. Similarly, you use the ‹xsl:text› tag to include literal text from your style sheet in your output document. The content of the ‹xsl:text› tag, including white space, is copied exactly to the output document.

XSL Processing in PHP

Because your format-independent content is in XML, and your markup for formatting your content is in XSL, you need a way to combine the two. Enter PHP's

XSL processor, based on the Sablotron processor from Ginger Alliance. It, like similar XSL processors for Java servlets and other server-side scripting systems, takes an XML document and an XSL document, creating a new XML document by following the formatting instructions within the XSL document.

The XSL module's API in PHP is simple. First, you create an instance—called *instantiation*—of the XSL processor because PHP doesn't waste time and memory initializing the processor unless you need it. Then you invoke the processor to transform your XML according to the template in your XSL document, returning a new XML document. Finally, you free the XSL processor. You saw an example of the process in Listing 9-2; let's look at each of these steps in more detail.

Before you can use the XSL processor, you must call `xslt_create` to instantiate the XSL processor. This function takes no arguments and returns a handle to the XSL processor.

Once you instantiate the XSL processor, you can process one or more documents using the `xslt_process` function. This function takes three strings: the XSL document, the XML document, and a string that contains the resulting XML after the function call exits. On success, `xslt_process` returns true, while if the processing fails for some reason, it returns `0`.

Finally, when your script finishes using the XSL processor, be sure to call `xslt_free` to free the processor you allocate with `xslt_create`. Doing so will help PHP's memory performance.

Developing with XSL can be frustrating due to the paucity of error messages. By accepted convention, XML and XSL parsers accept only well-formed, exactly correct documents. With HTML, you can often get away with the occasional mistake, but XML doesn't offer such latitude. Consequently, you must work carefully to avoid errors. Moreover, the PHP function calls don't report errors by design because that could interfere with the output from some scripts. Instead, you use the functions `xslt_error` and `xslt_errno` to obtain error messages from the XSL processor. Typically, you call one of these functions if `xslt_process` returns false, and you print the result or save it to your debugging log for later analysis. The `xslt_errno` function returns the numeric error code of the last error and is suited to in-code diagnosis of errors, while the `xslt_error` function returns an error string you can use to troubleshoot problems when they occur.

Content Abstraction in MobileHelper

Modifying MobileHelper to produce XML content transformed by XSL involves minor changes throughout the application. First, I need to describe the XML tags MobileHelper uses to represent tasks, locations, and user input. These tags become the basis of MobileHelper's style sheets, which MobileHelper's scripts now use after generating XML to produce either WML or HTML.

The changes to the scripts are quite extensive, although the changes are restricted to MobileHelper's output. Each script must now determine what format content the client accepts, produce output in XML rather than WML, and then use the XSL processor to create the final output.

The MobileHelper XML Application

MobileHelper content describes tasks that people carry out at specific locations. This, along with a look at MobileHelper's database schema (see Chapter 5), hints at a number of tags MobileHelper requires to represent its content. You can glean additional clues by reviewing how MobileHelper interacts with clients: tags or attributes must let the application specify links between scripts and prompt for user input when closing tasks.

To satisfy XML's requirement that all well-formed documents are contained within a single tag, the <mobilehelper> tag encloses all other MobileHelper content. A <mobilehelper> tag contains an entire document, either a page for an HTML browser or a deck for a WML browser. Consequently, the <mobilehelper> tag carries both WML soft key assignments as well as the MobileHelper session key scripts use to obtain per-session variables from the session table in the MySQL database. The <mobilehelper> tag has the required attribute key to hold the session key, while the four attributes action, prev, alabel, and plabel let you assign actions and labels to the two soft keys on wireless browsers. You use the action and alabel attributes to assign a URL and label to the **Accept** soft key (typically for navigation in the forward direction), while you use the prev and plabel attributes to assign a URL and label to the **Cancel** soft key.

I chose to make the navigation information attributes, rather than tags, because navigation doesn't directly affect the meaning of MobileHelper content. For example, the notion of a task stands on its own, regardless of whether you're looking at it in the context of a task list, task, or when closing a task. This decision—whether a piece of information should be an attribute or a task—is one you're faced with repeatedly as you design your XML application. In general, you should use tags to represent salient pieces of your content, and you should restrict attributes for information about your content, called *metadata*. When in doubt, create tags for your information because it's easier to access your information from tags than attributes.

Within the <mobilehelper> tag you can place one of four other tags: the <task> tag, the <location> tag, the <tasklist> tag, or the <taskcloseinput> tag. Each of these tags corresponds to one of the major views in MobileHelper.

The <task> tag contains information about a specific task. Within the tag, you include the task's name, start time, stop time, and owner, each within its own tags. Each <task> tag carries an id attribute with the value of the task's id column in the database so that the style sheet processor can create links (say, between task list items and tasks). The task tag must contain a `<name>` tag that encloses the task's name, and may include `<location>` and `<owner>` tags that identify the task's location and owner. It may also include the `<sstart>` and `<sstop>` tags, each bearing a `<date>` and `<time>` tag, to specify the task's start and stop times. Listing 9-10 shows a sample document containing a single `<task>` tag.

```
01: <?xml version="1.0" standalone="yes"?>
02:
03: <mobilehelper session="Nutmeg">
04:    <task id="1">
05:    <name>First Night</name>
06:      <sstart>
07:        <date>01-01-2001</date>
08:        <time>12:00</time>
09:      </sstart>
10:      <sstop>
11:        <date>01-01-2001</date>
12:        <time>14:00</time>
13:      </sstop>
14:      <owner id="8885554444">
15:        <name>Ray</name>
16:    </owner>
17:    <location id="1" action="location.php?">
18:      <name>Mountain Fire Dept</name>
19:      <address>7700 East Road, Hillsdale</address>
20:      <phone>888-555-1212</phone>
21:    </location>
22:  </task>
23: </mobilehelper>
```

Listing 9-10. The `<task>` *tag*

When referring to a specific location, the `<mobilehelper>` tag may contain a `<location>` tag. Like the `<task>` tag, `<location>` tags carry an id attribute that contains the value of the location's id entry in the database. Within the `<location>` tag, you use the `<name>` address to specify the location's name, the `<address>` tag to specify the location's address, and the `<phone>` tag to specify the location's phone number. Lines 17–21 of Listing 9-10 show an example of the `<location>` tag. To support the `<location>` tag and its children `<name>`, `<address>`, and `<phone>`, MobileHelper's database schema is modified to provide separate columns for a location's address and phone number, and for comments associated with the location (see "Food for Thought" in Chapter 5).

In Listing 9-6 you saw an example of the `<tasklist>` tag; the listing is shown again in Listing 9-11 for your convenience. A `<tasklist>` tag simply contains one or more `<task>` tags, each delineating one task in the list. The `<tasklist>` tag has two attributes, `name` and `action`. The `name` attribute contains a human-readable name the style sheet will use to label the task list, such as **Open Tasks**. The `action` attribute contains the base URL for the script to execute on the server when you select a task item.

```
01: <?xml version="1.0" standalone="yes"?>
02:
03: <mobilehelper session="Nutmeg">
04:
05:   <tasklist name="Open Tasks">
06:
07:   <task id="1">
08:     <name>First Night</name>
09:     <sstart>
10:       <date>01-01-2001</date>
11:       <time>12:00</time>
12:     </sstart>
13:     <sstop>
14:       <date>01-01-2001</date>
15:       <time>14:00</time>
16:     </sstop>
17:     <owner id="8885554444">
18:       <name>Ray</name>
19:     </owner>
20:     <location id="1">
21:       <name>Mountain Fire Dept</name>
22:       <address>7700 East Road, Hillsdale</address>
23:       <phone>888-555-1212</phone>
24:     </location>
25:   </task>
26:
27:   <task id="3">
28:     <name>Communications</name>
29:     <sstart>
30:       <date>02-12-2001</date>
31:       <time>08:00</time>
32:     </sstart>
33:     <sstop>
34:       <date>02-12-2001</date>
35:       <time>14:00</time>
36:     </sstop>
```

```
37:      <owner id="8885554444">
38:        <name>Ray</name>
39:      </owner>
40:      <location id="1">
41:        <name>Mountain Fire Dept</name>
42:        <address>7700 East Road, Hillsdale</address>
43:        <phone>888-555-1212</phone>
44:      </location>
45:    </task>
46:
47:    </tasklist>
48: </mobilehelper>
```

Listing 9-11. The `<tasklist>` *tag*

MobileHelper defines the `<taskcloseinput>` tag to allow client-independent input of the actual start and stop times for a closed task. Like the `<task>` tag, the `<taskcloseinput>` tag uses its id attribute to carry the task's id field, and its action attribute carries the script on the server to execute when you finish entering data. The `<taskcloseinput>` tag contains a `<name>` tag, containing the name of the task you're closing, along with `<dateinput>` and `<timeinput>` tags, which prompt you for date and time information. Each of the `<dateinput>` and `<timeinput>` tags have name and value attributes, which correspond to the input field's name and default value attributes. However, unlike HTML and WML input fields, these tags may contain content, which is displayed before the actual input item. Listing 9-12 shows a `<taskcloseinput>` tag.

```
01: <?xml version="1.0" standalone="yes"?>
02:
03: <mobilehelper session="Nutmeg">
04:    <taskcloseinput id="1" action="taskclosedo.php">
05:      <name>First Night</name>
06:      <dateinput name="startdate" value="01-01-2001">
07:        Actual start date
08:      </dateinput>
09:      <timeinput name="starttime" value="12:00">
10:        Actual start time
11:      </timeinput>
12:      <dateinput name="stopdate" value="01-01-2001">
13:        Actual stop date
14:      </dateinput>
```

```
15:    <timeinput name="stoptime" value="14:00">
16:      Actual stop time
17:    </timeinput>
18:   </taskcloseinput>
19: </mobilehelper>
```

Listing 9-12. A `<taskcloseinput>` *tag*

MobileHelper also defines the catch-all `<message>` tag, which you use to contain a generic text message within a `<mobilehelper>` document.

The MobileHelper Style Sheets

MobileHelper has two XSL style sheets, one each for generating XHTML and WML. These style sheets have templates that match the tags discussed in the last section, enabling the XSL processor to convert MobileHelper's content-focused tags into format-focused tags in XHTML and WML. In previous sections of this chapter you saw pieces of the XHTML style sheet html.xsl. It's shown in its entirety in Listing 9-13.

```
01: <?xml version="1.0"?>
02:
03: <xsl:stylesheet
04:   xmlns:xsl="http://www.w3.org/1999/XSL/Transform"
05:   version="1.0">
06:
07: <xsl:template match="/">
08:   <html>
09:     <head>
10:       <title>
11:         <xsl:value-of select="/*/name"/>
12:       </title>
13:     </head>
14:     <xsl:apply-templates/>
15:   </html>
16: </xsl:template>
17:
18: <xsl:template match="mobilehelper">
19:   <body>
20:     <h1>
21:       MobileHelper
22:     </h1>
23:     <xsl:apply-templates/>
24:
```

```
25:      <xsl:if test="@action|@prev">
26:        <p align="center">
27:          <hr/>
28:          <xsl:if test="@action">
29:            <a href="{@action}?key={@key}">
30:              |<xsl:value-of select="@alabel"/>|
31:            </a>
32:          </xsl:if>
33:          <xsl:if test="@prev">
34:            <a href="{@prev}?key={@key}">
35:              |<xsl:value-of select="@plabel"/>|
36:            </a>
37:          </xsl:if>
38:        </p>
39:      </xsl:if>
40:    </body>
41: </xsl:template>
42:
43: <xsl:template match="message">
44:   <p>
45:     <xsl:value-of select="."/>
46:   </p>
47: </xsl:template>
48:
49: <xsl:template match="tasklist[task]">
50:   <h2>
51:     <xsl:value-of select="@name"/>
52:   </h2>
53:   <p>
54:     <table>
55:       <xsl:for-each select="task">
56:         <tr>
57:           <td>
58:             <p>
59:               <xsl:value-of select="sstart/date"/>
60:               <xsl:text> </xsl:text>
61:               <xsl:value-of select="sstart/time"/>
62:             </p>
63:           </td><td>
64:             <p>
65:               <a href="{../@action}?id={@id}&#38;
    key={../../@key}">
66:                 <xsl:value-of select="name"/>
67:               </a>
```

```
68:              </p>
69:            </td>
70:          </tr>
71:        </xsl:for-each>
72:      </table>
73:    </p>
74: </xsl:template>
75:
76: <xsl:template match="tasklist[not(task)]">
77:    <p>
78:      <xsl:value-of select="."/>
79:    </p>
80: </xsl:template>
81:
82: <xsl:template match="task">
83:    <a name="{@id}"></a>
84:    <p>
85:      What: <b><xsl:value-of select="name"/></b><br/>
86:      When: <xsl:value-of select="sstart/date"/>
87:      <xsl:text> </xsl:text>
88:      <xsl:value-of select="sstart/time"/>
89:      -
90:      <xsl:value-of select="sstop/time"/><br/>
91:      Where:
92:      <a href="{location/@action}?id={location/@id}&#38;
   key={../@key}"
93:         target="_new">
94:        <xsl:value-of select="location/name"/>
95:      </a>
96:      <br/>
97:      Owner:
98:      <xsl:value-of select="owner/name"/>
99:    </p>
100: </xsl:template>
101:
102: <xsl:template match="location">
103:    <a name="{@id}"></a>
104:    <p>
105:      <xsl:value-of select="name"/><br/>
106:      <xsl:value-of select="address"/><br/>
107:      <xsl:value-of select="phone"/>
108:    </p>
```

```
109:    <p>
110:      <xsl:value-of select="note"/>
111:    </p>
112: </xsl:template>
113:
114: <xsl:template match="taskcloseinput">
115:    <h2>
116:      Task Completed
117:    </h2>
118:    <p>
119:      Please enter the following information for the task
120:      you've completed (<xsl:value-of select="name"/>).
121:      This will help your Coordinator track the number of
122:      hours we have contributed to the effort.
123:    </p>
124:    <p>
125:      <form method="POST" action="{@action}">
126:        <input type="hidden" name="key" value="{../@key}"/>
127:        <xsl:apply-templates select="dateinput|timeinput"/>
128:        <input type="submit" value="Close"/>
129:      </form>
130:    </p>
131: </xsl:template>
132:
133: <xsl:template match="dateinput">
134:    <xsl:value-of select="."/>
135:    <input type="text" name="{@name}" value="{@value}"
136:      size="10" maxlength="10"/>
137:    <br/>
138: </xsl:template>
139:
140: <xsl:template match="timeinput">
141:    <xsl:value-of select="."/>
142:    <input type="text" name="{@name}" value="{@value}"
143:      size="5" maxlength="5"/>
144:    <br/>
145: </xsl:template>
146:
147: </xsl:stylesheet>
```

Listing 9-13. The XSL style sheet to convert MobileHelper tags to XHTML

It's an excellent exercise to compare each template in Listing 9-13 with its counterpart in wml.xsl, the style sheet responsible for translating MobileHelper tags to WML. Listing 9-14 shows wml.xsl.

```
01: <?xml version="1.0"?>
02:
03: <xsl:stylesheet
04:   xmlns:xsl="http://www.w3.org/1999/XSL/Transform"
05:   version="1.0">
06:
07: <xsl:output
08:   doctype-system="http://www.wapforum.org/DTD/wml_1.1.xml"
09:   doctype-public="-//WAPFORUM//DTD WML 1.1//EN"/>
10:
11: <xsl:template match="/">
12:   <wml>
13:     <xsl:apply-templates/>
14:   </wml>
15: </xsl:template>
16:
17: <xsl:template match="mobilehelper">
18:   <xsl:if test="@action|@prev">
19:     <template>
20:       <xsl:if test="@action">
21:         <do type="accept"
22:          label="{@alabel}"
23:          name="accept">
24:           <go href="{@action}" method="post">
25:             <postfield name="key" value="{@key}"/>
26:           </go>
27:         </do>
28:       </xsl:if>
29:       <xsl:if test="@prev">
30:         <do type="cancel"
31:          label="{@plabel}"
32:          name="prev">
33:           <go href="{@prev}" method="post">
34:             <postfield name="key" value="{@key}"/>
35:           </go>
36:         </do>
37:       </xsl:if>
38:     </template>
39:   </xsl:if>
40:   <xsl:apply-templates/>
41: </xsl:template>
42:
```

```
43: <xsl:template match="message">
44:   <card title="MobileHelper">
45:     <p>
46:       <xsl:value-of select="."/>
47:     </p>
48:   </card>
49: </xsl:template>
50:
51: <xsl:template match="tasklist[task]">
52:   <card title="MobileHelper">
53:     <p mode="nowrap">
54:       <select name="id">
55:         <xsl:for-each select="task">
56:           <option value="{@id}"
57:             onpick="{../@action}?id={@id}&#38;
   key={../../@key}">
58:               <xsl:value-of select="sstart/date"/>
59:               <xsl:text> </xsl:text>
60:               <xsl:value-of select="sstart/time"/>
61:                <xsl:text> </xsl:text>
62:               <xsl:value-of select="name"/>
63:           </option>
64:         </xsl:for-each>
65:       </select>
66:     </p>
67:   </card>
68: </xsl:template>
69:
70: <xsl:template match="tasklist[not(task)]">
71:   <card title="MobileHelper">
72:     <p>
73:       <xsl:value-of select="."/>
74:     </p>
75:   </card>
76: </xsl:template>
77:
78: <xsl:template match="task">
79:   <card title="MobileHelper" id="task_{@id}">
80:     <p>
81:       <xsl:value-of select="sstart/date"/>
82:       <xsl:text> </xsl:text>
83:       <xsl:value-of select="sstart/time"/>
84:        -
```

```
85:        <xsl:value-of select="sstop/time"/><br/>
86:        <xsl:value-of select="name"/><br/>
87:        <anchor title="Where">
88:          <go href="{location/@action}">
89:            <postfield name="key" value="{../@key}"/>
90:            <postfield name="id" value="{@id}"/>
91:          </go>
92:          <xsl:value-of select="location/name"/>
93:        </anchor><br/>
94:        <xsl:value-of select="owner/name"/>
95:      </p>
96:    </card>
97: </xsl:template>
98:
99: <xsl:template match="location">
100:   <card title="MobileHelper" id="location_{@id}">
101:     <p>
102:       <xsl:value-of select="name"/><br/>
103:       <xsl:value-of select="address"/><br/>
104:       <xsl:value-of select="phone"/>
105:     </p>
106:     <p>
107:       <xsl:value-of select="note"/>
108:     </p>
109:   </card>
110: </xsl:template>
111:
112: <xsl:template match="taskcloseinput">
113:   <card title="MobileHelper" id="close_{@id}">
114:     <do type="accept" label="OK" name="accept">
115:       <go href="{@action}" method="post">
116:         <postfield name="key" value="{../@key}"/>
117:         <xsl:for-each select="dateinput|timeinput">
118:           <postfield name="{@name}" value="${@name}"/>
119:         </xsl:for-each>
120:       </go>
121:     </do>
122:     <p>
123:     <fieldset title="{@name}">
124:       <xsl:apply-templates select="dateinput|timeinput"/>
125:     </fieldset>
126:     </p>
127:   </card>
128: </xsl:template>
129:
```

```
130: <xsl:template match="dateinput">
131:   <xsl:value-of select="."/>
132:   <input type="text" name="{@name}" value="{@value}"
133:    format="NN/NN/NNNN" emptyok="false"
134:    size="10" maxlength="10"/>
135:   <br/>
136: </xsl:template>
137:
138: <xsl:template match="timeinput">
139:   <xsl:value-of select="."/>
140:   <input type="text" name="{@name}" value="{@value}"
141:    format="NN:NN" emptyok="false"
142:    size="5" maxlength="5"/>
143:   <br/>
144: </xsl:template>
145:
146: </xsl:stylesheet>
```

Listing 9-14. The XSL style sheet to convert MobileHelper tags to WML

Setting the XML output type

Unlike the XHTML style sheet, the WML style sheet must begin with an `<xsl:output>` tag (lines 3–5) to instruct the XSL processor to include the required XML preamble that identifies WML documents. Without this line, most WML clients would reject the output of the processor, although it would contain valid WML markup.

Matching the document root

The template matching the root of the document (lines 7–16 in Listing 9-13, lines 11–15 in Listing 9-14) is markedly different. The XHTML style sheet takes advantage of HTML's `<title>` tag, letting you assign a title to your MobileHelper document from the `<mobilehelper>` tag's name attribute (line 11). By comparison, the WML style sheet gets by with the bare minimum: the `<wml>` tag that must enclose all WML content. Note that unlike the original MobileHelper application, neither of these include directives such as a `<meta>` tag to control the cache; instead, I opt to control the client's cache directly using the HTTP Cache-control header from the scripts themselves, further separating content and its layout.

Matching the document tag

The next template, matching the `<mobilehelper>` tag (lines 18–41 in Listing 9-13, lines 17–41 in Listing 9-14), illustrates the different user interface characteristics of XHTML and WML. Because MobileHelper uses the soft keys on a smart phone, I need to find a similar navigation metaphor for HTML. By using the `<template>` tag in WML, and by including navigation elements at the tail of the XHTML body, the navigation elements you give to a `<mobilehelper>` tag can be included in both WML and in HTML. The XHTML style sheet begins by giving each page a simple `<h1>` header identifying the page, followed by the MobileHelper content included through the `<xsl:apply-templates/>` tag on line 23. After the MobileHelper content, the style sheet processor tests the `<mobilehelper>` tag for the presence of `action` or `prev` attributes; if either exists, the processor includes a horizontal rule and text with links to the given URLs in the final document. In contrast, the WML style sheet uses a `<template>` tag to define default user interface elements for each card in the deck, assigning the `action` and `prev` URLs to navigation tasks bound to the **Accept** and **Cancel** soft keys.

Matching the message tag

The third template matches the trivial `<message>` tag. Like the other top-level tags, the `<message>` tag copies its output to a paragraph in XHTML (Listing 9-13, lines 43–47), or a card containing a paragraph in WML (Listing 9-14, lines 43–49). Because the `<message>` tag can't contain other tags, it simply plucks out the contents of the incoming XML using `<xsl:value-of>`, selecting the value of the current tag.

Matching task lists

The fourth template matches task lists that contain tasks. The XSL matches this pattern when it scans a `<tasklist>` containing a `<task>`, seeing the `<tasklist>` as the current node. In XHTML, MobileHelper displays task lists as a bona fide table, while in WML it uses an unwrapped paragraph of `<option>` tags, as I showed in Chapter 5. The code for each of these is strikingly similar, although the resulting formatting is quite different because the actual content each includes (a task's start and stop times, along with its name and a hyperlink to the task) is the same. In the section "XSL Syntax," I dissected the XSL template for `<tasklist>` with tasks for XHTML, so I won't repeat it here. The corresponding code, on lines 51–68 of Listing 9-14, operates similarly. After matching task lists containing tasks, the processor creates a new WML card with the same name as the task list (lines 51–52). Then, the processor begins a new paragraph and creates an opening `<select>` tag to contain the `<option>` list (lines 53–54). The processor then iterates over each

<task> element in the task list, creating one <option> tag for each <task> tag, which contains the task's name, start date, and start time, and points to the <tasklist> action attribute (lines 55–63). The processor then closes the <select> list, paragraph, and card tags on the remaining lines (lines 65–68).

The template for an empty task list is significantly simpler because all it needs to do is output a paragraph containing the task list's message (see lines 76–80 of Listing 9-13, and lines 70–76 of Listing 9-14). The fundamental difference between the XHTML markup in Listing 9-13 and the WML markup in Listing 9-14 is that the WML markup must include a <card> tag to contain the paragraph with the message.

Matching tasks

The template for a task itself (lines 82–100 of Listing 9-13 and lines 78–97 of Listing 9-14) is similar for both markup languages, except for how each template constructs the hypertext link to the task's location (line 92 of Listing 9-13, line 78 of Listing 9-14). In XHTML, as with all other URLs, you concatenate the various variables and create an HTTP GET query bearing the server's session key and location ID. In contrast, the WML application continues to use HTTP POST queries throughout, including the <go> task on lines 88–91. Because MobileHelper uses PHP for its back end, I can freely mix HTTP GET and POST submissions, and let PHP bother with the protocol details. It's also worth noting that the XHTML version shows the name of the task before the task start time, whereas the WML version adheres to the convention that the start time comes first. In a mobile setting, people are more likely to want to know about their calendar (the when) than what they will be doing (the what).

Matching locations

The <location> template is wholly unremarkable. In the XHTML code on lines 102–112 of Listing 9-13, the template selects the location's name, address, and phone number, along with a note associated with the location. Similarly, the WML code on lines 99–110 of Listing 9-14 first creates a card and then formats the location's name, address, phone number, and note.

Matching input elements for task closure

By far the most challenging templates are for <taskcloseinput> and its children because these must deal with the differences between XHTML form elements and WML form elements. Whereas in XHTML a form's variables are implicit and sent to the server when you press the submit button, you must enumerate each of the

WML variables to send to the server with `<postfield>` elements. Moreover, the XHTML `<form>` tag must enclose form elements, while WML has no such restriction. (The `<fieldset>` tag is a good idea, but not necessarily required.) These differences result in very different approaches for the two templates for the `<taskcloseinput>` tag. The XHTML is straightforward (lines 114–131 of Listing 9-13), beginning with a brief caption and message, followed by a `<form>` element that the processor fills in accordance with the `<xsl:apply-templates>` instruction on line 127, which selects the `<dateinput>` and `<timeinput>` children of the `<taskcloseinput>` tag. In contrast, the WML template on lines 112–128 first begins by assigning a `<go>` task to the **Accept** key, gathering each of the WML variables it must post using an `<xsl:for-each>` loop on lines 117–119. After outputting the `<do>` task, the processor continues, outputting first the `<fieldset>` tag and then applying the `dateinput` and `timeinput` templates to create each input element.

Unlike `<taskcloseinput>`, the templates for `<dateinput>` and `<timeinput>` are similar for both markup languages, with only superficial differences that take advantage of WML's input validation features on lines 133 and 141 of Listing 9-14.

The MobileHelper Scripts

Let's look at some of the scripts that produce XML for the XSL processor, including the login, task list, task view, and task close scripts. For each of these scripts, I show you the script and the appearance of the output in both XHTML and WML.

Authenticating the user

The initial screens—the home page and login page—are separate for each platform. You sign on to MobileHelper by loading either the index.wml or index.html page, and then log in using either the login.wml or login.html page. While Mobile-Helper could use XML and XML tags for the markup on these pages, it was easier to use two different pages using the per-agent content technique I described earlier in the chapter. The login.php script uses this technique to select either the login.wml or login.html pages. These pages have straightforward WML and XHTML markup; Figure 9-4 shows the MobileHelper Login page in both XHTML and WML generated by login.php in Listing 9-15.

```
01: <?php
02: /*****************************************************
03:  * login.php
04:  *
05:  * This module examines the HTTP Accept header and sends
06:  * either an HTML or a WML file depending on the browser's
07:  * preference.
08:  *****************************************************/
09: if ( strstr( $HTTP_ACCEPT, "wml" ) )
10: {
11:    header( "Content-type: text/vnd.wap.wml" );
12:    readfile( "login.wml" );
13: }
14: elseif (strstr( $HTTP_ACCEPT, "*/*" ) ||
15:        strstr( $HTTP_ACCEPT, "html" ) )
16: {
17:    header( "Content-type: text/html" );
18:    readfile( "login.html" );
19: }
20: ?>
```

Listing 9-15. The login.php script

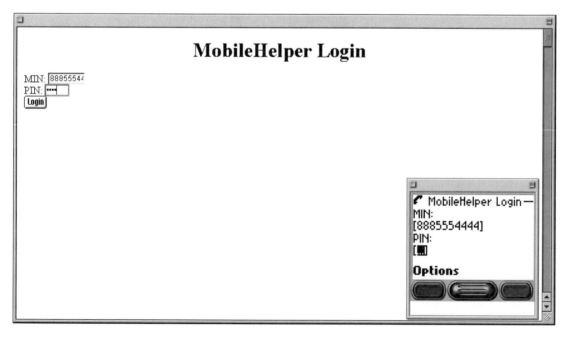

Figure 9-4. MobileHelper Login page viewed in Web and Wireless Web browsers

Selecting the style sheet

Once past the login page, MobileHelper turns to XML to represent all of its content. When using XML, MobileHelper must first determine the content appropriate for the client device and create a MIME string that identifies the content the client receives. Two functions in db.php do this: DBStyleSheetForClient and DBMimeTypeForClient. Listing 9-16 shows these functions taken from db.php.

```php
01: <?php
02:
03: // Excerpt from db.php
04:
05: /*******************************************************
06:  * FUNCTION: DBStyleSheetForClient
07:  *
08:  * DESCRIPTION: Uses HTTP headers to determine the
09:  * best style sheet for the client.
10:  *
11:  * RETURNED: string containing file name of style sheet.
12:  *******************************************************/
13:  function DBStyleSheetForClient()
14:  {
15:    global $HTTP_ACCEPT;
16:
17:    $result = "html.xsl";
18:
19:    if ( strstr( $HTTP_ACCEPT, "wml" ) )
20:    {
21:      $result = "wml.xsl";
22:    }
23:    elseif ( strstr( $HTTP_ACCEPT, "*/*" ) ||
24:      strstr( $HTTP_ACCEPT, "html" ) )
25:    {
26:      $result = "html.xsl";
27:    }
28:
29:    return $result;
30:  }
31:
```

```
32: /********************************************************
33: * FUNCTION: DBMimeTypeForClient
34: *
35: * DESCRIPTION: Uses HTTP headers to determine the
36: * best resulting MIME type for the client.
37: *
38: * RETURNED: string containing MIME type of returned data
39: ********************************************************/
40: function DBMimeTypeForClient()
41: {
42:   global $HTTP_ACCEPT;
43:
44:   $result = "text/html";
45:
46:   if ( strstr( $HTTP_ACCEPT, "wml" ) )
47:   {
48:     $result = "text/vnd.wap.wml";
49:   }
50:   elseif (  strstr( $HTTP_ACCEPT, "*/*" )  ||
51:     strstr( $HTTP_ACCEPT, "html" ) )
52:   {
53:     $result = "text/html";
54:   }
55:
56:   return $result;
57: }

58: ?>
```

Listing 9-16. The DBStyleSheetForClient *and* DBMimeTypeForClient *functions*

Both of these functions work the same way as the comparison in login.php. They begin by setting a default result value, and then test the HTTP Accept header to see if it contains either the string "html" or "wml", setting the result string appropriately. You can use these functions in your own script and change the default return values on lines 17 and 44 to meet your own needs.

Displaying open tasks

A good way to see these functions in use is to look at tasklistopen.php, which builds an XML listing of tasks and uses the XSL processor to convert the tasks to WML or XHTML. Listing 9-17 shows tasklistopen.php, while Figure 9-5 shows the output from tasklistopen.php in both XHTML and WML.

```
01: <?php
02: /*****************************************************
03:  * tasklistopen.php
04:  *
05:  * This script builds a list of open tasks in XML
06:  *
07:  *****************************************************/
08:
09: if ( !$dbLink ) include "db.php";
10:
11: // Filter our output through the client stylesheet.
12:
13: $xsltref = xslt_create();
14: $xslt = join( '', file( DBStyleSheetForClient() ) );
15:
16: // Is the user's session valid?
17:
18: $session = DBCheckUserSession( $key );
19:
20: if ( !is_array( $session ) || count( $session ) == 0 )
21: {
22:   include "logintimeout.php";
23:   exit();
24: }
25:
26: // Update the session variables
27: DBUpdateUserSession( $session );
28:
29: // Get a list of the tasks.
30:
31: $taskList = DBGetOpenTasks( $session[ "min" ] );
32:
33:
34: $content = '<?xml version="1.0" standalone="yes"?>' .
35:   "\n<mobilehelper key=\"$key\" " .
36:   "prev=\"tasklist.php\" plabel=\"Pend\" >\n";
37:
38:
39: $content .= "<tasklist name=\"Open Tasks\" " .
40:   "action=\"taskview.php\">\n";
41:
42: if ( $taskList && count( $taskList ) > 0 )
43: {
44:   for ( $i = 0; $i < count( $taskList ) ; $i++ )
```

```
45:    {
46:      $content .=
47:        "<task id=\"" . $taskList[ $i ][ "id" ] . "\" " .
48:        "state=\"" . $taskList[ $i ][ "state" ] . "\" " .
49:        ">\n";
50:
51:      $content .= "<sstart>";
52:      $content .= "<date>" .
53:        date( "n-d-y", $taskList[ $i ][ "start" ] ) .
54:      "</date>\n";
55:      $content .= "<time>" .
56:        date( "H:i", $taskList[ $i ][ "start" ] ) .
57:      "</time>";
58:      $content .= "</sstart>\n";
59:
60:      $content .= "<name>";
61:      $content .=$taskList[ $i ][ "name" ];
62:      $content .= "</name>\n";
63:
64:      $content .= "</task>\n";
65:    }
66: }
67: else
68: {
69:   $content .= "No open tasks.";
70: }
71:
72: $content .= "</tasklist>\n";
73: $content .= "</mobilehelper>\n";
74:
75: // Send results
76:
77: header( "Content-type: " . DBMimeTypeForClient() );
78: header( "Cache-control: no-cache " );
79:
80: xslt_process( $xslt, $content, $result );
81:
82: print( $result );
83:
84: // Clean up XSLT Processor
85:
86: xslt_free($xsltref);
87: ?>
```

Listing 9-17. The tasklistopen.php script

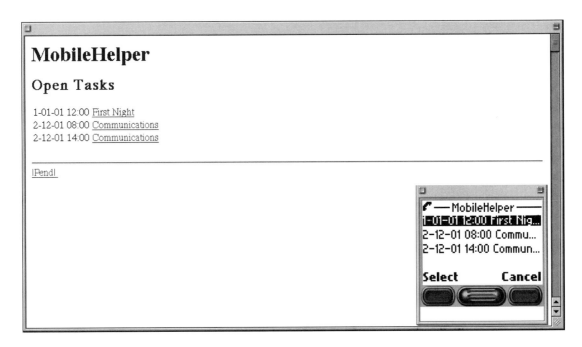

Figure 9-5. Task list viewed in Web and Wireless Web browsers

As part of the script's initialization, the script instantiates an XSL processor on line 13 and loads the style sheet selected by DBStyleSheetForClient on line 14 using the join trick I told you about back in the section "Getting Started with Content Abstraction." Next, the script performs the usual session and state initialization, fetching state information from the database on line 18, validating the session key on lines 20–24, and updating the session key on line 27. After getting a list of open tasks on line 31 with DBGetOpenTasks, the script begins accumulating the XML result in the $content variable.

The XML content begins on lines 34–36, which create the <?xml?> preamble and the <mobilehelper> tag. This tag assigns an action to the **Cancel** soft key; pressing **Cancel** from the open task list view brings you to the pending task list view, and vice versa. Lines 39–40 begin the <tasklist> tag, which specifies an action attribute taking you to the taskview.php script if you select a task. The script then loops over each task in $tasklist, creating a task tag for each with the start date and time and name (lines 44–66). If no tasks are in the list, the script instead puts the string "No Open Tasks" in the <tasklist> tag (lines 67–70). The script then closes the <tasklist> and <mobilehelper> tags on lines 72–73 and sends the results to the client on lines 77–82, finally freeing the XSL processor when the script completes on line 86. Note that the script uses the header function to send a "Cache-control:no-cache" message to the client on line 78, ensuring that the client doesn't cache old values of the open task list. Including cache control in the HTTP headers, rather than the XML, makes MobileHelper tag design and the XSL style sheets simpler.

Unlike the previous versions of MobileHelper, which used a variable sent from the client to select either the open or pending task lists, the XML-enabled version of MobileHelper uses two separate scripts, tasklist.php and tasklistopen.php. By using two separate scripts for the task lists, MobileHelper doesn't need an additional XML attribute in one of the tasks to track which task list a particular script should load. The logic in tasklist.php is identical to tasklistopen.php, save that the script enumerates your pending tasks rather than open tasks.

Displaying a task

When you select a task from the task list, you see the task display, shown in Figure 9-6. The layout is similar in both XHTML and WML, with a hyperlink from the location to a separate location view. The XHTML content shows locations in a separate window so you can see the location while looking at different tasks. Listing 9-18 shows the script taskview.php, which creates this content.

Figure 9-6. Task viewed in Web and Wireless Web browsers

```php
01: <?php
02: /******************************************************
03:  * taskview.php
04:  *
05:  * This script shows a selected task in WML for the
06:  * current user (indicated by $min and $task).
07:  ******************************************************/
08:
09: if ( !$dbLink ) include "db.php";
10:
11: // Filter our output through the client stylesheet.
12:
13: $xsltref = xslt_create();
14: $xslt = join( '', file( DBStyleSheetForClient() ) );
15:
16: // Is the user's session valid?
17:
18: $session = DBCheckUserSession( $key );
19:
20: if ( !is_array( $session ) || count( $session ) == 0 )
21: {
22:   include "logintimeout.php";
23:   exit();
24: }
25:
26: $task = $id;
27:
28: // Update the session variables
29:
30: if ( isset( $task ) )
31: {
32:   $session[ "task" ] = $task;
33: }
34: DBUpdateUserSession( $session );
35:
36: // Get details of this task
37:
38: $taskDesc = DBGetTaskDetail( $session[ "task" ] );
39:
40: // Build the response.
41:
42: $content = '<?xml version="1.0" standalone="yes"?>' .
43:   "\n<mobilehelper key=\"$key\" cache=\"no-cache\" ";
44:
```

```
45: // Decide which action is appropriate.
46:
47: if ( $taskDesc[ "state" ] == DBTASKOPEN )
48: {
49:
50: // Add this task to current user's queue
51:
52:   $content .= "action=\"taskassign.php\" " .
53:     "alabel=\"Accept\" ";
54: }
55: else if ( ( $taskDesc[ "state" ] == DBTASKPEND ) &&
56:   ( $taskDesc[ "owner" ] == $session[ "min" ] ) )
57: {
58:
59: // Close this task
60:
61:   $content .= "action=\"taskcloseinput.php\" " .
62:     "alabel=\"Close\" ";
63: }
64:
65: $content .= ">\n";
66:
67: // Show the task
68:
69: if ( $taskDesc && count ( $taskDesc ) > 0 )
70: {
71:   $content .= "<task id=\"" . $session[ "task" ] . "\" " .
72:     "state=\" " . $taskDesc[ "state" ] . "\">\n";
73:
74: // When is it in 1-01-01 2000-22000
75:
76:   $content .= "<sstart>";
77:   $content .= "<date>" .
78:     date( "n-d-y", $taskDesc[ "start" ] ) .
79:   "</date>\n";
80:   $content .= "<time>" .
81:     date( "H:i", $taskDesc[ "start" ] ) .
82:   "</time>";
83:   $content .= "</sstart>\n";
84:
```

```
85:    $content .= "<sstop>";
86:    $content .= "<date>" .
87:      date( "n-d-y", $taskDesc[ "stop" ] ) .
88:    "</date>\n";
89:    $content .= "<time>" .
90:      date( "H:i", $taskDesc[ "stop" ] ) .
91:    "</time>";
92:    $content .= "</sstop>\n";
93:
94: // What is it
95:
96:    $content .= "<name>";
97:    $content .=$taskDesc[ "taskName" ];
98:    $content .= "</name>\n";
99:
100: // Where is it
101:
102:    if ( $taskDesc[ "locationName" ] )
103:    {
104:
105:      $lid = $taskDesc[ "locationId" ];
106:
107:      $content .= "<location id=\"$lid\" " .
108:        "action=\"location.php\">\n";
109:      $content .= "<name>";
110:      $content .=$taskDesc[ "locationName" ];
111:      $content .= "</name>\n";
112:      $content .= "</location>\n";
113:    }
114:
115: // Who owns it
116:
117:    $oid = $taskDesc[ "owner" ];
118:    $content .= "<owner id=\"$oid\"><name>";
119:    $content .=$taskDesc[ "ownerName" ] ?
120:      $taskDesc[ "ownerName" ] : "Not assigned";
121:    $content .= "</name></owner>\n";
122:
123: // Notes
124:
125:    $content .= "<note>";
126:    $content .=$taskDesc[ "taskNote" ];
127:    $content .= "</note>\n";
128:
```

```
129:    $content .= "</task>\n";
130: }
131: else
132: {
133:    $content = "<message>No task matches the " .
134:       "given data.</message>";
135: }
136:
137: $content .= "</mobilehelper>\n";
138:
139: // Send results
140:
141: header( "Content-type: " . DBMimeTypeForClient() );
142: header( "Cache-control: no-cache " );
143: xslt_process( $xslt, $content, $result );
144:
145: print( $result );
146:
147: // Clean up XSLT Processor
148:
149: xslt_free($xsltref);
150:
151: ?>
```

Listing 9-18. The taskview.php script

This script is probably the longest script in MobileHelper, but its logic is simple, so only a quick walkthrough is in order. The script begins by initializing the XSL processor and loading the appropriate style sheet (lines 13–14), and performing the usual session key maintenance (lines 16–34). Note that the incoming task ID is now sent in the PHP variable $id, rather than the variable $task. I copy $id into $task on line 26 because the XML content refers to database IDs using the XML attribute id, and to keep things simple, I use the convention throughout the client-side implementation. Line 38 fetches the task description, while lines 42 and 43 build the <?xml?> and <mobilehelper> tag preamble and store it in the variable $content.

From a task view, you can accept a task if it's open, or close it if it's your task, but you can't otherwise change a task. The separate scripts taskassign.php and taskcloseinput.php perform these actions, and the taskview.php script must determine which action is appropriate when setting the <mobilehelper> tag's action attribute. The logic is identical to the logic MobileHelper uses to manage tasks in Chapter 5. If the state of the task is DBTASKOPEN, the task is open, and the action attribute should be "taskassign.php", to load the taskassign.php script (lines 47–54).

If the task's state is `DBTASKPEND` and you are the task's owner, the `action` attribute should be `"taskcloseinput.php"` so you can close the task (lines 55–63); otherwise, no `action` is set. The if-then statement on lines 47–63 also sets the `< mobilehelper >` `alabel` attribute to either `"Accept"` or `"Close"`, ensuring that the user interface correctly represents what will occur when you select the soft key.

The bulk of the script—lines 69–135—is a rather tedious construction of a simple `<task>` tag that contains `<owner>`, `<sstart>`, `<sstop>`, `<location>`, and `<note>` tags. Each tag is appended to `$content`, with a line feed after closing tags (such as the initial `<task>` tag on lines 71–72) to facilitate readability during debugging. The original `<task>` tag bears both the task's database ID (so that the style sheet can construct links if necessary) and the task's `state` field in the database, although the style sheet doesn't use it at present. The order of the tags within the `<task>` tag is unimportant because the style sheet dictates the order of the markup tags in the output, so the listing here follows the original order of information in earlier versions of MobileHelper. Of course, if the script didn't find a task description for the task, the script simply outputs a simple `<message>` tag on lines 133–134.

Once the script constructs the MobileHelper XML document, it sends the MIME type of the result to the client (line 141), and the `Cache-Control` header to the client to ensure the document won't be cached (line 142). Finally, the script invokes the XML processor and sends the formatted output to the client, freeing the style sheet processor when it's finished (lines 143–149).

As you saw earlier in the chapter, the style sheet uses information from the `<location>` tag to create a hyperlink to the location.php script, as directed by lines 107–108 of Listing 9-18. The code for location.php is quite similar to taskview.php, so I won't show it here; you can see sample output from the script in Figure 9-7.

Closing a task

Despite how tricky the style sheet entry for `<taskcloseinput>` is (see the previous section for details), the code to produce a `<taskcloseinput>` tag is as straightforward as the scripts you've seen so far. That's one of the beauties of using XML and XSL: you can often make your code simpler, moving some of the complexity to your style sheets. Moreover, once you understand XSL, it's easier to work with and test XSL tags than code; thus, you reduce the opportunity for error. Listing 9-19 shows the code for taskcloseinput.php, which builds a `<taskcloseinput>` tag to prompt you when you close a task. Figure 9-8 shows a task closure screen.

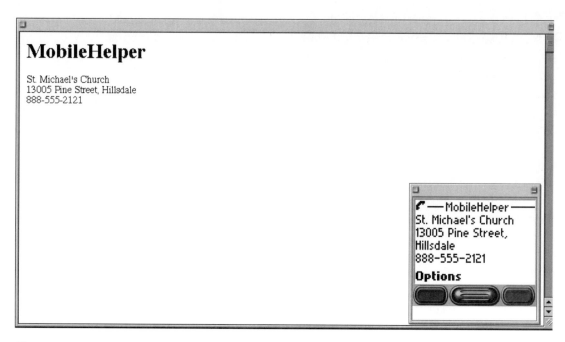

Figure 9-7. Location viewed in Web and Wireless Web browsers

```
01: <?php
02: /*****************************************************
03:  * taskcloseinput
04:  *
05:  * This script prompts the user for the information needed
06:  * to close a particular task.
07:  *****************************************************/
08:
09: if ( !$dbLink ) include "db.php";
10:
11:
12: // Filter our output through the client stylesheet.
13:
14: $xsltref = xslt_create();
15: $xslt = join( '', file( DBStyleSheetForClient() ) );
16:
17: // Is the user's session valid?
18:
19: $session = DBCheckUserSession( $key );
20:
```

```
21: if ( !is_array( $session ) || count( $session ) == 0 )
22: {
23:   include "logintimeout.php";
24:   exit();
25: }
26:
27: // Update the session variables
28:
29: DBUpdateUserSession( $session );
30: $task = $session[ "task" ];
31:
32: // Get details of this task
33:
34: $taskDesc = DBGetTaskDetail( $session[ "task" ] );
35:
36: // Set the default start and stop times for the task.
37:
38: $dstartdate = date( "m/d/Y", $taskDesc[ "start" ] );
39: $dstarttime = date( "H:i", $taskDesc[ "start" ] );
40: $dstopdate =  date( "m/d/Y", $taskDesc[ "stop" ] );
41: $dstoptime =  date( "H:i", $taskDesc[ "stop" ] );
42:
43: // Build the response.
44:
45: $content = '<?xml version="1.0" standalone="yes"?>' .
46:   "\n<mobilehelper key=\"$key\" >\n";
47:
48:
49: $content .= "<taskcloseinput id=\"" .
50:   $session[ "task" ] . "\" " .
51:   "action=\"taskclosedo.php\">\n";
52:
53: // task name
54:
55: $content .= "<name>" . $taskDesc[ "taskName" ] . "</name>\n";
56:
57: // start date input field
58:
59: $content .= "<dateinput name=\"startdate\" " .
60:   "value=\"$dstartdate\">" .
61:   "Actual start date</dateinput>\n";
62:
63: // start time input field
64:
```

```
65: $content .= "<timeinput name=\"startime\" " .
66:    "value=\"$dstarttime\">" .
67:    "Actual start time</timeinput>\n";
68:
69: // stop date input field
70:
71: $content .= "<dateinput name=\"stopdate\" " .
72:    "value=\"$dstopdate\">" .
73:    "Actual stop date</dateinput>\n";
74:
75: // stop time input field
76:
77: $content .= "<timeinput name=\"stoptime\" " .
78:    "value=\"$dstoptime\">" .
79:    "Actual stop time</timeinput>\n";
80:
81: // Closing tags
82:
83: $content .= "</taskcloseinput>\n";
84: $content .= "</mobilehelper>\n";
85:
86: // Send results
87:
88: header( "Content-type: " . DBMimeTypeForClient() );
89: header( "Cache-control: no-cache " );
90:
91: xslt_process( $xslt, $content, $result );
92:
93: print( $result );
94:
95: // Clean up XSLT Processor
96:
97: xslt_free($xsltref);
98:
99: ?>
```

Listing 9-19. The taskcloseinput.php script

The script begins with the now familiar XSL invocation and session key management, getting down to business on line 34 by loading the task's information from the database. The script uses this information on lines 38–41 to construct default input values for the actual start and stop times for the task.

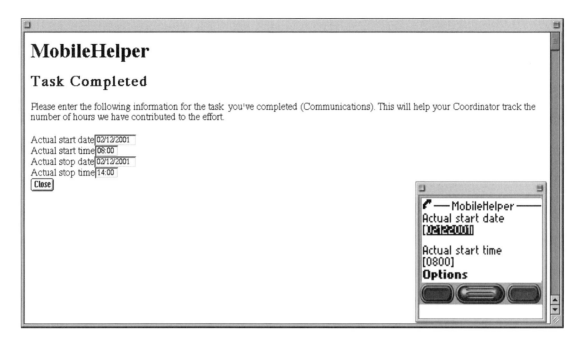

Figure 9-8. Location viewed in Web and Wireless Web browsers

The script builds the XML and `<mobilehelper>` preamble on lines 45–46, linking to the taskclosedo.php script in the `<taskcloseinput>` task on lines 49–51. A `<taskcloseinput>` tag must contain the task's name in a `<name>` tag, along with any information that the user must enter as either `<dateinput>` or `<timeinput>` tags. The script creates the `<name>` tag on line 55, constructing each of the input tags on lines 59–79. Unlike the `<task>` tag's style sheet entry, the `<taskcloseinput>` style sheet entry uses the `<xslt:apply-templates>` directive to select items from the `<taskcloseinput>` tag's content, so the various input lines will appear in the same order in the final output as they do in the XML generated on these lines. The script then closes the XML document (lines 83–84), generates the appropriate HTTP headers (lines 88–89), processes the result to generate either XHTML or WML (line 91), sends the result to the client (line 93), and frees the XSL processor (line 97).

Wrapping up

The logic in the other scripts is similar: fetch content from the database, wrap it in XML tags, merge the XML with the appropriate XSL style sheet, and send the results to the client. As you can see from the listings in this section, this approach has a number of advantages.

First, the code is simpler. When writing the PHP scripts, I don't have to worry about how the output will appear. Instead, I only need concern myself with including the appropriate tags for the output. In fact, I can even include *more* information in the XML output than the client will see because the style sheets determine which tags in the XML content get converted, thus limiting which information the client ultimately displays.

Second, you no longer need to worry about which clients have which capabilities. Instead, you only need determine what style sheet is appropriate for the client. In MobileHelper, I have only two style sheets, chosen by the HTTP Accept header, but I could easily have more. For example, Phone.com browsers handle soft key elements quite differently than the Nokia browser; by testing the HTTP User-Agent header and selecting a style sheet specific to Phone.com's browser, I could have a separate user interface carefully tuned to make the most of that browser's features.

Third, the division of content between database, scripts, and style sheets enables me to establish parallel work paths. Although it's not necessary in a small project like MobileHelper, in a large project different people can work on the database, scripts, and XSL style sheets, helping speed time-to-market.

The penalty for these benefits is performance and server configuration complexity. The XML version of MobileHelper is slower than the version shown in previous chapters because each script must access not just the database, but the file system to load a style sheet. Moreover, the style sheet processor consumes system resources (processor cycles and RAM), making performance a little slower. On the configuration side, configuring PHP to include the XSL processor takes more work because you must be sure to build and install the expat and Sablotron libraries before writing your code. These costs are easily absorbed on large projects with fast hardware and professional system administration experience.

On the CD-ROM

Although you won't find the Sablotron or expat sources on the CD-ROM, the Windows version of PHP include the Sablotron module. Regardless of which platform you're using, however, if you want to experiment with XSL and PHP, you should definitely visit http://www.php.net and download the latest implementation; this part of PHP changes almost daily.

Of course, the PHP, XML, and XSL for the version of MobileHelper described in this chapter are on the CD-ROM in the directory chap09. If you want to actually install these on a system running MySQL and PHP with the Sablotron module, you need to add a database named "MobileHelper" and seed the database with some new tables. To do this, connect to the server using the **mysql** utility and issue the command:

```
mysql> CREATE DATABASE MobileHelper;
```

Now you can seed the new database using the **mysql** command using

```
% mysql -u root < MobileHelper.dump
```

This seeds the database with the tables used by MobileHelper as well as a handful of tasks and Volunteers.

> **CAUTION** *You can't use the MobileHelper database you used in previous chapters with this version of MobileHelper because the* location *table is different. Although these scripts won't fail with earlier versions of the database, you won't get what you expect!*

As always, the listings are on the CD-ROM in the chapter directory, too. The two functions DBStyleSheetForClient and DBMimeTypeForClient, suitably renamed and modified, should help you greatly in your own work. Experiment and enjoy!

Food for Thought

- How would you modify Listing 9-1 to test the HTTP User-Agent header, say to work around the Phone.com UP.SDK problem I discussed in the section "Getting Started with Per-Agent Content"?

- Extend MobileHelper's XML tags to abstract the login screen, providing tags to prompt the user for his or her MIN and PIN. What attributes do these tags have?

- Extend MobileHelper's style sheets to support the XML tags you just created. Here's a hint: Look at how the existing style sheets format the <timeinput> and <dateinput> tags.

- How would you modify the login.php script to use the XML and XSL code you just created?

- Look at your Web site. Are there places you can use XML? Design an XML markup language for the data on your Web site. Alternatively, if you don't have a Web site yet, design an XML markup language for MobileHelper's administration interface, letting Coordinators enter new tasks and Volunteers.

- The `<task>` tag uses the `<sstart>` and `<sstop>` tags to represent the *scheduled* start and stop times for a task. How would you implement similar tags `<astart>` and `<astop>` to show actual start and stop times for tasks in an administration interface to MobileHelper?

- As an extension, PHP provides the XML-DOM library to give you easy-to-use functions to build XML documents, much as the wml.php file in previous chapters makes it easy to create WML without embedding markup in your PHP code. Investigate the XML-DOM library. Would it make MobileHelper's scripts easier to read and maintain? What are the tradeoffs in using such a package?

- How would you add support to your current debugging scaffold to support the PHP XSL processor's debugging functions?

APPENDIX A
Internet Resources

THE WIRELESS WEB is changing fast. While books such as this one earn a place on your bookshelf because they're easy to read, lightweight, and don't need to be plugged in, the Internet provides a valuable supplement.

This appendix provides a number of URLs for Web sites that can help you learn about Wireless Web development. Many of these sites provided me with valuable information while writing this book, and almost daily I refer to many other sites when developing wireless applications.

Of course, this appendix is by no means complete—for even more information, take a look on your favorite search engine for keywords such as *WAP*, *WML*, or *Wireless Web*.

WAP Specifications

The letter of the law is set in stone by the WAP Forum. While specifications make dry reading, they provide the ultimate answer as to how things should behave. You can find the WAP Forum's Web site with the current WAP specifications and other resources at `http://www.wapforum.org`.

Wholly unrelated to standards and specifications, you should grab a cup of coffee and go check out `http://www.coolwapsiteoftheday.com`. The URL describes it perfectly; this site can help you get a good idea of who's doing what with the Wireless Web.

Client-Side Tools

A crucial part of your development process is testing your Wireless Application on a number of browsers. One of the best ways to do this is to get as many different WAP toolkits as you can to see how your content renders on each. Several companies have announced free or subscription-based software development kits; you can visit their Web site for details.

jEdit

Vendor: Independent (Slava Pestov)

> URL: `http://jedit.sourceforge.com` or `http://sourceforge.net/projects/jedit`
>
> Platform: UNIX, Linux, Mac OS, Windows

This isn't a true SDK; rather, it's a Java-based text editor that provides auto indention, macros, and syntax coloring for a number of markup languages including XML, XSLT, and WML. It has more features than you can shake a stick at. Best of all, it's free.

Motorola

Vendor: Motorola Corporation

> URL: `http://www.motorola.com/developers/wireless/web-wo-wires`
>
> Platform: Varied

Provides developers with information and toolkits for testing WAP content on Motorola hardware.

Nokia WAP Toolkit

Vendor: Nokia Corporation

> URL: `http://www.nokia.com/wap/index.html`
>
> Platform: Microsoft Windows

Nokia WAP Toolkit for developing and debugging WAP content on a PC-based simulator.

Phone.com

Vendor: Phone.com

> URL: `http://www.phone.com`
>
> Platform: Windows, Solaris

Provides the Up.SDK simulator to view and debug HDML and WML applications, along with copious documentation and examples.

Yospace

Vendor: Yospace, LLC

> URL: `http://www.yospace.com`
>
> Platform: Windows, Macintosh, UNIX, Linux

> Provides the Yospace SPEDE to view and debug HDML and WML applications, along with copious documentation and examples.

Server-Side Tools

The client side is only half of the solution. These sites have software you can use to build your server applications.

Apache

Vendor: The Apache Software Foundation

> URL: `http://www.apache.org`
>
> Platform: UNIX, Linux, Mac OS X, Windows

> The Internet's most widely used Web server. Why not make it yours, too?

Nokia WAP Server

Vendor: Nokia Corporation

> URL: `http://www.nokia.com/wap/index.html`
>
> Platform: Varied

> Provides developers and networks with a reference server for gating WAP content from HTTP to WAP browsers using UDP over TCP/IP.

MySQL

Vendor: MySQL AB

URL: http://www.mysql.com

Platform: UNIX, Linux, Mac OS X, Windows

Freely available fast SQL database with reasonable feature set. Plays well with PHP, Perl, Java, and other software development tools.

PostgreSQL

Vendor: PostgreSQL, Inc.

URL: http://www.pgsql.com

Platform: Most flavors of UNIX and Linux

Open source object-oriented relational database with SQL and transaction support. Integrates well with PHP and scales well to support enterprise applications.

PHP

Vendor: The PHP Development Team

URL: http://www.php.net

Platform: UNIX, Linux, Mac OS X, Windows

APPENDIX B
WML Reference

THIS APPENDIX PROVIDES a reference to WML syntax and tags, discussed in Chapter 2.

Table B-1. Reserved WML Characters and the Corresponding Tags

CHARACTER	TAG	PURPOSE
<	&lt;	"less than" symbol
>	&gt;	"greater than" symbol
'	&apos;	apostrophe
"	&quot;	quotation marks
&	&amp;	ampersand
$	$$	dollar sign

Table B-2. Input Format Specification Characters

CHARACTER	ALLOWED INPUT TYPE
A	Any symbolic or uppercase alphabetic character
a	Any symbolic or lowercase alphabetic character
M	Any symbolic, numeric, or uppercase alphabetic character (changeable to lowercase)—for multiple-character input, defaults to uppercase first character
m	Any symbolic, numeric, or lowercase alphabetic character (changeable to uppercase)—for multiple-character input, defaults to lowercase first character
N	Any numeric character
X	Any symbolic, numeric, or uppercase alphabetic character (not changeable to lowercase)
x	Any symbolic, numeric, or lowercase alphabetic character (not changeable to uppercase)

Table B-3. WML Document Skeleton

TAG	PURPOSE
`<?xml version="1.0"?>`	States document is XML
`<!DOCTYPE wml PUBLIC`	Says document is WML
`"-//WAPFORUM//DTD WML 1.1//EN"`	Says document follows WML 1.1 standard
`"http://www.wapforum.org/DTD/ wml_1.1.xml">`	Provides validating gateway with WML 1.1. standard
`<wml>`	Begins WML document
`<template>…</template>`	Defines default event handlers and interface bindings
`<card>…</card>`	Defines one or more cards
`</wml>`	Ends WML document

Table B-4. WML Tags and Attributes

TAG	ATTRIBUTES	NOTE
`<a>`		Shorthand for the tags `<anchor><go href="url"/></anchor>`
	`href`	Destination URL
`<access/>`		Specifies access control for the deck
	`domain`	Domain that may refer to deck
	`path`	Path that may refer to deck in `domain`
`<anchor>`		Anchors a task to a region of formatted text
	`title`	Name of link
`<b>`		Indicates that text should be bold face
`<big>`		Indicates that text should be in a larger font than the default
` `		Indicates a line break

Table B-4. WML Tags and Attributes (Continued)

TAG	ATTRIBUTES	NOTE
<card>		Defines a new card
	id	Specifies a card's name
	onenterbackward	Specifies URL of card to present when the card is entered using a <prev/.> task
	onenterforward	Specifies URL of card to present when the card is entered using a <go> task
	ontimer	Specifies URL of card to present when the card is entered using a <timer> task
	title	Specifies a card's title for bookmarks or elsewhere
<do>		Binds a task to an interface item
	type	Target interface element to bind
	label	Human-readable label for interface element
	name	WML name for element
<em>		Indicates that text should be displayed with emphasis
<fieldset>		Indicates form elements
<go>		Navigation task
	href	URL to go to
	method	HTTP Method to use (GET, POST)
	sendreferer	Include this URL in request
	accept-charset	Specify supported character set transcoding for forms
<head>		Specifies the heading of a deck
<i>		Indicates that text should be in italics

Table B-4. WML Tags and Attributes (Continued)

TAG	ATTRIBUTES	NOTE
`<img/>`		Place image
	`alt`	Text label for image
	`src`	URL of image data
	`localsrc`	Name of image in ROM to use if available
	`height`	Height of image in pixels
	`width`	Width of image in pixels
	`align`	Screen alignment (`top`, `middle`, or `bottom`)
`<input/>`		Defines an input field
	`emptyok`	True if user may leave empty
	`format`	Format specification (see Table B-2)
	`maxlength`	Maximum number of characters allowed
	`name`	Name of WML variable to take input
	`size`	Number of characters to show in input field
	`type`	Type of input (`text`, `password`)
`<meta/>`		Provides meta data for client
	`content`	Value of meta data
	`http-equiv`	Names an HTTP header
	`name`	Name of meta data
	`user-agent`	Name of user-agent specific meta data
`<noop/>`		A task that does nothing
`<onevent>`		Binds an event to a task
	`type`	Type of event to bind
`<optgroup>`		Indicates related option choices in option list
`<option>`		Identifies option item in a select list
	`value`	Value to assign to `<select>` variable on selection
	`onpick`	URL to load on selection

Table B-4. WML Tags and Attributes (Continued)

TAG	ATTRIBUTES	NOTE
`<p>`		Paragraph
	`align`	Specifies left, center, or right alignment
	`wrap`	Specifies word wrap or no wrapping (one of `wrap` or `nowrap`)
`<prev/>`		Task that returns to the previously viewed card
`<postfield>`		Specifies name/value pair for HTTP POST request in task
	`name`	HTTP variable name
	`value`	Value to post
`<refresh/>`		Task that sets values of the indicated variables and redraws current card
`<select>`		Creates selection list
	`default`	Default selection value
	`name`	Name of WML variable to take input
`<small>`		Indicates that text should be in a smaller font than default
`<strong>`		Indicates that text should be displayed with strong emphasis
`<table>`		Indicates a table
	`columns`	Number of columns in the table
	`align`	Aligment of each table (left, center, or right)
	`title`	Title of table
`<timer>`		Establishes timer event
	`name`	Name of timer
	`value`	Duration in demiseconds
`<template>`		
	`onenterforward`	
	`onenterbackward`	
	`ontimer`	URL to load when timer elapses

Table B-4. WML Tags and Attributes (Continued)

TAG	ATTRIBUTES	NOTE
`<td>`		Demarcates a cell within a table
`<tr>`		Demarcates a row within a table
`<u>`		Indicates that text should be underlined
`<wml>`		Specifies a WML deck

WMLScript Reference

THIS APPENDIX PROVIDES a reference to WMLScript operations, functions, and libraries, discussed in Chapter 4.

Table C-1. Special Characters in WMLScript Strings

SEQUENCE	MEANING
\'	Single quote
\"	Double quote
\n	Linefeed (LF or 0x0A in ASCII)
\r	Carriage return (CR or 0x0D in ASCII)
\t	Horizontal tab (HT or 0x09 in ASCII)
\\	Backslash
\/	Slash

Table C-2. Common WMLScript Operators

OPERATION	ASSOCIATION	PURPOSE
!, ~, ++, –, isvalid, typeof	Right	Logical complement, binary complement, increment, decrement, complement equivalence to isvalid, returns type
*, /, %	Left	Multiplication, division, and modulo (remainder)
+, -	Left	Addition, subtraction, string concatenation
<<, >>	Left	Bitwise left shift, right shift
<, <=, >=, >	Non-associative	Less than, less than or equals, greater than or equals, greater than comparisons
==, !=	Non-associative	Equivalence, non-equivalence comparisons

Table C-2. Common WMLScript Operators (Continued)

OPERATION	ASSOCIATION	PURPOSE
&	Left	Bitwise and
^	Left	Bitwise xor
|	Left	Bitwise or
&&	Left	Logical and
||	Left	Logical or
? :	Left	Conditional operation
=, +=, -=, *=, /=, div=, %=, ^=, .=, &=, |=	Left	Assignment

Table C-3. Functions in the WMLScript Lang *Library*

FUNCTION	ARGUMENTS	RETURNS	PURPOSE
abort	string		Causes the interpretation of the WMLScript to abort and returns control to the caller of the WMLScript interpreter with the given string describing the error
abs	number	number or invalid	Computes the absolute value of the given number
characterSet		string	Returns an integer code indicating the character set supported by the WMLScript interpreter
exit	value		Causes the interpretation of the WMLScript to terminate and returns control to the caller of the WMLScript interpreter with the given value
float	*none*	Boolean	Returns true if the platform supports floating-point arithmetic, false otherwise
isInt	string	Boolean	Returns true if string can be interpreted as an integer, false otherwise

Table C-3. Functions in the WMLScript Lang *Library (Continued)*

FUNCTION	ARGUMENTS	RETURNS	PURPOSE
isFloat	string	Boolean	Returns true if string can be interpreted as a float, false otherwise
min	n1, n2	number or invalid	Computes the minimum of two given numbers
minInt		number	The minimum integer value supported
max	n1, n2	number or invalid	Computes the maximum of two given numbers
maxInit		The minimum integer value supported	
parseInt	string	integer or invalid	Returns an integer corresponding to an interpretation of the string, or invalid if the string could not be interpreted as an integer
parseFloat	string	float or invalid	Returns a floating-point number corresponding to an interpretation of the string, or invalid if the string could not be interpreted as a floating-point number
random	integer	integer	Returns a random integer between 0 and the value passed, or invalid if value is less than zero or not a number
seed	value	string	Initializes the random number sequence and returns an empty string

Table C-4. Functions in the WMLScript Float *Library*

FUNCTION	ARGUMENTS	RETURNS	PURPOSE
ceil	number	number	Returns the smallest integer value that is not less than the given number
int	number	number	Returns the integer part of the given number
floor	number	number	Returns the greatest integer value that is not greater than the given number
maxFloat		number	Returns the maximum supported floating-point number
minFloat		number	Returns the minimum supported floating-point number
pow	y, x	number	Returns an implementation-dependent approximation of the result of computing y^x
round	number	number	Returns the integer that is closest to number
sqrt	number	number	Returns an implementation-dependent approximation of the square root of number

Table C-5. Functions in the WMLScript String *Library*

FUNCTION	ARGUMENTS	RETURNS	PURPOSE
charAt	string, index	string	Returns a new string with one character containing the character in string at position index
compare	string1, string2	integer	Indicates whether string1 is less than, equal to, or greater than string2 based on the character codes of the native character set
element	string, sep	integer or invalid	Returns the number of elements in string that are separated by sep
elementAt	string, index, sep	string	Returns the index'th element of string as separated by sep

Table C-5. Functions in the WMLScript String *Library (Continued)*

FUNCTION	ARGUMENTS	RETURNS	PURPOSE
find	string, sub	value	Returns the index of sub in string or invalid
format	format, value	string	Uses the printf-style format string to format the value
insertAt	string, new, elem, index	string	Returns a new string where new is inserted at the index'th element of string separated by sep
isEmpty	string	Boolean	Returns true if the string length is zero or false otherwise
length	string	number	Returns the number of characters in string
replace	string, old, new	string	Returns a new string resulting from the replacement of all occurrences of the string old by new in string
removeAt	string, index, sep	string	Returns a new string in which element and sep at index have been removed from string
replaceAt	string, new, elem, index	string	Returns a new string in which the index'th element of string separated by sep has been replaced by new
squeeze	string	string	Returns a string in which all consecutive white spaces are reduced to single spaces
subString	string, start, length	string	Returns a new string consisting of the characters in string from start and extending length characters
toString	value	string	Returns a string representation of value
trim	string	string	Returns string where all leading and trailing white space has been removed

Table C-6. Functions in the WMLScript URL *Library*

FUNCTION	ARGUMENTS	RETURNS	PURPOSE
escapeString	string	string	Computes a new string where special characters have been escaped to create a valid URL
getBase	string		Returns an absolute URL of the current WMLScript file
getFragment	url	string	Returns the fragment in url
getHost	url	string	Returns the host in url
getPath	url	string	Returns the path in url
getParameters	url	string	Returns parameters in the last path segment of url
getPort	url	string	Returns the port number specified in url
getQuery	url	string	Returns the query part specified i n url
getReferer		string	Returns the smallest URL relative to the base URL of the current WMLScript file
getScheme	url	string	Returns the protocol (scheme) in url
isValid	url	Boolean	Returns true if url is a valid URL
loadString	string, type	string, integer, or invalid	Returns the content denoted by the given absolute URL and the given content type
resolve	base, embedded	string	Returns an absolute URL created from the given base and embedded URL strings
unescapeString	string	string	Computes a new string in which URL escaped characters are returned to their normal values

* Note: Relative URLs are not resolved in these functions.

Table C-7. Functions in the WMLScript WMLBrowser *Library*

FUNCTION	ARGUMENTS	RETURNS	PURPOSE
getVar	name	string	Returns the value of the WML variable name
go	string	string or invalid	Tells the browser to load the deck at the URL string when script exits
getCurrentCard		string	Returns the smallest relative URL (relative to the script) specifying the card being displayed by the browser
newContext			Clears all variables and the history of the browser
prev		string or invalid	Signals the browser to go to the previous card
refresh			Signals the browser to update its UI based on the current context
setVar	name, value	string	Sets WML variable name to value

Table C-8: Functions in the WMLScript Dialogs *Library*

FUNCTION	ARGUMENTS	RETURNS	PURPOSE
alert	message		Displays the message to the user and waits for user confirmation.
confirm	message, ok, cancel	Boolean	Displays message and two reply alternatives. Waits for the user to select a reply and returns true for ok and false for the cancel alternative.
prompt	message, default	string	Displays message and prompts for user input. Returns the user input.

Index

The Story Behind Apress

Apress is an innovative publishing company devoted to meeting the needs of existing and potential programming professionals. Simply put, the "A" in Apress stands for the "author's press™." Our unique author-centric approach to publishing grew from conversations between Dan Appleman and Gary Cornell, whose books are widely considered among the best in the area they cover. They wanted to create a publishing company that emphasized quality above all—a company whose books might not always be the first to market, but would always be the best to market.

To accomplish this goal, they knew it was necessary to attract the very best authors—established authors whose work is already highly regarded, and new authors who also have the kind of real-world practical experience that professional software developers want in the books they buy. If you look at the list of Apress titles on the following pages, you'll see that Dan and Gary's vision of an author-centric press has already attracted many leading software professionals to write for Apress.

Would You Like
to Write for Apress?

Apress is rapidly expanding its publishing program. If you can write and refuse to compromise on the quality of your work, if you believe in doing more then rehashing existing documentation, and if you are looking for opportunities and rewards that go far beyond those offered by traditional publishing houses, we want to hear from you! Consider these innovations that we offer every one of our authors:

- Top royalties with *no* hidden switch statements. For example, authors typically only receive half of their normal royalty rate on foreign sales. In contrast, Apress' royalty rate remains the same for both foreign and domestic sales.

- A mechanism for authors to obtain equity in Apress. Unlike the software industry, where stock options are essential to motivate and retain software professionals, the publishing industry has stuck to an outdated compensation model based on royalties alone. In the spirit of most software companies, Apress reserves a significant portion of its equity for authors.

- Serious treatment of the technical review process. Each Apress book has a technical reviewing team whose remuneration depends in part on the success of the book since they, too, receive a royalty.

Moreover, through a partnership with Springer-Verlag, one of the world's major publishing houses, Apress has significant venture capital behind it. Thus, Apress has the resources both to produce the highest quality books *and* to market them aggressively.

If you fit the model of the Apress author who can write a book that gives the "professional what he or she needs to know™," then please contact any one of our editorial directors, Gary Cornell (gary_cornell@apress.com), Dan Appleman (dan_appleman@apress.com), or Karen Watterson (karen_watterson@apress.com), for more information on how to become an Apress author.

Apress Titles

ISBN	LIST PRICE	AVAILABLE	AUTHOR	TITLE
1-893115-01-1	$39.95	Now	Appleman	Appleman's Win32 API Puzzle Book and Tutorial for Visual Basic Programmers
1-893115-23-2	$29.95	Now	Appleman	How Computer Programming Works
1-893115-09-7	$24.95	Now	Baum	Dave Baum's Definitive Guide to LEGO MINDSTORMS
1-893115-84-4	$29.95	Now	Baum, Gasperi, Hempel, and Villa	Extreme MINDSTORMS
1-893115-82-8	$59.95	Now	Ben-Gan/Moreau	Advanced Transact-SQL for SQL Server 2000
1-893115-85-2	$34.95	Now	Gilmore	A Programmer's Introduction to PHP 4.0
1-893115-17-8	$59.95	Now	Gross	A Programmer's Introduction to Windows DNA
1-893115-86-0	$34.95	Now	Gunnerson	A Programmer's Introduction to C#
1-893115-10-0	$34.95	Now	Holub	Taming Java Threads
1-893115-04-6	$34.95	Now	Hyman/Vaddadi	Mike and Phani's Essential C++ Techniques
1-893115-79-8	$49.95	Now	Kofler	Definitive Guide to Excel VBA
1-893115-75-5	$44.95	Now	Kurniawan	Internet Programming with VB
1-893115-19-4	$49.95	Now	Macdonald	Serious ADO: Universal Data Access with Visual Basic
1-893115-06-2	$39.95	Now	Marquis/Smith	A Visual Basic 6.0 Programmer's Toolkit
1-893115-22-4	$27.95	Now	McCarter	David McCarter's VB Tips and Techniques
1-893115-76-3	$49.95	Now	Morrison	C++ For VB Programmers
1-893115-80-1	$39.95	Now	Newmarch	A Programmer's Guide to Jini Technology
1-893115-81-X	$39.95	Now	Pike	SQL Server: Common Problems, Tested Solutions
1-893115-20-8	$34.95	Now	Rischpater	Wireless Web Development
1-893115-93-3	$34.95	Now	Rischpater	Wireless Web Development with PHP and WAP
1-893115-24-0	$49.95	Now	Sinclair	From Access to SQL Server

ISBN	LIST PRICE	AVAILABLE	AUTHOR	TITLE
1-893115-95-X	$49.95	Now	Welschenbach	Cryptography in C and C++
1-893115-05-4	$39.95	Now	Williamson	Writing Cross-Browser Dynamic HTML
1-893115-78-X	$49.95	Now	Zukowski	Definitive Guide to Swing for Java 2, Second Edition
1-893115-92-5	$49.95	Now	Zukowski	Java Collections

Available at bookstores nationwide or from Springer Verlag New York, Inc. at 1-800-777-4643; fax 1-212-533-3503. Contact us for more information at sales@apress.com.

Apress Titles Publishing SOON!

ISBN	AUTHOR	TITLE
1-893115-97-6	Appleman	Moving to VB.Net: Strategies, Concepts and Code
1-893115-99-2	Cornell/Morrison	Programming VB.Net: A Guide for Experienced Programmers
1-893115-96-8	Jorelid	Architecting a Servlet and JSP Based Application
1-893115-50-X	Knudsen	Wireless Java
1-893115-56-9	Kofler/Kramer	MySQL
1-893115-87-9	Kurata	Doing Web Development: Client-Side Techniques
1-893115-59-3	Troelsen	C# and the .Net Platform
1-893115-54-2	Trueblood/Lovett	Data Mining and Statistical Analysis Using SQL

Apress™

License Agreement (Single-User Products)